# Preparing College Teachers of Writing

# Preparing College Teachers of Writing

## Histories, Theories, Programs, Practices

EDITED BY

## BETTY P. PYTLIK
*Ohio University*

## SARAH LIGGETT
*Louisiana State University*

New York   Oxford

OXFORD UNIVERSITY PRESS

2002

Oxford University Press

Oxford New York
Athens Auckland Bangkok Bogotá Buenos Aires Calcutta
Cape Town Chennai Dar es Salaam Delhi Florence Hong Kong Istanbul
Karachi Kuala Lumpur Madrid Melbourne Mexico City Mumbai
Nairobi Paris São Paulo Shanghai Singapore Taipei Tokyo Toronto Warsaw

and associated companies in
Berlin Ibadan

Published by Oxford University Press, Inc.
198 Madison Avenue, New York, New York 10016
http://www.oup-usa.org

Oxford is a registered trademark of Oxford University Press

**Library of Congress Cataloging-in-Publication Data**

Preparing college teachers of writing: histories, theories, programs, practices /
edited by Betty P. Pytlik, Sarah Liggett.
    p. cm.
    ISBN 0-19-514309-4 (pbk : acid-free paper)
    1. English language—Rhetoric—Study and teaching. 2. Report writing—Study and
teaching (Higher) 3. Academic writing—Study and teaching. 4. English
teachers—Training of. I. Pytlik, Betty Parsons. II. Liggett, Sarah.
PE1404 .P64 2001
808'.042'0711—dc21
00-062400

Printing (last digit): 9 8 7 6 5 4 3 2 1

Printed in the United States of America
on acid-free paper

In memory of
Sara Leader Parsons
and
with thanks to
Marion and Lois Liggett

# Contents

## Part III.  Programs

## Part IV.  Practices

# Foreword: Preparing the Professors

## Richard Fulkerson

When I was young, my father, who had taught for forty years in public schools in southern Illinois, had finally reached the eminent position of Professor of Mathematics at a land-grant university with a Normal School history. Like most such universities, it had its own K–12 school on the campus, a school my father hoped to get me into eventually. One day, as we were walking around the campus from his office, I pointed at the building I thought housed grades K–12 and said, "Dad, that's the training school, isn't it?" My father, ever precise in usage and diction, said, "One *trains* animals. One *educates* people. That is our campus elementary and high school."

For this collection about how we now educate English graduate assistants for their teaching responsibilities, the editors' choice of title, *Preparing College Teachers of Writing*, would have pleased my father. As it pleases me, even though the word "train" crops up occasionally. These chapters remind us that effective teaching is nothing like the rote behavior for which one can be trained with some sort of Skinner-like stimulus/response conditioning. "What should I do if a student swears in class?" "How do I assign semester grades?" If future teachers could be "trained," presumably each would know *the* correct response for each situation, programmed in ahead of time. And English teachers would lead simpler lives. But the appropriate teacherly reactions must reflect a host of contextual variables: the student, the motive, the consequences, the teacher's personality, the program, and the current class activities, just to identify a few. Those of us who are responsible for TA programs, in whole or in part, simply hope that we have adequately *prepared* our charges to respond sensibly.

The story of how TAs used to be (not) "prepared" has achieved mythic status. New TAs, often fresh from an undergraduate literature curriculum the previous spring, were given in the fall one or more textbooks (and maybe a syllabus), then shoved into a classroom full of unruly and more or less baffled first-year students, and told to teach them to write. The story's mythic status shouldn't detract from its essential truth. As Betty P. Pytlik points out in the first chapter, although occasional isolated complaints had arisen about the failure of graduate English programs to prepare students for the realities of their professional lives, until around the 1970s, few graduate English students received much of any preparation for the classrooms they were put into—and in which they would spend their careers. Pytlik quotes William Irmscher about his experience at Indiana University. And a major MLA survey (published in *The Teaching Apprentice Program in Language and Literature* edited by Joseph Gibaldi and James Mirollo) reported that

> the programs we have surveyed vary drastically in quality, but those we especially deplore are weak in preparation of their trainees, whom they give little support, perfunctory supervision, and no pedagogical training; under the guise of a preferred informality or a desire to avoid dry pedagogy, they simply put young graduate students in front of a classroom to manage as best they can. (MLA 1981, 27)

My own experience at Ohio State University parallels Irmscher's. In the spring of 1963 I graduated with a degree in mathematics; in the fall, armed with three textbooks and a syllabus, I faced two sections of first-quarter composition with twenty-eight students in each. Over 100 of us were doing it, and we did occasionally have meetings in which the first-year director would lecture about some topic in the syllabus. I particularly recall a largely unsuccessful attempt to initiate us into the mysteries of the syllogism before we were to do the same for our students. I was observed teaching once that term and told I was doing a good job. I spent seven years as a teaching assistant, eventually being promoted so that I could teach three sections instead of two. In those seven years, I was never observed again. A high school friend of mine entered the University of Oklahoma about that same time and got even less guidance. She was handed a book but no syllabus and told to teach students how to write while they read literary selections. Her classroom experience was painful, and she eventually left the field.

Although the sporadic complaints dating back to the 1920s had attracted little attention, things changed somehow in the last three decades of the twentieth century. A significant number of graduate English programs as well as professional organizations such as the Conference on College Composition and Communication and the Association of Writing Program Administrators began to take seriously the preparation of teachers for college classrooms. In their bibliographic essays, Stephen Wilhoit and Kirsti Sandy attempt to account for the often dramatic changes documented and illustrated in the other chapters in this collection.

This collection is the third in what I regard as a progressive series of volumes addressing teacher preparation in graduate English programs. The first was the MLA-sponsored volume *The Teaching Apprentice Program in Language and Literature* edited by Joseph Gibaldi and James Mirollo in 1981. It included the (mixed) results of a major survey along with descriptions of eighteen preparation programs, nine in English, the others in foreign languages and linguistics. The second volume was the National Council of Teachers of English collection *Training the New Teacher of College Composition* edited by Charles Bridges in 1986. It included fourteen articles, more about what a preparation program ought to include or what new teachers ought to know than about existing programs.

In his preface, Bridges laments "the dearth of articles in major composition journals about teacher preparation" (viii). But as the Wilhoit and Sandy chapters in this collection indicate, after 1970 and growing into the 1980s and 1990s, we now have available a wealth of articles about TA preparation in American colleges (although not necessarily from "major composition journals"). In 1993, I edited an annotated bibliography of such articles (about 120, compiled under the auspices of the CCCC Committee on the Preparation of College Writing Teachers chaired by Richard Larson (ERIC 355 536). The introduction summed up the features of the programs represented: (1) A pre-service workshop to introduce the new teaching assistants to the goals and structure of the course they will teach and to help them with immediate problems. Textbooks and a syllabus have either been given out ahead of time or are distributed at this workshop. (2) Class visitation by an experienced writing teacher, often the Director of Composition. (3) Regular meetings with the Director, sometimes in new teacher staff meetings, sometimes in for-credit graduate courses. And (4) at least one graduate seminar with a name such as "Theory and Practice of Composition."

The chapters in this collection show how those features have evolved. The pre-service workshops have expanded and become more sophisticated, as have the courses in pedagogical theory, complete with the use of problematic scenarios, frequent observation of TAs by experienced teachers, and the use of videotapes and TA listservs. In addition, we now have a host of published materials designed precisely to use in preparing teaching assistants, ranging from college methods texts like Irmscher's *Teaching Expository Writing* (the first one in 1979) and Erika Lindemann's *A Rhetoric for Writing Teachers* (first published in 1982), to the various anthologies of major articles, to more specialized books such as *Scenarios for Teaching Writing,* by Chris Anson et al (NCTE 1993) or *12 Readers Reading* by Richard Straub and Ron Lunsford (Hampton 1995).

But these developments seem like natural evolution of the approaches from the 1970s and 1980s. What strikes me as essentially new in this collection is the pervasiveness of three key practices in current TA preparation: "mentoring," "reflection," and "portfolios." Virtually every program discussed uses some form of ongoing mentoring relationship, either between a professor and a new TA, or between an experienced TA and a new one, or sometimes both, and sometimes in groups. Although some mentoring was found in the 1981 MLA survey, the practice seems now to have become pervasive.

The idea that teaching is a "reflective" practice runs through these essays like a recurring *leitmotif.* Apparently the concept originates with Dewey (as Burnham and Jackson point out) before being elaborated by Donald Schön and then applied directly to English by Kathleen Blake Yancey in *Reflection in the Writing Classroom* (Utah State 1998). It is activity characterized by the conscious and conscientious attention of a prepared practitioner, rather than the essential mindlessness of a trained organism. As such it absolutely demands the use of writing as a tool. Although these chapters analyze and advocate the activity of written reflection for the novice teacher, they simultaneously enact the value of reflection *β kl ?* for the experienced practitioners, the authors themselves.

Finally, many of the contributors (Lindgren especially) refer to having current TAs keep various sorts of reflective teaching journals or logs, which eventually become part of the TA's teaching portfolio, a thoughtful (i.e., reflective) distillation of what the TA has learned, believed, and done in the classroom. A decade or so ago, we had not heard of teaching portfolios; now we regard them as a necessary sign of appropriate professional preparation and thus one requisite to success on the job market.

How I envy TAs today for the serious guidance and preparation they get. When I graduated from Ohio State University in 1970, not a single graduate composition or pedagogy course existed, even though Ed Corbett was there, and a member of my doctoral committee. There was no mentoring system, no one examined our teaching materials, and no one suggested that we employ writing as a way of reflecting on what we had done.

If I were to judge the preparation of prospective college English teachers by the contributions to this collection, I would conclude that the future of our profession and of first-year college writers is in good hands, and I would rush to tell colleagues in other disciplines that they had better get with the program. Professors of government, chemistry, or mathematics have no reason to be less fully prepared, with a solid basis in both *theoria* and *praxis,* than those in English.

And frankly, the same goes for teachers of literature. It's ironic that for some three decades, college English departments have been serious about preparing future college professors to teach writing, when the vast majority of doctoral TAs will also teach literature for at least a significant part of their load. Do we believe composition to be so complex that extensive preparation is needed to teach it effectively, but anyone who "knows literature" can therefore teach it well? Or is it time that doctoral programs in English also start to pay serious attention to issues of literary pedagogy?

English as a field thrives on theoretical controversy: Is writing a cognitive process or a social one? Is argument inherently antifeminist? Are all texts, even airline schedules, indeterminate? Do postmodern intertextuality and nonfoundational social construction theory mean the concept of authorship is meaningless? But far more important than such esoteric, yet to us glitzy, concerns is the pragmatic question of how graduate students seeking to enter the English academic arena can be effectively prepared for the daily realities of the classroom and the career, the issue addressed in this important collection.

Who ought to read this book? Anyone with administrative authority in an English department using graduate teaching assistants—from the WPA, to the director of the writing center, to the director of graduate studies and the department chair, not to mention anyone, TA or professor, who aspires to one of those positions. All will benefit from examining and reflecting on the theories, programs, and practices presented. As a Director of Graduate Studies and a professor of composition, in a program that I believe has done a good job of professional preparation for the last thirty years, I confess I did not expect to learn a lot from reading this collection. I expected confirmation of what we already do. But I also found that others are doing similar things, yet doing them in more elaborate and thoughtful (you might say more "reflective") ways than we do them at Texas A&M–Commerce. As a result, I find myself energized for the coming fall to institute several new or elaborated practices in our department, practices that will require yet more work from the TAs, the first-year director, the students I intend to mentor more effectively, and myself as well.

# Preface

SARAH LIGGETT AND BETTY P. PYTLIK

"Your students will teach you how to teach," Donald Murray assures new instructors in *A Writer Teaches Writing*. Contributors to this collection gratefully acknowledge the valuable lessons learned from undergraduate students in our writing classes and from the graduate teaching assistants in our orientations, practica, and theory courses. Yet, especially for beginning instructors, learning to teach by teaching can be an inefficient and frustrating method of professional development. As this book demonstrates, well-designed teacher preparation programs have much to offer novice teachers by way of theories and practices for teaching writing. Such programs also help new teachers reflect on their experiences in order to solve problems and gain insight into how college students develop as readers, writers, and thinkers. Throughout this collection, teacher educators also reflect on and interpret lessons they have learned from students; from scholarship in areas such as composition studies, rhetoric, cultural studies, curriculum and instruction, and postmodern theories of literacy; and from their ongoing research on effective ways to prepare college teachers of writing. The contributors speak from experiences as recent graduate students (TAs), adjuncts, new assistant professors, tenured faculty members; as WPAs and heads and chairs of departments; and as journal editors. The book's conversation among thirty-eight teacher educators from twenty-eight institutions (geographically and demographically diverse) discusses what new college teachers need to learn about writing and teaching writing and what kinds of programs facilitate their learning.

Chapters in *Preparing College Teachers of Writing* are grouped in four sections as indicated by its subtitle: *Histories, Theories, Programs, and Practices*. While most chapters address all four topics to some extent, we have grouped them to emphasize that preparation of new teachers of college writing, most often TAs, involves more than practical exercises. It has century-long historical roots, is grounded in theories from different disciplines, and is profoundly shaped by university, departmental, and programmatic structures and politics. The sections can be defined by four questions addressed in the collection: What are the historical contexts for current TA preparation programs? What theories inform TA preparation programs? How are successful TA programs structured? What teaching practices have proven effective in preparing TAs for college writing classrooms?

## WHAT ARE THE HISTORICAL CONTEXTS FOR CURRENT TA PREPARATION PROGRAMS?

The first five chapters of the collection recount how preparation for college writing teachers has developed from simple, informal tutorial arrangements in the mid-nineteenth century to complex, formal programs at the beginning of the twenty-first century in which TAs learn to teach writing in various settings, gain experience in writing program administration, and compete in a tight academic job market. In "How Graduate Students Were Prepared to Teach Writing—1850–1970," Betty P. Pytlik discusses how periods of rising college enrollments and students deficient in writing skills created a need to employ and to train teaching assistants as early as the late 1800s. She uncovers, too, faculty members' recurring apprehension about the writing abilities of graduate students who were sometimes no more proficient writers than their students.

Two bibliographical essays follow, summarizing more recent scholarship on preparing TAs to teach writing and to enter the profession: Stephen Wilhoit's "Recent Trends in TA Instruction: A Bibliographic Essay" accounts for "increased interest in TA preparation over the past thirty years," as evidenced in journal articles, conference presentations, and book chapters. His chapter explores patterns in the structure, practices, and content of TA preparation programs; recognizes ongoing concerns about the employment conditions of TAs; and identifies areas for further research. Kirsti Sandy's "After Preparing TAs for the Classroom, What Then? Three Decades of Conversation about Preparing TAs for the Job Market" looks at how a shrinking job market in academia has altered professional preparation, including additional course work in rhetoric and composition theory and practice, an emphasis on writing publishable seminar papers, and experience in writing program administration. Acknowledging some negative impacts of such preprofessionalization—overworked, exploited TAs who have less time for their studies—she describes efforts to help them prepare for the job market such as guidance in creating teaching portfolios, mentoring arrangements, and professional development courses and programs.

The last two chapters in the "History" section record developments in teacher preparation within two particular contexts. In "When Teaching Assistants Teach Teaching Assistants to Teach: A Historical View of a Teacher Preparation Program," Irwin Weiser traces Purdue University's nearly thirty-year history of mentoring TAs, initially through an informal support system in which faculty members mentored graduate students and currently through a formal structure in which experienced TAs also mentor TAs new to the writing classroom. His narrative shows how programmatic changes can be understood in light of disciplinary and institutional developments. In "TA Education as Dialogic Response: Furthering the Intellectual Work of the Profession through WPA," Darin Payne and Theresa Enos offer a historical perspective on the important role that the National Council of Writing Program Administrators has played as it "consistently *explicates* the forces that impact our work as writing teachers and TA educators, as well as the ways in which we respond to those forces." The forces that can shape a particular institution's preparation program are identified in the opening chapter of the next section.

## WHAT THEORIES INFORM TA PREPARATION PROGRAMS?

Theories influence how we create teacher preparation programs and how we structure the writing programs in which TAs teach. The first two chapters in the second section outline processes by which to design programs for TAs. In "The Professionalization of TA Development Programs: A Heuristic for Curriculum Design," Kathleen Blake Yancey categorizes a dozen forces that influence TA preparation programs, including local influences such as theories that underlie the writing programs in which TAs work and the graduate programs in which they study, as well as disciplinary forces such as current theories in composition studies and education. Her pivotal chapter gives readers a rubric by which to assess past and present programs and a heuristic for designing new ones. In "Thinking Together: Developing a Reciprocal Reflective Model for Approaches to Preparing College Teachers of Writing," Shirley K Rose and Margaret J. Finders propose that teacher educators work in teams. Built on the work of John Dewey and Donald Schön, their collaborative process uses a "dialogic model of reexamining and reconsidering, re-articulating, [and] redefining" the criteria by which they choose strategies for preparing writing teachers.

Other chapters in this section argue that the education of new teachers should include a solid grounding in theory since it informs and sometimes indicates suitable pedagogies and content for college writing classes. The authors differ, however, in their theoretical stances. Judith Goleman, in "Educating Literacy Instructors: Practice versus Expression," claims "it is . . . time to interrogate the transmission model of essential knowledge so that a new historical model of dialectical knowledge can supercede it as the basis for defining literacy." Using two case studies of TAs, Goleman problematizes the difficulties that new teachers encounter as they work with the dialogical and dialectical methods of postmodern pedagogy in the first-year writing classroom. In "Too Cool for School? Composition as Cultural Studies and Reflective Practice," Christine Farris asserts that preparing TAs is made more difficult as we revise "composition curricula to reflect postmodern notions of reading, writing, and representation." The first-year course she designed for students at Indiana University focuses on the analysis of popular culture and requires teachers who can skillfully apply a critical pedagogy to help students examine cultural attitudes and practices. As a teacher educator, Farris addresses resistance to the theory and practice of cultural critique that she sometimes encounters in new teachers (and their students) and describes methods to help them understand the intellectual work of teaching, including the use of experienced "peer consultants" who work with new TAs, a week-long orientation, and a semester-long proseminar. In "Feminist Approaches to Mentoring Teaching Assistants: Conflict, Power, and Collaboration," Rebecca J. Rickly and Susanmarie Harrington analyze the tensions that arose when they introduced feminist praxis in an experimental mentoring program for TAs at Texas Tech. Specifically, they examine how mentoring can encourage program coherence while attending to individual needs, how it can help untenured administrators speak from a position of authority while advocating the decentralization of authority, and how collaborative mentoring, based in a desire to value all voices, can respond to voices that resist the collaboration of mentoring.

The coauthors of the last chapter in the "Theories" section do not promote a singular ideology. Rather, in "Negotiating Resistance and Change: One Composition Program's Struggle Not to Convert," Katrina M. Powell, Peggy O'Neill, Cassandra Mach Phillips, and Brian Huot describe how TA preparation at the University of Louisville has addressed a resistance to theory voiced by some new teachers more immediately concerned with practice. In an intensive five-week summer seminar on "Teaching College Composition," co-taught by the Director of Composition and three experienced TAs who serve as Assistant Directors, TAs learn to choose and articulate for themselves theories and practices upon which to build a writing course.

## HOW ARE SUCCESSFUL TA PROGRAMS STRUCTURED?

The third section provides six models for TA preparation programs in different sites and configurations. Katherine K. Gottschalk and Betty Bamberg, for instance, describe programs that prepare TAs from disciplines other than English and that provide multiple sites for training. In "Preparing Graduate Students across the Curriculum to Teach Writing," Gottschalk discusses how developments in Cornell's writing-in-the-disciplines program, begun in the 1960s, have necessitated changes in the preparation of TAs from thirty-eight disciplines. She describes Cornell's multiple sites for today's preparation, including course work, a summer intern/mentor program, and continuing supplementary programs such as peer collaboration and tutorials on responding to essays. Bamberg, in "Creating a Culture of Reflective Practice: A Program for Continuing TA Preparation after the Practicum," recounts how TAs from more than a dozen departments at the University of Southern California receive instruction first through an orientation and then in a weekly practicum in order to teach writing courses linked to large-lecture social issues courses. After the practicum, TAs continue to develop classroom expertise through reflective practices; they attend advanced workshops, analyze and respond to student evaluations of their teaching, contribute descriptions of successful teaching practices and assignments to the program's "Rhetorical Resource File" (more evidence of their growth as instructors), and create teaching portfolios.

In "Experience and Reflection in Multiple Contexts: Preparing TAs for the Artistry of Professional Practice," Chris Burnham and Rebecca Jackson briefly narrate the twenty-year evolution of New Mexico State University's teacher education program, emphasizing ways it has been influenced by Schön's notion of a "reflective practicum." TAs in the program now learn in a five-day orientation, a full-semester course entitled "Composition Theory and Pedagogy," and a first-semester appointment to the Writing Center supported by an orientation and ongoing professional development through staff meetings, a Writing Center listerv, and a goal-centered evaluation process. Throughout the program, TAs reflect upon and reconcile tensions among their roles as graduate students, writing teachers, and Writing Center consultants.

The remaining three chapters in this section describe nationally known TA preparation programs for professional writing courses, computerized classrooms, and a Writing Center. In "The Three-Part Program for Preparing TAs to Lead Professional Communication Courses at Miami University (Ohio)," Paul Anderson and former TAs Todd DeLuca and Lisa Rosenberger reflect upon the teaching partnership and seminars that prepare TAs in Miami's master's degree program in technical and scientific communication to teach undergraduate students in professional writing courses. During the first semester, new TAs, usually without teaching experience and often with degrees in disciplines other than English, assist veteran faculty members in an undergraduate business or technical writing course. They also take a teaching seminar and other seminars on organizational communication, rhetoric, and technical and scientific editing. During the second semester, TAs use a common syllabus to teach their own business or technical writing classes and continue to meet weekly in a teaching seminar. This chapter is unique in the collection for its dialogue among the teacher and TA apprentices on the value of teacher preparation.

In the next chapter, Christine Hult and Lynn Meeks describe approaches to "Preparing College Teachers of Writing to Teach in a Web-Based Classroom: History, Theoretical Base, Web Base, and Current Practices" at Utah State University. The coauthors attribute the success of SyllaBase, their English department's Web-based classroom, to administrators who support technological innovation, teachers who commit to learn new technologies, and technical support personnel who respond to inevitable problems. While completing assignments for their Writing Practicum during the first semester they teach, TAs first learn to work in an on-line teaching environment before gradually incorporating SyllaBase assignments into their first-year writing courses in the second semester. In-service training continues through teaching demonstrations. Hult and Meeks conclude their chapter with basic rules for on-line instruction.

"What Would You Like to Work on Today?" is the opening question that Muriel Harris prompts tutors to ask when she uses "The Writing Center as a Site for Teacher Training." Harris's chapter discusses various approaches she takes to prepare inexperienced undergraduate peer tutors and experienced TAs in one-on-one writing pedagogy appropriate for the diverse students who seek help at Purdue's Writing Lab. Harris details what tutors learn—writing processes, individual differences among writers, and instructional strategies for responding to ambiguous assignments and to students' drafts—and how they learn it—through observation and reflection, interviews with other writers, analyses of personality styles, collaborative reports, and discussions.

## WHAT TEACHING PRACTICES HAVE PROVEN EFFECTIVE FOR PREPARING TAS FOR COLLEGE WRITING CLASSROOMS?

While authors throughout the collection describe their practices as teacher educators, the final section focuses especially on mentoring, orientation sessions, practica and other course work, writing assignments, strategies for evaluating writing, and teaching portfolios and notebooks. Mentoring new teachers is the topic of three essays: Sally Barr Ebest's "Mentoring: Past, Present, and Future" surveys mentoring practices in the academy's early years; examines present goals and arrangements for mentoring relationships including WPAs, faculty members, and peers as mentors; and alerts readers to possible misuses of mentoring given the power differential. In "Mentors, Models, and Agents of Change: Veteran TAs Preparing Teachers of Writing," Wanda Martin and Charles Paine describe the week-long orientation at the University of New Mexico, where experienced TAs propose and develop sessions based on their own classroom experiences and on curriculum innovation. They mentor less-experienced teachers and model the kind of reflective practice the program administrators feel is essential to preparing TAs. In "Orientation and Mentoring: Collaborative Practices in Teacher Preparation," Gita Das Bender discusses New York University's Expository Writing Program in which program directors and graduate student mentors collaboratively plan and lead the summer orientations for new and returning teachers. These peer mentors also conduct weekly mentor meetings, which provide a structure for year-long staff development. She elaborates benefits to the writing program that arise from collaboration between administrators and teachers.

Summer orientation is also integral to teacher preparation at the University of Oklahoma, as detailed by Michael C. Flanigan in "From Discomfort, Isolation, and Fear to Comfort, Community, and Confidence: Using Reflection, Role-Playing, and Classroom Observation to Prepare New Teachers of College Writing." Flanigan describes the ten-day intensive workshop in which new teaching assistants are given repeated opportunities for written reflection on their fears and sources of stress as well as on their changing attitudes and new knowledge as the workshop progresses. He also advocates using role-playing in response to video and written scenarios to help TAs anticipate how they might handle classroom situations such as racial tensions or grade disputes. The chapter ends with a model for classroom observations that either TAs or teacher educators can adopt to evaluate the teaching of others.

Although it has long been common knowledge in our discipline that students learn to write by writing, authors in the next three chapters demonstrate that teachers can learn to teach by writing as well. Thomas E. Recchio, in "Essaying TA Training," describes a teacher preparation program that achieves coherence from its essayist orientation toward students' and TAs' learning, one that is "open, receptive, adaptable, curious, responsive, and self-aware." He describes how the first-year English course at the University of Connecticut (focused on academic writing in response to difficult academic readings) "reflects the pedagogical ideals of the required TA graduate course." Through a series of three writing assignments, the TAs experience "a concrete sense of the work they are asking their students to do" as they respond to professional readings in their graduate course and reflect on their teaching experiences.

Barry Thatcher also demands much writing from TAs assigned to teach technical writing at Ohio University. In "Orientation for Teachers of Technical Writing," he explains his motive for having the TAs write four complex assignments in a three-day summer orientation: The TAs lack experience with the rhetorical situations of the technical writing assignments they are about to teach. Using Bakhtin's constitutive dimensions (the material/physical, cognitive/ethical, and emotional/volitional) as a theoretical frame, he helps TAs understand the contexts and rhetorical and ethical challenges of the resumés and cover letters, proposals, instructional manuals, and Web pages they write and evaluate. In the graduate practicum that follows the orientation, TAs continue to write, composing literature reviews, Web pages, and reports of peer observations.

In "Learning to Evaluate and Grade Student Writing: An Ongoing Conversation," Donna Qualley addresses a major worry of every TA: "No other aspect of learning to teach composition is fraught with as much anxiety and concern as the assigning of grades." Qualley lays out two key assumptions: (1) "Evaluating and grading are necessarily subjective processes, and TAs need to learn to use their subjectivity consciously." (2) "Any program-wide system of evaluation needs to be dynamic and open to continual adjustment and modification by the members of the community." She then explains her system for teaching TAs to rank sample student essays by identifying criteria that lead them to claim one essay is better than another; they also articulate a language of grading to distinguish between letter grades. Finally, she describes an all-day, end-of-quarter portfolio reading session that encourages TAs to reexamine and calibrate their grading practices.

The last two chapters describe long-term projects that offer insight into TAs' professional development. In "The Teaching Portfolio: Practicing What We Teach," Margaret Lindgren describes the teaching portfolio as the culminating assignment for a full-year practicum at the University of Cincinnati. She analyzes features of nine TAs' portfolios for patterns and inconsistencies in the way that new teachers represent themselves to their imagined audience—a postsecondary hiring committee. For example, she studies (among other things) how they address issues of classroom authority and position themselves within the field of composition studies. She concludes by showing how close analysis of TAs' portfolios can lead us to evaluate our preparation programs. In the final chapter, Sarah Liggett explains the "Evolution of a Teaching Notebook: Contents, Purposes, and Assessment." The main project in her practicum, the Teaching Notebook helps TAs understand how assignments, readings, and practices in the graduate course relate to the pedagogy of the undergraduate course they are teaching. In their notebooks, TAs collect and organize unit plans and lesson plans, reflections on classroom experiences, reading notes, reading lists, sample graded essays, peer observations, and proposals to solve teaching problems. Liggett also suggests ways to assess the effectiveness of practicum assignments such as the Teaching Notebook.

While this introduction has summarized chapters as they are grouped in the book with an emphasis on histories, theories, programmatic structures, and practices, there are certainly many other ways to read the collection. For example, a reader interested in a particular practice such as mentoring would find informative chapters in all four sections, perhaps starting with Barr Ebest's overview of mentoring practices through time; then studying chapters by Weiser, Anderson and colleagues, Martin and Paine, and Bender to see how variations work in particular programs; and finally learning from Rickly and Harrington's frank discussion of potential problems with mentoring as a feminist practice. Or a reader interested in reflective teaching would find the ideas of Schön's *Educating the Reflective Practitioner* especially influential in chapters by Bamberg, Farris, Liggett, Rose and Finders, and Burnham and Jackson. Or a reader curious about the structure and influence of one university's program, in this case Purdue's, could read together chapters by those who teach there (Weiser, Rose and Finders, and Harris) and by those who learned to teach there (Liggett, Yancey, and Thatcher). We believe teacher educators as well as TAs studying writing program administration will find this a useful text no matter which reading pattern they follow.

What this book does not offer readers is a "best" model for teacher preparation. Complex questions such as the four that organize this collection are seldom answered simply. Rather, as Yancey's heuristic shows, teacher educators must adapt the ideas, practices, and programmatic structures offered in this collection to their own situations as they design preparation programs that are suitable for their TAs, their institutions, and their writing programs and that reflect current disciplinary knowledge of writing and teaching. Nor has this book covered all issues related to teacher education, such as how to prepare TAs to work effectively with nonnative speakers of English or how to combine teacher preparation with teacher research. As several contributors have suggested, there are many topics worthy of further study.

In conclusion, the editors wish to recognize people, in addition to the contributors, who helped make this collection possible. Betty is appreciative of her supportive friends and support staff in Ohio University's Department of English, especially Barbara Grueser. Sarah wishes to thank Jerry Kennedy, her helpful and encouraging husband who understands firsthand the demands of scholarly writing, and Molly, her daughter whose playfulness, good-natured wit, and refusal to take her parents' academic concerns too seriously bring a refreshing perspective to our work. Sarah is also appreciative of Valerie Hudson's assistance. Both editors benefited from administrative backing through sabbatical leaves at Ohio University and Louisiana State University, respectively. We have also appreciated the support of Anthony English, our editor at Oxford University Press, who was quick to see the value of the collection even as a proposal, and Lisa Grzan, who saw the manuscript through production.

Recognizing that graduate students come to us having spent sixteen or more years in various classroom settings, we also value the indirect contributions of their previous teachers who model effective practices and shape TAs' notions of good teaching even before they enter our programs. Finally, we acknowledge the contributions of the TAs whom we have taught and from whom we have learned. They are the reason for this collection.

# PART 1

## HISTORIES

# 1. How Graduate Students Were Prepared to Teach Writing—1850–1970

## Betty P. Pytlik

Before the proliferation of TA training programs in the 1970s, a history of how colleges prepared TAs to teach writing would have documented public and professional pleas for a better prepared professoriat rather than have described formal teacher education programs. Frequently, though, descriptions of the formal preparation of the 1970s lead one to assume that the plethora of methods courses simply sprang forth as if from the head of Zeus. In fact, some models for those 1970s programs were developed in the early 1900s, in real programs like Chester Noyes Greenough's course begun at Harvard in 1912 and in ideal programs like the one proposed in 1916 by Ohio State University English department chair, Joseph V. Denney. This chapter provides a historical context for the innovative and theoretically grounded programs and practices available to today's TAs. In this sprinting tour through the early history of TA preparation, I will occasionally detour to comment on one of the recurring themes in literature about early TA preparation—the inadequate writing skills of TAs.

The antecedents of today's TAs were postbaccalaureate students who tutored undergraduates. In *Memories of Yale Life and Men, 1854–1899*, Timothy Dwight's 1903 memoir of his fifty-some years at Yale, he describes how, in 1849, he became the first recipient of a scholarship that allowed him to remain at Yale as a graduate for two years to study under faculty direction (97). In this early graduate program, five or six graduates met with Yale President Woolsey twice a week during 1849–1850 to read Thucydides and, in the next year, to study Pindar. Four months after he had begun as a graduate student, Dwight was asked to take over recitations when tutors were absent for a few days or a few weeks.

Dwight's account makes several points about the use of graduate assistants to teach writing. First, graduate students learned to teach through example: "The President," Dwight wrote, "was always ready to give us what was best in his teaching ... [and] what was best in himself—the opportunity of seeing his own scholarship and his own intellectual power" (101). Second, much graduate student writing took the form of translations of the classics, as had been the case with previous generations of students in grammar school, in the academies, and in undergraduate school. Third, once graduate students were available, college professors turned to them to help handle the heavy undergraduate paper load and recitations.

Although Dwight's pre–Civil War opportunity to assist as a graduate student was a rarity, in the next couple of decades, calls for better preparation for the professoriat and for graduate student assistance were frequent. In 1869, respected Yale professor Noah Porter made an early plea for a special group of short-term instructors to teach writing. In a series of articles for *New Englander,* Porter argued that every large college should have a corps of doctoral fellows assigned special teaching duties "as examiners, as critics of composition, as coaches to the timid or the halting, above all as private or parlor teachers." He maintained that if Yale or Harvard College spent $100,000 on six or eight such fellowships, "terminable in from five to eight years, . . . such a body of Fellows would also serve as a school for the training of permanent instructors" (159–61).

Three of Porter's 1869 concerns resonate with graduate teachers today: First, it was clear then, as it is today, that graduate students needed special preparation for their teaching careers. Second, colleges were dealing with an increased number of undergraduate students deficient in skills (such as writing) and knowledge that had been assumed of earlier students. And, third, cost-effectiveness was even then an argument for employing graduate assistants.

Pleas for a better prepared professoriat continued to appear occasionally in popular journals after the Civil War, when colleges, which had always served the elite, began to serve the middle class, too. In the 1870s, college enrollments increased as the economy flourished and society required new skills, among them effective writing. Recent historians of rhetoric and composition have described the social and economic changes that brought about the demand for an improved professoriat, in particular one better prepared to teach composition, but here, I'll make one point: For at least 100 years after the Civil War, the preparation of college teachers in general was largely shaped by the belief that a good man will learn to teach by teaching, and the preparation of college English teachers in particular was shaped by the belief that if one could write English, he could teach others to write it.

Despite increased enrollment of poorly prepared students following the Civil War, instruction remained predominately recitation, with students memorizing texts and repeating them verbatim to their teachers or tutors, just as generations of students before them had done. Indeed, even in the early 1890s, as Edwin M. Hopkins recounts in a 1931 *English Journal* (hereafter *EJ*),[1] the undergraduate program in English consisted of "college elocution and college rhetoric, but college courses in writing were almost unheard of; the current academic discipline for prospective writers or speakers was to read and recite upon a textbook, and become acquainted with specimens of the work of famous writers and speakers" (321).

By the end of the nineteenth century, though, most freshmen were taking a one- or two-semester writing course that focused on technical skill in grammar and usage, paragraph coherence, and the modes of discourse. It was believed, Patricia Bizzell and Bruce Herzberg remind us, "that knowledge came from the sciences and from careful observation" and that writers were "to record and transmit this knowledge with a minimum of distortion" (903). To do so required a great deal of practice—and correction. New professors could not handle the papers generated by the weekly themes so graduate students joined new teachers, sometimes referred to as "rhetoric slaves," in correcting students' themes. In 1894, according to Albert Kitzhaber, the first two such assistants in English helped a staff of four full-time teachers correct the weekly themes of nearly 1200 students at the University of Michigan (*Rhetoric* 44).

The graduate-level emphasis on rigorous scientific investigations of language, that is, philological studies, angered some turn-of-the-century humanists, most notably Irving Babbitt, who, in a series of essays published in the early 1900s, articulated some views common in the professional literature: Departments were failing to prepare college teachers. Furthermore, doctoral programs concentrated on factual knowledge at the expense of comprehending and applying ideas. The degree, Babbitt complained, "[put] a premium, not on the man who has read widely and thought maturely, but on the man who has shown proficiency in research" (141).

The emphasis on methods of investigation in most graduate programs, some educators argued, resulted in graduate students who themselves could not write well. M. Lyle Spencer of Lawrence College described the situation most passionately:

> To me the most lamentable situation in English teaching is that of the young Ph.D. from some big university, trained in all the highly specialized knowledge of Shakespeare, mediaeval literature, Old English, Germanic and Romance philology, and the rest . . . , but with no adequate idea at all of how to conduct a composition class. . . . He himself cannot write readable English. His doctor's thesis was a conglomeration of Latinisms, Germanisms, sesquipedalian-worded sentences, and unrhetorical expressions. And when during his college course the head of his department took him to task for the unreadableness of his dissertation, he excused himself on the ground that he was thinking too much of *what* he was saying, and not enough of *how* he was saying it. But as a matter of fact he could not then, and he cannot now, write clear, forceful, graceful English. Yet that man is to teach the one fundamental course in the college curriculum—composition. (Greenough 117–8)

At the beginning of the twentieth century, then, it was acknowledged that new teachers needed better preparation for their "real" task of teaching writing, including more experience in writing. Responses to a 1900 MLA questionnaire, for example, indicated that the majority of the respondents favored the study of Rhetoric at the graduate level. Some thought that future instructors in Rhetoric "should be trained in methods of teaching the subject" and "that practical exercise in composition should be included in the graduate work, though several were careful to exclude that as counting for a degree" (Stewart 740).

Undergraduates' weak writing was sometimes attributed to the bad conditions in which writing instructors worked—too many hours, too many students, too many themes for the individual teacher (Miller 120)—and too little individual teaching and poor cooperation between teachers. To eliminate the last two problems, George Miller, of the University of Cincinnati, argued for "a change in standards for the selection and promotion of college [composition] teachers. . . . Appointment and promotion of teachers of college composition should be based upon the ability to teach . . . and not upon scholarship in literature and linguistics" (121). A graduate methods course would be the best way to ensure that writing teachers met departmental standards for retention and promotion. If such courses weren't feasible, he suggested, carefully organized and well-supervised graduate teaching fellowships would help.

Still, there was much resistance to formal programs for graduate students, and much of it stemmed from faculty attitudes about teaching writing. Donald C. Stewart, who studied the first twenty-seven annual MLA programs, tells us that, in general, faculty were mainly interested "in demonstrating that the study of English and modern literatures was as intellectually legitimate and pedagogically beneficial as studying Latin and Greek" (734). The prevailing attitude toward preparing composition teachers was reflected in a 1914 MLA paper: MLA's purpose was to advance philological study of modern life and culture; it was not "a teacher's agency nor was it centrally concerned with pedagogical problems" (737).

Raymond M. Alden, advocating better college teacher preparation, told his 1913 National Council of Teachers of English (NCTE) audience (and his subsequent *EJ* readers) that "[W]hen it comes to finding a teacher, we generally look for the right kind of *man* [Alden's italics], and are sure that defects in his training will take care of themselves in time" (355). Alden acknowledged that he had omitted a discussion of

> the most difficult element in my whole subject—the relation of the teacher's preparation to the demand for the teaching of English *composition* [again, Alden's italics] as distinguished from literature. . . . [N]o special staff, and no special training [are] necessary [to teach composition] which is genuinely collegiate instruction, concerned with the development of the student's powers of expression in the subject-matter of his intellectual life, after he has mastered the elements of correct and orderly writing. . . . [A]ny competent scholar can give [those students] the requisite aid. (footnote on 355)

However, courses that are "designed to correct deficiencies" were another case altogether. New college teachers did need help in dealing with rapidly expanding remedial programs. "What that preparation ought to be, and how, if at all, it can be combined with preparation for very different things, I leave it to experts in the subject to discuss," Alden added (footnote continued on 356).

Experts were being heard, and despite the attitudes mentioned above, some faculty publicly supported graduate preparation in the teaching of composition. In a 1916 *EJ*, for example, J. M. Thomas, at the University of Minnesota, argued that composition requires "that men should come to it with high qualifications as far as teaching ability is concerned, and with unmistakable enthusiasm for the work" (449). Therefore, graduate students who were looking forward to composition-teaching opportunities should have "to connect their graduate study more definitely with their after-work [teaching composition]" (454). And graduate methods courses had already begun to appear. The one that received the most attention was Harvard's English 67 course for new teachers of college writing In 1913, Greenough described it to the newly formed College Section of NCTE. Half of the course was based on his belief that "[T]he chief requisite for success in teaching Freshmen to write is to be able to write everything that a Freshman would be required to write, and to do it enough better than a Freshman can be expected to do it to make everybody concerned feel that the instructor belongs behind the desk and not down among the beginners on the benches" (110). In addition, because the impulse to write needs to be genuine, graduate students in English 67 submitted to their peers their theses and reports for other courses or pieces about outside interests and revised writing from previous years (110).

The other half of English 67 was about writing pedagogy. The assignments the graduate students completed are worth noting here because they targeted problems that continue to vex methods teachers today—how to teach TAs to respond to papers, teach usage and mechanics, and handle the paper load. Each graduate student was assigned ten freshmen whose themes he read in search of errors, which he recorded in a notebook. By classifying the students' errors each month, TAs could prepare themselves for their future classes, "carrying their notebooks with them, to go to their teaching with a kind of diary by the use of which they can ward off, through advice and explanation given in advance, a very considerable number of typical errors" (113). In the methods class, TAs critiqued sample freshman themes.

As for gaining experience with conferencing and developing class exercises, graduate students observed classes of experienced teachers, wrote lectures for an imaginary freshman class which they presented to their classmates for discussion, and simulated the conference situation by going over with the course instructor the themes of the ten freshmen. These candidates for apprenticeships in freshman composition met weekly for informal sessions on practical matters like textbook selection and "the problem of co-operation with other courses to secure better written work" (115).

While some colleges followed Harvard's lead, most graduate programs did not develop courses to prepare teachers. In 1916, in an address to the College Section of NCTE, Denney called for two kinds of courses to prepare teachers of undergraduate English students. First were courses to remedy undergraduate deficiencies, like a course in historical English grammar to acquaint the TAs with the history of idiom. Second were "courses that [dealt] directly with the educational problems involved in the teaching of English" (322). The problems that would be investigated would be the specific aims, necessity, and content of the first-year courses in writing and literature; "the bearings of psychology on current practice; the order of topics; the best basis of differentiating students into groups for instruction; the use of the conference period"; cooperation among departments; the grammar question; oral composition; and assessment (325). Graduate students would learn how other institutions were handling freshman writing, and perhaps they would student teach. Experienced faculty members, especially those who directed the first-year composition and literature courses, would lead the seminars. Senior faculty would visit classes, thus creating "a live interest among all members of the department" (326). Denney's proposed—but not implemented—graduate program for preparing TAs incorporated the best of what was known about teacher preparation.

Graduate students' inadequate writing skills remained a topic in popular and professional journals. Greenough had developed his methods course because the inadequacy of Harvard's graduate students had "been perceptible both in the very moderate skill displayed by most graduate students in writing theses and reports, and in the dismay with which even the best of them have approached the unfamiliar task of teaching Freshmen to write" (109).

In "Twenty-five Years of Trying to 'Teach' English," written in 1935, Franklin B. Snyder bemoaned the effort he had put into useless MA theses. He speculated that, while graduate students probably had "receive[d] valuable training in accuracy, initiative, and half a dozen other desirable qualities . . . it would have done most of them far more good, would have better prepared them for the teaching profession they were entering, to have taken a good stiff course in English history, or even a semester's work in advanced English composition" (199).

In the 1920s, Charles Gott reported in a 1929 *EJ* article that selecting and preparing teachers to teach composition was usually

> a very casual matter. Sometimes the new teachers are recruited from students in a graduating class who have assisted the composition teacher by reading papers or even by holding conferences; very often a yearling graduate is considered amply qualified if he be but fortified with an M.A. degree, earned in the study of Chaucer, Spenser, Milton, the Romantic poets, and Anglo-Saxon. But not infrequently, untrained students just out of college are turned loose on the unoffending Freshmen, armed possibly with a syllabus which names the required texts and specifies the size of paper to be used, and with little else except the number of the classroom. (589–90)

In 1927, in response to situations like Gott described, Tufts College began to recruit nationally for teaching fellows, men *and* women (italics mine) who were committed to two years of studying and teaching. In the teacher preparation program, work of the freshman course was used as instructional material in the three weekly meetings during the first semester and the single weekly meeting in the second semester. Graduate students discussed rhetorical theory, including the best order in which to teach the modes; marked and graded papers and developed standards of grading; prioritized errors to determine when to emphasize them in the semester's work; and discussed differences between subjective and objective comments, the way to conduct class, and how to lead class (590–1).

Fellows were given lesson plans that suggested day-to-day activities. "Everything that might be regarded as lecture-material is given to the Freshmen in textbooks, and the teaching fellow simply carries on a discussion or socialized recitation upon that material, upon the students' reading, or upon errors appearing in the students' compositions" (592). The Director of Composition visited each fellow's classes three times to teach a lesson as a demonstration to the new teacher, to participate in the class, and then to observe and critique the fellow's teaching. In addition, senior teaching staff either held conferences with the 120 freshmen taught by new TAs or each week read several of the themes corrected by the fellow (592–3).

Although the need for programs like Tufts' was discussed in the 1930s, few existed. In *The Preparation and In-Service Training of College Teachers,* Homer L. Dodge quoted a New York University dean's 1930 response to "What should be the role of subject-matter departments in preparing college teachers?" The university was "not . . . convinced that formal course instruction in methods of teaching college subjects should be required for the Ph.D. . . . , nor that such courses are necessary, or are advisable, in all cases to the making of a successful college or university teacher" (155). Queried again in 1938, the dean said, "[N]one of our subject-matter departments is making any special efforts toward preparation for teaching other than through an organized and thorough grounding in subject matter" (155).

While Dodge's late 1930s survey indicated that the dean's response typified that of administration at most universities, he was heartened by discussions at the Universities of Illinois, Nebraska, Michigan, and Oregon and at Clark and Harvard Universities, all of which were considering or were offering preparation programs for college writing teachers. He was also encouraged by initiatives from subject-area professors who believed that departments, not "educationists " from schools of education, should be responsible for preparing teachers.

In 1936, Warner Rice initiated an internship program at the University of Michigan. A TA was assigned to a professor who visited the TA's classes two or three times in the fall and two or three times in the spring. The TA met with the professor to go over assignments, check on paper grading, and discuss classroom methods and problems. At the end of the term, the chairman or Director of Composition met with the TA to discuss sample themes from students. Records from those meetings provided the department with useful information when TAs sought positions elsewhere (Allen 7). (Thus, concern about helping TAs find positions began to appear in publications in the 1930s.)

That graduate students' writing ability was still a concern during the 1920s and 1930s is reflected in an *Educational Review* critique of the writing of the English PhDs who authored freshman composition textbooks. "Their style," Harry T. Baker wrote in 1925, "is heavy and commonplace and no spark of animation touches their pages" (148). Did the authors write badly because they had practiced the turgid style of dissertations too long or because they had had no instruction to improve their writing? In either case, during those decades, articles in *EJ* and other periodicals urged curricular changes to improve the writing of graduate students through more rigorous examination of the language—but not through practice in writing.

The 1940s and early 1950s saw more than 2 million veterans arrive on campuses, and first-year composition, which in many schools had been dropped to allow more room for war-related courses, was *now* reinstituted and created an even greater staffing problem. "The dramatic, overnight impact on the facilities, faculty, curricula, heterogeneity, and atmosphere of campuses," more than one historian has noted, "has drawn extensive historical attention" (Peeps 524). But the short- and long-term impact of the GI Bill on freshman composition and TA preparation has not been extensively documented. Our literature, especially after the appearance of *College Composition and Communication* (hereafter *CCC*), offers many anecdotal accounts of individuals' experiences with (and as) veterans in freshman composition and as new teachers of freshman composition. The literature of this period boasts of accommodating hundreds of thousands of freshmen in composition classes in converted naval depots and army barracks, but methods classes were slow to appear.

One dilemma faced by universities after World War II is outlined by Robert S. Hunting in "A Training Course for Teachers of Freshman Composition," a 1951 *CCC* article: On the one hand, a TA couldn't afford to take a great interest in teaching composition because "a wholesome regard for his own professional advancement compels him to think of [teaching composition] as a mere stepping-stone . . . a not-too-demanding way of earning a living while [he] gave his primary attention . . . to getting his degree, preparing learned articles, and generally getting ready to teach advanced courses" (3). On the other hand, working with undergraduates to improve their writing was important, and TAs were obligated—and needed—to do it. Thus, Hunting argued, TAs must be prepared for the task through "intelligent, but not oppressive, guidance at the right time" (5).

Despite the interest of organizations like the American Association of Colleges and the Conference on College Composition and Communication (CCCC), colleagues and friends who entered graduate school in the mid- and late-1940s have reported that preparation to teach composition at their institutions either did not exist or was minimal. One reported that, in a new apprenticeship program at Berkeley, he taught four or five classes of whatever his mentor told him to teach and graded his mentor's papers. At Tulane another had no set syllabus but was required to assign *Using Good English.* He was observed once and was required to attend occasional meetings about administrative matters. At the University of Connecticut, TAs at first had weekly meetings in which they led discussions about, for example, how to teach a particular concept or how to grade papers. Later TAs met biweekly to address textual matters, assignments, teaching strategies, "whatever was thrown on the table for discussion." At Ohio State University, one friend was handed a syllabus, a text, a class roster for her composition class, and an office number. (Later, to teach a sophomore introduction to literature class, however, she was required to apprentice with a senior faculty member.)[2]

Here I offer what, from my reading and interviewing, appears to be a fairly typical experience for those veterans who returned to graduate school—an excerpt from a 1993 interview I conducted with Professor William Irmscher about his post–World War II experience as a TA:

> I applied to the Indiana program, having done an MA at Chicago. I arrived on the scene, and not knowing very much about teaching assistantships or anything of that sort, I went in to see the department chair and said, "I will need some kind of work. If you have something in the English Department, I would prefer doing that rather than having to go out and do something else."

Although classes were already in the first week, the chair offered him an unstaffed class of composition and handed him a syllabus,

> which wasn't much of a syllabus. It was really certain grading standards and a list of the books—I was handed the books and so forth, and he said, "Go do it." I think I would have been quite lost, except for the fact that as an undergraduate I had done teacher preparation and a year of practice teaching, and then right before the war, I had taught seventh grade in junior high school. And I simply utilized whatever skills that I had to teach that class. Of course, lots of times there wasn't much to do because we had a workbook. I can't recall having any essays. We just did things in the workbook, the textbook, and so forth. At that time, they had absolutely nothing to prepare new teachers.

According to early CCCC workshop reports on teaching preparation, most instructors usually relied on methods "they vaguely recall having been used on them from six to ten years earlier" and committee members believed that graduate programs should develop the candidate's abilities to write ("Teacher-Training for Composition or Communication" 31). Committees reported that some universities were beginning to offer help to TAs. In 1946, for instance, Charles Roberts, of the University of Illinois, introduced "Theory and Practice of Composition."[3] In 1948, at the University of Washington, Porter Perrin offered a seminar on backgrounds for teaching composition, unique in that TAs worked out practical applications of the theories of language, psychology, rhetoric, and critical reading they were discussing in class (Allen 6).

In 1956, CCCC workshop participants listed reasons why TA preparation warranted a committee to continue the activities of the workshops. The participants' arguments bear citing because they demonstrate that, in the 1950s, decades of pleas for TA preparation programs were paying off.

> (1) A clear need exists for more adequate professional preparation for teachers of composition/communication. (2) The professional training of teachers of composition/communication is the prerogative and the duty of Departments of English, rather than of Schools or Departments of Education. (3) A program of in-service training for teachers . . . is desirable, this training to consist of (a) a course syllabus, (b) staff meetings, (c) some measure of supervision of teaching and theme-grading, and (d) a special course in the teaching of composition/communication. (4) Certain changes need to be made in the graduate curriculum to insure better training of teachers of composition/communication. (5) More latitude should be permitted in M.A. and Ph.D. theses so as to permit a student to do research problems related to composition/communication. ("Preparation of Composition/Communication Teachers" 138)

The need for courses to prepare TAs to teach composition had always existed and, as noted, had occasionally been met. But in the 1950s, the need for TA preparation was critical. Not only were colleges and universities trying to accommodate the returning veterans, but they were also facing a severe shortage of qualified college teachers in all disciplines.[4] Considering that most undergraduates during this period had to enroll in at least one first-year composition course, staffing was going to be a nightmare. What was to be done *quickly* to prepare college teachers of English?

Throughout the 1950s, *CCC* published articles about TA courses, one of which may be considered a model for the 1960s and 1970s courses in which current rhetorical and pedagogical theories were introduced. Albert Kitzhaber's "Rhetorical Background of Written English," first offered in 1950 at the University of Kansas, grew out of a need for experienced writing teachers, but the university also wanted to help "beginning teachers form the same sort of professional attitude toward the teaching of composition as they already [had] toward the teaching of literature" (196). New teachers met two hours every other week; the first hour was devoted to lectures on the announced topic, the second hour to "a discussion that aims to work out some of the practical applications of the theoretical material presented in the lecture" (196). To give a sense of the new ground that was broken in this course, here is the list of the biweekly topics: The first semester covered rhetorical traditions, British rhetoric of the eighteenth century, nineteenth-century American tradition, psychology and rhetoric, linguistics and rhetoric, grammar and usage, punctuation, and paragraphs. The second semester covered literary theory, English prose style, reading and grading compositions, subjects for composition, semantics and rhetoric, rhetoric and logic, English placement exams, and various types of composition courses around the country. New teachers wrote "a sort of intellectual autobiography, [at the start] of the term, in which the students . . . examine critically those beliefs they hold that have led them to choose English teaching as a career, and to determine as exactly as they can what their attitudes are toward the teaching of composition and literature" and a study of disputed usage (197).

The notion that "A good scholar *is* a good teacher [and you] don't have to train him to be one" still prevailed, Harold B. Allen reported in 1952 in "Preparing the Teacher of Composition and Communication—A Report" (4). Allen, however, happily reported progress: The University of Michigan had begun to offer a course in the teaching of composition as early as 1925, and Indiana University had required a seminar with informal reports and discussions and with the unique feature of TAs visiting high schools and conferring with secondary teachers (5). Allen found informal, noncredit seminars at Ohio State, Wayne State University, Pennsylvania, and New York University (6). In some smaller colleges and universities, like Pace, Western Michigan, Bridgeport, and the Naval Academy, TAs joined departmental staff to compare grades on freshman papers (8). One common preparation exercise, used at NYU, Pittsburgh, Iowa, Purdue, and the Naval Academy, for instance, was the common syllabus. While syllabi did not deal with general problems in teaching writing, they did provide information about textbooks and "course machinery" (8).

Although methods courses offered at Duquesne and Marquette in the late 1950s included writing assignments—at Duquesne, "a research paper analyzing any pivotal problem related to the teaching of Freshman Composition" (Hazo 120), and at Marquette, "a seminar paper in which [TAs] give form and expression to some individual research" (Schwartz 203)—little attention was paid to

TAs' writing in the 1960s and the 1970s. It was assumed that TAs could handle their composition classes without any particular preparation and without any attention to their own writing, except as it had always been attended to in course papers, theses, and dissertations. One graduate student in the mid-sixties described his experience this way:

> I have learned many facts, but few writing skills. In only one course this year did the instructor read our papers as pieces of writing. It came in my last term, and I realized then how unimproved my writing has remained. Papers in other courses were judged on the basis of length, perfection of mechanics, and material—largely in that order. In a system which perpetuates publish or perish, it seems contradictory that good writing is not more highly valued. (Macrorie 218)

In the early 1960s, NCTE, the Modern Language Association (MLA), College English Association (CEA), and the American Studies Association sponsored a collection of essays for the NCTE Curriculum Series in which leading scholars in English reported on programs that "pointed beyond the best of today to the possibilities of tomorrow" (*College Teaching* viii). Several contributors noted in passing a need to include in the graduate study direct preparation for the college classroom, as 90 percent of the PhDs in English teach in college. "Training in seminars is good, as far as it goes," Roger P. McCutcheon noted, "but does it go far enough? Graduate departments of English have some responsibility to equip their students for the careers in which they expect to earn a livelihood" (251). Encouraged by the growing number of graduate departments recommending teaching experience for PhD candidates, McCutcheon proposed that English TAs take a course in rhetoric and "should satisfy the speech department that [their] speech is adequate or can be made adequate with special exercises" (251). He also proposed that the English department offer an apprenticeship and an introductory course in college teaching.

In the 1960s, some universities experimented with innovative ways to prepare the increased numbers of TAs responsible for first-year composition. What the TA training programs at those institutions had in common, John S. Bowman of Pennsylvania State University writes, was a service commitment to supervision and preparation (73). At Pennsylvania State University four or five TAs teamed with a master teacher to instruct 120–150 students. The master teacher lectured three times a week, with TAs present; two days a week TAs met with recitation sections to address the week's lectures through discussion, repetition, textbook exercises, and supplementary materials. At Loyola University, TAs took "Studies in Methods of Language Analysis," a course that moved "from a consideration of traditional grammar through the study of structural linguistics to a concluding period on generative grammar" (Barry 77). Problems that arose in composition classes were not discussed in graduate class but rather during conferences with the master teachers. At Arizona State University, TAs took a three-credit seminar on classroom practice that emphasized grading themes; there were frequent guest lecturers on such topics as grammar and the teaching profession (Ferrell 79). At the University of Illinois, ranking members of the department were given released time to advise new TAs. They conducted group meetings, visited TAs' classes, checked graded papers, and met individually with advisees (Moake 82).

With increased attention to preparing TAs came an occasional statement about the professional status of TAs. TAs themselves occasionally found forums in which to express their concerns, as in "The Graduate Assistant Reviews His Role," a *CCC* article based on Doris McCrosson's 1958 CCCC presentation. McCutcheon, too, observed that TAs were a cheap labor source "and can be exploited, overworked, and underpaid; there is strong temptation to keep an assistant long after he has learned the essentials and is no longer getting very profitable experience out of his teaching" (251–2). Finally, as Philip R. Wikelund's *CCC* "'Masters' and 'Slaves': A Director of Composition Looks at the Graduate Assistant" indicates, TAs were beginning to find advocates in their Directors of Composition.

By the 1970s, then, English departments, which were scurrying to establish graduate programs to prepare TAs to teach first-year composition, knew some proven strategies to incorporate into their new programs: class visitations, mentors, apprenticeships, rhetoric courses, group grading of papers, reading assignments from professional journals, student-instructor conferences, writing about teaching. What was to come in the 1970s was the appointment of Directors of Composition who had an interest and a background in the teaching of writing; increased concern about the status of TAs; formal, credit-bearing methods courses; summer workshops on rhetoric and composition; graduate programs in rhetoric and composition; and emerging respectability for the teaching of writing—in short, the beginning of a new discipline documented by Steve Wilhoit and Kirsti Sandy in their respective bibliographies in this collection.

I carry my opening metaphor to this terminus: If this sprinting tour of the history of how TAs were prepared had been more leisurely, I would have stopped frequently to point out how developments in the freshman composition course itself, textbooks, social and economic contexts, the teaching of literature, and a myriad of other forces shaped the preparation of TAs. Instead, this has been, per force, a Gray Line tour that one takes to get one's bearings so she can return to the interesting points for a closer look.

## NOTES

1. The sources on which I relied most heavily in preparing this chapter—the *English Journal, College English,* and *College Composition and Communication*—began publication in 1912, 1938, and 1950, respectively. Robert J. Connors wisely reminds us that even those journals "were long read by a minority of teachers" (69).
2. During 1992, three Ohio University colleagues and a friend from Youngstown State University allowed me to interview them about their TA training in the mid-1940s and early 1950s: Lester Marx (University of Connecticut), Roland Swardson (Tulane), Calvin Thayer (UC Berkeley), and Gratia Murphy (Ohio State).
3. Roberts's course is detailed in "A Course for Training Rhetoric Teachers at the University of Illinois," *College Composition and Communication* 6 (1955): 190–4.
4. For example, between 1930 and 1955, the percentage of Southern students going to college had risen from 6 to 22; between 1951 to 1955, the percentage had risen from 17 to 22. It was

predicted that by 1965, Southern colleges could expect an 85 percent increase over that of 1955; by 1970, the South alone would need 42,000 college teachers (*Preparing College Teachers: A Project Report* 9–10).

## WORKS CITED

Alden, Raymond M. "Preparation for College English Teaching." *English Journal* 2 (1913): 344–56.

Allen, Harold B. "Preparing the Teacher of Composition and Communication—A Report." *College Composition and Communication* 3 (1952): 3–13.

Babbitt, Irving. *Literature and the American College: Essays in Defense of the Humanities.* Intro. Russell Kirk. Washington, DC: National Humanities Institute, 1986.

Baker, Harry T. "English and the Ph.D." *Educational Review* 69 (1925): 147–9.

Barry, James D. "Training Graduate Students as Teachers At Loyola University (Chicago)." *College Composition and Communication* 14 (1963): 75–8.

Bizzell, Patricia, and Bruce Herzberg. *The Rhetorical Tradition: Readings from Classical Times to the Present.* Ed. Patricia Bizzell and Bruce Herzberg. Boston: Bedford, 1990.

Bowman, John S. "Training Graduate Students as Teachers. At Pennsylvania State University." *College Composition and Communication* 14 (1963): 73–5.

Connors, Robert J. *Composition-Rhetoric: Backgrounds, Theory, and Pedagogy.* Pittsburgh: U of Pittsburgh P, 1997.

Denney, Joseph Villiers. "Preparation of College Teachers of English." *English Journal* 7 (1918): 322–6.

Dodge, Homer L. "The Place of the Subject-Matter Department in the Preparation of College Teachers." *The Preparation and In-Service Training of College Teachers.* Ed. William S. Gray. Chicago: U of Chicago P, 1938. 153–72.

Dwight, Timothy. *Memories of Yale Life and Men, 1854–1899.* New York: Dodd, Mead, 1903.

Ferrell, Wilfred A. "Training Graduate Students as Teachers. At Arizona State University." *College Composition and Communication* 14 (1963): 78–80.

Gott, Charles. "An Experiment in Teacher-Training for College Instruction." *English Journal* 18 (1929): 589–93.

Greenough, Chester Noyes. "An Experiment in the Training of Teachers of Composition for Work with College Freshmen." *English Journal* 2 (1913): 109–21.

Hazo, Samuel J. "The Graduate Assistant Program at Duquesne University." *College Composition and Communication* 8 (1957): 119–21.

Hopkins, Edwin M. "Forty Years of College English: History and Prophecy." *English Journal* 20 (1931): 320–30.

Hunting, Robert S. "A Training Course for Teachers of Freshman Composition." *College Composition and Communication* 2 (1951): 3–6.

Irmscher, William. Interview. Seattle, WA. November 23, 1992.

Kitzhaber, Albert R. *Rhetoric in American Colleges, 1850–1900.* Intro. John T. Gage. Dallas: Southern Methodist UP, 1990.

———. "The University of Kansas Course in the College Teaching of English" *College Composition and Communication* 6 (1955): 194–200.

Macrorie, Ken. "The Graduate Experience in English." *College Composition and Communication* 15 (1964): 209–52.

McCrosson, Doris Ross. "The Graduate Assistant Reviews His Role." *College Composition and Communication* 9 (May 1958): 71–5.

McCutcheon, Roger P. "Graduate Programs in English." *The College Teaching of English.* New York: Appleton-Century-Croft, 1965. 230–55.

Miller, George M. "Discussion." *English Journal* 2 (1913): 119–21.

Moake, Frank B. "Training Graduate Students as Teachers. At the University of Illinois." *College Composition and Communication* 14 (1963): 81–4.

National Council of Teachers of English. Commission on the English Curriculum. *The College Teaching of English.* Ed. John C. Gerber. New York: Appleton-Century-Croft, 1965.

Peeps, J. M. Stephen. "A B.A. For the G.I. . . . Why?" *History of Education Quarterly* 24 (1984): 513–25.

Porter, Noah. *The American Colleges and the American Public.* New Haven, CT: Charles C. Chatfield, 1870.

"Preparation of Composition/Communication Teachers: Toward a Comprehensive Program." *College Composition and Communication* 7 (1956): 138–40.

*Preparing College Teachers: A Project Report.* The University of Kentucky and the Southern Regional Education Board, 1959.

Roberts, Charles W. "A Course for Training Rhetoric Teachers at the University of Illinois." *College Composition and Communication* 6 (1955): 190–4.

Schwartz, Joseph. "One Method of Training the Composition Teacher." *College Composition and Communication* 6 (1955): 200–4.

Snyder, Franklin B. "Twenty-five Years of Trying to 'Teach' English." *English Journal* 24 (1935): 196–208.

Stewart, Donald C. "The Status of Composition and Rhetoric in American Colleges, 1880–1902: An MLA Perspective." *College English* 47 (1985): 734–46.

"Teacher-Training for Composition or Communication." *College Composition and Communication* 2 (1951): 31–2.

Thomas, J. M. "Training for Teaching Composition in Colleges." *English Journal* 5 (1916): 447–57.

Wikelund, Philip R. "'Masters' and 'Slaves': A Director of Composition Looks at the Graduate Assistant." *College Composition and Communication* 10 (1959): 226–30.

# 2. Recent Trends in TA Instruction: A Bibliographic Essay

STEPHEN WILHOIT

In his 1972 article "Preparing College Teachers of English," Kenneth Eble concluded that few English departments effectively prepared TAs to teach. By 1988, when Paul Puccio presented "Graduate Instructor Representation in Writing Programs" at the Conference on College Composition and Communication (CCCC), the situation had changed; most of the fifty departments he surveyed required TAs to participate in pre-service workshops, take credit-bearing courses in composition theory and pedagogy, and have their classroom teaching evaluated by faculty members. Catherine Latterell's 1996 survey of thirty-six graduate programs found wide use of teacher apprenticeship programs, in-service practica, theory seminars, teaching journals, classroom observation, and teaching portfolios.

What accounts for this increased interest in TA preparation over the past thirty years? Jody D. Nyquist, Robert D. Abbott, and Donald H. Wulff cite the need to replace the large numbers of professors expected to retire toward the end of the century with professionally accomplished applicants prepared to teach increasingly diverse student populations. Others cite calls from organizations such as the Council of Graduate Schools, the Pew Charitable Trusts, the American Association for Higher Education, and the Carnegie Foundation for improved undergraduate instruction (Svinicki; Tice, Gaff, and Pruitt-Logan). Over the past three decades, numerous articles, book chapters, and conference papers have suggested ways to improve the education new TAs receive as composition instructors. A review of this literature reveals general agreement concerning the structure of TA instructional programs but ongoing debates over which instructional procedures to employ and concern about the working conditions of TAs.

## TRENDS IN TA PROGRAM STRUCTURE

### PRE-SERVICE ORIENTATIONS

Perhaps the most commonly employed component of TA instruction is the pre-service orientation program. Over the years, these workshops have tended to become longer and more comprehensive. Early advocates of orientation programs, such as Lynn Bloom and Michael Flanigan in the 1970s, recommended meeting with students a few days before classes begin to discuss writing pedagogy, composition theory, and their school's writing program, three topics most often covered in orientation sessions today as well. Throughout the 1980s and 1990s, educators expanded the topics to be addressed (such as diverse student populations, research methodologies, and composition theory) and suggested that orientation sessions should last a number of weeks, not just a number of days (Haring-Smith; Svinicki).

## IN-SERVICE PRACTICA

Another common component of TA instructional programs over the years has been in-service course work or practica in composition pedagogy or theory. While early in-service practica focused on pedagogy, the trend lately has been to place more emphasis on theory. In a 1977 article, Frank D'Angelo recommended course work in the history of rhetoric, the form and structure of writing, and contemporary writing pedagogy. That same year, Richard Gebhardt suggested that course work in pedagogy be balanced with course work in composition theory and rhetoric, a position endorsed by many writers, including Gene Krupa, William Gracie ("Serving"), and John J. Ruszkiewicz. By the late 1980s and 1990s, writers were arguing for an even greater emphasis on theory in TA education, many citing Tori Haring-Smith's 1985 article, "The Importance of Theory in the Training of Teaching Assistants."

Yet this move toward theory met with some resistance. For example, Wendy Bishop ("Attitudes") examined how efforts to encourage TA adherence to a particular theory of composition can be complicated by the theories TAs bring with them to graduate school, while Douglas Hesse examined graduate student resistance to "difficult" readings in his composition theory course. In her 1993 article "Resisting the Faith," Nancy Welch critiqued a TA training program that, in her view, attempted to "convert the non-believers," TAs who adhered to a theory of writing different from the one endorsed by the department.

The 1990s saw the content of in-service practica expand significantly beyond the study of theory and practice. Educators pointed out, for example, that practica can help TAs learn how to engage in research projects of their own (Wilhoit, "Toward"), prepare them for the job market (Hattenhauer and Shaw), provide needed moral support (Hunt), build a sense of community in English departments (Dunn), and improve the quality of TA instruction across the curriculum (Svinicki). Despite these changes, however, Latterell argues that current in-service courses are still overly "skills based" and too frequently confined to the TAs' first year of study.

Today, TA in-service programs must balance three related needs: to educate TAs in composition theory and pedagogy, to maintain a theoretically coherent writing program, and to respect the TAs' own theories of writing and teaching. Longitudinal studies of TA education, such as those conducted by Christine Farris, Sarah Liggett, and Elizabeth Rankin, can help identify the long-term outcomes of in-service education and effective ways to meet the diverse needs of new and experienced TAs.

## APPRENTICESHIP AND MENTORSHIP PROGRAMS

Over the past thirty years, a dominant guiding metaphor in the literature on TA education has been the TA as "apprentice" teacher. In most apprenticeship programs, TAs are seen as teachers-in-training who, as a group, work under the supervision of a faculty member, perhaps even team teaching a course with their supervisor (Simpson). Although the degree of supervision can vary widely, this faculty member typically works with all or most of the TAs in a program and guides or dictates what and how the TAs teach. While most writers praise apprenticeship programs (Gefvert; Krupa), lately such methods have received more critical scrutiny. William Gracie ("Positive") argues that faculty will not value TAs and attend to their instruction as long as TAs are viewed merely as apprentice teachers, a position endorsed by Timothy R. Donovan, Patricia Sprouse, and Patricia Williams. In fact, Mark C. Long, Jennifer H. Holberg, and Marcy M. Taylor argue that "apprenticeship" programs fail to promote inde-pendent teaching and inadequately prepare TAs for research and service. Despite these criticisms, though, apprenticeship programs still dominate TA education (Barr Ebest; Latterell). Increasingly, however, TAs are seen not only as apprentice teachers, but also as apprentice researchers and apprentice adminis-trators. Expanded professional training and experience are helping today's TAs more quickly gain the status of junior colleague (Nyquist and Sprague), necessi-tating a reevaluation of their working conditions and compensation.

Advocates of faculty mentorship programs believe that with close, one-on-one rather than group supervision, TAs will learn to improve as classroom teachers; receive experienced, informed responses to their teaching; obtain ready advice and guidance; and have a role model to emulate (Flanigan; Hansen et al.; Tice, Gaff, and Pruitt-Logan). Over the years, however, a clear trend has emerged—a shift from faculty mentor programs toward peer mentor programs. Although a few writers in the 1970s mentioned peer mentoring as an instruc-tional technique (Hairston), it received greater attention in the 1980s and 1990s. In 1986, both David Foster and Marvin Diogenes, Duane H. Roen, and C. Jan Swearingen argued that TA peer support groups promote collegiality and improve teaching (see also Back et al.; Chase; Puccio, "TAs"; Weiser). These instructional techniques have proven effective: Linda Williams notes that TAs who participate in consultant observation and peer mentor programs experi-enced less anxiety when teaching than do TAs who do not have faculty consult-ants or peer mentors.

## WRITING TUTORS

Training TAs as writing tutors prior to assuming responsibility for their own writing classes is a movement that emerged strongly in the 1980s. Irene Clark's 1988 article, "Preparing Future Composition Teachers in the Writing Center," explained how experience as a writing tutor can improve a TA's class-room teaching (see also Blalock). Peggy F. Broder offered testimonials from for-mer tutors who later became classroom teachers explaining how their work in a writing center benefited their classroom teaching, findings supported by Jane

Cogie's 1997 study of ten TAs. Muriel Harris, on the other hand, argues that TAs should have experience as classroom instructors before becoming writing center tutors. All of these educators agree, however, that working as a tutor helps TAs learn how to talk to students about their writing, offer precise and constructive commentary on student work, and gain confidence as teachers.

## TRENDS IN TA PROGRAM PRACTICES AND CONTENT

### CLASSROOM OBSERVATION

Since the 1970s, many educators have advocated classroom observation as a central TA instructional practice. Some educators suggest that faculty observe TAs in class and evaluate their performance (Flanigan; Diogenes, Roen, and Swearingen; Haring-Smith; Svinicki). Others advocate peer observation, either alone or in combination with faculty observation (Cooper and Kehl; Hairston; Weiser). Some argue that TAs should watch other teachers conduct class (Back et al.; Reagan). Although these educators advocate a range of classroom observation programs, they agree that TAs benefit when feedback from observations are detailed, descriptive, and supportive rather than general, judgmental, and critical. All also agree on the importance of pre-observation conversations in which TAs can explain their course goals and class plans and post-observation discussions where TAs can ask questions and get advice.

### ROLE-PLAYING

Other widely advocated TA-preparation practices involve various role-playing techniques, including classroom simulations and teaching scenarios. Over the years, these instructional techniques have become increasingly complex and rhetorically sophisticated, addressing a wide range of concerns. In his 1982 article, Krupa maintained that role-playing exercises promote reflective teaching. Irvin Hashimoto agreed, suggesting that in orientation sessions TAs be required to work through a series of "writing problems" that force them to articulate and challenge their often tacit assumptions about writing and teaching. More recently, TA educators have suggested that classroom scenarios—elaborate and sophisticated descriptions of situations teachers are likely to face in a writing class—encourage reflective instruction (Anson, Jolliffe, and Shapiro), help TAs reflect upon diversity issues in the classroom (Swyt), and encourage TAs to connect theory with practice, drawing on their tacit knowledge of teaching and learning (Rose and Finders). Scenarios used during both pre-service orientations and in-service practica help TAs anticipate classroom situations, practice alternative methods of presenting material or solving problems, and apply composition theory.

### TEACHING JOURNALS AND PORTFOLIOS

In the 1980s and 1990s, a number of writers began recommending that TAs keep teaching journals and portfolios as a part of their education. For example,

Nancy Comley maintained that composing informal journal entries helps TAs connect composition theory with their own teaching practices and lessens their anxieties, a position endorsed by Gebhardt and by Bishop ("Teachers"). In fact, several writers, including Mary Kay Tirrell and Geraldine McBroom, suggest that keeping a teaching journal is central to a TA's growth as a teacher because it promotes critical reflection. Recently, writers have recommended that TAs maintain teaching portfolios as well, collections of classroom materials, course evaluations, and self-reflective essays. John Webster argues that TAs and administrators can use teaching portfolios to improve instruction, assess and review the TAs' progress in a program, and help TAs get jobs when they graduate (see also Hutchings). Documenting their experiences as instructors through teaching journals and portfolios enables TAs to reflect on their growth, express their anxieties, formulate their educational philosophies, and critique their classroom performance.

## REFLECTIVE PRACTICE

Today many practices for preparing TAs promote "reflective teaching," a movement that emerged forcefully in the 1990s (Hillocks). Most articles on the topic, like Robert Tremmel's "Beyond Self-Criticism: Reflecting on Teacher Research and TA Education," explore how "reflective practice" can improve TA class performance. These instructional methods require TAs to identify and critique their practices as teachers and their plans for the future through a series of exercises: role-playing, writing about their experiences in teaching journals, discussing their plans with peers. Recently writers have argued that reflection exercises such as these can help TAs understand the important relationship between their personal histories as writers and students and their teaching practices (Cleary and Seidman), examine their own often tacit assumptions about writing and writing instruction (Bishop, "Attitudes"; Hashimoto; Swyt), and advance through various stages of professional development (Nyquist and Sprague). For these writers, reflective teaching holds the key for lifelong professional development. If new TAs learn to reflect on their teaching practices, assess the effectiveness of their teaching, and consider alternative pedagogies that might improve the instruction they offer their students, they will continue to grow as teachers throughout their careers.

## RESEARCH AND PUBLICATION

Establishing connections between TAs and the wider academic community is one motive behind recent calls to teach TAs how to develop research projects and publish their results. Both Stephen Wilhoit ("Conducting") and Thomas A. Angelo and K. Patricia Cross recommend introducing TAs to the teacher-researcher movement in practica by having them conduct research projects that link composition theory and pedagogy. Diogenes, Roen, and Swearingen suggest that, as a part of TA training, faculty and TAs engage in joint research projects aimed at publication. Such projects, they argue, contribute to the professional development of TAs. This trend, however, is not without its detractors. Janice Lauer, for example, maintained that some graduate students are pushed to publish material prematurely, and Carrie Leverenz and Amy Goodburn believe that a heavy emphasis on professional development in TA instructional programs may result in too little attention to the preparation of TAs as classroom teachers. As always, balance is required. While new TAs may well need to focus on pedagogy, more experienced TAs, especially those who plan a career in academia, would benefit from a program that encourages them to enter into professional conversations, to engage in the type of research projects studied in composition theory classes, and to develop classroom applications like those studied in pedagogy seminars.

## WRITING PROGRAM ADMINISTRATION

In addition to instruction in pedagogy and research, writers have recently argued that TAs should receive instruction in writing program administration as a part of their preparation program (Barr Ebest; Long, Holdberg, and Taylor; Thomas; Tice, Gaff, and Pruitt-Logan; Wilhoit, "Toward"). In his 1993 essay "Tales Too Terrible to Tell," Michael Pemberton condemns the lack of administrative preparation provided by most current doctoral programs given that many faculty trained in rhetoric and composition can expect to serve as writing program administrators.

Today, many TA educators offer instruction in writing pedagogy, composition theory, research, and administration. TAs applying for entry-level jobs may well have extensive experience as teachers, a thorough education in pedagogy and theory, academic publications, conference presentations, and administrative experience. As TAs become more professionalized, however, questions arise about their working conditions: How should the TAs' teaching duties and compensation reflect their professional status?

## TRENDS IN EMPLOYMENT CONCERNS

TAs generally face poor working conditions, labor-intensive classes, low pay, few benefits, and little respect, conditions that have changed little over the past few decades. In 1972, Eble concluded that most colleges and universities undervalue teaching and give TAs no voice in department affairs. In two studies of TA working conditions conducted in 1987 and 1997, Robert M. Diamond and Peter J. Gray reached similar conclusions. In fact, Ward Hellstrom argued that full-time faculty in English departments are not committed to TA education because the faculty benefits from a system that overworks TAs (see also Crowley; Sledd). Concerns over the continuing problems TAs face surfaced forcefully in the recent debate over The Wyoming Resolution, a statement documenting TA working conditions and recommending changes (Robertson, Crowley, and Lentricchia; Sledd).

Those interested in improving the working conditions of TAs have proposed several changes, arguing that TAs need fair financial compensation and a work load that supports progress toward their degrees (CCCC Task Force on the Preparation of Teachers of Writing; Syverson and Tice). In 1991, the CCCC reiterated its 1989 "Statement of Principles and Standards for the Postsecondary Teaching of Writing" and recommended steps that writing programs should take to improve the working conditions of TAs (CCCC Committee on Professional Standards 1991; Weiser and Dwyer). Others suggest that TAs can best improve their working conditions through increased education and professional development, maintaining that TAs who improve their teaching, engage in research, serve on committees, publish, and attend conferences will be in a better position to demand and expect better working conditions (for a discussion of this position, see Leverenz and Goodburn). Others, however, maintain that the biggest impediment to improving the working conditions of TAs is the title "teaching *assistant*," a title that helps justify giving TAs less pay, lower status, and fewer privileges (Hattenhauer and Shaw; Long, Holberg, and Taylor; Schell).

Recently writers have advocated a more "collegial" model of TA instruction in which TAs enjoy the same privileges as full-time faculty members (Long, Holberg, and Taylor), such as funding for professional activities (Jolliffe) and merit pay (Weiser). Others, like Eileen E. Schell, maintain that TAs can only improve their working conditions by unionizing. Current efforts to recognize TAs as full members of the profession—including the growing trend toward unionization—demonstrate the changing status of TAs in universities across the country. As their instructional programs have matured and they have become more "professionalized," TAs have assumed more responsibilities in their departments, necessitating changes in work loads and salaries to compensate them fairly for their work.

## FUTURE DIRECTIONS

Over the past three decades, programs to prepare new TAs have increased in coverage and complexity, moving from pre-service workshops that introduced only survival skills to various combinations of pre-service and in-service colloquia and courses that address pedagogical, theoretical, and professional issues. The literature also reveals several areas deserving additional research. For example, additional longitudinal studies of TA development would help determine which instructional techniques have lasting value for TAs. Are some methods of instruction most helpful to TAs early in their teaching and some most helpful as they near graduation? What is the best way to sequence instruction throughout the years of a TA's service? Research that examines the relationship between TA instructional techniques and gender, race, age, and teaching style is also needed. For example, are some methods of instruction best suited for female TAs and some best for male TAs? Is the experience of minority TAs in the classroom different than the experience of other TAs? If so, what additional instruction might be needed to prepare all TAs for the classroom?

Much more attention also needs to be paid to TA preparation at comprehensive universities. How does the experience of TAs working in MA programs differ from those working in doctoral programs? Additional research might help develop more effective ways to prepare TAs for increasingly diverse student populations and an increasingly technological workplace. We also need more research on preparing TAs to work in a variety of instructional settings, such as two-year colleges and high schools. Which techniques work best to prepare TAs to teach in these different types of institutions? Finally, TA employment concerns need more study: How can TAs, faculty, and university administrators work together to improve TA working conditions and ensure TAs a living wage, a reasonable work load, and adequate support? Although educators have made great advances in TA preparation over the past three decades, much work remains.

## Works Cited

Angelo, Thomas A., and K. Patricia Cross. "Classroom Research for Teaching Assistants." *Teaching Assistant Training in the 1990s.* Ed. Jody D. Nyquist, Robert D. Abbott, and Donald H. Wulff. San Francisco: Jossey-Bass, 1989. 99–107.

Anson, Chris M., David A. Jolliffe, and Nancy Shapiro. "Stories to Teach By: Using Narrative Cases in TA and Faculty Development." *WPA* 19.1–2 (1995): 24–37.

Back, Lillian, Susan Carlton, Merla Wolk, and Robin Schulze. "Training TAs to Teach Writing: Four Perspectives on Creating a Community for Composition Instruction." *Preparing the Professoriate of Tomorrow to Teach.* Ed. Jody D. Nyquist, Robert D. Abbott, Donald H. Wulff, and Jo Sprague. Dubuque: Kendall/Hunt, 1991. 198–204.

Barr Ebest, Sally. "The Next Generation of WPAs: A Study of Graduate Students in Composition/Rhetoric." *WPA* 22.3 (1999): 65–84.

Bishop, Wendy. "Attitudes and Expectations: How Theory in the Graduate Student (Teacher) Complicates the English Curriculum." *Teaching Lives: Essays and Stories.* Logan: Utah State UP, 1997. 192–207.

———. "Teachers as Learners: Negotiated Roles in Writing Teachers' Learning Logs." *Journal of Teaching Writing* 10.2 (1991): 217–40.

Blalock, Susan E. "The Tutor as Creative Teacher: Balancing Collaborative and Directive Teaching Styles." *The TA Experience: Preparing for Multiple Roles.* Ed. Karron G. Lewis. Stillwater, OK: New Forums P, 1993. 348–52.

Bloom, Lynn. "The Promise and the Performance: What's Really Basic in Teaching TAs." Conference on College Composition and Communication. Philadelphia. Mar. 1976.

Broder, Peggy F. "Writing Centers and Teacher Training." *WPA* 13.3 (1990): 37–45.

CCCC Committee on Professional Standards. "A Progress Report from the CCCC Committee on Professional Standards." *College Composition and Communication* 42 (1991): 330–44.

CCCC Task Force on the Preparation of Teachers of Writing. "Position Statement on the Preparation and Professional Development of Teachers of Writing." *College Composition and Communication* 33 (1982): 446–9.

Chase, Geoffrey. "A Professional Development Program for Graduate Students: Fostering Collaboration in the Writing Program at Northern Arizona University." *Making Teaching University Property.* Ed. Pat Hutchins. Washington, DC: American Association for Higher Education, 1993. 85–8.

Clark, Irene Lurkis. "Preparing Future Composition Teachers in the Writing Center." *College Composition and Communication* 39 (1988): 347–50.

Cleary, Linda Miller, and Earl Seidman. "In-Depth Interviewing in the Preparation of Writing Teachers." *College Composition and Communication* 41 (1990): 465–71.

Cogie, Jane. "Theory Made Visible: How Tutoring May Effect Development of Student-Centered Teachers." *WPA* 21.1–2 (1997): 76–84.

Comely, Nancy. "The Teaching Seminar: Writing Isn't Just Rhetoric." *Training the New Teacher of College Composition.* Ed. Charles W. Bridges. Urbana, IL: NCTE, 1986. 47–57.

Cooper, Allene, and D.G. Kehl. "Development of Composition Instruction through Peer Coaching." *WPA* 14.3 (1991): 27–39.

Crowley, Sharon. "Terms of Employment: Rhetoric Slaves and Lesser Men." *Composition in the University: Historical and Polemical Essays.* Pittsburgh: U of Pittsburgh P, 1998. 118–31.

D'Angelo, Frank J. "Strategies for Involving Graduate Students in the Teaching of Composition." *ADE Bulletin* 54 (1977): 34–6.

Diamond, Robert M., and Peter J. Gray. "A National Study of Teaching Assistants." *Institutional Responsibilities and Responses in the Employment and Education of Teaching Assistants.* Ed. Nancy Van Note Chism. Columbus: Ohio State University Center for Teaching Excellence, 1987. 80–2.

———. *1997 National Study of Teaching Assistants.* Syracuse, NY: Center for Instructional Development, Syracuse University, 1998.

Diogenes, Marvin, Duane H. Roen, and C. Jan Swearingen. "Creating the Profession: The GAT Training Program at the University of Arizona." *WPA* 10.1–2 (1986): 51–60.

Donovan, Timothy R., Patricia Sprouse, and Patricia Williams. "How TAs Teach Themselves." *Training the New Teacher of College Composition.* Ed. Charles W. Bridges. Urbana, IL: NCTE, 1986. 139–47.

Dunn, Richard J. "Teaching Assistance, Not Teaching Assistants." *ADE Bulletin* 97 (1990): 47–50.

Eble, Kenneth E. "Preparing College Teachers of English." *College English* 33 (1972): 385–406.

Farris, Christine. *Subject to Change: New Composition Instructors' Theory and Practice.* Cresskill, NJ: Hampton P, 1996.

Flanigan, Michael C. "Variety, the Key to Training Programs for Faculty and Teaching Assistants." *ADE Bulletin* 57 (1978): 44–6.

Foster, David. "Training Writing Teachers in a Small Program." *WPA* 10.1–2 (1986): 43–50.

Gebhardt, Richard C. "Balancing Theory with Practice in the Training of Writing Teachers." *College Composition and Communication* 28 (1977): 134–40.

Gefvert, Constance J. "An Apprenticeship for Teaching Assistants." *Freshman English News* 10.3 (1982): 16–19.

Gracie, William J., Jr. "A Positive Program in a Negative Climate: Training the First Year Graduate Student to Teach Freshman English." Rocky Mountain Modern Language Association. Albuquerque. Oct. 1979.

———. "Serving Our Teaching Assistants and Our Profession: Teaching Graduate Students to Teach Composition." Conference on College Composition and Communication. San Francisco. Mar. 1982.

Hairston, Maxine. "Training Teaching Assistants in English." *College Composition and Communication* 25 (1974): 52–5.

Hansen, Kristine, Phillip A. Snyder, Nancy Davenport, and Kimberli Stafford. "Collaborative Learning and Teaching: A Model for Mentoring TAs." *The TA Experience: Preparing for Multiple Roles.* Ed. Karron G. Lewis. Stillwater, OK: New Forums P, 1993. 251–9.

Haring-Smith, Tori. "The Importance of Theory in the Training of Teaching Assistants." *ADE Bulletin* 82 (1985): 33–9.

Harris, Muriel. "Selecting and Training Undergraduate and Graduate Staffs in a Writing Lab." *Administrative Problem-Solving for Writing Programs and Writing Centers.* Ed. Linda Myers-Breslin. Urbana, IL: NCTE, 1999. 14–29.

Hashimoto, Irvin Y. "Sensitizing Beginning Teachers of Writing." *Journal of Basic Writing* 3 (1984): 55–62.

Hattenhauer, Darryl, and Mary Ellen Shaw. "The Teaching Assistant as Apprentice." *College Composition and Communication* 33 (1982): 452–4.

Hellstrom, Ward. "Economics, Elitism, and Teacher Apprentice Programs." *ADE Bulletin* 77 (1984): 26–32.

Hesse, Douglas. "Teaching as Students, Reflecting Resistance." *College Composition and Communication* 44 (1993): 224–31.

Hillocks, George, Jr. *Teaching Writing as Reflective Practice.* New York: Teachers College P, 1995.

Hunt, Maurice. "Preventing Burn-out in Teaching Assistants." *Freshman English News* 15.1 (1986): 12–15.

Hutchings, Pat. "Teaching Portfolios as a Tool for TA Development." *The Professional Development of Graduate Teaching Assistants.* Ed. Michele Marincovich, Jack Prostko, and Frederic Stout. Bolton, MA: Ankor, 1998. 235–48.

Jolliffe, David A. "Programs of Note in English and Composition." *Preparing Graduate Students to Teach: A Guide to Programs That Improve Undergraduate Education and Develop Tomorrow's Faculty.* Ed. Leo M. Lambert and Stacey Lane Tice. Washington, DC: American Association for Higher Education, 1993. 77–85.

Krupa, Gene H. "Helping New Teachers of Writing: Book, Model, and Mirror." *College Composition and Communication* 33 (1982): 442–5.

Latterell, Catherine G. "Training the Workforce: An Overview of GTA Education Curricula." *WPA* 19.3 (1996): 7–23.

Lauer, Janice M. "Graduate Students as Active Members of the Profession: Some Questions for Mentoring." *Publishing in Rhetoric and Composition.* Ed. Gary A. Olson and Todd W. Taylor. Albany: State U of New York P, 1997. 229–35.

Leverenz, Carrie Shively, and Amy Goodburn. "Professionalizing TA Training: Commitment to Teaching or Rhetorical Response to Market Crisis?" *WPA* 22.1–2 (1998): 9–32.

Liggett, Sarah. "After the Practicum: Assessing Teacher Preparation Programs." *The Writing Program Administrator as Researcher.* Ed. Shirley K Rose and Irwin Weiser. Portsmouth, NH: Boynton/Cook, 1999. 65–80.

Long, Mark C., Jennifer H. Holberg, and Marcy M. Taylor. "Beyond Apprenticeship: Graduate Students, Professional Development Programs and the Future(s) of English Studies." *WPA* 20.1–2 (1996): 66–78.

McBroom, Geraldine. "A New Crop of Teaching Assistants and How They Grew." *WPA* 15.3 (1992): 62–8.

Nyquist, Jody D., Robert D. Abbott, and Donald H. Wulff. "The Challenge of TA Training in the 1990s." *Teaching Assistant Training in the 1990s.* Ed. Jody D. Nyquist, Robert D. Abbott, and Donald H. Wulff. San Francisco: Jossey-Bass, 1989. 7–14.

Nyquist, Jody D., and Jo Sprague. "Thinking Developmentally about TAs." *The Professional Development of Graduate Teaching Assistants.* Ed. Michele Marincovich, Jack Prostko, and Frederic Stout. Bolton, MA: Ankor, 1998. 61–88.

Pemberton, Michael A. "Tales Too Terrible to Tell: Unstated Truths and Underpreparation in Graduate Composition Programs." *Writing Ourselves into the Story.* Ed. Sheryl I. Fontaine and Susan Hunter. Carbondale IL: Southern Illinois UP, 1993. 154–73.

Puccio, Paul M. "Graduate Instructor Representation in Writing Programs." Conference on College Composition and Communication. St. Louis. Mar. 1988.

———. "TAs Help TAs: Peer Counseling and Mentoring." Conference on Employment and Education of Teaching Assistants. Columbus. Nov. 1987.

Rankin, Elizabeth. *Seeing Yourself as a Teacher: Conversations with Five New Teachers in a University Writing Program.* Urbana, IL: NCTE, 1994.

Reagan, Sally Barr. "Practicing What We Preach." *CEA Forum* 20 (1990): 16–8.

Robertson, Linda R., Sharon Crowley, and Frank Lentricchia. "The Wyoming Conference Resolution Opposing Unfair Salaries and Working Conditions for Post-Secondary Teachers of Writing." *College English* 49 (1987): 274–80.

Rose, Shirley K, and Margaret J. Finders. "Learning from Experience: Using Situated Performances in Writing Teacher Development." *WPA* 22.1–2 (1998): 33–52.

Ruszkiewicz, John J. "Training Teachers Is a Process Too." *College Composition and Communication* 38 (1987): 461–4.

Schell, Eileen E. "Teaching under Unusual Conditions: Graduate Teaching Assistants and the CCCC's 'Progress Report.'" *College Composition and Communication* 43 (1992): 164–7.

Simpson, Isaiah. "Training and Evaluating Teaching Assistants through Team Teaching." *Freshman English News* 15.3 (1987): 4, 9–13.

Sledd, James. "Why the Wyoming Resolution Had to Be Emasculated." *Journal of Advanced Composition* 11 (1991): 269–81.

Svinicki, Marilla D. "The Development of TAs: Preparing for the Future While Enhancing the Present." *The Department Chairperson's Role in Enhancing College Teaching.* Ed. Ann F. Lucas. San Francisco: Jossey-Bass, 1989. 71–80.

Swyt, Wendy. "Teacher Training in the Contact Zone." *WPA* 19.3 (1996): 24–35.

Syverson, Peter D., and Stacey Lance Tice. "The Critical Role of the Teaching Assistantship." *Preparing Graduate Students to Teach.* Ed. Leo M. Lambert and Stacey Lane Tice. Washington, DC: American Association for Higher Education, 1993. 1–11.

Thomas, Trudelle. "The Graduate Student as Apprentice WPA: Experiencing the Future." *WPA* 14.3 (1991): 41–51.

Tice, Stacey Lane, Jerry G. Gaff, and Anne S. Pruitt-Logan. "Preparing Future Faculty Programs: Beyond TA Development." *The Professional Development of Graduate Teaching Assistants.* Ed. Michele Marincovich, Jack Prostko, and Frederic Stout. Bolton, MA: Ankor, 1998. 275–92.

Tirrell, Mary Kay. "Teaching Assistants as Teachers and Writers: Developmental Issues in TA Training." *Writing Instructor* 5 (1986): 51–6.

Tremmel, Robert. "Beyond Self-Criticism: Reflecting on Teacher Research and TA Education." *Composition Studies* 22.1(1994): 44–64.

Webster, John. "Great Expectations: Introducing Teaching Portfolios to a University Writing Program." National Council of Teachers of English. Louisville. Nov. 1992.

Weiser, Irwin. "Teaching Assistants as Collaborators in Their Preparation and Evaluation." *Evaluating Teachers of Writing.* Ed. Christine A. Hult. Urbana, IL: NCTE, 1994. 133–46.

Weiser, Irwin, and Karen Dwyer. "The CCC's 'Statement of Principles and Standards for the Postsecondary Teaching of Writing': Implications for Writing Program Administrators and Teaching Assistants." *The TA Experience: Preparing for Multiple Roles.* Ed. Karron G. Lewis. Stillwater, OK: New Forums P, 1993. 19–24.

Welch, Nancy. "Resisting the Faith: Conversion, Resistance, and the Training of Teachers." *College English* 55 (1993): 387–401.

Wilhoit, Stephen. "Conducting Research: An Essential Aspect of TA Training." *Kentucky English Bulletin* 39.1 (1989): 48–55.

———. "Toward a Comprehensive TA Training Program." *Kansas English* 78.2 (1993): 66–74.

Williams, Linda Stallworth. "The Effects of a Comprehensive Teaching Assistant Training Program on Teaching Anxiety and Effectiveness." *Research in Higher Education* 32 (1991): 585–98.

# 3. After Preparing TAs for the Classroom, What Then?
## Three Decades of Conversation about Preparing TAs for the Job Market

KIRSTI A. SANDY

Preparing TAs for positions upon graduation has been an aim of TA educators for the last thirty years. As a freshly minted PhD and newly appointed tenure-track faculty member, I am grateful that my program emphasized professional development. At Illinois State University and elsewhere, TAs not only learn theories and practices about the teaching of composition, but new TAs take part in a mentoring program in which they co-teach a first-year writing class with veteran TAs, and they begin early in their graduate program to prepare teaching portfolios. As a former mentor to two new TAs, I was able to fully examine my teaching and to revise it when appropriate. Co-teaching allowed me to reflect upon my strengths and weaknesses as a teacher, gaining knowledge that proved useful when I prepared my teaching portfolio and responded to interview questions.

Graduate programs have, in fact, become so concerned about preparing their students for the job market that Carrie Shively Leverenz and Amy Goodburn have observed, "Calls for an increased emphasis on the professional development of graduate students have begun to generate some opposition" (11). They claim, "The relationship between TA preparation and a graduate student's professional development needs to be examined in more depth" (10) As this chapter will show, debates about whether and how TA preparation should focus on employment issues are not altogether new. In this collection Betty P. Pytlik notes that preparing TAs for the job market has been a concern of professional organizations and teacher educators in recent decades. However, several ways to prepare TAs to face the job market have emerged from these conversations—both in English and in other disciplines—creating today's increased interest in professional development as part of teacher education.

Debates about professionalizing graduate student education always, in some fashion, refer to the job market crisis. In other words, the glut of PhDs and the shortage of tenure-line positions together offer an imperative for increased professionalization. In the 1970s, professionalizing TA education in English studies often meant integrating the study of composition with that of literature in graduate degree programs. In the 1980s, it often involved offering TAs apprenticeship opportunities and supervision beyond the first-year classroom. In the 1990s, professionalization often meant encouraging TAs to publish and present papers at professional conferences. Throughout the past three decades, then, universities have sought ways to prepare TAs to meet the demands of the competitive market by modifying the graduate curriculum, including adding preparation for the job search to their agenda. They have, for instance, given more varied job assignments to TAs, as is evident in the administrative positions some TAs hold (see chapters in this collection by Irwin Weiser and Katrina Powell and colleagues). Others have revised their curricula to attend more to issues of professionalization in course work (see Margaret Lindgren's chapter on teaching portfolios in this collection).

What accounts for such changes? Is the job market worse now than it was ten, twenty, or thirty years ago? Actually, according to Raul Sanchez, it is improving slightly. Although Sanchez suggests that the job market for most literary fields remains tight, he claims, "In both absolute and comparative terms, [rhetoric and composition PhDs] are still actively sought by departments around the country, and at this moment it is misleading to suggest otherwise" (96). He adds, "If the job market is any indication, rhetoric and composition is still quite a vibrant field" (96). While professional development in graduate school began as a response to a tight job market, it has continued to evolve and expand as compositionists have understood and articulated the relationship between learning theories and practices for the classroom and job preparation. In other words, preparing professionally no longer ends with professional employment but continues as one builds a career. The remainder of this chapter will explore how our concepts of professional development, especially our ideas about what graduate students need to do to prepare for the market, have evolved in the last thirty years.

## TA PROFESSIONAL DEVELOPMENT AS A SOLUTION TO THE JOB MARKET CRISIS

In 1976, Allan Cartter and Lewis Soloman, estimating that the unemployment rate for English PhDs was 33 percent, predicted, "Since about 41,000 new Ph.D.s will be produced annually during the remainder of this decade, total academic demand will be about a third of the graduate school outflow in the next few years" (38). Cartter also predicted that by the 1980s graduate schools would produce 46,000 new PhDs per year across the disciplines (38). In 1977, the MLA began, according to Kurt E. Müller and R. Douglas LeMaster, "to monitor the production and placement of Ph.D'.s" (51). Two years later, the language used in the *ADE Bulletin, College English,* and *College Composition and Communication* to describe the job market was just short of apocalyptic. Ward Hellstrom, in "Academic Responsibility and the Job Market," observed, "we must not delude ourselves [into believing that] the market is not so bad as it is painted; it is worse" (98). Hellstrom recommended that departments act to combat the problem: Cut back current graduate programs, refrain from adding new programs, raise admissions standards, and eliminate postdoctoral programs that "provide cheap labor for composition" (97–8).

Many, however, worried that the tight job market would not only diminish enrollment in their graduate programs but also rob English departments of the perspectives and innovations that new faculty can offer. Dan McLeod, in his 1979 "Watching Our Discipline Die," insisted, "If intelligent graduate students realized what was facing them when they finished their doctorates, they would certainly want to reconsider their choice of a career" (34). The waning job market, he added, will "kill" the profession, since "Denying young professors the full and active roles that most of us played in our first tenure-track jobs simply transforms a lively intellectual stream of a department into an unattractive, stagnant pond" (34). "These are perilous times," declared Nancy Lenz Harvey in 1981. "[T]he party is over" (1). The toll of the waning job market on graduate students and faculty was evident in the 1970s. Robert B. Hinman, in 1977, told about a colleague's receiving an envelope containing tiny shreds of paper, the remains of a PhD diploma of a student whose dissertation the colleague had directed. Hinman lamented, "Probably every one of us has suffered some pangs of guilt, felt a few twinges of futility, as we have meditated upon our sins of unworldliness and reflected on our failure to prepare our graduate students for the 'real world' of the job market" (36).

Although the job market for literature specialists declined in the 1970s, the demand for rhetoric and composition specialists was growing. As a result, many graduate programs in English responded to the job market crisis by reintegrating rhetoric into their graduate course requirements; this move, when added to the growing use of teaching apprenticeships, paved the way for many of our discussions regarding the professionalization of graduate education today. According to Marilyn L. Williamson. "During doctoral training, students should have some formal instruction in linguistics, rhetoric, and cognitive processes with specialists, not so that the graduate students will become such specialists, but so that they will be able to fulfill adequately a major professorial responsibility" (7). Williamson's implication that courses in linguistics, rhetoric, and cognitive processes inherently prepare graduate students in English programs for the job market reflects a larger trend of the late 1970s—that of preparing graduate students in English programs as generalists rather than as literature specialists.

Jonathan Culler, in his 1979 "Rethinking the Graduate Curriculum," pointed out that graduate students need to prepare for teaching a wide variety of courses. Culler argued, "graduate programs should be more professional, should explicitly set out to offer thorough preparation for the teaching profession" (19) rather than focusing exclusively on preparing TAs to teach traditional literature courses. According to Culler, "the advocates of 'back to basics' in graduate studies have not given sufficient thought to the situations their students will encounter when they begin, or seek to begin, teaching" (19). Graduate students, Culler suggested, should be given opportunities to develop innovative approaches to teaching. Since enrollments had dropped and the job market had become more competitive, Culler argued, "a department may be better served by an assistant professor who can develop new courses that are attractive to students than by one who can take over the Elizabethan literature course and offer a Spenser seminar" (20). To be well-prepared for the job search, graduate students should have a course of study that involves "something other than a reimposition of the tough requirements and high standards of yester-year" (20) such as "extensive work on the relationship between literature and other forms of writing and modes of representation" (20). Such work would require "the revival of rhetoric and rhetorical categories to describe the production of meaning in discourse" (21).

Others, like E. D. Hirsch, viewed the "double vocation in literature and literacy" as a back-to-basics approach, rather than as an alternative to one. Hirsch, in his 1979 "Remarks on Composition to the Yale English Department," claimed, "[a] good Ph.D. program in English ought to . . . turn out professors of rhetoric *and* belles lettres, as in the days of yore" (65). Hirsch stated that "the composition problem" (63) is one caused by professors' neglect of the course, one that could be solved by "restoring in its Ph.D. program the historical connection between the teaching of literature and the teaching of literacy" (64). Since, as he claimed, "students are flooding into writing courses" (63), it was imperative to pay attention to those courses.

Because many graduate programs were rethinking their curricula, the 1970s saw a greater emphasis on implementing and offering graduate courses in rhetoric and improving teacher preparation programs. In 1976, Winifred Horner observed the positive effect of the job market on the TA preparation program at the University of Missouri, Columbia. She claimed, "Too often economic pressures and the demands of the job market limit our options and take us in directions we do not always choose. For the composition program at the University of Missouri, such has not been the case" (62). In 1974, the University of Missouri had offered a graduate course entitled "Rhetorical and Linguistic Theory Applied to the Teaching of English Language." According to Horner, this course, mandatory for all TAs, "seriously changed the nature of the composition program" (61). Horner claimed, "As enrollments in literature courses continue to decline, graduate students recognize the teaching of writing as part of a lifelong commitment" and "recognize that their expertise in the teaching of composition may well be the decisive factor in securing a position when they graduate" (59) since expertise in teaching writing was increasingly in demand by colleges and universities.

Teacher preparation for the writing classroom was also beginning to be considered a professional development activity and not merely a way to "train" TAs to teach courses as temporary labor. For example, the University of Iowa's Professional Development Program in Rhetoric was, according to Cleo Martin in 1976, designed "primarily for the purpose of providing teachers with regular opportunities to exchange ideas and information and to discuss teaching theories and techniques" (77). The program assumed "that teachers continue to 'develop professionally' throughout their careers," which made the program unlike the usual "staff training" programs at many other schools (77). Since teaching composition was beginning to be a permanent commitment on the part of many TAs and faculty, TA education in teaching writing was considered as integral to graduate study as course work.

## THE 1980s: A TIME OF GRADUAL CHANGE

In "Graduate Programs in the Eighties," Edward Sharples discussed his survey of 139 English departments in which he asked, among other questions, "What, then, is being done by these departments to prepare [graduate] students adequately for entry into college teaching in these times?" (13) According to Sharples, "Typical answers on the conservative side were 'we give seminars and our students teach freshman English'; 'All features of our program prepare them: seminars, examinations, and teaching assistantships'; 'Our standard Ph.D. prepares them to teach. Our students take courses, seminars, field examinations, foreign language exams, and write theses'" (13–14). Sharples identified these responses as "conservative" because he saw in them "little recognition of how circumstances have altered since most of us entered the profession ten, twenty, thirty, or more years ago" (14). However, Sharples noted, "Some responses . . . reflect greater sensitivity to current conditions; these three are representative: One chairman wrote, 'We are beginning to concentrate more on the teaching of composition and rhetoric, since more schools are asking specifically for this kind of preparation'" (14). According to Sharples, "Fully seventy percent replied that their graduate programs did have composition components" (18) and, of those, "Approximately twenty-three percent of these departments require all graduate students to take work in composition, and twenty-eight percent require that some of their students (usually their graduate teaching assistants) take courses in teaching composition" (18). Sharples described these trends as evidence of "the law of supply and demand and the law of natural selection" (19). "Nothing," Sharples added, "neither the power nor the inertia of graduate faculties, can withstand such forces" (19).

Maxine Hairston noted in 1981 that the more rhetoric and composition programs grew, the more job opportunities would be available. According to Hairston, "[G]raduate programs are proliferating, and the demand for writing courses and writing teachers continues to increase" (12). She claimed to "know of no discipline that promises to be more productive and exciting during the eighties than that of composition and rhetoric" and suggested that the early 1980s was "a good time to be a writing teacher," predicting, "[I]n ten years it will be an even better time" (14). Constance Gefvert agreed, adding, "Composition is becoming increasingly professional" (41). Gefvert observed, "[A] number of new journals have recently been founded, and established journals are broadening their fields to include composition research, rhetorical theory, and interdisciplinary links between English and other academic fields. The teaching of composition is . . . gradually gaining the prestige that it rightfully deserves" (41). Gefvert also noted a "growing sense of professionalism" in the field (43).

This "sense of professionalism" meant that TAs would need more preparation in teaching, publishing, and presenting conference papers first to get academic jobs and then to be promoted. In 1981, Paula Backscheider suggested that departments help graduate students publish, which meant, "[W]e must be alert to the promising seminar paper and be willing to read successive drafts and to guide submissions" (18). In addition, Backscheider claimed, faculty must provide graduate students "with varied teaching experience" that may require faculty to teach "elementary composition classes" (18). She noted that new PhDs must "enter the job stream as assistant professors who are ready to compete at a level not required of most associate professors ten years ago" (18).

Darryl Hattenhauer and Mary Ellen Shaw, as Stephen Wilhoit notes in the previous chapter, also commented upon the increasing professional responsibilities of graduate students and noted that the key to preparing graduate students for professional positions is not to eliminate the supervision of graduate students but to treat them "like apprentices, rather than like temporary labor" (452). Apprenticeship opportunities, claimed Hattenhauer and Shaw, including observing and working with experienced teachers, administrative work, and committee work, will better enrich the professional development of graduate students, who need these opportunities to ensure future employment.

The increasing opportunities for TAs in rhetoric and composition brought a number of additional responsibilities for them as well. The CCC Executive Committee's 1989 "Statement of the Principles and Standards for the Postsecondary Teaching of Writing," which was the result of an investigation of TAs' working conditions, found, "The quality of writing instruction today is seriously compromised" because "English graduate students who staff many writing programs are regularly assigned teaching duties that they cannot responsibly discharge without neglecting their own course work" (329). The Executive Committee issued a reminder: "Graduate students are primarily students," (330) and their "special status . . . should be recognized and their compensation, benefits, class size, and course load should be adjusted accordingly. . . . Attention should be given to hours spent outside and inside of class and to the increased responsibility for grading, classroom management, and preparation." (332) That the CCCC Executive Committee took up the issue of exploitation of the graduate students suggests that the profession itself had begun to recognize TAs as future professionals and not merely as temporary labor. However, the report's suggestion that TAs take on fewer responsibilities also meant fewer opportunities for them to have a variety of teaching and administrative experiences.

The 1980s also saw a growing recognition that graduate school could not do it all—that some job preparation had to be the result of TAs' own initiative and not necessarily part of a department mandated program. Trudelle Thomas, in her 1989 "Demystifying the Job Search: A Guide for Candidates," suggested that graduate students find creative ways to merge their professional and "school" work. One creative way, as one of Thomas's headings recommends, is to "View the Job Search as a Research Project" (312). Thomas claimed that the best way to prepare for the market was to "Read at least a few of the journals important in your field" and to "Turn seminar papers into conference presentations and later submit them for publication in professional journals" (314). Becoming involved in one's university, whether it be through administrative experience, graduate student organizations, or university committees, is crucial, according to Thomas.

During the 1980s, rhetoric and composition provided job opportunities not available in other areas of English studies. The result of this trend in graduate preparation for the job market was tremendous; it meant more opportunities for graduate courses in rhetoric and composition, and it meant that teaching writing was considered professional preparation rather than temporary employment. More opportunities for apprenticeships and increased teaching responsibilities followed, as did a greater emphasis on publishing. With all of these changes, however, came the caution that graduate students can become overwhelmed with too much professional preparation. This concern was part of the conversation about TA preparation that continued into the next decade.

## THE 1990s AND BEYOND: CONTINUING (AND ACTING UPON) THE CONVERSATION

Like Thomas, many others are asking, "How can we help TAs see themselves as professionals?" Scott L. Miller, Brenda Jo Brueggemann, Bennis Blue, and Deneen M. Shepherd claim that graduate students today "evince far less satisfaction with and far less understanding about the broader professional realm of rhetoric and composition" (397) than they do about other aspects of graduate school. This "dissatisfaction and ignorance manifests itself most especially regarding professional development issues, job market difficulties, or the transition from graduate school into the professoriate," (397) they add. Miller et al. claim, "Most graduate students are already required to take some sort of 'Introduction to English Studies' course and a composition [theory] course and even, perhaps, for those pursuing a degree or emphasis in rhetoric and composition, at least one course in composition and rhetoric research methods." (403) "Why," they ask, "isn't anything consistently required in relation to their professional development at large—to the summation of all these other requirements?" (403)

According to Teresa Mangum, "Graduate programs need to give more attention to the difficulties students have learning to integrate and balance the complex, competing responsibilities they will face as professionals" (20). Mangum argues that graduate students need mentors who will "guide them more explicitly as they learn to integrate research and pedagogical questions" (20). Too many faculty members avoid taking on this responsibility; they need to "understand the job market and work harder to help candidates" (23).

How well have many colleges and universities addressed the concerns that Mangum and Miller et al. discuss? As I indicated at the beginning of this chapter, institutions and programs have met the challenge of professionalizing TA education in several ways.

### MENTORING PROGRAMS

Irwin Weiser claims, in "When Teaching Assistants Teach Teaching Assistants to Teach: A Historical View of a Teacher Preparation Program" in this collection, that "[M]entoring is professional development, of a kind not available through class work, and as such, . . . it has an important role to play in the preparation of soon-to-be faculty" (47). Many compositionists suggest that mentorship opportunities—situations in which new TAs work closely with experienced TAs in the classroom and beyond—are essential. A mentor in this sense is not only one who supervises another's teaching, but also one who provides assistance and guidance throughout one's graduate career. Miller et al. suggest, "Rhetoric and composition programs ought to have a well-planned and well-developed mentoring system" which could include "both faculty members paired with graduate students, throughout their professional careers" or "'experienced' graduate students paired with 'new' graduate students particularly in their first year" (405). Such a system would work particularly well in large programs, Miller et al. claim, since "Graduate students easily get lost in the system." A mentoring program, they add, would "give graduate students a chance to make informed decisions and the best sorts of progress in their teaching, coursework, and overall professional path" (405).

Mentorship can be defined in a number of ways. In some cases, it occurs when experienced TAs work with new TAs, as Weiser describes (for more on peer mentoring, see Wanda Martin and Charles Paine and Gita Das Bender, in this collection). Mentoring can also mean faculty support, as Theresa Mangum describes. Mentors can play a number of roles—that of "contact" in the field, advocate, supervisor, guide, colleague, and advisor. While these roles can conflict, opportunities can arise from them as well. For example, three of the essays in this collection are coauthored by faculty and graduate students. It is this kind of professional development opportunity that Miller et al. promote.

To support the spirit of mentorship, many institutions provide graduate faculty with incentives. For example, the "Graduate College Outstanding Mentor Award," "recognizes exemplary efforts of members of the graduate faculty in advising and serving graduate students." The criteria for selection includes "Excellent guidance of individual research and creative projects, including theses; general assistance to graduate students, including advising for graduate student organizations, conflict resolution, and advocacy for graduate students; impact on students; and other contributions to the professional development of graduate students, including supervision of teaching assistants and research assistants, and career preparation and advancement."

## TEACHING PORTFOLIOS

Margaret Lindgren notes in this collection that she is "certain that teaching portfolios help our TAs to be more competitive on the job market" and also that "Several TAs have won departmental and university-wide teaching awards after having used their portfolios when representing themselves to judges [while] others have found jobs and used all or pieces of their portfolios when writing application letters and submitting materials" (301). According to Chris Anson, "While the portfolio may seem at first glance like a typical faculty 'file,' it differs from dossiers in important ways. First, although it can contain personal materials, [the teaching portfolio] benefits from arguments among a community of teachers about what it should contain and what purposes it should serve"

(187). Additionally, Anson states, it "is not simply a repository of the outcomes of teaching; it contains documents that show teachers in action, both creating their teaching and reflecting on it during moments of introspection" (187). Anson suggests, "The portfolio may become several portfolios, each displaying different materials depending on its purpose and audience" (187).

For my own job search, I was encouraged by my professors to create mini-portfolios for each job interview, using my larger teaching portfolio as a base. Composing my teaching portfolio allowed me to see the job search as a rhetorical situation, one that offered me the opportunity to better understand each institution and to demonstrate how I met the needs of each one. For many graduate students, the teaching portfolio has become an indispensable part of graduate school and of the job search.

## PROFESSIONAL DEVELOPMENT COURSES

Graduate courses in professional development are usually devoted exclusively to the job search. In other words, such courses require graduate students to develop teaching portfolios, compose cover letters, and participate in mock interviews, among other activities. For example, in 1995 Texas A&M University implemented a one-credit course to prepare graduate students for the job search. According to Maura Ives, who designed and teaches the course, it "worked, both administratively and pedagogically" (14). Says Ives, "[I]t isn't enough for placement directors and committee chairs to point PhD candidates in the right direction with a reading list and some extra office hours. After teaching English 681, I would argue that it is unacceptable for placement directors to hand out a bibliography of useful sources without sitting down with students to discuss it" (14). Ives suggests, "We have to teach the market, just as we teach cultural studies or Shakespeare, because it is our responsibility as faculty members to know our profession and to share that knowledge with our students" (14).

The design of the course, according to Ives, "was shaped by the timetable of the fall academic job search" (15). Ives explains that "the course began with an overview of the academic job market and for the first few weeks focused on the preparation of letters, vitae, dissertation abstracts, and other written materials for the search" (15). According to Ives, this process helped her view the job search as "an exercise in professional writing" (15). Ives adds, "The classroom format of reading, listening, and debating allowed students to take control of their job searches and of their professional identities" (16).

Some programs offer TAs courses in writing program administration as well. Shirley K Rose at Purdue University states in her 1998 syllabus for "English 680W: Writing Program Administration" that most rhetoric and composition scholars "at one or more points in their academic careers" will most likely "be expected to work for a period as writing program administrators." According to Rose, her seminar attempts to answer the question, "What does it take to qualify as a Writing Program Administrator—good 'people skills,' on-the-job experience, or disciplinary expertise in writing studies?" The course, claims Rose, addresses "Ethical implications of defining the responsibilities of writing program administrators; rhetorical strategies for documenting writing program administration; and institutional politics of characterizing writing program administration as 'service,' 'teaching,' and/or 'research.'" Courses such as Rose's can offer TAs opportunities to understand the responsibilities of a WPA, which would prove invaluable when applying for positions that may include such appointments.

## PREPARING FUTURE FACULTY PROGRAMS: PROFESSIONAL DEVELOPMENT ACROSS THE DISCIPLINES

Some professional development incentives involve graduate students from a number of disciplines. According to Richard A. Cherwitz, the University of Texas also offers Graduate School Professional Development courses, which "address such topics as writing, pedagogy, technology, ethics, consulting, communication, and multiculturalism." According to the Web page, "Professional Development courses are one way the Graduate School is preparing students to be intellectually rigorous scholars and teachers (the next generation of professors), as well as professionally astute citizens qualified to meet the needs of society." The curriculum teaches TAs "how to adapt to a variety of audiences—so that they can write scholarly articles, develop grant proposals, and secure book contracts," among other achievements.

Preparing Future Faculty (PFF), another program that helps graduate students across the disciplines prepare for the job search, is "a national network of academic leaders reshaping graduate education to include preparation for the full range of faculty roles subsumed by the terms teaching, research, and service" (http://www.preparing.faculty.org). The National PFF program consists of fifteen colleges and universities, including Syracuse University, the University of Washington, Howard University, and the University of New Hampshire. PFF institutions were persuaded to "plan their programs in accordance with their students' maturity and stage of development; to include mentoring in teaching and other aspects of professional development; to provide direct, personal experience with diverse institutions; and to emphasize emerging and future expectations of faculty."

Professional development activities promoted by PFF include developing teaching and professional portfolios, peer review of vita and dossier documents, simulated job interviews, and participation in search committees. PFF also provides graduate students opportunities to "get acquainted with the professional lives of faculty members at institutions markedly different from the research universities where they are earning their degrees."

## IN THE NEW MILLENNIUM

Although graduate English programs will continue to emphasize preparing TAs to teach writing to ensure the quality of instruction in undergraduate writing courses, the exigencies of the market make it imperative that we also continue to help TAs gain entry into the writing class through tenure-track positions. Despite the numerous professional development opportunities for graduate students in rhetoric and composition, Mark C. Long, Jennifer L. Holberg, and Marcy M. Taylor remind us that although "graduate students are being trained for jobs in the profession, there is increasing evidence that these jobs will be more varied and will require broader skills than the positions as they are defined today" (76). Thus, teacher preparation courses must remain abreast of these changes, and those responsible for preparing teachers and for preparing future professors must continue to find innovative ways, such as the ones mentioned in this chapter, to meet the demands of the profession and of the market.

As the recent discussions of teacher education and professionalization demonstrate, the fact that these conversations are taking place is proof that the discipline has not, as some predicted, died. It is alive. But we must keep in mind Clyde Moneyhun's admonition: "New rhet/comp PhDs must investigate and prepare to enter a job market that is quite different from the one their teachers faced ten or fifteen or twenty years ago, and different even from the one their friends faced five or six years ago" (92). The only certainty in the quest for professional employment is that the stakes will continue to change, and we must be sure that preparation for the job search is a part of the broad conversation of our discipline.

## WORKS CITED

Anson, Chris. "Portfolios for Teachers: Writing Our Way to Reflective Practice." *New Directions in Portfolio Assessment: Reflective Practice, Critical Theory, and Large-Scale Assessment.* Ed. Laurel Black, Donald A. Daiker, Jeffrey Sommers, and Gail Stygall. Portsmouth, NH: Boynton Cook, 1994. 185–200.

Backscheider, Paula. "Into All the World." *ADE Bulletin* 68 (1981): 17–20.

Cartter, Allan M., and Lewis Solomon. "Implications for Faculty." *Change* 8 (1976): 3–8.

CCC Executive Committee. "Statement of Principles and Standards for the Postsecondary Teaching of Writing." *College Composition and Communication* 40 (1989): 329–36

Cherwitz, Richard A. "Graduate School (GRS) Professional Development Program." University of Texas Web page. Accessed June 9, 2000. http://www.utexas.edu/ogs/grs/pd_board.

Culler, Jonathan. "Rethinking the Graduate Curriculum." *ADE Bulletin* 62 (1979): 19–26.

Gefvert, Constance J. "The Composing Process: Bringing Order out of Confusion." *ADE Bulletin* 70 (1980): 41–3.

"Graduate College Outstanding Mentor Award." University of Illinois at Urbana-Champaign Web site. Accessed June 8, 2000. http://www.grad.uiuc.edu/mentoring 2000.html.

Hairston, Maxine. "Some Speculation about Writing Programs in the Eighties." *ADE Bulletin* 67 (1981): 12–4.

Harvey, Nancy Lenz. "We Can Get There from Here." *ADE Bulletin* 70 (1980): 1–4.

Hattenhauer, Darryl, and Mary Ellen Shaw. "The Teaching Assistant as Apprentice." *College Composition and Communication* 33 (1982): 452–4.

Hellstrom, Ward. "Academic Responsibility and the Job Market." *ADE Bulletin* 62 (1979): 95–9.

Hinman, Robert B. "Imagining What We Know." *ADE Bulletin* 55 (1977): 32–6.

Hirsch, E.D. "Remarks on Composition to the Yale English Department." *ADE Bulletin* 62 (1979): 63–5.

Horner, Winifred. "The Graduate Student Teacher-Training Program at the University of Missouri, Columbia." *Options for the Teaching of English: Freshman Composition*. Ed. Jasper Neel. New York: MLA, 1978. 58–62.

Ives, Maura. "Teaching the Market: Graduate Placement in the Classroom." *ADE Bulletin* 119 (1998): 14–8.

Leverenz, Carrie Shively, and Amy Goodburn. "Professionalizing TA Training: Commitment to Teaching or Rhetorical Response to Market Crisis?" *WPA* 22 (1998): 9–32.

Long, Mark C., Jennifer L. Holberg, and Marcy M. Taylor. "Beyond Apprenticeship: Graduate Students, Professional Development Programs and the Future(s) of English Studies." *WPA* 20 (1996): 66–78.

Mangum, Teresa. "Identity and Economics, or, The Job Placement Procedural." *ADE Bulletin* 114 (1996): 19–24.

Martin, Cleo. "The Rhetoric Program at the University of Iowa." *Options for the Teaching of English: Freshman Composition*. Ed. Jasper Neel. New York: MLA, 1978. 70–8.

McLeod, Dan. "Watching Our Discipline Die." *ADE Bulletin* 66 (1980): 34–5.

Miller, Scott L., Brenda Jo Brueggemann, Bennis Blue, and Deneen M. Shepherd. "Present Perfect and Future Imperfect: Results of a National Survey of Graduate Students in Rhetoric and Composition Programs." *College Composition and Communication* 48 (1997): 392–409.

MLA Committee on Professional Employment. "Final Report of the MLA Committee on Professional Employment." *ADE Bulletin* 119 (1998): 27–45.

Moneyhun, Clyde. "Still Dressed Up but OTJ: Beyond the Quest for Perfection in the Rhet/Comp Industry." *College Composition and Communication* 50 (1998): 91–5.

Müller, Kurt E., and R. Douglas LeMaster. "Criteria Used in Selecting English Faculty in American Colleges and Universities." *ADE Bulletin* 77 (1984): 51–7.

"Preparing Future Faculty." Web site. Accessed June 8, 2000. http://www.preparing.faculty.org.

Rose, Shirley K. "Syllabus for English 680 W: Writing Program Administration." Web site. Accessed June 8, 2000. http://iedweb.cc.Purdue.edu/w/skrose/eng1680.html.

Sanchez, Raul. "No Time for Panic." *College Composition and Communication* 50 (1998): 95–7.

Sharples, Edward. "Graduate Programs in the Eighties." *ADE Bulletin* 59 (1978): 13–9.

Thomas, Trudelle. "Demystifying the Job Search: A Guide for Candidates." *College Composition and Communication* 40 (1989): 312–28.

Williamson, Marilyn L. "Reviewing Graduate Programs: Have You Looked at JIL Lately?" *ADE Bulletin* 56 (1978): 5–8.

Percy Long PmLA 64 (1949): 1-12

# 4. When Teaching Assistants Teach Teaching Assistants to Teach: A Historical View of a Teacher Preparation Program

IRWIN WEISER

In 1974, I began my career as a composition teacher: A second-year doctoral student, I was assigned a composition class in the spring and told when and where it would meet in the fall. I was told where the sample textbooks were shelved and when and to whom to submit my textbook order. I talked with one or two TAs who had taught the course before, borrowed their syllabi, perused the bookshelves, ordered two books that I was unable to recognize as theoretically at opposite ends of the composition spectrum, and prayed when fall came I'd "first, do no harm," and second, not be hated by the students I would teach (or perhaps it was the other way around). My previous teaching experience had been one semester as a grader in a literature lecture course and one semester as the leader of a discussion section and grader in a composition/literature course. My previous formal preparation for teaching composition: none.

In 1976, after apparently not doing harm to any students, I began teaching as a part-timer in a composition program at another university. There, under the leadership of a new composition director, the whole composition staff met for two days prior to the start of the semester. The director and his assistants talked about their sense of the program, gave us copies of the book we'd be using, and led us through the sample syllabus they'd developed for us. We read and evaluated and discussed some papers. Then the semester began and we taught.

What I'm describing is probably not unfamiliar to readers who began to teach writing in the mid-1970s and early 1980s. I'm afraid it's not completely unfamiliar to some of you who may have begun your teaching much more recently. And I'm not recalling these early memories to criticize the two research universities where I began teaching. I simply want to remind us of how recently we've begun to take seriously the preparation of new teachers of writing, of how recently most universities have acted upon the belief that anyone who could write well enough to be in graduate school in English could teach writing without any instruction or support.

In 1981, I came to Purdue University and for the first time participated in a teacher preparation program that seemed the result of viewing the teaching of college composition as an activity requiring some specialized knowledge, some disciplinary familiarity, if not expertise.

Purdue was not institutionally significantly different from the other places I had taught. All were state-supported universities, and all but one had PhD programs (and the one that did not had offered the MA in English). All but one enrolled well more than 20,000 students at the time. (Purdue's current enrollment is nearly 37,000.) Three were broad-based institutions focusing primarily on social and natural sciences, liberal arts, and education; two, including Purdue, had heavy emphases on technology and engineering. (Purdue is a land-grant university and offers programs in agriculture, veterinary medicine, nursing, pharmacy, sciences, liberal arts, education, management, technology, and education.) As was the case at the other universities where I taught, all students were required to take at least one semester of composition. But despite its institutional similarity, there was clearly an attitudinal difference in Purdue's Department of English toward the preparation of teachers of writing.

## A HISTORY OF TEACHING ASSISTANT PREPARATION AT PURDUE

Like many large research universities, Purdue University has long depended upon graduate student teaching assistants to teach most sections of first-year composition courses. This has been the case since as early as 1963–1964, when the department head, Russell Cosper, indicated that "graduate assistants [were] assuming most of the burden of teaching freshman composition" (Department of English Annual Report).[1] Unlike English Departments at many other institutions, including those where I had previously taught, however, Purdue's English Department recognized very early the importance of providing those TAs with support and preparation for their work. Because records are sketchy, I have been unable to discover exactly when, but sometime during the tenure of Professor Barnet Kottler as Director of Composition between 1962 and 1966, the English department instituted a mentoring program. A memo concerning salaries for TAs from Professor Kottler to Professor Cosper dated October 10, 1966, refers to TAs' raises being based on satisfactory progress toward their degrees and "favorable recommendations for their teaching from their Mentors." An undated sheet titled "The Mentor Program for Training and Supervising Teaching Assistants," written by Robert A. Miller, who began his term as Director of Composition in 1969, begins, "In order to train and supervise the large number of teaching assistants who teach our basic composition courses, the Purdue Department of English has for years used a 'mentor system.'"

According to a description of Professor Kottler's responsibilities found in a 1976 promotion document, mentors were "regular staff members" who supervised "groups of five or six new teaching assistants." This description indicates how seriously the English Department took its responsibility to support and prepare new teachers of writing: "regular staff members"—tenured and tenure-track faculty–mentored as part of their teaching responsibility and worked with very small groups of new TAs to do so. Again, records about the number of mentors and TAs cannot be found, but one document does refer to "well over a hundred sections of the composition courses" and "a large corps of teaching assistants" (Promotion Document, 1976, 6). Mentoring remained primarily a faculty responsibility through the 1970s. A report by department head Jacob Adler in 1976 refers to mentors as "full-time faculty members experienced in teaching composition [who] are put in charge of groups of five new teaching assistants."

However, as Purdue grew, and as the demand for more sections of composition grew, the mentoring system began to change. The undated description of the mentoring system I referred to above, which had to be written no later than the Adler report since Miller's term ended in 1976, indicates that by that time, not all mentoring was done by faculty: "Each mentor is an experienced teacher (regular member of the professorial staff or advanced teaching assistant with unusual ability as a teacher) who has volunteered to serve in the program as a regular part of his teaching assignment. His duties as mentor are considered equivalent to the teaching of one three-hour course a semester, and he is given a reduced teaching load accordingly" (Miller.) Thus, apparently at the same time that one report identified mentors as "full-time faculty," another document indicated that advanced graduate students could serve as mentors.

The use of graduate student mentors was mentioned in minutes of the Composition Committee in 1979, the year in which a graduate Practicum in Teaching College Composition was established to formalize mentoring. In the minutes of the December 7, 1979, Composition Committee meeting, Professor Leonora Woodman, Director of Composition, was quoted as saying "only graduate faculty can be mentors" but "it is possible to arrange an internship whereby a graduate student can work with a mentor." This issue was raised because by 1979, several graduate students were serving as mentors, but since the practicum was being proposed as a 600-level course, graduate students would not be eligible to be instructors of record. Although the available records do not mention this, at some point between the time the proposal passed the Composition Committee and the course's being finally approved, it was made a 500-level course. I speculate that part of the reason for this change is that 500-level courses are technically dual-level (undergraduate and graduate) and therefore could be taught by graduate students. The new practicum addressed not only TAs new to the first-year writing program but also "teaching assistants in their initial semester(s) in English 100 [Developmental Writing] . . . 420 [Business Writing], and special composition-related programs [such as the Writing Lab and the English as a Second Language courses]" (Minutes of the Composition Committee, Feb. 20, 1980).

Thus, when I arrived at Purdue in August 1981, the mentoring program had been in existence for at least fifteen years and had been formalized as a course for a year. The one-credit practicum in place in 1981 offered TAs practical support in teaching. While each mentor was responsible for choosing the textbook and designing the syllabus for the TAs enrolled in his or her section of English 502, common features of the practicum included discussions of the specific material being taught in the upcoming week, approaches to commenting on and evaluating student writing, designing writing assignments, designing small-group activities, and issues of classroom management, including developing and applying course policies for attendance and late work, working with unmotivated or resistant students, and so on. As time permitted, mentors assigned articles in composition studies, typically those with direct practical applications like Nancy Sommers's 1982 *College Composition and Communication* article "Responding to Student Writing." Each mentor observed TAs in her section twice per semester, following those observations with conferences to discuss what the TA was doing well and how to improve. Mentors also reviewed sample sets of commented on or graded papers from each teacher in the practicum and provided comments and advice on the TAs' practices as evaluators. While mentors provided most of the structure for the first semester, most included the TAs in the planning for the second semester course and offered some flexibility in designing assignments or sequencing papers. Teaching assistants were evaluated each semester by their mentors, receiving written evaluations and usually meeting with their mentors for a conference to discuss their performances.

To the extent possible, mentoring was done by faculty, perhaps with graduate students serving as assistants or "apprentices" (Minutes of the Composition Committee, Sept. 23, 1981). In 1981, in fact, only one TA mentored new TAs, while the other four mentor groups were taught by faculty in the newly established rhetoric and composition graduate program. And from the earliest available records in 1980 through 1987, there was at most one experienced TA serving as a mentor for new TAs, nearly always the current or former assistant Director of Composition.

Since 1988, the number of TA mentors and the ratio of faculty to TA mentors have fluctuated a bit. In the years between 1988 and 1994, there have been as many as four TAs serving as mentors, but there have also been three years in which no TAs mentored. Some of this fluctuation reflects the ebb and flow of graduate enrollments. For instance, in 1994, the last year no TAs mentored, there were only thirty-one new TAs, so that four faculty mentors could work with relatively small groups, but in 1989, when forty-six new TAs were appointed, five faculty members and three graduate students mentored. In part, the fluctuation reflects the availability of faculty to mentor, since as the graduate program grew, faculty were needed to teach other graduate courses. Exacerbating the issue of faculty availability were two reductions in teaching loads for faculty as Purdue recognized that its teaching loads had to be comparable to those of other Research I universities in order to recruit and retain faculty. In 1981, when I arrived, assistant and associate professors taught three courses per semester; full professors taught five per year. In the mid-1980s, all faculty moved to a five-course-per-year load, and in 1991, faculty teaching load was again reduced, this time to two courses per semester. This course reduction and the growth of the graduate program together meant that either the available pool of mentors had to be expanded or mentor group size would have to increase—or, as gradually happened, both. Finally, the fluctuation reflects the ambivalent attitudes of department heads and Directors of Composition (myself, for most of the years between 1986 and now) about the use of graduate student mentors.

## RESISTANCE TO TAs TEACHING TAs

Why has our department resisted having TAs teach other TAs, preferring instead to appoint faculty to mentor whenever possible? In part, that reluctance can be attributed to concerns about the potential problems of graduate students/TAs having supervisory and evaluative authority over their peers. As the 1966 memo I mentioned earlier suggests, mentors' evaluations played a significant role in whether or not a new TA received a merit raise. While the implementation in the mid-1980s of teaching portfolios in which the mentor's evaluation was only one of a number of artifacts helped reduce this potential source of conflicts among graduate students, faculty were, understandably, I think, concerned about the potential for problems this situation carried with it. Further, mentors' evaluations and less formal reports also provided the Director of Composition with information about the performance of new TAs that could lead to a graduate student's losing his or her assistantship. This, in fact, occurred in 1990, the first year that the number of graduate student mentors equaled the number of faculty mentors. During that year, three first-year TAs were not reappointed. Two were being mentored by other TAs, and while the decision not to reappoint them was mine, as Director of Composition, nevertheless, the complex issue of having TAs supervise one another raised its head.[2] For the next two years, no TAs mentored, even though this meant that mentor groups increased in size. And size has always been an issue for us. Because mentors not only meet weekly with the TAs in their groups but also observe classes, review selected papers the TAs have evaluated, and meet individually with group members to discuss class observations, papers, student problems and so on, we have always tried (although not always successfully) to keep group size as low as possible. Certainly, the original limit of five is a thing of the past, largely because there are not enough faculty or advanced graduate students (although in part because economic pressures across the university have led to larger classes at both the graduate and undergraduate levels).

There is one final reason that I believe our department has resisted, at least until recently, shifting our mentoring program from being primarily faculty taught to being largely a TA-taught program. That the department has been willing to devote significant resources in the form of faculty teaching assignments to mentoring (mentoring that still takes place in relatively small sections) is an indication of the seriousness with which the department takes the preparation of new teachers of composition.[3] When graduate students begin at Purdue and are assigned to a mentor group taught by a member of the graduate faculty in rhetoric and composition (and at Purdue, that has included people such as James Berlin, Patty Harkin, Janice Lauer, and Shirley Rose), the message is, I believe, clear: Teaching first-year composition is not simply something anyone can do; it requires disciplinary knowledge and support, and one way to get both that knowledge and support is to work with an experienced teacher/scholar. And the message, I would argue, has merit. Faculty such as those I have mentioned above are leaders in rhetoric and composition studies; they have both theoretical knowledge and practical experience to share with the TAs they supervise, and their experience is based on more than two or three years of teaching experience and course work, as is the case for graduate student mentors.[4]

## WHY TAs SHOULD TEACH OTHER TAs

But there is another side to this story. There are good reasons to provide opportunities for TAs to mentors their peers. As I suggested above, to keep the size of mentor groups small, we have had to increase the number of mentors. There are several ways that this could have been done. One would be to hire new tenure-track faculty, part of whose role would be mentoring new writing teachers. Certainly, this is desirable, but unfortunately impractical. Increasing enrollments at Purdue have not been accompanied by an increase in the size of the faculty. Our number of faculty on the whole has stayed at about the same size for several years, but like most large English departments, we are a diverse lot—our faculty is composed of people in rhetoric and composition, in literature, in theory and cultural studies, in English language and linguistics, in creative writing, and in English education. Growth in majors as well as other students taking English courses as electives has occurred along with the growth in the graduate program, and every area I have mentioned has competed for the faculty lines made available to us. Often, we find that our hiring is not a matter of growth, but a matter of maintenance, as colleagues retire, move to other institutions, or move into administrative posts. Another way to address the desire to keep mentor groups small would be to appoint more of the existing faculty, both those in and those not in rhetoric and composition, to serve as mentors. This is also impractical, if not impossible. One of the reasons we have increased the number of TAs who are mentoring is that nearly all of the rhetoric and composition faculty hold some sort of administrative responsibility as well, and all are needed to teach in the graduate program. And while faculty not specializing in rhetoric and composition have occasionally mentored in the past, the increased enrollment I mentioned above means that faculty in other specializations find their teaching entirely taken up by courses in those areas. Even if a faculty member who specializes in literature or creative writing wanted to mentor, it is unlikely he or she would be able to. The third, and only practical option, is to rely more heavily on TAs to mentor their peers. And keeping mentor groups small is an important enough value for us to accept this solution.

Another good reason to appoint TAs as mentors involves disciplinary knowledge. Faculty in other areas of the department simply do not have the familiarity with scholarship in rhetoric and composition that many of our graduate students do. Since the 1991 course reduction, few faculty in any area, including rhetoric and composition, have taught composition courses, so even those outside the field with interest in rhetoric and composition have little incentive to stay current in the scholarship. But our graduate program in rhetoric and composition attracts talented students and familiarizes them with theory, research, and practice in the discipline. Not only do students for whom rhetoric and composition is the primary area become familiar with this work, but a

number of graduate students in other areas take rhetoric and composition graduate courses as a secondary field.[5] Our graduate student mentors must have
completed their PhD preliminary examinations before they can be appointed to
mentor, so we are able to appoint students in their third, fourth, or fifth year of
doctoral work, often with one or two years of composition teaching experience
at the master's level prior to their entering the PhD program. Our graduate student mentors are, then, more familiar with the scholarship and more recently
experienced in the pedagogy of composition than the majority of our non-
rhetoric and composition faculty. Because of their background, we are able to
maintain a mentoring program staffed by people with disciplinary knowledge
and to have a more professional mentoring program than we would if we
staffed mentor groups with faculty unfamiliar with the field.

Finally, mentoring provides TAs with valuable professional development
opportunities. TAs who serve as mentors can apply their disciplinary knowledge and teaching experience in a way that is quite different from simply teaching their own classes. As mentors, they find themselves having to generalize
from their own experiences and to find ways to apply what they have learned,
both as students and as teachers. They discover that what works (or doesn't
work) for them in the classroom may not (or may) work for another teacher.
They learn to recognize that what they have learned about teaching over a number of years of experience can't always be easily explained to or adopted by
another person. They have to theorize their practice. For many of our graduate
student mentors, mentoring allows them to apply their expertise and in doing
so to contribute to our program's diversity in ways that might not otherwise
occur. For example, until fall 2000, we did not have faculty in the introductory
writing program with expertise in the applications of computers to composition. But a number of our graduate students have made technology and writing
a focus of their studies and research and have taught in our professional writing program, where they have been mentored by faculty with that expertise.
When these graduate students mentor, they not only bring what they have
learned about computers and writing to the introductory writing program, but
they also have an opportunity to see how the theories and pedagogies they have
practiced in professional writing change when they are moved into the first-
year writing course.

Indeed, the increasing numbers of graduate student mentors have led those
of us who administer the introductory writing program to recognize our
responsibility in the professional development of these new teachers of new
teachers of writing. When the mentoring was done exclusively, or nearly so, by
faculty, we all operated independently. Occasionally, we talked with one
another about our approaches to mentoring or shared experiences with one
another, and we discussed with the Director of Composition any particularly
vexing or serious problems. In recent years, however, as the number of graduate student mentors has begun to equal or surpass the number of faculty mentors, mentors have begun meeting regularly for "mentor lunches"—opportunities to discuss in an informal setting issues that concern us all. And it has not
been only the graduate student mentors who have benefited from these lunches:
Their insights into teacher preparation have been useful to the faculty mentors

as well. At a recent lunch, the graduate student mentors pointed out that the narrative evaluation form that the TAs complete about their mentor and the experience of being mentored has not been revised for a number of years and agreed that we should spend time at the next lunch discussing possible changes. It was a graduate student mentor who suggested that we hold a spring meeting of all the people who have been appointed to mentor the following year as a way to share ideas and approaches.

The shift from a primarily faculty-led teacher preparation program to one I anticipate will continue to be at least equally led by TAs has been, as I think my narrative here has indicated, a process of circumstance more than one of deliberate action. I am still concerned about some of the issues of authority and responsibility that are raised when TAs teach and evaluate their peers. We are, perhaps, lucky that over the years very few problems have occurred. As a writing program administrator, I know that my own responsibility for supporting mentors is increased when graduate students mentor one another. I am concerned as well that the shift away from faculty mentors may mean a loss of status for composition in English Studies, since, as I said earlier, the willingness of a department to assign faculty to mentoring is an indication of its support for the teaching of composition. Yet, I certainly recognize that the opportunity to mentor in an established program such as ours, with appropriate support from the Director of Composition, contributes to our graduate students' professional development, particularly by providing them with experience in a very common activity for those who go on to become writing program administrators, as many of our graduates do.

The inevitable question remains: "Should TAs teach TAs to teach?" The inevitable answer—my inevitable answer: "Yes, but . . ." Yes, but only if those TAs are selected carefully and supported adequately. Yes, but only if reliance on TAs does not mean that teaching composition and preparing teachers of composition are considered unworthy of the faculty's attention. Yes, but only if the working conditions of those TAs are comparable to those of faculty doing the same work. If I could design the ideal program for preparing new teachers of writing, it would not look exactly like ours. Prospective teachers would not have to learn on the job; they would take a course in composition pedagogy before they began teaching. But they would be supported during their initial year of teaching by a program that, like ours, provides them with opportunities to work in small groups led by a person with extensive teaching experience and disciplinary knowledge of composition. And in my ideal program, that person would be—more often than is currently our case—a faculty member. But I don't think I would want to return to the days when TAs could not mentor because, as I said above, mentoring is professional development, of a kind not available through class work, and as such, I believe it has an important role to play in the preparation of soon-to-be faculty.

Structurally, the mentoring program at Purdue is little different from the one in place when I arrived in 1981, although in the fall of 1999, mentoring in first-year composition moved from a one-credit to a three-credit course, now entitled "Approaches to Teaching College Composition." This change occurred for two related reasons. First, we recognized that the time required of TAs who were being mentored was substantially more than one hour per week. Second, as mentors and TAs became increasingly interested in discussing published research and scholarship in composition, we needed to be able to acknowledge that the course was shifting from a practicum model to a teaching seminar model. For TA mentors, this shift has provided an additional professional development opportunity, since they now have the opportunity to identify, select, and lead discussions about research and scholarship, in addition to their previous focus on practical classroom pedagogy.

But of course, as this chapter points out, changes in teacher preparation occur in ways beyond the structural. The shift from a faculty-led mentoring program to one in which TAs play at least an equal role in mentoring has challenged faculty, particularly those of us with responsibility for administering the writing program, to reflect on issues of importance to any program that relies on TAs, particularly inexperienced TAs, to teach its classes. We have had to consider why we were so committed to a faculty-led TA preparation program, to think about whether our commitment was based on legitimate concerns about authority, disciplinary status, and the role of TAs in large universities. We have had to consider what has been gained and what has been lost in this shift. Such reflection has been beneficial, since it has enabled us to see that, at least in our particular context, much has been gained by providing experienced TAs with the opportunity to support their peers in their development as teachers of writing. TA mentors now have professional development opportunities only available to a very few in previous years. Both faculty and TA mentors have benefited from the more regular opportunities to meet and talk about our work.

The changes in our mentoring program I have been describing demonstrate how our writing program has addressed changes in resources, both in terms of faculty available for mentoring and funds to support teacher preparation. These changes reflect our continuing commitment to providing the best possible preparation for TAs by drawing on the department's strengths. The increased reliance on TA mentors has worked at Purdue; however, I acknowledge that other institutions with different strengths and resources will and should draw upon them to shape their TA preparation programs. At Purdue, the continuing value placed on preparing new teachers through a small-group mentoring model and the large number of new TAs who enter our program each year meant that we chose not to respond to changes in resources by trying to offer teacher preparation through a single large course. Instead, knowing that we had the support of a strong graduate program in rhetoric and composition, which provides graduate students with opportunities for formal study of the field, we have chosen to retain small sections through the appointment of experienced TAs as mentors.

## NOTES

1. It is not coincidental, I imagine, that the increasing number of TAs parallels the time at which graduate enrollments at Purdue began to grow. Cosper's report is written the year prior to the first year Purdue offered the PhD in English.
2. I do not want to suggest that these situations do not arise with faculty; they do. But when faculty find it necessary to give poor evaluations or even to advise TAs that their performance is weak in some particular way, the power/status differential makes it easier to do

so. It is the peer relationship between TAs that complicates these situations. Graduate student mentors should not be in the position of being subjects of formal grievances or informal vendettas when they themselves are in the process of developing as professionals.

3. I imagine that the desire to present mentoring as a professional activity accounts for the discrepancy between Adler's 1976 annual report and Miller's undated description of who mentors at about that same date. When reality conflicts with the ideal, administrators may sometimes choose to publicly represent the ideal as if it were real.

4. Since the mentoring program was in place prior to the establishment of the graduate program in rhetoric and composition, it is clear that Purdue's commitment to TA preparation precedes that program. However, I believe it is also the case that the professional commitment to composition and rhetoric at Purdue has played a role in the development of the mentoring program. That TAs could be taught by prominent scholars in the field assured that their preparation, even if primarily practical in focus, would be grounded in current theory, research, and scholarship.

5. At the time I am writing, in spring 2000, three of the graduate student mentors are in rhetoric and composition, one is in English education, and one is in literary studies.

## WORKS CITED

Adler, Jacob. Annual Report. Department of English. West Lafayette, IN: Purdue University. 1976.

Cosper, Russell. Annual Report. Department of English. West Lafayette, IN: Purdue University. 1964.

Kottler, Barnet. Memo to Russell Cosper. West Lafayette, IN: Purdue University. 10 October 1966.

Miller, Robert A. "The Mentor Program for Training and Supervising Teaching Assistants." Department of English. West Lafayette, IN: Purdue University. Mimeographed sheet, n.d.

Minutes of the Composition Committee. Department of English. West Lafayette, IN: Purdue University, 7 December 1979.

Minutes of the Composition Committee. Department of English. West Lafayette, IN: Purdue University, 20 February 1980.

Minutes of the Composition Committee. Department of English. West Lafayette, IN: Purdue University, 23 September 1981.

Promotion Document for Professor Barnet Kottler. 1976, 6.

Sommers, Nancy. "Responding to Student Writing." *College Composition and Communication* 33 (1982): 148–56.

# 5. TA Education as Dialogic Response: Furthering the Intellectual Work of the Profession through WPA

DARIN PAYNE AND THERESA ENOS

*Hi Jean. Can you tell me if your TA training courses count towards their grad degrees? There's a move afoot here to keep our course in Teaching Composition (we only have one) from counting toward the MA, in part because it "distracts from the students' important work in literature." Of course, the people suggesting this idea will still want our MA students to continue teaching comp. (!) Carol.[1]*

—from the WPA listserv, 1999

We begin with the above quotation because it embodies the complex and often frustrating tensions surrounding and shaping the intellectual and political work of composition: it also exemplifies the work of the National Council of Writing Program Administrators (WPA) in response to those tensions, particularly in relation to educating teaching assistants. While the above request was spammed to an entire listserv by accident, it is hardly accidental that the listserv in question was the WPA-L, a daily support network for approximately 1,000 college writing teachers throughout the country.[2] A significant—and highly representative—forum for WPA members,[3] the WPA-L is a relatively safe site for those charged with running writing programs and educating TAs amidst a myriad of institutional, academic, cultural, and economic conditions that can often be political minefields. For better or worse, those conditions shape our discipline and our efforts to teach TAs.

The quotation above, for example, speaks to several such conditions, among them the lowly status of composition relative to other "more important" disciplines like literature. As demeaning as such status may be—and it needn't be rearticulated here, for most readers will be familiar with the all-too-common lament that composition departments reside in academia's metaphorical basement, several floors beneath literature programs—more than self-esteem is at stake. The political clout behind decision making is at stake, as are programmatic course structures (such as the kind that would prevent courses in teacher education from counting toward degree programs), promotion and tenure requirements (which delimit what kind of graduate education is valued and in effect permitted), and, of course, funding (often the bottom line in determining how TAs are educated). Writing program administrators struggle to achieve and maintain the respect and recognition of other academics, particularly those who see composition as a set of skills to be drilled and the teaching of composition as an unfortunately necessary service. Carol, the sender of the above email post, is struggling to keep alive *one* course in teaching composition. She notes that it is the only such course available at her institution, a clear indicator of the value placed on teaching writing by those with whom she works. Further, Carol's tone reveals the lack of understanding—and the exploitation—she feels coming from those behind "the move afoot": "Of course, the people suggesting this idea will still want our MA students to continue teaching comp. (!)"

The responses Carol received to her post on the WPA-L reveal one of WPA's most significant contributions to TA education: namely, its *explicit dialogic responsiveness.* By that phrase we mean more than dialogue and more than response, at least in their vernacular senses. We are drawing on a Bakhtinian framework, one that recognizes centrifugal and centripetal social forces that both tear apart and impose order on (and therefore give shape to) existing social relations and formations. The institutional and academic conditions that Carol's post indexes were both explicated and addressed on the WPA-L through a variety of responses that included emotional support; intellectual, philosophical, and political positioning; and administrative pragmatics. Some respondents, for example, suggested increasing mentoring for TAs and restructuring faculty reward systems to promote more TA education by tenured and tenure-track faculty. Still others suggested straightforward research—number gathering—to prove that required composition pedagogy courses are the national norm.

It may seem an obvious point to make that any TA education must inevitably respond to the centrifugal and centripetal conditions giving it shape. A model of TA education that is economic and efficient, for example, is often a response to a typical rhetorical situation—one in which a large institution finds itself in need of staffing numerous sections of First-Year Composition (FYC) on a limited budget. Such a model would surely be informed by other factors as well, such as the extent to which composition studies is locally realized as a legitimate discipline, the current market demands that may be influencing the curriculum, and of course the educational background of those running FYC. Nevertheless, such factors often remain quietly underneath the surface of TA education. It is still common for TAs to be led through a practical, nuts-and-bolts "training course" that enables them to simply get through their very first semester of both graduate school and teaching. Yet such TAs often do not gain the theoretical background many deem necessary for adequate instruction in composition, nor are they given the opportunities to understand why their preparation takes the form that it does (Latterell; Haring-Smith; Hesse).

WPA, on the other hand, consistently *explicates* the forces that impact our work as writing teachers and TA educators, as well as the ways in which we respond to those forces. By laying bare that dialogic process at work, WPA enables TA education itself to participate in the dialogue, rather than to remain a mere result of it. Through explicit dialogic responsiveness, WPA thus lays a foundation for effecting change and for furthering the intellectual work of both

TA education and the field of composition as a whole. In this chapter we wish to develop this claim by examining WPA as a historically motivated response to conditions often elided in TA education. We begin with a brief sketch of WPA's history, articulating in the process some of the centrifugal and centripetal social forces that not only led to the creation of the organization but that have also remained as the subject matter of its work during the past twenty-five years. We then follow that brief sketch by looking more closely at a few interrelated conditions that have given—and are giving—TA education its particular shape: namely, the professional status of composition as a discipline; the knowledge of the field that informs our pedagogical work; and the demands of the marketplace that delimit what we do and for whom we do it. We conclude by suggesting that WPA has given us a useful model to draw from and that explicit dialogic responsiveness can and should be embedded in TA education as a way to move the discipline and the profession forward.

## WPA AS RESPONSE: DIALOGIC BEGINNINGS

In 1976, as part of the first MLA "Teaching of Writing Division" convention program in New York City, Kenneth Bruffee, WPA's founder, edited and published a pamphlet called "Issues in Writing Program Administration." Of the seven sessions at the convention devoted to issues in teaching writing, one had been reserved for an organizational meeting to serve the interests of people administering writing programs in American and Canadian colleges and universities. That association became WPA: the National Council of Writing Program Administrators (Bruffee 5). The purpose of Bruffee's pamphlet, which was the beginning of WPA: Journal of the Council of Writing Program Administrators, was to suggest to whoever showed up at that organizational meeting, and to interested others, some issues such an association might address. Since that first meeting in 1976, the issues have not changed much, and WPA's pragmatic approach to them is still dominant. WPA has, since inception, been concerned with the politics and practices of developing, running, and evaluating writing programs, evaluating writing teachers, and preparing TAs to teach writing.

Looking back, it is clear that much of WPA's mission has involved reconfiguring the professional context within which TA education has primarily existed. The Portland Resolution,[4] drafted by WPA in 1992 and a milestone in its history, exemplifies such reconfiguration. The resolution addresses, in its very title, "Working Conditions Necessary for Quality Writing Program Administration." Among them, the resolution defines as valuable scholarly work various forms of teacher education, including teaching, supervising, and evaluating TAs. By defining such work as scholarship, WPA has given it a foothold on a slope made slippery by tenure and promotion guidelines that have traditionally devalued (and thus discouraged appropriate commitments to) TA education.

WPA's "intellectual work document,"[5] released in 1998, develops this agenda even further. The document argues that teacher education "is one of the most salient examples of intellectual work carried out within an administrative sphere" (97) and that "it requires specific expertise, training, and an understanding of disciplinary knowledge" (92). That document is complemented by the recently developed "WPA Outcomes Statement for First-Year Composition." As a response to increasing pressures—from many outside rhetoric and composition—to standardize assessment and curricula in first-year composition courses, the statement "articulates what composition teachers nationwide have learned from practice, research, and theory."[6] The document can thus be used to inform TAs of current directions in our field, to justify local curricular developments, and to argue for particular content in TA education. WPA's focus on improving working conditions—hence, on context—has thus helped to give administrators the necessary room to develop substantive TA education programs; moreover, such focus has often informed and empowered TA education by bringing it into direct dialogue with those working conditions. In the next section, we illustrate that process by examining some of the ways in which WPA has worked to configure TA education as an explicit response to specific contextual conditions.

## TA EDUCATION AS RESPONSE: DIALOGIC PARTICIPATION

At least one guiding philosophy behind the eponymous *WPA Journal* (hereafter *WPA*) is that contextual conditions are indeed addressed, that interconnections among programmatic structures and educational quality are *assumed. WPA* editor (1976–1979) Bruffee writes that "this is an important assumption. It underlies, for example, the difference between the editorial policy of *WPA* and the editorial policy of *CCC* and other journals that publish articles on teaching writing. *WPA* does not publish articles on classroom practice, theory of composition, or research in composition unless they deal with the relationship of these topics to program administration"(6). The explication of context that *WPA* looks for in publishing thus demands response and dialogue as we are defining those terms here. Consider, for example, Catherine Latterell's explication and critique of TA "training" programs, published in *WPA* and referenced elsewhere in this collection. Such programs, according to Latterell, lack a great deal of pedagogical context or theories, and they consist primarily of practical "how to" strategies and idea sharing.[7] She writes,

> [T]here is a danger that these practica devolve writing pedagogy from a critical practice with an epistemological grounding to sets of lesson plans and activities disconnected from a teaching philosophy. . . . By dispensing "training" in one to two hour doses once a week for one (possibly two) terms, this model encourages the passing out of class activities and other quick-fixes—an inoculation method of GTA education. We need to examine the message we are sending GTAs and our other colleagues in English studies by maintaining such practices. (19–20)

Significantly, Latterell connects the above problem not just to common disheartening perceptions of composition studies but also to concrete centrifugal and centripetal forces that affect the daily defining work of the field. She argues that "this type of teacher preparation perpetuates traditional administrative power structures that may neutralize the discipline's efforts to redefine teaching and administrative activities for tenure and promotion cases as well as for the professionalizing of the discipline" (19). In other words, Latterell recognizes and draws attention to the context of TA training, as well as the implications of that context and of the training itself. She articulates the relationship between the two, thus completing what Michael Holquist calls the triad of any Bakhtinian dialogue: the "I," the "other," and the relationship between them. She makes explicit the lowly status of composition we referenced in our introduction, and she situates TA education both against and within that condition.

Carrie Leverenz and Amy Goodburn, also writing for *WPA*, express related concerns over the status of composition as it gets reproduced in current TA "training" programs. They wish to encourage in TAs professional*ism* over professional*ization*—the former being concerned with understanding the discourses of the field and the institutional forces that shape the teaching of writing, the latter with *representing* that understanding. Leverenz and Goodburn's recommendations are ultimately geared toward furthering the intellectual work of the discipline through the future workers of the discipline, through making TAs knowledgeable and willing participants in dialogues about subjects like promotion and tenure, by inviting them "to help shape the programs they teach in" (23). What is obvious from Leverenz and Goodburn's work, and from Latterell's, is that the conditions impacting TA education are interrelated and need to be negotiated as such.

Just as the status of composition shapes and is shaped by the working conditions of teaching writing and educating TAs, so is our field's disciplinary knowledge base. Even knowledge seemingly taken for granted, like process pedagogy, often gets reduced to universalized boiler-plate steps that new teachers can follow. The complexity of elements of the writing process, such as recursion, for example, or social-epistemic collaboration, can be lost in untheorized TA discussions that attempt to instill the linear logistics of freewriting, drafting, revising, and editing. TA education is particularly susceptible to this kind of reductionism because of the need to provide new instructors with concrete working plans, something immediate to guide them through the day, week, or unit, and to give shape to their syllabi.

In addition to its journal articles, its listserv discussions, and its policy statements, WPA has responded to this kind of "watering down" of disciplinary knowledge in TA education through its Consultant/Evaluator visits. Currently led by Edward M. White and Deborah Holdstein, the Consultant/Evaluators routinely suggest to departments that first-year TAs should *not* be thrust immediately into the classroom, that they should instead be given the space and time to be introduced to the discourses of the field (White). When they are not given such time, TAs—most of whom are *not* rhetoric and composition students—often end up skimming the surface of the discipline, reading only the section titles of detailed articulations of knowledge made in composition. Their understanding remains skeletal at best, misguided at worst. As Doug Hesse writes,

> Because for many graduate students the reason they're in graduate school is not to learn how to teach writing but to write fiction or to talk about literary or cultural ideas, those interests challenge, at least to them, the assumptions and practices of the writing program. [To] such students the writing program is often deemed "repressive" or "hegemonic" or "workmanlike" or "dull." Interestingly, those teachers often hyperconstruct a stereotypical teacherly identity, becoming the very dogmatic teachers against which they complain. "I would never do this as a fiction writer," they suggest, "but I'll become a rule-bound grammar cop (for example) in my teaching freshman composition, because it's not 'real' or 'important' writing anyway."[8]

Indeed the attitudes of the students Hesse paraphrases are not unlike those of the colleagues Carol mentions in our opening passage. Her struggles to keep afloat a single course in composition theory are a result of such attitudes. The singularity of that course, paradoxically, is also a *cause* of such attitudes; that is, when the teaching of the field's knowledge is so restricted, how can it be considered "real" or "important"?

Christine Farris, in this collection, describes one possible response to such a paradox. Her institution now approaches composition through cultural studies, which demands that TAs be educated to work with cultural critique, with the analysis of cultural representations of race, class, and gender. She notes, "How TAs come to this intellectual work, which is, one hopes, connected to their scholarship and understanding of the field of English studies, shapes how they view [composition] and teaching from then on."[9] Thus, her approach, on at least one level, has been to configure the discipline to better meet the academic interests of TAs not directly in rhetoric and composition. In fact, Farris laments WPA's seeming inability to devote more of its work toward such theoretical developments:

> WPA tends to focus less, perhaps out of necessity, on the implications of theoretical and research-driven changes in composition studies for curriculum design and, consequently, for TA training. . . . Changes in the field make it harder work, all while the socioeconomic and political conditions of that work remain largely unchanged. The newest members of the profession are doing perhaps the hardest work for the least money . . . and [writing program administrators] are caught in the middle.[10]

We suggest, nonetheless, that the middle is a good place to be. It is a necessary location for responding to local conditions that impact the translation and productive use of the discipline's knowledge base. For example, while WPA's consultant/evaluators "routinely" recommend that TAs not be immediately thrust into the classroom, those recommendations only come, according to White, in response to localized politics, resources, and institutional and pedagogical goals. Within such a model, knowledge of the field becomes explicitly situated and realized in its local context; in turn, so does TA education. As Tim Peeples has written on the WPA-L, "what I'm realizing . . . is that I—and many of the [participants discussing] TAs—essentialize the TA *according to my own institutional experience*" (italics original). We believe that if such recognition can be embedded in TA education, and in dialogues surrounding and informing TA education at specific institutions, then the work of WPA will intersect with the work of the discipline in mutually enriching ways.

That intersection can in fact be seen in the recent development of graduate courses in writing program administration, which are generally directed toward TAs in English and are thus a significant contribution to TA education. WPA courses have been offered at Purdue, Iowa State, Kansas, The University of Arizona, and other major institutions. Shirley K Rose's multicourse sequence at Purdue includes readings and discussions that address ethical implications of defining the responsibilities of writing program administrators, rhetorical strategies for documenting WPA work, and institutional politics of characterizing writing program administration as service, teaching, or research (Barr Ebest 74–5). Edward White and Theresa Enos's WPA course at The University of Arizona covers similar ground, engaging TAs in required reading in *WPA* and on the WPA-L, forums that—as we hope we have shown—lay bare the interrelations among disciplinary knowledge, teacher education, and relevant economic and institutional conditions.

Such courses are, to be sure, a form of dialogic response to yet another contextual condition impacting TA education and the intellectual work of the discipline: namely, the marketplace. Beyond institutional politics, local attitudes, and resource allocations, TA education is unmistakably shaped and constrained by the larger political economies of the job market. Anyone who has served on search committees in English knows how competitive conditions have led to an emphasis—some would say overemphasis—on professionalization. Graduate students are now in the position of needing to enter their careers with a level of professional experience that at one time they were expected to earn *after* becoming assistant professors. This trend has been termed "*pre*professionlization" by John Guillory, who argues along with Leverenz and Goodburn that graduate education is becoming conflated with self-marketing. While graduate courses in writing program administration might seem on their surface to be contributing directly to preprofessionalization by teaching TAs how to be good administrators, such courses, when informed by the discourses of WPA, inevitably expose TAs to the tensions between TA development and TA self-marketing, tensions promoted by pressures that begin at the level of the marketplace and move inward to TA education programs, graduate student professional opportunities, and TA/faculty mentoring relationships.

Beyond the academic marketplace, the corporate marketplace also shapes TA education in ways that need to be acknowledged and responded to. Undergraduates, for example, are coming to us in need of instruction that will meet the demand for communicative competencies in the technology-rich corporate world. Composition studies is answering those demands through computer-mediated writing instruction—an answer that inevitably must translate into educating TAs to teach their students using new technologies. At The University of Arizona, for instance, the English Department's "Computers in Composition Working Group" (CICWG) is comprised mainly of TAs, who have been charged with exploring, testing, and implementing various forms of computer-enhanced writing instruction.[11] Their work, while contributing to the discourses of the field and to putting theory into practice, falls into a category of intellectual work normally associated with writing program administration; they have become direct participants in conversations surrounding the administrative logistics of securing lab access, writing grants for equipment and training funds, competing with other departments and disciplines for such resources, and establishing curricular guidelines for computer-enhanced writing instruction.

Although this is not an example of a direct contribution by WPA to TA education, we offer it here because it so aptly embodies the dialogic responsive function of WPA as we have been articulating it. It also exemplifies Marvin Diogenes, Duane Roen, and C. Jan Swearingen's assertion in *WPA* that "since the future of literacy may depend on the teachers, scholars, and researchers who will replace us, we have the responsibility of shaping the profession as we perform what seem to be routine administrative duties" (53). One of us writing this chapter, Darin, has moved from being a TA in the CICWG to teaching computer-mediated pedagogy to new TAs at another institution. In that role, he works to explicitly situate technology-enhanced composition instruction amidst the administrative and institutional conditions within which they are working; that is, after all, the model in which he was educated. As a result, the character of composition that Darin's TAs are currently coming to understand is one far removed from lofty notions of a pure or unfettered disciplinary corpus; the discipline of composition is evolving amidst the development of new technologies, their integration into the writing classroom, and a host of administrative and intellectual conditions impacting such work.

## WPA AS MODEL-IN-PROCESS

We end with the above example because it embodies the kind of work we have been ascribing to WPA without actually being directly under the purview of WPA. WPA's contribution to TA education has historically been to respond to conditions within which such education has been situated and to explicate the relations among those conditions, TA education, and the discipline of composition. That model of teacher education is one that, we believe, can and should be adopted beyond the bounds of WPA's domain. It is in fact a model that *responds*—an appropriate term—to Latterell's call for teacher development beyond "training." In supporting her call, she cites a TA educator's observation:

> As teachers, I think, we always feel a centripetal pressure that centers our attention on the mechanics of the classroom. What should we assign today? . . . What should we ask our students to write about? By what objective standard should we grade our students' work? But when we consider the context—institutional, disciplinary, social, and personal—of our students and ourselves, we feel a range of centrifugal pressures that complicate what at first glance seems to be the safely enclosed world of the classroom. Those centrifugal pressures make it impossible to see the classroom as a neutral site of learning where the key ques-

tions are about the effective presentation and objective evaluation of material. The classroom is not a safe haven; it is a contested site where learning results from an active process of questioning, dialogue, and negotiation. (17)

We submit that just as a classroom is a contested site, so are our writing programs and our discipline. As we attempt to move them forward, we would do well to recognize and respond to the pressures that complicate such work.

With that in mind, then, we wish to offer WPA as a model-in-process for TA education, one that may *serve*—another appropriate term—the professoriate of the future as well as the profession itself. Such a model suggests that TA educators construct their work at the intersections of theory, practice, and pragmatics, of academic, institutional, and cultural contexts; indeed, that is what we are here calling for. Our call is complemented, reaffirmed even, by the call for the 2000 WPA Conference in Charlotte, North Carolina. While certainly open to more issues than TA education, the call exemplifies WPA's role in the dialogic processes of our discipline's intellectual work. Titled "In the Thick of Things," the call is as follows:

> A common observation is that WPA's work in the middle: between teachers and "higher" administrators, between managerial and scholarly interests, between disciplinary and institutional concerns, between programmatic dreams and budgetary realities, between student needs and public desires. . . . We must also confront the implications of distance education, for-profit education, increased consumerism, legislative intervention in teaching methods, growing interest in learner-centered education, and general education reform. How might we work effectively—for our students, our colleagues, our profession, our culture, ourselves—within this often messy middle?[12]

Our short answer to this question—how might we work effectively within this often messy middle?—is that we remain there, and that we bring TAs with us. If we are to educate them, we need to do so in ways that do not elide the conditions that impact their development and in ways that give them some agency amidst those conditions. Engaging them as dialogic respondents is one possible way, the necessary work for which can be found in WPA.

## NOTES

1. The names in this quotation are not the participants' real names.
2. As of April 2, 2000, there were 966 subscribed users to the WPA-L.
3. The WPA-L, created by David Schwalm, does not officially belong to WPA; nonetheless, its integral affiliation with WPA members and its central role in mediating their discussions make clear WPA's de facto "ownership."
4. WPA. "The Portland Resolution: Guidelines for Writing Program Administrator Positions."
5. WPA. "Evaluating the Intellectual Work of Writing Administration."
6. See the Outcomes Statement at http://www.mwsc.edu/~outcomes.
7. We have consciously avoided using the term *training* throughout this article, for it invokes that which we have long labored against in this field: the external (and sometimes internal) impression that our work is devoid of rigorous scholarship, that writing is a set of mechanical skills separate from "real" academic work, and that the teaching of writing is

similarly reducible to practical activities that drill those skills. Indeed, amidst the many responses Carol received from her question that we opened with, several respondents sought to revise her use of the term *training.*

8. Email correspondence with the authors, December 1999.
9. Ibid.
10. Ibid.
11. See the homepage of the CICWG at http://www.coh.arizona.edu/comp/cic/index.html.
12. From the 2000 WPA Conference call at http://www.cas.ilstu.edu/English/Hesse/2000annwkshp.htm.

## WORKS CITED

Bakhtin, M. M. *The Dialogic Imagination.* Ed. C. Emerson and M. Holquist. Trans. V. M. McGee. Austin: U of Texas P, 1981.

Barr Ebest, Sally. "The Next Generation of WPAs: A Study of Graduate Students in Composition/Rhetoric." *WPA* 22.3 (1999): 65–84.

Bruffee, Ken. "The WPA as (Journal) Writer: What the Record Reveals." *WPA* 9.1–2 (1985): 5–10.

Diogenes, Marvin, Duane H. Roen, and C. Jan Swearingen. "Creating the Profession: The GAT Training Program at the University of Arizona." *WPA* 10.1–2 (1986): 51–9.

Farris, Christine. E-mail correspondence with authors. December 1999.

Guillory, John. "Preprofessionalism: What Graduate Students Want." *Profession 1996.* New York: MLA, 1996. 91–9.

Haring-Smith, Tori. "The Importance of Theory in the Training of Teaching Assistants." *ADE Bulletin* 82 (1985): 33–9.

Hesse, Douglas. "Teachers as Students, Reflecting Resistance." *College Composition and Communication* 44 (1993): 224–31.

———. E-mail correspondence with authors. December 1999.

Holquist, Michael. *Dialogism: Bakhtin and His World.* New York: Routledge, 1990.

Latterell, Catherine. "Training the Workforce: An Overview of GTA Education Curricula." *WPA* 19.3 (1996): 7–23.

Leverenz, Carrie Shively, and Amy Goodburn. "Professionalizing TA Training: Commitment to Teaching or Rhetorical Response to Market Crisis?" *WPA* 22.1–2 (1998): 9–32.

Peeples, Tim. Response on WPA-L. May 16, 1997.

White, Edward M. E-mail correspondence with authors. December 1999.

WPA. "Evaluating the Intellectual Work of Writing Administration" *WPA* 22.1/2 (1998): 85–104.

———. "The Portland Resolution: Guidelines for Writing Program Administrator Positions." *WPA* 16.1–2 (1992): 88–94.

WPA-L Archives: http://lists.asu.edu/archives/wpa-l.html.

# PART 2

## THEORIES

# 6. The Professionalization of TA Development Programs: A Heuristic for Curriculum Design

## KATHLEEN BLAKE YANCEY

Composition studies, as we currently know it, is typically regarded as a discipline born in the late twentieth century. Ironically, it's a discipline that has ardently served the needs of one population while attending little to another. More specifically, we've focused on how to teach students to write, while thinking very little, at least systematically, about the kinds of assistance we might offer the graduate students—the so-called TAs, the teaching assistants who by any other name are instructors who teach a considerable number of the first-year composition courses offered in this country.

To make such a claim—that TA development programs suffer from some neglect—isn't to say that there aren't good models of TA development; this collection makes the opposing argument eloquently. But in their diversity, the models offer very little general guidance about how to develop a program or sense even of what features these programs might share. Without a general picture of these programs, it can be understandably difficult to relativize our own and difficult as well, then, to design, maintain, and redesign such a program. Too, the kinds of institutions that populate higher education—historically black colleges, liberal arts colleges, comprehensive schools, doctoral granting institutions, and even two-year colleges (where TAs are learning to teach through programs like the Preparing Future Faculty Program), to name but some of the kinds of schools we inhabit—with their own particularities underscore the difficulty we have in thinking about a generalized model. Not that the goal necessarily is a common model; given the wealth of sites in which composition is offered, a common model seems neither possible nor desirable. At the same time, however, the WPAs responsible for TA development programs are likely to find useful a common understanding and explanation of the components that define these programs—at the least to see what's possible, at the most, perhaps, to use in the design of their own programs.

Instead of working from a common understanding, we tend, I suspect, to think principally in terms of local needs. Local needs will of course continue to focus our attention; context, as we know, is critical. But practice suggests that when local needs *determine* rather than *influence* a TA development program, it's all too easy to find that one's program is rich with technique but absent theory, or sensitive to experience but unable to reframe it. In other words, it's useful to ask, What other kinds of needs would we identify for TA development if our central concern were not local exigence but TA development more generally? Put another way, two questions: First, how is TA development a curriculum issue, and thus, second, what should we expect in a curriculum created expressly to prepare TAs to teach?

Curriculum theorist Gunther Kress's work can be helpful here, especially his emphasis on the role of design in curriculum. Kress suggests that curriculum is two-sided. One side enables students to consume and critique, and we have seen ample evidence of this in the scholarship of composition studies. A second side of curriculum, in Kress's model, reflects an interest in design, and this plays out in the creation of our own curricula: "The contents and processes put forward in curriculum and in its associated pedagogy constitute the design for future human dispositions. They provide one set of important means and resources for the individual's transformative shaping action in making herself or himself as social humans" (87–8). The key here, to critique and to design, is made analogously through the metaphor of consumption and production, and both of these metaphors operate on three levels. First, within the composition course, students have historically been asked to "consume" and critique. That's one way of understanding David Bartholomae's "inventing" of the university, for instance—as an exercise in consuming sufficiently and well enough that students can replicate or invent university thinking and writing. Increasingly, through programs like service learning and projects like class Web pages, students are also asked *to produce and to design,* both texts and knowledge. As important is the choice of design as a trope in the context of the composition classroom. It suggests, of course, that there is an aesthetic quality to the production that is itself a function of purpose and an understanding of the parts and how they relate to each other and to the whole.

Second and likewise, WPAs want TAs in their development programs to consume—the relevant institutional and cultural materials, for example, as well as the theoretical orientations of the specific programs. At the same time, WPAs also want TAs to design—syllabi, writing assignments, journal entries, portfolio templates. Third, WPAs themselves are designing TA development programs based on consumption and critique. In these programs, WPAs move beyond critique to think in terms of the elements we choose—what language, what materials, what pedagogies?—and about how to design a curriculum that interrelates these elements in a coherent way, particularly for a specific group of TAs seeking to teach a specific group of students. Finally, and not least, the local design can itself be relativized against a common understanding of a TA development program.

One means of relativization and design is provided through a heuristic that allows us to define and consider the various dimensions of a TA development program. It seems reasonable, for example, to assume that if we could identify a limited set of models, such as those informing this collection, we might also be able to talk about those models in a generalized way and to identify common features and common ways of thinking about TA development. Taken together, such common features form a heuristic that will allow all of us who work with TA development programs to design such programs, to review them as our writing programs change, and to revise them as needed. In other words, like all educational programs, TA preparation programs constitute a rhetorical response to a given local need; they want to be sensitive to such needs. At the same time, to design *good* programs, we must consider not only the local context but also the larger rhetorical contexts of writing programs. This chapter maps these features as the components of a heuristic available for both design and review.

One additional note: I've referred above to a good program as though it were a given. I'm not sure it is. It is, however, a possibility, the likelihood of which we increase by conscious attention to design of new programs and by inference, to review of extant programs. As important is definition: For my purposes, a good program is one that first, serves the needs of the students; second, prepares graduate students to teach both curriculum and individual students; and third, encourages the developing faculty member to reflect upon and learn from practice. It thus is a model that is itself theorized and that fosters the identity of a developing teacher. As important, it's a model of TA development that welcomes and socializes the TA without scripting him or her.

What follows, then, is an overall heuristic with each component then examined in some detail.

## A HEURISTIC FOR DESIGNING AND REVIEWING TA DEVELOPMENT PROGRAMS

1. What are the characteristics of the TAs for whom the program is designed?
2. What are the material conditions of the local program?
3. What is the nature of the graduate program within which the TA program is housed?
4. How is the undergraduate program designed, taught, and administered?
5. What sites for teacher preparation are available?
6. What kinds of pedagogical strategies are appropriate for the teacher preparation program? How do they fit with the strategies that the TAs are being asked to adopt in their own classrooms?
7. What is the role of the textbook in the TA development program?
8. Who is responsible for preparing teachers of college writing?
9. Historically, how have TAs been prepared at the institution and why?
10. How are identity issues woven into a TA development program?
11. What ethical implications of identity are predicated in this model of TA development?
12. How is the TA development program itself reviewed, assessed, and enhanced?

## 1.   WHAT ARE THE CHARACTERISTICS OF THE TAs FOR WHOM THE PROGRAM IS DESIGNED?

Just as we begin a writing course by considering the students who will enroll, we can begin the design of the TA development program by thinking about who the TAs are. Demographically, are TAs recent college graduates or older, more experienced graduate students? Are they primarily women or men? What ethnicity are they? What about class identity? And more generally, what kind of fit do we see between TA demographics and those of the undergraduate population? This last query suggests how much information about the student writers will need to be addressed as the TAs begin to teach and perhaps even before they walk into the classroom. If the TAs share their students' demographic characteristics, for example, they may be able to think specifically and realistically about the students they'll be teaching; they will know and understand what motivates the students they'll work with as well as how and why they see the world as they do. If not—if, for instance, the TA is a Yankee from Connecticut and the students have never traveled outside their Southern state (as is frequently the case at my home institution)—a little demographic and cultural introduction might be wise. As is the case in any cultural mix, exploring how the students may be different from us and how we might accommodate those differences can make the classroom experience more beneficial for students and TA alike.

Similarly, did the TAs themselves complete a first-year course in composition? Anecdotal evidence suggests that many, perhaps most, have not. Defining the first-year course—perhaps by reference to the course as a type—provides one means of context, and in its statement about what first-year students should know and do, the WPA Outcomes Statement serves this need well. A related concern has to do with how well the TAs write, how frequently they write, and how they understand writing as an activity foundational to a successful academic career. It's axiomatic that a writing instructor is in fact an instructor who writes, so exploring the role and place of writing in the TA's life is a central activity in TA preparation—as well as a first step in this heuristic for design.

## 2.   WHAT ARE THE MATERIAL CONDITIONS OF THE LOCAL PROGRAM?

A TA development program, like the writing program it connects to, is a function of the local context. What are the salient material features of that context? How can it be understood demographically, economically, and politically? For instance, what is the size of the institution, and what is its stipulated mission? A small school with a service orientation is likely to offer a general curriculum and different opportunities than a public school with considerable resources, thousands of students, and large classes. Likewise, what are the demographics of its undergraduate students? Are the undergraduates trying to work full-time and care for families while attending classes? Are they full-time residential students? Given their backgrounds, do the students see education as a "natural" part of life, or are they first-time college students who need to figure college out before they undertake much else? And how are these material conditions foregrounded and addressed in the TA development program? Does a staff member from Student Services profile the undergraduates for the TAs? Can students themselves be asked to speak to the material conditions of their learning?

In a related fashion, the material conditions of the institution, which of course are related to the material conditions of its students, tend to translate almost directly into the economic support provided to the writing program. Some writing programs, like those at Cornell and Miami of Ohio (as the chapters in this collection by Katherine Gottschalk and Paul Anderson and colleagues suggest), have the luxury of introducing TAs slowly to the process of teaching. Other programs find the exigence of students needing a teacher more compelling; in these cases the TAs enter the classroom sooner than anyone would wish. Clearly, of course, these considerations are general in nature; the purpose is to use them to think about the context as it exists. This is not to say that conditions cannot be changed, as we know. Indeed, the way we—WPAs, tenure-line faculty, part-timers, and TAs—teach, the way we frame the program, is one means of changing such conditions.

### 3. WHAT IS THE NATURE OF THE GRADUATE PROGRAM WITHIN WHICH THE TA PROGRAM IS HOUSED?

Graduate programs vary. They can offer a very focused program: an MA in English, for instance. Or they can offer a full range of degrees and specializations: MAs, PhDs, MFAs, and postdoctoral fellowships, in fields like rhetoric and composition, of course, but in creative writing, American studies, cultural critique, linguistics, as well as in literatures of various kinds. (And in some cases, the TAs aren't specializing in any field of English studies.) Still, since the TA development program is typically located within the graduate program, the vision of graduate education held by the department will shape the way that preparation for teaching is construed. (In some institutions, in fact, teaching assistantships are awarded without consideration of an applicant's potential for teaching, but rather purely as a means of support for graduate student study.) Given the nature of the graduate program, then, are TAs being "trained" as writing teachers principally to fill a need within the institution—so they can earn support until they graduate and get jobs teaching literature? Are the TAs hoping to work, after graduation, as technical editors and writers, so that the teaching of writing is both a means of making a living and a way of learning about the processes of writing itself? Is there a specialization in rhetoric and composition? Frequently, institutions that have graduate programs in rhetoric and composition take stronger theoretical approaches to teacher preparation. Such departments have a different kind of faculty expertise, and the TAs might expect to find themselves participating in a model connected to faculty research, one that is highly systematic and the object of professional, often national attention, as, for instance, has been the case for compositionist graduate students at Purdue.

Even assuming that the graduate program doesn't offer a specialization in rhetoric and composition, however, how else might TAs be socialized into the teaching of writing? One option is to provide multiple experiences for TAs so that they can participate more fully in the discipline: (1) different kinds of teaching assignments within first-year composition, for instance, teaching within a computer classroom or including service learning as a component of First-Year Composition, as at Michigan Technological University and at Clemson University; (2) experience as assistants to WPAs, as at the University of Louisville (as documented in this collection in the Powell and colleagues' chapter), so that the TAs both see the curriculum from a wider angle and take on administrative tasks that enact curriculum; and (3) teacher research leading to presentations and publications, as at UNC Greensboro. The general question: In the graduate program, are TAs seen as potential colleagues whose pedagogical and professional development is as important as their scholarly development? as important as their need to make a living?

## 4.   HOW IS THE UNDERGRADUATE PROGRAM DESIGNED, TAUGHT, AND ADMINISTERED?

Writing programs have theoretical stances, of course, even those that claim no particular stance (which itself is a theoretical stance, as we know). Accordingly, this program, this theoretical stance of the writing program, and the one undergirding the teacher preparation program (rhetorical context), should be considered as well. Does a clearly identifiable rhetorical theory construct the writing program, as in the case at Indiana University (discussed in this collection by Christine Farris)? Or is the program one where the newer "trends" in writing—first, process theory, then writing as social process, then the role of genre and the desire of cultural critique, for example—can seem to be added without a coherent plan, perhaps as a function in a change in leadership of the program or the addition of new faculty members? The approach we'd design would be different in each case, of course. Again, a general question can tell us much: Is there only one rhetorical theory acceptable to the department—either implicitly or explicitly? Or as in the writing programs at New Mexico State University and the University of Louisville, are WPAs and TAs free to work within different theoretical frameworks as long as students are learning to write? Who decides what "learning to write" means, and by what means?

A second set of related questions clusters around how the theoretical stance of the writing program matches the theoretical stance of the teacher preparation program. As a first premise, we might look at how the students are positioned in first-year composition. As consumers? As producers? The answers to these questions suggest parallel stances for TAs. Thus, in writing programs that emphasize production of knowledge by students, we hope to find that TAs are likewise understood to be producing their own teaching knowledge in their own classrooms. Put generally, then, how much agency is awarded to the TAs?

## 5.   WHAT SITES FOR TEACHER PREPARATION ARE AVAILABLE?

The situational context provided in any site brings with it particular opportunities for understanding and learning. As this collection attests, TA development takes place in multiple sites: in Writing Labs (Purdue and UNC Charlotte); in computer labs (Utah State and Michigan Tech); in sites of graduate study, as we see in orientations, practica, methods courses, and formal coursework in rhetoric and composition; and in undergraduate classrooms where most often TA learning is experiential rather than formal. As suggested above, sites we might call extracurricular—like the offices of a WPA—can also be a component of TA development programs. Some authors, building on Catherine Latterell's suggestion, have argued for preparing teachers for administrative roles as well. TA development in this kind of program is writ large: The developing faculty member is socialized widely as well as specifically through the work and the discourses of departmental offices, in meetings across campus, and with faculty in other disciplines. A general question for this category, then: What is the scope or focus of the preparation? And a related question: What does writing mean in the TA development program? Is it exclusively first-year composition? Is it first-year composition for a target population, ESL, for example, or basic writing? What about delivery: Is the course assumed to take place within a classroom, or is it delivered electronically? Does writing mean writing across the curriculum, and if so, which variety thereof? Is it a combination, say, of first-year composition and another course like technical communication? In the latter case, what is the link between the courses and the preparation to teach them?

### 6. WHAT KINDS OF PEDAGOGICAL STRATEGIES ARE APPROPRIATE FOR THE TEACHER PREPARATION PROGRAM? HOW DO THEY FIT WITH THE STRATEGIES THAT THE TAs ARE BEING ASKED TO ADOPT IN THEIR OWN CLASSROOMS?

The strategies, as we know, seem limitless, from reading professional literature in rhetoric and composition and using reflection—observational logs, reflective letters, case studies, exploratory assignments, portfolios—to providing mentors, offering methods courses or practica, arranging apprenticeships, setting up classroom observations, staging experience in preparing syllabi and course materials, reviewing case studies and scenarios, and introducing classroom management techniques (questioning strategies, guidelines for using email, etc.). Design provides the means by which the other components of the heuristic are brought into relationship with each other. It asks, what are the strategies that we choose, why do we choose them, and how do we fit them together?

One way to choose the relevant strategies and design them into a coherent whole is to think in terms of design features like repetition, alignment, and contrast. Thus, we might take a single explicit component like scholarly readings and ask first how they repeat and align with our own experiences as writers and then, second, with the writing and school curricula that our students have experienced already. By the same token, we can ask TAs about contrasts, for instance about a contrast between what the readings claim and what TAs experience in the classroom, and we might ask that they record this kind of thinking in an observational log, on a daily basis, or at the conclusion of a course in a portfolio.

A second way of thinking about the design issue here is through the lens of the rhetorical situation. Who is the teacher/author, and what does he or she bring to the teaching context? What are the topics/subject—the readings and formal knowledge—that frame the teaching context? And who are the students/audience, and how do they learn best—through discussion, workshop, writing groups, email, or portfolios? Not least, how do we make knowledge from bringing these components together, or what is the scholarship of teaching composition and how might we practice it? Seen this way, the strategies are selected according to the needs they serve on the points of a rhetorical triangle of teaching, and they are organized so as to connect those points with each other.

Finally, we might think about design of the curriculum through the lens of chronology. What will TAs need to know and when? Can we create a kind of parallel model in which TAs are introduced to practical strategies when they need them, like the creation of syllabi early and the practices of grading later? Perhaps at the same time and throughout, we'd weave theory in the form of readings, lectures, and discussions. Can we stagger and build upon similar activities, like variations on a theme? Here, we'd assign readings throughout the term and introduce specific strategies according to the time during the semester when they would be useful: for instance, reflective logs for an early part of the term, to help TAs learn to observe; reflective analysis of student work or a case study later in the term, when classroom management starts becoming routine, and a portfolio that synthesizes and culminates as the term concludes.

## 7.   WHAT IS THE ROLE OF THE TEXTBOOK IN THE TA DEVELOPMENT PROGRAM?

Again, programs vary in the roles that they assign to textbooks. In some programs, the textbook drives the curriculum, and TAs may or may not be asked to think beyond the textbook as they project into another term. In other cases, TAs help choose the textbook; they may be asked to work together to create a syllabus based on, but not driven by, the textbook; and may be asked as well to assess the value of the textbook for first-year composition at that particular school. In some situations, TAs also serve on the committee recommending texts. In some rare instances, such as at the University of New Mexico, TAs may even write their own textbook. Historically, textbooks have influenced the development of first-year composition in some surprising ways, so for that reason at least, the role of the textbook needs to be included and possibly foregrounded.

## 8.   WHO IS RESPONSIBLE FOR PREPARING TEACHERS OF COLLEGE WRITING?

Some contributors to this collection argue that a fuller involvement by faculty is desirable so that TAs see varying methods for teaching and for thinking about teaching. In such a model, WPAs, faculty members in rhetoric and composition, experienced TAs, and adjunct instructors play a role in "welcoming and socializing" new writing teachers, in an academic version of the "it takes a village to raise a child" model. As suggested earlier, some of these participants may include nonfaculty support personnel who can speak to student issues like student life, college safety, and risk signs for alcohol abuse. And in some cases, the socializing focuses on areas of inquiry so that the mentoring becomes more of a co-mentoring kind of dynamic as faculty and TAs take up questions about topics such as ways students revise and the appropriate role that technology should play in the classroom.

Other institutions view this leadership issue differently, arguing that the WPA should carry primary, and sometimes exclusive, responsibility and authority for TA development. For one thing, they claim, the WPA is the presumed expert, so it makes sense to have that person play the pivotal role. For another, TAs can perceive conflicting messages when perhaps too many voices are engaged, which in turn can lead to a coherence problem at odds with the design of the program. Not least, when only the WPA is preparing TAs, they tend to develop a kind of loyalty to the program that can be healthy for them and the program alike. To a certain extent, how one designs this feature is a function of the faculty and other leaders available, their interest and resources, and the needs of the program. Finally, how much support the WPA is awarded likewise influences this feature. A WPA with a single course release, for instance, will have less time to devote to TA development, given the other tasks that compose the job.

## 9. HISTORICALLY, HOW HAVE TAs BEEN PREPARED AT THE INSTITUTION AND WHY?

The way we have developed TAs isn't the way that we always have to prepare them to teach, but past does tend to prologue. We read out of our own experience as well as out of the experiences of the institution itself. What this means is that we are always carrying forward what was. Relative to TA development, it means that what we do needs to be contextualized within the past practices of TA development, and this is especially so, I think, when we make major curricular changes as can happen with the inclusion of digital media, with the addition of electronic portfolios, or with major pedagogical and assessment changes like collaborative writing groups producing a single (and singly assessed) document. Frequently, major changes in what is being taught require similarly different ways of preparing TAs, ways that differ precisely in their contrast to past practices.

Even when the curricular changes we are making don't require a change in the way that we prepare TAs, other factors can call for a change. Perhaps TAs perceive that too much is asked during an orientation, so they are asked, even paid, to arrive a week earlier for a more extensive session. Perhaps an ungraded practicum becomes a graded graduate seminar. Or perhaps the portfolios are used later to acquire a job. These changes, like those listed above, all affect how we see and understand the TA: The TA's subject position—how we understand him or her—provides another point of departure for curriculum design.

## 10.   HOW ARE IDENTITY ISSUES WOVEN INTO A TA DEVELOPMENT PROGRAM?

Just as a student walks into a classroom with a rich text of lived experience, so too does the new TA. Accordingly, attention to the TA's identity, both the pre-conceived identity the TA brought to the experience of development and the new/revised identity developed over time, is critical. Such attention includes consideration of questions having to do with the TA's construct of teacher/faculty member. How does the new TA understand the identity of a teacher? A faculty member? In other words, what experiences and education have shaped the TA's construct of a teacher, and how does he or she construct his or her relationship to that identity?

Likewise, what "larger" theories—from new historicism to feminist theory—does the TA bring to the experience of teaching, and how can they be used to enhance the teaching of writing? These theories might be the same ones invigorating the writing program, but they might be different as well, as Rebecca Rickly and Susanmarie Harrington experienced at Texas Tech (described in this collection). It's the TA's task to identify them and to synthesize or disambiguate them. Also, what new identity is encouraged by the TA development program? Is it an identity congruent with our understandings, as expressed above? Is it an identity expressed for the duration of the program only, or is it an identity that can be carried forward into the TA's larger, more diverse pedagogical career?

## 11.   WHAT ETHICAL IMPLICATIONS OF IDENTITY ARE PREDICATED IN THIS MODEL OF TA DEVELOPMENT?

Our work with TAs is constructive, it is rhetorical; it is therefore ethical. We need to remember this as we plan curriculum, as we deliver it, as we review it. Is the course we ask TAs to teach one that we teach ourselves? that other tenure-line faculty teach? What kind of teacher have we imagined and do we construct in our materials and discussions? one with her own agency or one who is limited to enact a priori institutional prerogatives? And increasingly, we understand the relationship between conditions under which TAs teach—the number of students per class, for instance, and the number of classes per term; the kind of office space that TAs inhabit; access to technology, be that pens and pencils or phones and faxes—and the ethics of TA development programs. To develop as professionals and as teachers, TAs need certain kinds of support systems. Where and how do they appear in our TA development program?

## 12.   HOW IS THE TA DEVELOPMENT PROGRAM ITSELF REVIEWED, ASSESSED, AND ENHANCED?

Program assessment has become regular institutional practice, and so too should the TA development program be reviewed so that what works can be made to work better and what isn't working can be addressed as well. How we define work—from the arts of constructing a syllabus and leading a class discussion to helping students create Web pages and responding helpfully to print texts—is a first step. A second is collecting the materials—school documents, surveys of student and TA perceptions, follow-up studies of TAs as they complete their graduate work—to review and analyze them systematically. A third is interpreting these data, and a fourth is recommending and implementing change on the basis of the findings. The heuristic provided here can also provide a lens through which the data can be understood.

Raymond Williams has talked about the significance of key words, how they can identify for us a center for a discipline, a way of articulating what we know, how we know it, what we might know. *Design,* I think, is one such word. With this heuristic, I hope, we can do a more comprehensive job of thinking about what we want to design into our TA preparation programs—and why. Perhaps as important, we can use this heuristic, this sense of design, and our own experiences to think about what works in our current models. Without a map of where we've been, it's difficult to know how or where to go next.

We also have practice to guide us; teaching is, after all, both practice and art. And weaving by design seems an apt metaphor for an art that is practice. Reflection, woven throughout, provides the means by which identity is explored, articulated, and acquired. Theory provides backdrop and application; its usefulness in application is reflectively questioned. Techniques are likewise reflectively chosen and assembled to support certain aims; their facility is also an open question. With this heuristic as map, then, we can do a better job of beginning to answer it for the purposes of curriculum design. With the assistance of TAs, we can chart where to go next.

This is a much different model than the one in which many WPAs learned to teach. I began as a TA many years ago as a twenty-two-year-old at Virginia Tech. Nearly broke, I brought with me a BA in English and a lot of enthusiasm. With my peers, I arrived on campus a week before the term commenced to learn how to teach the first-quarter class in nonfiction discourse. The first thing I had to learn, of course, is that there is such a thing as nonfiction discourse. After that, the learning came fast and furious: We talked about how to help students analyze texts, we discussed how to create a syllabus, we practiced how to grade papers, and—not least—we learned how to run the ditto machine.

What we didn't do was in part a function of the times: read theory, keep a log, consider possible syllabi or alternative textbooks, work in other sites (since there weren't any other sites), talk to peers very much about the teaching, compose a portfolio, think of ourselves as learning, think of what we might do differently the next time or the next term. We didn't think of ourselves as a faculty in the making. But we were.

Since that time, I've worked with TAs in several settings: in a composition program at Purdue and in the Writing Lab there and in a testing center; in a Writing Lab practicum at UNC Charlotte. Here at Clemson several of us—some new TAs, some experienced TAs, a new instructor we've just hired from UNC Charlotte, and a tenure-line faculty member or two—are working to develop an electronic portfolio. So the work continues, in ways new and interesting and informative. What we do today, in other words, is far different than what I experienced some quarter of a century ago. It often includes the practices I engaged in as well as those I didn't. It does so, we hope, in an informed, thoughtful, and reflective way.

In its design, a TA development program constructs us all—students, TAs, faculty, and administrators—in ways we plan, in ways we do not. It's therefore more than prudent to plan it well; it's fundamental.

## WORKS CITED

Bartholomae, David. "Inventing the University." *When a Writer Can't Write: Studies in Writer's Block and Other Composing Process Problems.* Ed. Mike Rose. New York: Guilford, 1985. 134–65.

Kress, Gunther. "'English' at the Crossroads: Re-Thinking Curricula of Communication in the Context of the Turn to the Visual." *Passions, Pedagogies, and 21st Century Technologies.* Ed. Gail Hawisher and Cynthia Selfe. Logan: Utah State UP, 1999. 66–89.

Latterel, Catherine G. "Training the Workforce: An Overview of GTA Education Curricula." *WPA* 19.3 (1996): 7–23.

Williams Raymond. *Keywords: A Vocabulary of Culture and Society.* Rev. ed. New York: Oxford UP, 1985.

"The WPA Outcomes Statement for First-Year Composition." *WPA: Writing Program Administration* 23 (1999): 59–67.

# 7. Thinking Together: Developing a Reciprocal Reflective Model for Approaches to Preparing College Teachers of Writing

## SHIRLEY K ROSE AND MARGARET J. FINDERS

When students of writing become teachers of writing, an initial step in applying for that first job is to send to potential employers a teaching philosophy or a teaching statement. Those of us in university settings may be all too familiar with such a task that asks us to articulate fundamental beliefs. We may prepare such statements for grant applications, teaching awards, or annual reviews. To some, it may seem a mere exercise of appropriating the right buzzwords. Over our professional lives, however, we have struggled to make such an exercise more meaningful. We believe that reflecting on and articulating one's beliefs about teaching—whether in philosophies, vision statements, curricular goals, or course syllabi—can serve a generative purpose. But the image of a lone writer crafting a coherent, clearly articulated statement may not be a particularly effective model. We now believe that creating a static statement may be going in the wrong direction altogether. We advocate a reciprocal, reflective process, one done collaboratively with others.

If we take at face value that it is a good idea to articulate a set of guiding principles, then what purposes should such a statement serve? In this chapter we will explain why creating a set of criteria or guiding principles is necessary for preparing writing teachers. Our goals are the following: to present and justify our own criteria for selecting and using particular approaches to prepare teachers of writing; to argue that every teacher educator needs to develop his or her own criteria in dialogue with other teacher educators within a teaching community; and to demonstrate our own ongoing process of identifying, articulating, developing, and refining our criteria.

We are colleagues at Purdue University—Margaret is the senior faculty member in English Education and Shirley regularly mentors new graduate teaching assistants in the Introductory Writing Program.[1] Though we are both engaged in preparing writing teachers—Margaret for the secondary schools and Shirley for first-year college composition—we do not take our professional collaboration for granted. We are well aware that at many institutions the isolation of the English Education program from the faculty development program for teachers of first-year composition parallels the separation between these fields as professions. We consider ourselves fortunate to have found opportunities to work together that have resulted in this chapter as well as other collaborative writing projects (see Finders and Rose, Rose and Finders) for which we have drawn on our teacher preparation experiences in our respective areas.

## WHY ARE CRITERIA FOR TEACHER PREPARATION STRATEGIES NEEDED?

How can teacher educators prepare their students to be reflective practitioners? Reflection is often held up as the key to successful teaching. When we build our course syllabi and design our courses, we list reflection as a central goal. But do we support our students in understanding this term in a more meaningful way than simply transferring it from our course syllabi to their teaching philosophies?

What does reflection look like for our students? And, more importantly, for us? Since the publication of Donald Schön's *The Reflective Practitioner* in 1983, the notion of "knowledge-in-action" has held sway in teacher education programs. But how can we prevent "reflective teaching" from becoming a mere slogan? We're in danger of becoming so familiar with the term that we make it less meaningful, less useful—that is, we may become less reflective about reflection. How can we as teacher educators hold on to the term *reflection* yet make it strange enough to need examination, to prevent it from becoming a taken-for-granted goal statement on our course syllabi?

We are perhaps too comfortable with our conventional reflective practices. As we teacher educators develop curricula that help to instill the disposition and skills necessary to study one's own teaching practices, how can we become uncomfortable with the act of reflection and its results?

## THE LINEAR MODEL OF CURRICULUM DEVELOPMENT

Many conceptions of reflection do not challenge a traditional curricular model, a model that does not allow for the kind of deep thinking for which teacher educators might hope. While teacher preparation practices may have changed to some extent, many have not given up the assumption that a teaching philosophy developed early provides a bedrock for later professional development. When one looks closely at such practices, one can see that they most often rest on a conventional linear design. Goals and philosophy are articulated first. Second, scope and sequence or another curricular model is designed and developed based upon the guiding principles articulated within the vision statement. Instruction follows. Strategies and techniques are developed to meet our goals, and finally assessment tools are chosen to check for understanding and measure achievement. In the linear model, a teaching philosophy comes first and assessments come last. And where does reflection come into play in this model? How might we build concrete strategies to integrate reflection throughout the model? How might we redesign this linear model to make the entire process more recursive and more reflective?

## A RECIPROCAL MODEL OF REFLECTIVE CURRICULUM NEGOTIATION

For engaged teachers, the process of establishing pedagogical principles is always under revision. We have become convinced that this revision is best accomplished in an interchange in which two or more teachers reflect together—an interchange in which each participant reciprocates the contributions of the others. This mutual interaction allows the flow of our actions to be interrupted, suspended for examination. This process is, in fact, as valuable as the product that is created. Furthermore, this reciprocal model of curricular design we now adhere to in our work as teacher educators is built on our recognition that examining one's own teaching beliefs and practices in broader sociopolitical frameworks is rarely productive in isolation.

Kenneth Zeichner cautions that efforts to teach reflective practice might actually undermine what he calls "genuine teacher development" because many practices that facilitate teachers' reflections about their teaching ignore the social and institutional contexts in which teaching takes place and because many reflective practices emphasize helping teachers reflect individually (206). Thus, we advocate a reciprocal model in which reflections must be more than *individual* responses. Reciprocal reflection, because it occurs between and among members of a teaching community—indeed, can work to discursively construct that community—is necessarily conscious and cognizant of its situatedness. While it is now recognized that reflection is a social act, as Kathleen Blake Yancey's recent book *Reflection in the Writing Classroom* argues and demonstrates, most conceptions of reflection still assume an individual thinking alone within a social situation. We are attempting to characterize a kind of reflection that is instantiated in face-to-face interaction in real time. Our reciprocal model still provides us with a working set of principles and teaching practices, but it is the process of negotiating, of a kind of assessment at every turn, that we find so productive for our teaching. It places reflection at the center of the process, rather than at the end.

When reflection is performed by two or more teachers, the interchanges are complementary—contributions complete, extend, challenge, and answer one another. As the discussion moves back and forth, reciprocal reflection can (1) make visible the assumptions that an individual teacher takes as "natural," (2) invite considerations of the immediate context from which beliefs/assumptions/practices emerged; and (3) solicit considerations beyond the immediate context of classrooms.

Reciprocating reflection is important to developing principles for teacher preparation for two key reasons. First, the examination of one's beliefs and behaviors is a concrete act of reflection. Second, it situates the principles within a learning community.

To demonstrate this process, what follows is a transcribed snippet from a reciprocal reflection session in which we were revisiting the set of guiding teaching principles for preparing future writing teachers that we had created a year earlier. As friends and colleagues, we engaged in multiple conversations about creating learning opportunities for our writing students. In designing our courses, we both faced the dilemma of how to teach reflective practice when our students have little or no teaching experience on which to draw. Together, we struggled to provide teaching experiences that would best serve future writing teachers. These informal conversations led to more formal discussions and finally to writing together. We began working on a set of criteria when we were coauthoring an article about a pedagogical strategy we created, the situated performance. To clarify our views and find common ground, we decided to list criteria for effective teaching strategies. We started with practices that we both valued and attempted to tease out why we valued particular strategies and not others. In our collaboration, we had established a common set of criteria for creating and selecting strategies for teacher preparation that would provide educative experiences for future teachers. When we began our session, our list looked like this:

*Teacher preparation strategies must*

1. Allow prospective teachers to develop and draw from both disciplinary expertise and experiential learning
2. Be guided by a confidence in teacher efficacy, that is, a belief that teachers can be taught
3. Acknowledge the importance of affect in teaching and learning
4. Recognize that teacher knowledge is situated
5. Develop habits of reflective practice
6. Model the critical discourse of teaching
7. Be learner centered yet allow for critical intervention by the teacher educator
8. Not depend upon mediating technological accessories.

## UNDER REVISION: A CONCRETE ACT OF REFLECTION

While this process of articulating a concrete set of principles is time intensive, we found it to be extremely generative for our writing and teaching. A year later we decided to revisit our criteria. As we began to re"view" our list, Shirley brought up concerns about number 7: *Be learner-centered yet allow for critical intervention by the teacher educator:*

**M:** My first reaction is to say, "This is good. I agree with it completely. It's great." And move on, but then I know you'll say, "But what do we mean by 'critical intervention'?"

**S:** Well, okay, but let's say, "What do we mean by learner centered?" I'm a little afraid that that is a bit of a slogan. So are we saying that the strategies give the teacher educator a critical role? Does this contradict itself? Be learner centered yet allow for critical intervention? What do *we* mean by "learner centered"? What do *you* mean by "learner centered"?

**M:** I think what you just said is very important. It would be very easy for us and quick if we ask someone to do this. Set up a list of criteria. It is easy to come up with the slogans. "Be learner centered. Tend to diversity. Blah, blah, blah." But the whole point of the conversation is to say what it means to us. We can set down the slogan, but what does it mean to us?

**S:** We're talking about critically entering the discourse of teaching. Ha.

**M:** And it's easy to take it up without being critical.

**S:** To pick it up and use it. Also it has become a kind of shorthand. It becomes so cryptic that it can mean all things to all people.

**M:** And then it means nothing. We could make a list of slogans and be done.

**S:** If we look at the words the way we wrote this one . . . the "yet" implies that there is some presumed opposition or conflict.

**M:** And I think that is wrong. One view of "learner centered" is that the role of the teacher is to facilitate and never to push. And I've been working against that notion all along. So our statement implies that if you do intervene you are not being learner centered. And I think we both agree that that is not the case.

**S:** How about "and allows the teacher educator the critical role of directing the students' attention?" We need to emphasize the attention.

As this brief exchange shows, these discussions are sustained by mutual respect and collegiality, a sense of playfulness and seriousness. Our shared task is to interrogate and challenge our beliefs and practices, so we invite and encourage each other to complicate or simplify one another's formulations, to refine and clarify our language. We prod and probe, coax and cut each other short to help each other discover what we think and why.

In the section that follows, we will place this exchange in its context—our project of articulating a set of principles for developing and using particular strategies in our work as writing teacher educators. Just as we would not hand our students/teachers-in-training a bag of tricks, we do not offer our teacher educator peers a bag of tricks either. Here our purpose is not to authorize or recommend a particular set of strategies or propose a top-ten approved list of approaches to teacher preparation. To do so would be to do the kind of thinking that we are arguing against. Instead, we hope to demonstrate the process and outcome of our reciprocal reflection and to affirm that other writing teacher educators can benefit from engaging in a similar reciprocal reflective practice in their teaching communities.

## OUR FIRST SET OF CRITERIA

This first set of criteria for evaluating, selecting, and employing approaches to teaching writing teachers had been developed through our shared reflection on our teaching experiences, our critical work of revising our teaching practices, and our engagement with and participation in pedagogical theory and research on literacy. While you have overheard a bit of our revision of our first set of criteria, we'll step back and explain how we came to this first set. We began with informal talk over lunch and coffee. The rich conversations led to more organized sessions. We told each other stories about successes and failures in our English education classrooms and TA mentoring meetings. We shared memories of learning critical lessons—inside and outside the classroom. We talked about our research projects and repledged our allegiances to our favorite theorists (particularly John Dewey and Donald Schön). In short, we held each other accountable—that is, each listened to, asked questions of, and answered the other in her attempts to construct a coherent practice of writing teacher preparation. One outcome is the following version of our criteria, developed two years ago.

*A teacher preparation strategy must*

- Allow novice teachers to develop and draw from both disciplinary expertise (knowledge of writing theory and research findings) and experiential learning
- Be guided by a confidence in teacher efficacy, that is, a belief that writing can be taught and that teachers can be taught
- Acknowledge the importance of affect in teaching and learning
- Recognize that teacher knowledge is situated
- Model the critical discourse of teaching
- Be learner centered yet allow critical intervention by the teacher educator
- Offer multiple, flexible options for use that may be enhanced by, but are not dependent upon multimedia technologies (computers, videotape, etc.)
- Develop habits of reflective practice.[2]

Our process of identifying these criteria was not, in the beginning, systematic. We looked at specific teacher preparation strategies we had embraced, such as teaching journals, teaching portfolios, teaching philosophies, and collaborative writing assignments, and tried to characterize their features, strength, and constraints. We started with our concrete experience—not with abstract philosophies of teacher education. We identified strategies we value as teachers and asked ourselves why they were effective and why we used them. Then we worked at finding the precise, refined language we wanted, crafting at word and sentence level, exploring the possibilities and suggestiveness of particular word choices such as "learner centered."

We talked and revised and talked and looked for unintentional contradiction and for what was missing. As we explored together what hadn't worked for us, one would suggest an idea and the other would develop it. We began to suspect that we needed each other to draw out what the other meant, and we reminded ourselves that each teaches in a context, in a community, and no one can do this kind of work by oneself. We also realized that our thinking and talking together were themselves a part of the process of building a community that could encompass both the undergraduate English Education majors and the graduate teaching assistants with whom the two of us worked.

## WHY EVERY TEACHER EDUCATOR SHOULD DEVELOP HIS OR HER OWN CRITERIA

*The process of developing criteria that are always under revision is as important if not more important than the criteria themselves.* This process is our own reflective practice as teacher educators. By developing our own criteria, we as teacher educators engaged in the very kind of reflective practice we ask novice teachers to learn. We must be as willing to forego comfortable and familiar concepts as we expect our students to be.

*To embrace/accept the process of revision allows us continually to adapt our criteria to specific teaching situations, which are themselves in flux.* The institutional context—with constraints such as program design and sequencing of courses—is always subject to change. Our individual positions as teacher educators shift over time as our experience deepens and our specific job responsibilities evolve. Most significantly, our students' needs change as the classrooms they prepare to enter alter. High school and college student writers have experiences, interests, and anxieties that differ substantially over time and across geographic and demographic boundaries.

*Teachers need to think deeply about criteria for themselves and should not accept slogans or formulae.* Because we developed our own criteria, not only are we more committed to using them to plan our work with novice teachers, but the criteria are also more available to us to draw from consciously. They are grounded in vivid experiences and lively conversations we can remember.

*Individually developed criteria can be specific to the teaching situation.* They are available to rationalize what must be a contingent practice, one that asks, "What is needed now, in this specific instructional situation, with these individual teachers in preparation?" The importance of this last point was brought home to us when one of Shirley's students in a seminar on writing program administration developed the following criteria for workshops for adjunct composition faculty:[3]

- Will the program build on knowledge the instructors have already gained through experience?
- Will it situate that knowledge/lore into current theoretical arguments?
- Will it better instructors' chances of getting better working conditions or better their chances at access and admission to graduate school?
- Will it be manageable with their current teaching load?
- Will it be compensated with release time or funds if the program requires extensive outside work?

These criteria are clearly sensitive to the economic and political situations of adjunct writing faculty, and they remind us that committed professional writing instructors never outgrow the status of "teachers-in-preparation."

## WHY CRITERIA MUST BE ARTICULATED

*The process of articulating criteria makes the underlying beliefs and values that inform them more explicit.* This explicitness has several advantages: (1) It allows us to determine whether any of our criteria are in conflict, and if so, to explore critically the reasons why we might simultaneously espouse apparently conflicting criteria. (2) It allows us to rationalize our selection of particular teacher preparation practices. (3) It makes them transformable: We can choose to alter them or reinterpret them.

*Once criteria are articulated, they can be interrogated*—by our peers, ourselves, our students. By making our criteria available to our students' critique in class discussions, we model reflective practice. For example, our teachers-in-preparation can learn to develop their own criteria and learn to consider and review their own teaching methods. In the high school methods course, for instance, future teachers begin the semester-long course by selecting from and revising sample lists of criteria. Working within a small group, students create a tentative list of guiding principles for selecting strategies for teaching writing. Throughout the semester, the future teachers are asked to "check for alignment," measuring a particular strategy against their evolving list. Where students note a misalignment, they have two choices: revise their principles or revise their practices. Being explicit about beliefs and practices provides future teachers with tools to make informed judgments about commercial and self-created pedagogical materials.

*Once articulated, criteria can be used in a disciplined, systematic way.* Teachers can operate more consciously from clearly stated criteria. Until articulated, self-contradictory criteria may remain unrecognized and unintentional; once articulated, contradictory criteria need not be eliminated but can be placed in intentional juxtapositions that generate new understandings and insights. For example, we were able to articulate our criterion that a strategy must be "learner centered yet allow critical intervention by the teacher educator" only after we recognized an implied contradiction in wanting both to be "learner centered" and to fulfill our responsibility to provide direction to the teachers with whom we work.

*Once articulated, criteria can be meaningfully ordered.* They may be ordered hierarchically, categorically, in terms of importance, or chronologically, suggesting stages of development. Our set of criteria can be subject to several different orders, depending upon the way that ordering might inform our planning. We might prioritize them by their relative importance or centrality to our teaching goals. Sequencing the criteria by stages of teacher development might be of generative/heuristic use in planning a teacher preparation curriculum. For example, "modeling the critical discourse of teaching" might be more important at an early stage of teacher preparation than "allow[ing] novice teachers to develop and draw from both disciplinary expertise and experiential learning." If criteria can be ordered, they can be reordered, prompting us to explore the purposes of our ordering. For example, our current ordering of our criteria (see below) reflects a sequence beginning with selection and moving through implementation to outcomes of a strategy for teaching teachers.

## A RECIPROCAL MODEL OF REFLECTION FOR REVIEWING/RECONSIDERING CRITERIA

By now, it should be clear that, for us, the process of developing criteria for selecting and using approaches to teaching writing teachers has been collaborative. This collaboration has been essential to an effective practice of reflection. We have named this dialogic model of reexamining and reconsidering, rearticulating, refining our criteria *reciprocal reflection*. The term "reflection" often suggests (or assumes) the lone thinker; but our work together has led us to question that figure. It has been through our dialogues—probing, challenging, and elaborating one another's ideas—that we've produced a useable set of criteria choosing strategies in our preparation of teachers of writing.

In the remainder of this chapter, we describe a process we share—both to demonstrate that process and to make it available to our readers' critical scrutiny. We feel good about our criteria, yet we have resisted the temptation to offer them as a template for others to adopt wholesale. In the process of making explicit our criteria, we have become invested in them and have validated their usefulness to us as tools to guide our own practice. When we began work on this chapter, we imagined our task was to convince readers that our criteria were not only sound, but superior—we had come through a process that was productive for us and wanted to share the results with others. After reflecting together, we realized that doing so would not be consistent with our own criteria and that it would be a mistake to think that the criteria will not change—even for us.

Not only are our criteria subject to change, but what we mean by any one criterion may change over time. For example, it is no longer easy to think about teaching without a class email list. Just two years after articulating the criterion that an approach to teacher preparation should not depend upon mediating technologies, we are prepared to revise that criterion. We've revisited the issue of dependence upon technologies and realized that the important considerations for us are the costs of the technologies—costs in money, time, and energy. As we discussed these considerations in regard to use of technology, we quickly understood their necessary extension to other issues. We have identified and substituted a more inclusive criterion: The strategy must effectively use resources of available time, physical space (including the metaphorical "spaces" of distance learning), technologies, and money.

In fact, because there is a self-reflective aspect in each criterion, we have already changed our list more than once. Certainly, we cannot present it as the *final word*. Our criteria are articulated but not fixed, continually revisited, constantly under revision. We present our criteria because we are invested in them and have thought about them. But we also present them because we believe that the sharing of criteria and the dialogue it can lead to will promote reflection.

At the same time, we believe that our fellow writing teacher educators must develop their own criteria, taking responsibility for articulating them. That is, we believe both (1) the development of criteria for teaching strategies should be every teacher educator's work and (2) the development of criteria will be most rewarding when it is done through dialogue with other teacher educators— especially within a local teaching community. This kind of dialogue—this reciprocal reflection—is more than trading lore—although teacher lore is rich, valuable, and sustaining, and the exchange is critically important to building a teaching community (see Harkin). By engaging in reciprocal reflection, we draw from one another's store of disciplinary knowledge, making our different experiences and expertise available and accessible to one another. We're fortunate that we teach in the same department and have offices within a few feet of each other, which allows us many opportunities to meet. Other teacher educators may have to go further afield to find a colleague with whom to engage in this reciprocal reflection; and their collaboration will surely be aided, as ours has, by having specific writing projects to work on together. Engaging in reciprocal reflection is time consuming and requires a commitment of considerable effort. But it is worth the time and effort for us because we are able to model the working relationship we hope to develop with future teachers and for them to develop with each other.

In reciprocal reflection, we also make our teaching visible to one another. Usually, we know very little about our colleagues' teaching practices. But by engaging in critical discussion of our teaching with a colleague, we make that action public—available to recognize and subject to scrutiny. We may be uncomfortable with exposing our teaching to the scrutiny of our peers, but to not do so is to also make it unavailable to their understanding and appreciation.

## OUR MORE RECENT SET OF CRITERIA

As we were writing this chapter, we began by rearticulating our revised, refined set of criteria to the following version:

*A teacher preparation strategy must*
- Value and bring into play students' interests, knowledges, experiences, and needs as well as require them to draw from their developing knowledge of writing theory and research
- Be grounded in both the teacher educator's and the students' confidence that those teachers can be taught; it must confirm, demonstrate, and make participants conscious of the progress of their learning
- Allow beginning teachers to affirm the importance of affect in teaching and learning
- Demonstrate that teacher knowledge is situated
- Lead teachers-in-preparation to enter critically the discourse of teachers

- Provide teacher educators opportunities for critical intervention in their students' learning by directing students' attention
- Effectively use resources of available time, physical space, technologies, and money
- Encourage novice teachers to develop the habits of reflective professional practitioners

We articulate our criteria within a community, just as we teach within a community; the negotiation, the process of articulation, builds consensus and community. But as we were presenting this revision, we began to question our terms once more. Is "criteria" the right word? Doesn't it imply a rigid application? Do we mean a set of "standards"? a set of "guiding principles"? what about "a set of considerations" . . . ?

What we've described and advocated here is a postmodern practice of teacher preparation, one that acknowledges the instability, provisionality, and contingent nature of what constitutes good teaching practices. It is an approach to teacher preparation that seeks not closure and definition but a commitment to keep thinking together.

## NOTES

1. For a fuller description of how mentors prepare new TAs in Purdue's writing program, see Irwin Weiser's "When Teaching Assistants Teach Teaching Assistants to Teach" in this collection.
2. We understand reflective practice to be more like a habit than like a routine or a discipline. A habit can become internalized, almost second nature, while "discipline" implies an externally imposed set of constraints.
3. These criteria were developed by Christine Norris, a student in Purdue's graduate program in rhetoric and composition.

## WORKS CITED

Dewey, John. *Experience and Education.* New York: MacMillan, 1938.

———. *How We Think.* New York: Heath, 1910.

Finders, Margaret J., and Shirley K Rose. "'If I Were the Teacher': Situated Performances as Pedagogical Tools for Teacher Preparation." *English Education* 31.3 (1999): 205–22.

Harkin, Patricia. "The Postdisciplinary Politics of Lore." *Contending with Words: Composition and Rhetoric in a Postmodern Age.* Ed. Patricia Harkin and John Schilb. New York: MLA, 1991. 124–38.

Rose, Shirley K, and Margaret J. Finders. "Learning from Experience: Using Situated Performances in Writing Teacher Development." *WPA* 22.1/2 (1998): 33–52.

Schön, Donald. *The Reflective Practitioner: How Professionals Think in Action.* New York: Basic, 1983.

Yancey, Kathleen Blake. *Reflection in the Writing Classroom.* Logan, UT: Utah State UP, 1998.

Zeichner, Kenneth. "Teachers as Reflective Practitioners and the Democratization of School Reform." *Currents of Reform in Preservice Teacher Education.* Ed. Kenneth Zeichner, Susan Melnick, and Mary Louise Gomez. New York: Teachers College P, 1996. 199–214.

# 8. Educating Literacy Instructors: Practice versus Expression

## Judith Goleman

> When I was at the Centre for Cultural Studies, young students wanting to get into politics were sometimes impatient, asking, "Why should we go through all of this and study books? Let's just get out there!" It took a lot of time to convince them. They were not street kids; they were extremely privileged middle-class graduate students. To make a political link with other people requires a practice, not an expression.
>
> —Stuart Hall

Those of us who work with graduate students toward their development as advanced literacy instructors are likely to recognize in Hall's story a version of our own experience—students dying to teach, impatient with theory, eager for methods of effective transmission. Unlike Hall, however, I have avoided trying to convince graduate students why they should "go through" all that we ask of them, choosing instead to apply what Hall says about educating people "out there" to the education right here of graduate students: "To make a political link with other people requires a practice, not an expression" (Drew 181).

In this chapter, I want to argue that the graduate education of literacy instructors offers an important opportunity for advanced pedagogical practices where the teacher-student relationship becomes an occasion for reflection and critique. It is a time to interrogate the transmission model of essential knowledge so that a new historical model of dialectical knowledge can supercede it as the basis for defining literacy. However, unless graduate educators design courses and experiences that require instructors to explore these models of knowledge, not just as subject matter but as subject positions composing complex structures of feeling, discourse, and relationality, the graduate students we are preparing will find it next to impossible to sustain pedagogically the shift to a new model of knowledge in their own work as literacy instructors. This is because they will not have had sufficiently complex experiences with the new model—which after all does not offer a stable alternative subjectivity, but, rather, a critical dialogical one—nor will they have had sufficient experience negotiating a position for themselves among these models' competing subjectivities—something that is crucial for a literacy instructor who will be asking this of her students while continuing to go through it herself. Preparation for this kind of literacy instruction must embody and reveal what Mariolina Salvatori has called "pedagogy's complexity . . . as a discipline" (66).

What I am particularly interested in pursuing is the look and sound of novice literacy instructors negotiating positions for themselves among competing models of subjectivity. Two graduate students, Jan and Amy, who are becoming literacy instructors working their way into a historical model of dialectical knowledge and out of a transmission model of essential knowledge, exemplify this transition. They are students in the master's program in English at the University of Massachusetts–Boston. The composition track of this program offers teacher preparation in three stages: co-teaching with a composition mentor, studying the teaching of composition in a seminar, and teaching English 101 as part of a staff that collaboratively designs the course under the supervision of the same faculty member who has taught the seminar. This is a small program: Only five TAs a year are chosen to participate, the rest of the freshman writing program being taught by full- and part-time faculty. Because of the three-stage process, TAs do not begin teaching until their third semester in the program. As a result, many new TAs will already have taken more than the one required seminar in composition studies. Through the work of various theorists, practitioners, and historians, including Paulo Freire, Mikhail Bakhtin, Michel Foucault, Richard Ohmann, James Berlin, Ann Berthoff, David Bartholomae, John Brereton, and Robert Connors, TAs learn the assumptions and methods of critical composition studies.

One assumption is that American college students are confronted with multiple, often contradictory discourses that they struggle to resolve through the unifying methods of the foundational systems they have been taught. Limited by these foundational systems of truth and knowledge that they have not yet learned to problematize, students attempt to resolve the startling array of social realities that they confront in texts and in experience. The inadequacies of these resolutions reveal the severely limited capacities of their literacies to address their situations, including their academic situations. In the teaching of composition seminar, a TA learns dialogical and dialectical methods that enable first-year students to grapple with and expand their ways of composing meaning. Dialogical methods invite students to reflect on and compare the knowledge produced by different discourses so that they can make choices among them; dialectical methods offer students a means to understand the social functions of these discourses. Together, these methods represent an alternative approach to postsecondary literacy (see Goleman).

To these new instructors in the process of learning alternative literacy practices, I want to bring close textual readings. For my purposes, the most useful texts contain moments of difficulty that reveal the tension between residual and emerging forms of knowledge in the novice educator. One such moment occurred when Jan, a new graduate instructor I was working with on the staff-designed English 101 course, came to talk to me about a class she had just taught. The staff's plan had been to work in class with our students' literacy narratives, which they had collected into a class book. For homework, the instructors asked students to read and gloss the class book and to form a set of three or four papers around a concept that they could name and explore. The instructor had asked eight or so students to list their related titles on the board and to say in what ways they saw them as sets. With so many lists of titles on the board, the instructor found herself at a loss for something to say after each student explained briefly what connections she or he had found. In my office afterward, the instructor was very upset as she descibed the blankness and inadequacy she had felt. In her mind, she had failed because she could not form a rich, thought-provoking response after each student had spoken. This assumption that she should immediately see the nut in the shell of each student's list and crack it open with pointed questions is a highly concentrated effect of traditional, expressivist relations to knowledge; it is easy to see here how traditional knowl-edge relations translate into traditional pedagogical relations.

One of my purposes is to consider a pedagogy for literacy instruction that prepares instructors for problematizing such moments in their teaching. For me, the instructor's expectation that she would be able to see into each student's set instantly is particularly poignant considering the assignment's requirement that the students form sets that went beyond the easy, obvious, or quick connection. In our staff meetings, we had developed the assignment sequence to this point in order to enact critical reflection and revision toward what Richard Rodriguez calls the longer, more adequate response. These first-year students were learn-ing through their reading and writing assignments to notice and question authoritative discourses, to see their historical function and their effects on the students' own writing so as to forge less automatic connections among texts and experiences. The dialogical and dialectical theories for these practices had been the subject of graduate seminars and staff meetings. Still, for this instructor, tears threatened when her success at getting her students to generate complex sets contradicted her unreflected desire for quick mastery, making such a per-formance impossible.

I have to assume that experiences like this one occur dozens of times a week across the country among novice instructors whose commitments to dialogical and dialectical approaches to knowledge are unevenly integrated as subject positions, thus producing scenes of pedagogical contradiction and silenced, dis-abled instruction. Yet we see very little written about how the educators of instructors can read these scenes not only to prop up novices for the next day's work but also as occasions for instructors to reflect on their own evolving rela-tionship to a new model of knowledge.

If such moments are understood in terms of an instructor's ideological development, which consists, as Bakhtin says, of "an intense struggle within us for hegemony among various available verbal and ideological points of view" (346), they can be valuable occasions for the advance of one's practice. This, in part, is what I meant earlier when I wrote that graduate educators need to design not only courses but also experiences that invite new instructors to explore with their mentors and peers the models of knowledge they are prac-ticing—not just as competing subject matter but as competing subject positions.

In the case of Jan, I responded to her description of her class by raising a few questions: Why did she expect to be able to respond to a student's set if she had not reread the papers in light of the proposed connection? What assumptions about reading and interpreting student work were implicit in her expectation? These questions, at first, took her aback. On the one hand, I was posing them from a position of authority, but on the other, they were questions that exposed how self-defeating *her* concept of authority was. I followed quickly by asking why she would make such a harsh demand on herself in front of students. Only when these questions were linked did Jan start to perk up and to reflect on the scene. Inclined toward self-blame, she was reticent to trade her internally persuasive discourse of the romantic individual who rises or falls alone for a more dynamic analysis. However, my question about knowing the sets without rereading the papers struck at our freshman course's deepest theme of dialogue and dialectic as the engines of meaning. We were not teaching students how to find the hidden meaning; we were not taking the position that one meaning was to be found, and yet this premise underlay Jan's position to the students' knowledge that day, contributing to her subsequent feelings of muteness and incompetence.

Having contradicted the approach to knowledge she was trying to teach her students, Jan was now more troubled by *that* contradiction than by her performance. As a result, Jan became more inclined toward questioning her subject position and the way it had disrupted a fellowship with her students by privileging mastery over learning. "I guess we could have *all* stopped to reread the papers on someone's list before trying to respond," she said, still a little glum. Giving up authoritative relations in exchange for a common process with one's students can feel like defeat. It's such a slow, decentralized vision of the reading and writing classroom that at first it can seem like no vision at all.

In my experience, only by piling up and continuously reflecting on such contradictory experiences at the micro-level of daily practice in seminars and staff meetings through the use of teacher research can one transform authoritative concepts of knowledge, discourse, and subjectivity into dialogical concepts. As classroom researchers, these new instructors learned to return to their preparatory staff notes after teaching a class, commenting on what occurred and reflecting on the relationship between theory and practice as they had in their teaching seminar, using prepared materials. Making notes on their notes, new instructors learned to form pointed questions and to determine the appropriate means for addressing them—for example, a reference text, a staff meeting, a conference, or a peer conversation. Each of these means has been consciously structured into our program through the content and design of the mentor experience, the teaching seminar, and the staff meeting. With practice over time, TAs discover the heuristic power of these methods, and, as a result, their commitment to dialogical practices for both themselves *and* their students intensifies. A pedagogy for preparing literacy instructors needs to include time and space and faculty for the piling up of such research experiences to occur in a meaningful context of guided reflection and critique. Otherwise, the pedagogical complexity of a dialectical model of knowledge will be overwhelming and more than likely cause a retreat into the traditional model of essential knowledge that resides in Western consciousness as a subject position of tremendous authority and truth value.

In Jan's case, she appeared to have taken from our discussion a more specific understanding of how to read *with* her students rather than for them. The attraction for her was its consistency with the dialogical theory of reading we were teaching and its capacity to spare herself the pressure of masterful performances. The unattractive aspect, which caused her to remain skeptical and glum as we spoke, was that she would have nothing intellectually interesting to do in the classroom. She told me that she had enjoyed the idea of finding a thesis to transmit to her students even though she found herself at a painful loss trying to name a student's thesis. I asked her to consider transforming her desire to deliver a thesis to delivering an *occasion* for one to be imagined collaboratively. She invited me to observe her next class and to see how far along she could come in these changes.

In some ways the class I observed was a classic version of the new pedagogy: Students read excerpts from Nancy Sommers's research comparing what student writers and professional writers say about revision; the students offered interpretations of Sommers's data; the instructor put these interpretations on the board for the students to synthesize. Next, they worked in groups to evaluate a student draft and revision in terms of Sommers's contrast between the revision methods of student and professional writers. The groups then reported their analyses and argued among themselves about where the revision fell on the continuum between a student writer's methods and an experienced writer's methods.

As I observed the class and transcribed the discussion, I found myself inserting comments to the instructor in brackets: Here you have a chance to articulate a connection between the student's comment and Sommers's text; here you can press the students to say *why* they marked the revision on the continuum where they did, and so on. A pattern emerged that I was not surprised to see—one in which the instructor would not allow herself to participate directly in furthering students' knowledge. The scaffolding Jan had built for the students to work in— which admittedly was strong and useful—now had to do all the work. In reaction to her earlier problems, it seemed she was now mistaking any practice that involved using her knowledge to stimulate students' transformative processes with that of an authoritative (or in Hall's terms an expressive) pedagogy. And in discussion afterwards, she did not understand the historical reasons why the immediate difference between such a practice or expression would not always be self-evident or even matter. While my work with Jan continued, I am going to depart from her case now to complicate—even contest—my own main point by saying that it does not really matter if a particular teaching activity can be typified as a critical practice or an authoritative expression, and I am going to consider what the alternative is to such a binary opposition.

In *Marxism and Literature*, Raymond Williams writes, "Hegemony is always an active process" (115). By implication we can add: Counterhegemony is always an active process too. As such it is always going to be a complex, even dismaying mix of residual and emerging elements whose relationships to one another are unstable and shifting. "It is exceptionally difficult," writes Williams, "to distinguish between . . . elements of some new phase of dominant culture . . . and those which are substantially alternative or oppositional to it" (123). If it is impossible to determine the exact social function of a particular practice, it is also impossible to be purely counterhegemonically aligned.

Thus, the very concept of a counterhegemonic or nonauthoritative practice is an idealism. One's practice will always consist of residual and emergent elements, and these elements themselves will not maintain a fixed status. For these reasons, it could be argued that the ambiguous circumstances of the instructor who is beginning a nonauthoritative practice stands for the circumstances of every other nonauthoritative instructor, writ large.

Seen this way, ongoing revision of one's subjectivity as an instructor is the common work of the graduate educator and the novice instructor of literacy, and in neither case should it be driven by an attempt to forge a purely nonauthoritative project in the classroom, such as I guessed Jan was trying to do in the class I observed, and such as I guessed she imagined that I expected. The classroom, James Berlin has written, is the place in which "theory and practice engage in a dialectic interaction, [not an ideal application] where one can work out a rhetoric [and I would add, a subjectivity] more adequate to the historical moment and the actual conditions of students and teachers" (25).

Problematizing the difficulties of the instructor in transition allows us to consider what might constitute not so much a purely nonauthoritative rhetoric and subjectivity but a more *adequate* rhetoric and subjectivity for literacy instructors today. In Jan's case, such a rhetoric would position her as a historical subject in transition, stimulating reflection in her students regarding their knowledge while negotiating and renegotiating her position to her knowledge and theirs.

When I try to think of a model for this rhetoric, I am drawn to Bakhtin's discussion of double-voiced discourse in the English comic novel where the author incorporates "another's speech in another's language, serving to express authorial intentions but in a refracted way" (324). Double-voiced discourse in the classroom would mean the "relativizing of [one's] linguistic consciousness in the perception of language borders—borders created by history and society . . . and [would] permit expression of a feeling for the materiality of language that defines such a relativized consciousness" (323–4).

In short, the comic impossibility of a pure pedagogical practice can be negotiated by playing with and refracting—not controlling—the discourses that compose us and our subject relations as teachers. To achieve this negotiation, however, one must be in active dialogue with the specific, historical discourses that compose us as composition instructors. "It demands . . . a lively to-and-fro movement in [one's] relation to language" and the verbal-ideological belief systems that compose it (302). This internally dialogized double-voiced discourse of the literacy instructor in transition represents a pedagogical form of the rhetoric we are teaching our first-year students to construct when they work with essays by such writers as Adrienne Rich, Susan Griffin, and John Edgar Wideman. It is the rhetoric we represent as constructing the conscious and credible writer reading herself and the world. Educating instructors to practice double-voiced discourse as a rhetorical style and subject position for the literacy classroom challenges graduate programs that marginalize composition pedagogy and deny its complexity as a subject matter and subject position. It is challenging to such programs because it requires incremental and recursive study of composition theory, history, and pedagogy in relation to one's teaching experience.

As a graduate educator reflecting on the preparation of composition instructors, I have come to realize that studying composition history offers novice instructors opportunities to discover the context for many of their assumptions about the teaching of writing. For instance, it enables novice instructors to understand the specific context for the rise of freshman English—its standardized, class-based rhetoric; its exclusionary emphasis on mechanical correctness; its authoritative, judgmental pedagogy; its passifying effect on the student as a theme writer, not an author. Seeing a larger problematic of power/knowledge/discourse relations at work in the field, novice instructors can see how these relations structure their own pedagogical choices and reactions as well—not so much as personal acts of failure or success but as features of a larger social process of which they are part. They come to see the traditions of which they are part as a various, contradictory mix of residual and emerging rhetorical elements that will structure their own teaching practice in various and contradictory ways.

In a moment we will look at the halting, interrogative sentences of Amy, a novice instructor reflecting on these mixed traditions in relation to her classroom work, and we will see a new method of response becoming internally persuasive. This slowed-down, questioning method is above all what I want to hear in a novice instructor because it makes possible the analysis of her personal practice in terms of a larger historical process. We should not, after all, expect novice writing instructors to sustain dialectical meaning-making methods with their mentors or their students if they haven't been guided to establish these relations with themselves as a way of knowing.

In what follows, I want to examine the writing of Amy, who was learning to problematize her place in the history of composition and to negotiate a position for herself in relation to her students. What we can hear in excerpts from her own course writing is an excitement about the problems of a unified teaching practice and subjectivity that we could not hear in Jan's case.

Amy, who was studying the history and politics of college composition, was not having difficulties with her teaching. In Jan's eyes, Amy was simply a better teacher—a natural. And it is true that Amy was a little more easy-going and had taught study skills courses for a private company before returning to graduate school. My purpose in looking now at Amy's writing is not to make claims for what *determined* her easier approximation of a dialogic discourse in the classroom. All I want to do is to offer for consideration what one may be in a position to think about, to say, and to write as an instructor when doing the kind of work Amy has done.

The context for Amy's writing was an elective seminar in the history and politics of college composition in which Jan had not chosen to enroll. Students read numerous histories of college writing and compared them with various primary sources to which the histories refer. (These sources are available in John Brereton's documentary history, *The Origins of Composition Studies in the American College, 1875–1925*.) At a point of near saturation with these materials, I asked students to read Lester Faigley's 1989 article, "Judging Writing, Judging Selves," which begins to draw out the implications of freshman English's history on present practice. In that article, Faigley compares responses to student writing by college entrance examiners in 1931 with modern compositionists of the 1970s and concludes that compositionists' ways of responding to student writing cannot be separated from compositionists' ways of judging the students doing the writing. When examiners apply their unreflected presuppositions about students to texts, the effects on students' lives can be extreme—resulting in success or failure, acceptance or rejection. From our current vantage point, Faigley makes it easy to see that both the examiners and their reviewers were reading these entrance exams in order to find *themselves* among the applicants—that elite one-tenth—giving high scores for identity and failing difference.

Faigley also uses William Coles and James Vopat's *What Makes Writing Good?* to discern a pattern of response among modern compositionists who were asked to contribute the best student paper they had ever received and to explain what made it so good. What Faigley explores in great detail is the way that these student writers and teacher readers from the 1970s are just as identified by a traditional blend of class and aesthetic values as the 1931 students and examiners. Both groups read their students through the dominant ideology of Western humanism and continue to do so despite the postmodern dismantling of humanism's key features: the unified, ahistorical self, the autonomous text, and the transparency of language.

In the context of her seminar on the history of college composition, Amy responds to Faigley's article in a mostly positive way. She grants legitimacy to Faigley's claim that throughout the history of writing instruction "writing instructors have been as much or more interested in *who* they want their students to be as in *what* they want their students to write." Next, she states that in his critique of the largely confessional narratives named as best essays in *What Makes Writing Good?* Faigley "seems to be lumping all writing teachers into one group: those who enjoy receiving and responding to autobiographical student writing." This is not an abstract issue for Amy: Faigley has launched a serious social and historical critique of expressivism in general and autobiographical writing in particular, placing it in a tradition of authoritative discourse relations that Amy sees herself countering in her own teaching even though that teaching makes use of autobiographical writing.

Using Faigley's critique of expressivism's notion of the unitary self, she talks back to Faigley in the following excerpt and offers (in a novice's voice of reaction and defense) a complex historical representation of the teacher as subject to multiple discourses about language, self and knowledge. Here is part of what she writes:

> But aren't we as individual as the students we're teaching? Don't we also possess contingent and partial selves, constantly changing selves who privilege different qualities in student writing just as we privilege different qualities in our constantly changing selves? Faigley advocates teachers' attempts at understanding that the students we teach are not unified, rational selves. My claim is

that neither are the teachers, and to present ourselves as though we are unified, rational beings perpetuates an imbalance of power in the classroom.

... If we—both teachers and students—are simultaneously uniquely individual and subject to cultural, social, and historical ways of knowing, how do we account for the different ways such contexts affect us?

My interest in this paragraph lies in the interrogative, problematizing method Amy is finding to organize the disruptions to traditional notions of students' and teachers' subjectivities that Faigley's article, in the context of composition's history, has stimulated. Even her answers are provisional and stated as questions: "Can't authority come from students' understanding that their teachers too are human beings with values, with likes and dislikes, that their teachers are equally subjected to cultural and historical ways of knowing?" Here we can see a novice instructor reading against the grain of composition's long history of reading its students, but not itself. Cultivating a reflexive (yet very public) voice, Amy offers an unstable open response to a question typically posed in a fixed, either-or way: Where does authority reside? Can it reside, she wonders, in not one person or another, but in their shared understanding of the hierarchical situation itself?

Again, I am not making claims for the completeness or satisfactoriness of this response to the problem of authority in the classroom. I am only suggesting that a novice instructor who is given chances to think and write her way into a historicizing method for understanding her subject position is less likely to, say, plan classes that rise or fall on her ability to perform master readings of student texts—or at least is less likely to be without means of reflection and critique after doing so. Reading herself in relation to her students, she will know she is in the middle of a historical struggle that "is always going to be a dismaying mix of residual and emerging elements whose relationships to one another are unstable and shifting" (Williams 123). She will know that a successful pedagogy does not require her to side-step the problems of history and subjectivity, but to model the negotiated stance that these problems constantly require through the critical reflexivity of a double-voiced discourse.

In a later section of her paper, Amy pursues the question of authority in relation to the writing of assignments and the decisions students make when they read assignments. In the language she uses to set up this section, we can overhear her practicing this negotiated stance, making it her own.

It's time for me to get to my own work as a teacher. ... Of course, because of what I've said this far, I'm in sort of a bind: I cannot ... get much distance from my own social situatedness to make an analysis of my own practice that could in any way be said to be objective. ... [E]ven my choice of which student papers to work with is political. I'm obviously going to choose those papers that illustrate part or all of what I've been arguing so far, the papers I understand best, maybe even those I like best. I also know [as Robert Schwegler has written] that "simply by deciding to read a student paper as a text, an instructor becomes socially (and ideologically) situated with regard to it" (213).

Reading herself preparing to read her students in the context of composition's history and politics, this novice instructor is developing her internal dialogue in a complex and double-voiced way that, with ongoing support, will fulfill itself as a style of classroom discourse as well.

Preparing literacy instructors to construe their classroom discourse as just such an ongoing negotiation is sufficiently different from traditional practices to warrant the development of an explicit pedagogy. The predominant quick-start model of TA preparation is the residue of an earlier rhetoric that concerned itself mainly with arrangement and mechanical correctness. Preparing TAs in the old way for a new rhetoric constitutes a contradiction that will produce inadequately transformed writing instruction. In what I have offered here a reader will notice the basic features of a new pedagogy: attention to composition as both a subject matter *and* a subject position, ongoing reflection and critique of one's practice via teacher research, familiarity with composition's history and politics, and institutional commitment to teacher preparation as an accretive, scholarly activity.

## WORKS CITED

Bakhtin, M. M. *The Dialogic Imagaination.* Trans. Caryl Emerson and Michael Holquist. Austin: U of Texas, 1981.

Bartholomae, David. "Inventing the University." *When a Writer Can't Write: Studies in Writer's Block and Other Composing Process Problems.* Ed. Mike Rose. New York: Guilford, 1985: 134–65.

Berlin, James. "Poststructuralism, Cultural Studies, and the Composition Classroom: Postmodern Theory in Practice." *Rhetoric Review* (1992): 16–33.

Berthoff, Ann E. *The Making of Meaning.* Montclair, NJ: Boynton/Cook, 1981.

Brereton, John C., ed. *The Origins of Composition Studies in the American College, 1875–1925.* Pittsburgh: U of Pittsburgh P, 1995.

Coles, William E., Jr., and James Vopat. *What Makes Writing Good?* Lexington, MA: D.C. Heath, 1985.

Connors, Robert. *Composition-Rhetoric: Backgrounds, Theory, and Pedagogy.* Pittsburgh: U of Pittsburgh P, 1997.

Drew, Julie. "Cultural Composition: Stuart Hall on Ethnicity and the Discursive Turn." *JAC* 18.2 (1998): 171–96.

Faigley, Lester. "Judging Writing, Judging Selves." *College Composition and Communication* 40 (1989): 395–412.

Foucault, Michel. *Discipline and Punish: The Birth of the Prison.* Trans. A. M. Sheridan Smith. New York: Pantheon, 1972.

Freire, Paulo. *Pedagogy of the Oppressed.* Trans. Myra Bergman Ramos. New York: Seabury Press, 1968.

Goleman, Judith. *Working Theory: Critical Composition Studies for Students and Teachers.* Westport, CT: Bergin and Garvey, 1995.

Ohmann, Richard. *English in America: A Radical View of the Profession.* New York: Oxford UP, 1976.

Rodriguez, Richard. *Hunger of Memory: The Education of Richard Rodriguez.* Boston: Godine, 1981.

Salvatori, Mariolina Rizzi, ed. *Pedagogy: Disturbing History, 1819–1929*. Pittsburgh: U of Pittsburgh P, 1996.

Schwegler, Robert A. "The Politics of Reading Student Papers." *Politics of Writing Instruction: Postsecondary*. Ed. Richard Bullock and John Trimbur. Portsmouth, NH: Boynton/Cook, 1991. 203–26.

Sommers, Nancy. "Revision Strategies of Student Writers and Experienced Adult Writers." *College Composition and Communication* 31 (1980): 378–88.

Williams, Raymond. *Marxism and Literature*. Oxford: Oxford UP, 1977.

# 9. Too Cool for School? Composition as Cultural Studies and Reflective Practice

CHRISTINE FARRIS

*Private Benjamin to her Basic Training Commander: "I think they sent me to the wrong place. See, I did join the Army, but I joined a different army. I joined the one with the condos and the private rooms."*

Even in its so-called current-traditional past, when we presumably both practiced *and* believed in composition as a set of transparent skills to be learned and applied to any situation, comp made for some hard teaching. Now that programs like my own are revising composition curricula to reflect postmodern notions of reading, writing, and representation, it's even harder work.

My first composition teaching job almost twenty-five years ago was for the European Division of the University of Maryland on a NATO base in Iceland. In summer under the midnight sun and in winter under the northern lights, I drove fifty miles each way across a lunar landscape between Reykjavik and Keflavik to teach—with no training or supervision—from the regulation *Harbrace Handbook* and Decker's *Patterns of Exposition*. My students, mostly homesick and bored nineteen-year-olds on "hardship duty," would study model essays that compared General Grant to General Lee and then write papers comparing Jello to pudding and M-16 rifles to their best friends. I was required to keep a chart (in *Harbrace Handbook* code) logging every error students made on every paper they wrote. At the end of each semester, I dutifully sent these charts back to the States. I never heard from a soul at the other end. *I had this comp teaching thing down cold.* Of course, the writing my students produced had no intellectual consequences whatsoever. But I would have to say that the ennui that accompanied my teaching the modes of exposition or, a few years later, the stages of the writing process, at least made possible a gradual comfort with a teaching authority that postmodern composition specialists now question at every turn.

As Director of Composition at Indiana University, nine years ago I redesigned the required one-semester three-credit academic writing course taught almost exclusively by TAs in over 100 sections to approximately 2500 freshmen per year. I shifted the focus from argument to the critical analysis of popular culture. This move made sense as our TAs became increasingly familiar with semiotics and cultural studies in their graduate courses. Ideally, this shift in approach would allow us to introduce the future professoriate to pedagogy in theorized ways tied not only to composition. It was part of our larger efforts to bust up the literature/composition, theory/practice binaries that divide departments and the field of English at large.

At the same time that I am attracted to cultural studies as a scholar and a teacher of things other than composition, my motivation to steer the composition curriculum in this direction came about honestly, bottom-up—from practice as a teacher, writing program administrator, and writing across the curriculum consultant. I find that a lot of what we consider ineffective, boring, and bad about undergraduate writing is rooted in students' cultural misunderstandings, that is, in their perceptions that experience is universally the same for everyone and that cultural texts of all sorts mirror that experience unproblematically. When instructors in English and other disciplines are disappointed with student writing in ways that don't have to do with error, it is often because students can't get beyond their first responses to cultural phenomena, beyond merely agreeing or disagreeing, delivering back "commonplaces," or ventriloquizing the positions of expert critics they read. Merely learning to write academic papers "in conversation with sources" is not enough to develop the tolerance for complexity that most college instructors would like to see their students not so eager to reduce when writing about issues with global, not just personal, implications. Our students need, as my colleague John Schilb says, "to study relations within and between spaces in the contemporary world" (138).

Cultural studies, most often defined as the analysis of the complex relationships between culture and power in the production, reception, and use of texts (Giroux 5), can help us enlarge the inquiry tied to the reading and writing in a first-year course. We work with our students to become more active critical subjects, aware not only of how academic discourse works but also of how language and visual representations of gender, race, class, and sexual orientation in ads, TV, and films make for interesting contradictions that invite us to occupy various—even conflicting—roles as spectators and consumers. Our use of popular media as primary texts has leveled the playing field for analysis at the same time that our use of essays about popular culture as critical lenses has made it possible for our students to try on the moves of academic and professional discourse. Students come to understand better their "guilty pleasures" as consumers even as they resist some of the moves that academic and professional discourse makes.

It's problematic, however, to just call any classroom practice or program "cultural studies" because it makes use of popular culture or assigns critique— especially when the program depends on 100 or more new and nearly new teachers, some of whom may ask for the "formula" that will enable them to reproduce cultural critique in their classrooms, and some of whom fear political advocacy or indoctrination. The efforts of programs like ours to reconfigure traditional composition in ways that reflect changes in the rest of English studies have sometimes met with resistance from graduate teaching assistants (Welch). Reasons for TA resistance are varied and complex. Research has found new TAs in practice work from "convergent" theories (Bishop) that meld their perceived classroom needs and their prior experience and beliefs about writing with those of the programs for which they work in ways that are not unified (Farris; Farris and Anson), but this process is never a smooth one, particularly when we up the curricular ante. Arguments that a composition curriculum be more open to difference—including acknowledgment of the effects of cultural background on students' writing and the ideologies students bring to the classroom—along with new emphases on representations of gender, race, class, and sexuality, must also consider the institutional position of the first-year composition course. TAs, presumed through the ages to be sufficiently qualified to teach the current-traditional version of composition, may indeed want, need, and expect their first-time teaching experience to be familiar, successful, and uncomplicated in the very ways that seasoned compositionists have come to complicate and professionalize it.

Despite the contemporary theories underlying their graduate course work, new TAs may assume a prototype of uncomplicated teaching and learning. Especially given the persistence of composition's "modern" conservative service role (Crowley 218), it is understandable that they may view all composition as foundational and any syllabus, however hip, as monolithic. After all, if a requirement remains in place, it can be assumed that students are expected to master the composing process, academic discourse conventions, grammar, and style, even if they are now also expected to become critics of their culture. TAs not yet accustomed to thinking of teaching in the postmodern age as "overdetermined" may argue when they find that "Jason can't *do* cultural critique" that we should return to what they consider an ideologically neutral approach—in short, to *"just* the teaching of writing." Understandably, they would like to reduce the conflicts that arise among their authority in the classroom, the syllabus, and the students in front of them. When composition specialists try to reconfigure composition in new ways, we may find ourselves handing new teachers postmodern tools to do what is institutionally configured as a modern job. It is no wonder TAs (along with those who prepare them) are frustrated.

One challenge in teaching composition as cultural studies is, of course, that the curriculum not be a top-down dissemination of a theory by a program or instructors but a bottom-up inquiry that does more than replace one "banking model" with another and that includes the classroom culture in its examination of representation and practices. We are continually urged to remain alert to why our students might resist cultural critique and attentive to our own power and motives for encouraging such critique (George and Shoos).

Joseph Harris, in reexamining Mary Louise Pratt's discussion of the "Culture, Ideas, Values" course at Stanford and her notion of the classroom "contact zone" as a contested space where students can examine competing worldviews, urges us to do more than merely apply the agenda of recent cultural criticism to our teaching (121). Particularly in working with students "who voice beliefs which are not so much 'oppositional' as they are simply opposed to our own," we need, Harris says, "to find ways of keeping them an active part of the conversation of the class" (122). The goals of such a critical pedagogy thus become "not the forcing of a certain 'multicultural' agenda through an assigned set of readings or lectures but the creating of a forum where students themselves can articulate (and thus perhaps also become more responsive to) differences among themselves" (123). The contact zone is then "more like a process or event than a physical space," a "shifting series of interactions among perspectives and individuals" (122). I want to expand on Harris's challenge to critical pedagogy to include the examination of the vexed positions of TAs, who, as members of a conscripted labor force, must implement such new curricula, often not of their making, sometimes at the point they first enter the profession. Their power and authority are similar to and yet different from that of regular faculty. Their resistance is different from and yet, in some ways, similar to that of the undergraduates they teach. However, resistance, along with TAs' deviation from a "master syllabus," can be the impetus for a theorized "shifting series of interactions," (122) for healthy reflection and change in both individual and program praxis.

In the nine years since we shifted the emphasis in our first-year composition curriculum from argument to the analysis of popular culture, both formal and informal evaluations of the course indicate that TAs, along with the freshmen, show greater interest in the curriculum. As satisfaction with required comp courses goes, most of our TAs prefer a course that invites students to use the ideas of cultural critics like Susan Willis and Michael Omi (anthologized in *Signs of Life in the USA*, Maasik and Solomon) as lenses for the reexamination of cultural attitudes and practices. Most would rather view with their students a series of Madonna videos in light of bell hooks' claims of racial exploitation than teach the enthymeme or revise tiresome claims about seat belts or the drinking age. But *showing an interest in* and *having an interest in* the curriculum are not the same thing.

This interest is nevertheless fraught with uneasiness about a nontraditional writing curriculum. It is an uneasiness intertwined with first-time teaching anxiety and a growing awareness of the place of composition (and of non-tenure track labor) in institutional politics. While they are becoming more at ease questioning traditional notions of literature and culture in their graduate courses, some TAs did not anticipate that the interpretive turn would extend to their teaching lives, or that they would even *have* a teaching life, much less a theorized teaching practice. Just as first-year undergraduates may cling to unified worldviews when confronted with our demands for problematization, TAs at first may cling to an expectation that there is a conflict-free transcendent state of teacher/student work on "good writing." Similar to the freshman who resists examining how his own position is shaped by cultural myth and representation ("I *choose* to wear a nose ring because it is comfortable"), a new TA may at first stake out a position as the lone individualist, selectively aware of developments in composition and English studies, institutional history, or even lore, blazing a trail toward the better pedagogy ("I'll be lecturing on Bourdieu, requiring abstracts rather than drafts, and giving a lot more grammar quizzes"). Like their undergraduate counterparts, graduate students new to teaching are also, to borrow David Bartholomae's phrase, "inventing the university," only from a position on the other side of the desk. And like the undergraduates, TAs also nego-tiate their way through a paradoxical combination of imitation and misreading, insecurity and bravado.

Individual cases of resistance, however, are imbedded in larger institutional structures. In most English departments, composition is marginalized; the teach-ing of writing is separated from the teaching of reading. Consequently, the practicum or proseminar, like the freshman composition course, by virtue of who takes it and who teaches it, may be viewed as a-disciplinary and un-theorized by those first coming to teaching. TAs may assume that the teaching of writing to freshmen will not be as fraught with complexity as the "sacred" texts, theories, and rituals they are encountering in the rest of the profession.

For many graduate students, teaching may be the first thing in their aca-demic lives that has not gone really well from the beginning—the first thing they could not control with smarts and verbal skills. Doing college was easy. Many of them come to us unaware of what was even taught in the composition courses they tested out of, not to mention what is at stake in the power relations between those who can play the academic game and those who can't. So when a student can't get the point of an article by a cultural critic and "join the con-versation" or when a student's analysis of a Calvin Klein ad is simply that "Sex sells. If you have a product, you want to sell it, right?" the reaction of new TAs might be that the program directors are asking too much, because if we're not, then they must be teaching comp *wrong.*

It is understandable that teaching a set of skills would seem more comfort-able than entanglement with students' resistance to critiquing the culture of late capitalism. Further, TAs may have expected that if there is a master syllabus and a sequence of assignments, then there must be "ideal types"—teachers who teach writing and students who learn it—*perfectly.* So if at first teaching does not go well, then it must be the fault of (a) the syllabus, (b) the textbook, (c) the approach to composition, (d) the director, (e) the students, (f) the TA, or, on any given day, all of the above. The idea of teaching as struggle rather than crisis is a new one. It might still be a new idea (or the best kept secret) for some of our faculty colleagues, who, often out of guilt and self-interest, pass on to graduate students the myth that comp teaching is no-brainer, common sense easy work, something anyone can do until he or she moves up and out of it. The more polit-ically self-conscious version of this position now includes decrying the practice of hiring poorly paid TA "apprentices" and part-timers to teach composition—a practice in which all of us in English and the university are complicit. So far this socially responsible position almost never leads to the restructuring of English departments in ways that are responsive to the public or to the market for PhDs (e.g., relocating literature more responsibly in relation to rhetoric, lit-eracy, technology, and culture). Even more obvious is the failure of most English departments to radically downsize their graduate programs and work with their institutions to redistribute the teaching of first-year courses to tenured and tenure-track faculty.

If there is a solution to all of this, short of burning down the house, it lies in getting our new graduate instructors to think of teaching neither as meaningless grunt-work nor as the same sort of work they put into the A+ seminar paper. Composition teaching, especially when it involves cultural analysis, can be more a dialogue than a performance, in which not every student and teacher begins and ends in the same place. This reconsideration of teaching, however, must include giving TAs more of a stake in the composition course, even as we strive for some standardization in a large program.

From an administrative perspective, we want confident, reflective teachers whom we know will grow and change in interesting ways at the same time that we want a certain amount of consistency across hundreds of sections of composition. We want a reading and writing course, the requiring of which we can justify outside the English department, at the same time that we want to maintain some disciplinary independence and integrity in the approach we take. But rather than merely encouraging the deconstruction of the very thing they are learning to do, we try to make visible the teaching moves we would like to see TAs making—just as we would make academic writing and cultural analysis moves visible to first-year undergraduates who might not intuit or invent them on their own.

However, if TAs are going to assume more ownership of a course with a common syllabus, the Director of Composition can't be the only one "making the moves visible." At the center of the success we have had with our shift to a cultural studies approach and with our TA preparation in general are the eight peer "consultants" we appoint every year. A consultantship carries with it one course release from the usual three-course-per-year TA load. Consultants play a collaborative role in the planning and execution of the freshman composition course, the week-long August TA orientation workshop, and the two-hour/two-credit weekly proseminar taught by the Director of Composition (and additional composition faculty if needed). New TAs take the required proseminar (graded on a satisfactory/nonsatisfactory basis) while they are teaching the freshman course for the first time. The consultants are divided up among the four sections of the proseminar and attend the same section as their "consultees." There was a time when I taught a new group of forty TAs in one section; we've since gone to four sections to make productive discussion possible. The Director of Composition and any additional faculty teaching the proseminar meet as a group with all the consultants once a week. A portion of each meeting is devoted to what we call "forecasting," reminding ourselves of what lies ahead in the freshman course so that we can prepare new TAs well in advance with lesson guidelines, materials, and potential pitfalls. We spend the second half of each meeting discussing what consultants have learned in their small groups about new TAs' concerns, problems, and innovations.

In addition to their strengths as teachers and team players, the senior TAs who become consultants have typically distinguished themselves with the innovations they have made to the common syllabus. One may have found a better way to articulate in an assignment what we're asking students to do when they engage the theories of critics in the evolution of their own critique of a Hollywood film. Another may have designed a successful class exercise around the production of original ad campaigns that commodify desire in the marketing of new products. Still another may have worked out a computerized system for responding to drafts. Rather than enforce theory into practice, it could be argued that the consultants' function is to circulate our program's teaching "lore." As Patricia Harkin maintains, lore, as postdisciplinary *theory,* can be knowledge-making that allows for practitioners' often contradictory attempts to solve writing problems with more than one cause (134). The consultants demonstrate that they can negotiate with and reshape the knowledge about teaching writing that the program offers; new TAs see that they can do likewise.

In our week-long (thirty-hour) August orientation workshop and the weekly proseminar course during the fall semester, the consultants' contributions enhance the explanation of our course goals and assignment sequence; their testimonies and demonstrations concretize the introduction we provide to teaching semiotic analysis and cultural representation. Several TAs typically share with the new group the activity they have planned for the freshmen to explain how the meaning of a "sign" like the McDonald's Golden Arches exists within a system of cultural concepts, not in the thing itself. Our Greatest Hits collection of subjects-for-analysis continues to grow and includes new and vintage print ads, commercials, sitcom episodes, game shows, and films. While TAs are most likely to share in the orientation workshop how we might analyze those cultural artifacts that have been "field-tested" with skeptical students, we routinely like to present to the group popular phenomena and visual texts that offer "anomalies" (a favorite term of David Rosenwasser and Jill Stephen, the authors of one of our key textbooks in the course, *Writing Analytically*). Public response and media coverage surrounding the O. J. Simpson trial, the death of Princess Diana, and the custody battle over Elian Gonzalez have provided us with rich and timely material that cannot be easily explained.

Both before our August workshop and during the weekly class meetings of the required proseminar, we expect that TAs will read essays that exemplify cultural criticism (both in and beyond our course anthology, *Signs of Life in the USA*) as well as pieces on critical pedagogy (see, for example, Berlin and Vivion; Fitts and France; Gilyard; Harris) and some classic essays on topics like revision and grading. Our August orientation workshop materials have grown from a folder with pockets to a ten-pound three-ring binder that includes a six-assignment sequence of my design that now has spawned a host of retooled assignments, prewriting exercises, and sample student papers from many TAs' teaching portfolios over the last nine years.

Both practically and theoretically, the proseminar in the teaching of composition extends the discussion begun in the August workshop. Requirements include classroom observations of other instructors and an end-of-semester teaching portfolio containing a reflective teaching statement, two classroom observation reports, a brief case study of either a revised assignment or one student's experiences/progress over the semester, a week-by-week syllabus annotating the changes to be made the following semester, and a sample set of student papers, reflecting a range of grades and including several marked drafts. If TAs, as they move on to teach other courses, continue to update their teaching portfolios, they can request a review by a faculty member each year they remain in the department. Teaching portfolios have helped our graduate students tremendously as they prepare materials for their academic job dossiers. Hiring departments have been able to consider them as both scholars and reflective teachers who take course design and student learning seriously.

One aim of the proseminar is to engage new TAs in theorizing the course they are teaching without necessarily seeming to. Each week the new TAs, the consultants, and I address topics important to new teachers of composition and of this course in particular (Responding to and Grading Papers, Analyzing Visual Texts, Teaching Revision, The Writing Conference, Representations of Gender and Race, Leading Discussion, Collaborative Learning, Grammar and Style). Along with articles by pedagogy experts in composition and cultural studies, materials from the consultants' own teaching portfolios provide the basis for our discussion and help concretize what seems abstract to new teachers with day-to-day concerns. Consultants will share case studies, including their revisions of an assignment and accompanying classroom activities that model, for instance, several ways to pair readings about representations of race, gender, and class with films like *Long Kiss Goodnight* or *Devil in a Blue Dress*, which invite various critical combinations students might work with in their papers.

Sharing case studies of revised assignments convinces TAs that, while part of a sequence (Summary and Response, Making Connections, Ad Analysis, Comparative Analysis of a Film, Researched Cultural Analysis of Trend or Film Genre), assignments in the program are not set in stone. In a Comparative Analysis paper assignment, for instance, one TA's revision indicates that her new goal for the assignment is to get her students' interpretive positions to grow from an analysis of their critical sources rather than from their simply using the sources to bolster a fact-based thesis. She decides to break the assignment into steps to better work in a purposeful comparison of two theoretical approaches to the same issue. Another TA's revision of the same assignment indicates that he redesigned the comparative analysis so that students are now directed to identify gaps in how critic #1's theory explains a cultural phenomenon such as fascination with the Kennedys. He wants them to search and read until they find a critic #2 who better analyzes in ways they can work with what the obsession with the Kennedys says about American myths and values.

In the proseminar we might talk about the advantages and disadvantages of both approaches to the same assignment. We look at old student papers written to those two versions of the assignment. In examining the materials of other teachers, comparing them to what they are currently trying in their own classrooms, TAs come to realize better how to get at what their students need to work on and what the aims should be of the assignment and the composition course overall. I'm modeling what movement through the course I designed can look like. At the same time, I am showing them that when something didn't work, others did not despair but, in fact, in keeping with Harkin's notion of "lore," they theorized to solve the problem in front of them. I am communicating that there *are* options and that I trust them to tailor the course in smart ways. As a teacher of teachers, what I am saying with our use of portfolios is that teaching is messy, but you can clean it up. Your life in English may have gone smoothly until this point; teaching never does, but you get another chance.

Having provided the guidance through the course and all its assignments, at the end of the proseminar we concentrate on writing and sharing reflective teaching statements, case studies of students and assignments, and annotated syllabi with changes we can all learn from.

In addition to the two-hour proseminar, groups of about five new TAs meet for one hour a week with their consultant. As a supplement to the professor-led sessions, these mentoring sessions enable new TAs to voice skepticism, share lesson plans and materials in progress, and learn from their consultant and one another what's both desirable and possible.

Revisions to a writing course brought about by a shift to a cultural studies approach (e.g., analysis of visual texts, ethnographic fieldwork) have to be melded with rhetorical and writing process concerns (e.g., evolving a thesis, paragraph development, writing multiple drafts, using peer review) that veteran composition teachers carry along with them as a matter of course, but which new instructors may never have considered. In examining materials from past TA portfolios like assignment sheets or prewriting and peer review exercises, new TAs can see how this melding takes place—how, for example, the reading of film criticism and the examination of representation of gender in action films can be merged with work on developing a thesis that gives a student's paper some critical work to do.

I've come to view the construction of the teaching portfolio and the critical exchange of their contents from year to year as key to our program's effectiveness and to a workable labor-management relationship. (I hesitate to use "collaborative" in referring to TA/faculty writing program administration because it implies an equal power relationship and economic status that simply does not exist.) Most important for new teachers to understand is how much those of us who teach the course reflect on what hasn't worked, how much we revise our plans in light of that, and how, particularly in a writing course that takes as its subject the representation of race, gender, and class, we don't know what we're teaching until we see what we get, and then we change everything in an effort to work with the students who are actually in the room. While we certainly have objectives for our students tied to proficiency in composition, teaching is also learning to live in that space where you are comfortable saying, "I know what I want to do next time," and then accepting that as your praxis, not your shortcoming or failure.

In addition to the case studies of assignments and students that TAs write, I also write case studies for the proseminar of tough teaching situations, often involving student resistance to issues like race and gender, not just in class discussion, but in journals and drafts of essays. A case study, for instance, of a student paper that accuses the author bell hooks of reverse racism in her critique of Madonna ("Madonna: Plantation Mistress or Soul Sister?"), suggesting that "she stick to her own kind," will get us talking not only about what to do immediately in the situation (what to write on the draft or say to the student), but also about how we might have introduced the representations of race differently, and, further, how tough situations illuminate and test the goals of a course aimed at reading and writing about culture.

I use the case studies of students, including their progress on multiple drafts and changes in their critical thinking over the course of the semester, both on the first day of orientation and throughout the semester, to give new TAs a sense of what is good, not so good, and even possible in a fifteen-week course. Freshmen do not become sophisticated cultural critics with papers that advance highly theorized claims. And this is nobody's fault. It doesn't mean we have to give up and just teach Strunk and White. What were once just hallway stories about terminally weak thesis statements or racist remarks in the classroom can be mined for their "teaching moments."

Case studies are particularly useful in illuminating the ways in which our undergraduate students negotiate such a course in cultural analysis. Not surprisingly, they do not end up occupying the subject positions invited by the ads and films we examine together any more than they automatically take on the positions offered by much of what constitutes our course. Both the undergraduates and the TAs who work on critiques with them inevitably resist and reshape these positions to meet their own ends, and that is both humbling and encouraging. I am also encouraged by the extent to which our TAs view teaching and curriculum design as intellectual work; recent changes called for by organizations like MLA and WPA that would better integrate scholarship and teaching are only as good as the future professoriate we are now preparing and hiring.

## WORKS CITED

Bartholomae, David. "Inventing the University." *When a Writer Can't Write: Studies in Writer's Block and Other Composing Process Problems.* Ed. Mike Rose. New York: Guilford, 1985. 134–65.

Berlin, James A., and Michael J. Vivion, eds. *Cultural Studies in the English Classroom.* Portsmouth, NH: Boynton/Cook, 1992.

Bishop, Wendy. *Something Old, Something New: College Writing Teachers and Classroom Change.* Carbondale: Southern Illinois UP, 1990.

Crowley, Sharon. *Composition in the University: Historical and Polemical Essays.* Pittsburgh: U of Pittsburgh P, 1998.

Farris, Christine. *Subject to Change: New Composition Instructors' Theory and Practice.* Cresskill, NJ: Hampton P, 1996.

Farris, Christine, and Chris M. Anson, eds. *Under Construction: Working at the Intersections of Composition Theory, Research, and Practice.* Logan: Utah State UP, 1998.

Fitts, Karen, and Alan W. France, eds. *Left Margins: Cultural Studies and Composition Pedagogy.* Albany: SUNY P, 1995.

George, Diana, and Diana Shoos. "Issues of Subjectivity and Resistance: Cultural Studies in the Composition Classroom." *Cultural Studies in the English Classroom.* Ed. James A. Berlin and Michael J. Vivion. Portsmouth, NH: Boynton/Cook, 1992. 200–10.

Gilyard, Keith, ed. *Race, Rhetoric, and Composition.* Portsmouth, NH: Boynton/Cook, 1999.

Giroux, Henry A. "Who Writes in a Cultural Studies Class? Or, Where Is the Pedagogy?" *Left Margins: Cultural Studies and Composition Pedagogy.* Ed. Karen Fitts and Alan W. France. Albany, NY: SUNY P, 1995. 3–16.

Harkin, Patricia. "The Postdisciplinary Politics of Lore." *Contending with Words: Composition and Rhetoric in a Postmodern Age.* Ed. Patricia Harkin and John Schilb. New York: MLA, 1991. 124–38.

Harris, Joseph. *A Teaching Subject: Composition Since 1966.* Upper Saddle River, NJ: Prentice-Hall, 1997.

hooks, bell. "Madonna: Plantation Mistress or Soul Sister?" *Black Looks: Race and Representation.* Boston: South End Press, 1992. Rpt. in *Signs of Life in the USA: Readings on Popular Culture for Writers.* Ed. Sonia Massik and Jack Solomon. 2nd ed. Boston: Bedford, 1997. 223–30.

Maasik, Sonia, and Jack Solomon, eds. *Signs of Life in the USA: Readings on Popular Culture for Writers.* 3rd ed. Boston: Bedford, 2000.

Pratt, Mary Louise. "Arts of the Contact Zone." *Profession 91* (1991): 33–40.

Rosenwasser, David, and Jill Stephen. *Writing Analytically.* 2nd ed. Fort Worth: Harcourt, 2000.

Schilb, John. *Between the Lines: Relating Composition Theory and Literary Theory.* Portsmouth, NH: Boynton/Cook, 1996.

Welch, Nancy. "Resisting the Faith: Conversion, Resistance, and the Training of Teachers." *College English* 55 (1993): 387–401.

# 10. Feminist Approaches to Mentoring Teaching Assistants: Conflict, Power, and Collaboration

REBECCA J. RICKLY AND
SUSANMARIE HARRINGTON

A year ago, as new visiting assistant professors serving as Associate Directors of Composition at Texas Tech University, we designed a mentoring program for TAs.[1] Building on existing program structures, we designed two initiatives, one involving all TAs and another involving those whose teaching evaluations raised concerns. Each was prompted by our professional interests and by a local need, and each had the full support of the department administrators. In this chapter, we analyze our activities as feminists and mentors, situating our work in feminist and writing program administration scholarly traditions. In so doing, we problematize our original thinking about terms like *feminist* and *mentor* and conclude with principles to help teacher educators and administrators consider conflict, power, and collaboration as key elements in preparing college teachers of writing.

Some program particulars are helpful here (although more details are available in Myers-Breslin). Texas Tech University is a mid-sized PhD-granting, state-supported school that offers approximately 250 sections of introductory composition for more than 5,300 undergraduates each year (all students must take two semesters of composition to graduate, and some must take basic writing before beginning the two-semester sequence). The writing program has had strong, stable leadership for more than a decade. Sections are taught by more than seventy TAs and fifteen lecturers, although the five tenure-line faculty in rhetoric and composition occasionally teach in the program as well. Some TAs are in the technical communication and rhetoric MA or PhD programs, but most are pursuing literature or creative writing degrees.

All TAs, regardless of degree program, receive a structured introduction to composition pedagogy and theory. Before receiving a teaching assignment, incoming graduate students must take a course in the history and theory of composition (usually in the summer, before teaching for the first time in the fall; this requirement is waived for PhD students who have taken such a course elsewhere). New master's students who lack the credit hours and teaching experience required by accrediting associations[2] are supported for a full semester before they teach. After taking the history and theory course, TAs take a practicum in the fall in what the department calls an "apprenticeship program." Each new TA is paired with an experienced mentor TA or lecturer. Each week the "apprentices" observe their mentor's class, meet with their mentor to discuss the class for an hour, and meet with the practicum group to discuss experiences, problems, applications, and readings for an additional hour. Mentors are selected by the composition faculty, and they earn a small stipend for the fall semester for their work with apprentices.

All TAs, new and returning, have access to on-line and print resources, including a TA handbook, a core syllabus and assignments, and an interactive Web application that the program recommends for all classes, regardless of whether they meet in a computer lab. The pedagogical materials (core syllabus and assignments) are constructed by a team of TAs and composition faculty before each year begins, and a curriculum committee (open to any TA who would like to participate) suggests revisions during the year. New TAs are strongly encouraged to follow the core syllabus; after they've gained experience, TAs are free to adapt the syllabus and assignments to their own teaching style (major alterations, such as incorporating a regular film component, must be approved by the Director or Associate Director of Composition). All TAs who teach first-year composition must also attend two of six composition workshops held each semester on topics such as grading, portfolios, or conferencing. The TAs vote on the workshop topics at the beginning of the semester, and faculty members or graduate students conduct the workshops.

This program works well, and we joined it most enthusiastically. But we recognized two areas in which we could build on the program's structure. First, we could link program workshops to broader professional development and job search preparation. To do this, we developed a program encouraging TAs to reflect on their teaching and to create and share both course and teaching portfolios. Second, we could support TAs who struggled beyond the first semester of teaching. To that end, we developed a formal mentoring system to help TAs reflect on their development as teacher–scholars and to interpret course evaluation data. After a year with those changes in place, we'd learned a great deal about power, collaboration, and conflict; what seemed simple at the start now seems incredibly complex. In this chapter, we explore how feminist beliefs and practices both shaped our approaches to mentoring and continue to be a lens for analyzing our work.

## FEMINISM AND MENTORING: COLLABORATION OR CONFLICT?

Conflict is not the first term many people associate with feminism. Recently, a student in Becky's research methods class who was also taking her first graduate women's studies class asked for further reading on feminist methodology. During the conversation, she became increasingly agitated, and finally blurted out, "When I started taking [women's studies courses], I was really excited, because I thought I'd learn what 'feminism' was. Instead, I'm learning that no one agrees what it is, and everyone seems to be fighting about who's right. I'm not even sure I want to *be* a feminist anymore!" Her reaction is not unusual, and feminist scholars like Susan Jarratt might contend that such conflict is in fact healthy and necessary in our process of reflection and action as we integrate the concept of *feminisms* into our evolving ideology and practices.

One conflict we faced immediately was the complexity of feminist responses to mentoring. Some feminist scholars have compared mentoring's associations to an old boys' network. Mentoring, in practice, grows out of a master/apprentice model, a model that invokes patriarchal and hierarchical power issues. Such a model indeed fits nicely into an academic institution, with its stratified power structures and hierarchical organization, yet reports from women in academia illustrate that women frequently are not given a "place in or access to the master-apprentice model of mentoring" (Enos, "Mentoring" 137).

Differences in what it means to be a mentor—and what it would mean to be a feminist mentor—can affect how we position ourselves within the TA preparation programs we design. For example, we bring very different assumptions about mentoring to our work. Becky is more sensitive to Theresa Enos's critique of mentoring—like many of the women Enos surveyed for *Gender Roles and Faculty Lives in Rhetoric and Composition,* Becky doesn't identify a single mentor in her academic career. She's wary of the implied power differential that is associated with the formal, institutional version of "mentoring." She does not think of the important professional and collegial relationships she's experienced as "mentoring" relationships. For her, they resemble Mary Ann Cain's description of her relationship with Lil Brannon: a "partnership, one based in mutuality—of learning, trust, risk, care, and challenge" (113). Susanmarie, on the other hand, reacts more positively to the term because of her experiences with male and female mentors in academic and extracurricular settings. The individual attention she received from Girl Scout leaders, piano teachers, and undergraduate and graduate faculty members has shaped her professional sense of self. She sees mentoring as key to academic development—and views teacher preparation programs as a site for building structures within which good mentoring takes place naturally. While we both consider teaching/research communities to be important influences, and we approach our work from a shared base of feminist theory, our different views about what it means to mentor are immediately apparent in the programs we initiated, one which organized teaching groups (led more by Becky), the other which focused on one-on-one contact (led more by Susanmarie).

That said, we share a commitment to mentoring as an activity, and we've puzzled together over whether it's necessary to *feel like* a mentor in order *to mentor.* Our feminist sensibilities tell us that mentoring's impact is created through fluid and flexible relationships; our shared commitment to the activity of mentoring makes it easy for us to collaborate. Because of our experiences in academic collectives, we're convinced that effective writing programs allow all participants, from most novice to most experienced, to feel some ownership and power. Yet while we feel strongly about the importance of mentoring and collaboration, our positions as Associate Directors sometimes seemed to conflict with the values that we sought to foster through mentoring. The teaching community sets the context for decisions about individual classroom matters as well as program policy, yet the institution must sanction these decisions. Our emphasis on community context reflects the kind of women's moral reasoning that Carol Gilligan identifies; as administrators, teachers, and individuals, we value connections, contexts, and situated analysis, rather than universal, abstract, and impersonal analysis (19). Gilligan's theory has been applied to writing programs by Marcia Dickson, who outlines an administrative model that examines the needs of each instructor, rather than the power of a single administrator, purposely blurring authority and control. In our efforts to institute mentoring programs, we tried to capture this blurring of power and emphasize collaboration in the context of programmatically imposed mentoring. Yet "administration" and "collaboration" seem often to be in conflict. We needed models for mentoring, and we drew ours from feminist scholarship.

Sara Ruddick's notion of "maternal" thinking posits that maternal caretaking constitutes feminist actions that can influence all aspects of life (348–57). Carol Stranger takes this concept into the composition classroom, arguing that collaborative learning is, in fact, a form of maternal teaching, building knowledge through support and consensus, as opposed to the more traditional (and patriarchal) competitive activities associated with institutional higher learning (41). Others have labeled collaborative learning and teaching as "feminist" based on maternal activities such as responsiveness to others, support, awareness of context, and the goal of consensus (see Caywood and Overing). Emily Jessup and Marion Lardner draw on their experiences with (grand) mothering as they reflect on teaching and challenge us to "learn to be as caring, as tender, as responsive to the needs of [students] as we might be to a first grandchild. For real learning to occur, a great deal of listening must happen: we need to listen as children find ways to tell us who they are, what is important in their lives, what they worry about, what they are interested in" (191). Caring and listening are two important elements of mentoring TAs: we care for them (and for the undergraduates who study writing in our institutions); we also listen to them. Sometimes these activities conflict: To ensure that undergraduates have a positive experience, sometimes we need to act rather than listen. We hoped to lessen this conflict by including more voices—talking *and* listening—in TA preparation.

The literature on maternal thinking in composition, however, led us to another site of conflict. Portraying maternal practices as feminist is a complicated intellectual move. It can undercut how women are perceived, particularly if they hold positions of authority, such as a director or mentor. Such critiques run through our reflections on our work. While Becky uses "maternal thinking" as a way to reimagine power structures, Susanmarie worries that an emphasis on such reimagining consistently stereotypes and subordinates women's roles. Some respondents in Enos's research argue that being drawn to maternal models threatens productivity and identity, putting relationships over "our own time, privacy, and voice" (*Gender Roles* 31); Doug Hesse's analysis of masculinity and writing program work reminds us that caretaking is not only left to women. Yet generally, women do spend more time caretaking (Enos, *Gender*

*Roles* 77), and if mentoring remains an undervalued caretaking activity, those who mentor may not then have the time to participate in more institutionally sanctioned activities such as publishing. We extended our consideration of such critiques to the TAs as well. While Enos looked primarily at junior faculty and administrators, perhaps, we mused, similiar conflicts might arise when we asked TAs to participate in the mentoring process. If we want the relationship between teacher educators and TAs to have positive elements of that between a mother and child, how can we balance a practice based on care with concerns for professional satisfaction and advancement?

As feminist teachers of graduate students, we find ourselves further challenged. How do we cultivate collaborative relationships with the TAs we mentor? How do we encourage peer mentoring among TAs? How do we, as coadministrators, bridge the differences between our own feminisms? How do we become aware of and use conflict productively to promote the growth of individuals and a program? And how does feminism make a difference in our work?

Despite—or perhaps because of—these conflicts, we continue to view our work as teacher educators and mentors as involving an ethic of care. This principle cuts across our own differences and is the basis for the way we approach relationships in the workplace. For instance, a concern for others, Patricia Bizzell reports, involves noticing details that others might miss, using those observations to help individuals "do their work better and enjoy it more" (ix). As we discovered, however, good mentors also notice the minutiae of people's working lives that some people do not want observed. While our approach to mentoring was certainly designed to "help [TAs] do their work better and enjoy it more," our work was not always received that way. Mentoring—particularly the forced mentoring that occurs in graduate programs that institutionalize mentoring—challenges teachers to make their teaching public within a program hierarchy, and that can intimidate some TAs. Others may resist the extra work involved in reflecting on and making teaching public. And some may find it challenging to articulate minority views on issues of teaching or practice, to admit mistakes, or to reimagine their pedagogy.

Mentoring relationships are the key to making these challenges productive. Mentoring should contribute to a greater sense of teacher agency, choice, and power. At the same time, in a graduate program where many teachers have little training (or even interest in) composition, we recognize that our role includes educating TAs about the nature of our scholarly field. It also demands empathy and a willingness to understand the program from the point of view of TAs who are, as Louise Wetherbee Phelps notes, "sometimes misplaced in a writing program by the accidents of institutional history" (313) which mandates that all English students teach writing. Like Phelps, we found that some TAs saw composition and rhetoric as "an ambitious project they thought irrelevant or even antithetical to their own intellectual interests" (313). Furthermore, as Phelps notes, different theories and assumptions govern TAs' experiences. Lives of TAs are complex balancing acts, and we need to understand their positions as well as our own.

Our challenge was to help TAs see these conflicts as generative. For the TAs, this was difficult, since they had to work through conflicts, both individually and collaboratively; it was difficult for us, as well, since we had to embrace our power as mentors and administrators. And since we considered ourselves working within a feminist paradigm that worked to redistribute power, coming to terms with power was a conflict for us. Professional development is normally seen as an individual act, and our approach asked TAs to collaborate reflectively with faculty and each other. We had to balance program coherence against individual needs, our own positions as new faculty against our desire for change, and enthusiastic voices against resistant ones.

## PEER COLLABORATION/PORTFOLIO TEAMS

Becky introduced a new professional development program—peer collaboration/portfolio teams—during the fall semester. This initiative integrated the concepts of peer editing and peer observation borrowed from composition pedagogy and encouraged reflection and collaboration in small groups. All TAs who were teaching either of the first-year composition classes were required to participate.[3] The initiative linked peer collaboration for teachers to classroom pedagogies, arguing that teachers gain a better understanding of audience, learn to read more critically and analytically, and become practiced at solving problems in a collaborative setting. In essence, TAs mentored each other in fourteen teams of three to five members, assigned by Becky based on TA preferences. The teams' goal was to identify a problem or topic to explore during the semester. They were given several options as to how they might address problems but were encouraged to develop other strategies. Groups were to choose three different forums for dialogue: attending (and reflecting on) workshops, meeting during the semester, using email, observing each other's classes, and so forth. The goal was to encourage reflection on the individual theories and practices used in teaching composition.

During the spring semester, TAs had an additional option: Instead of participating in a peer collaboration team, they could work individually to construct a course portfolio. They could reflectively analyze their syllabus, they could analyze an assignment or sequence of assignments according to the course goals, or they could discuss how a particular assignment would elicit student work that would correspond with course and individual goals. TAs had to reflect on their teaching in some way, but we offered choice, hoping that TAs would select the materials for reflection most in keeping with their individual needs. As mentors, we met with those who weren't sure about what they wanted to do (or which activity would benefit them most), and we reviewed the group and individual proposals that TAs gave to us. We also offered workshops on observations and on portfolios. Finally, when TAs submitted the final portfolio, we read it and provided written feedback the following fall semester. Interestingly, most TAs opted to continue in a collaborative setting; the perception (gained by informal discussions with TAs) was that the final product—a collaborative, reflective portfolio—

would require less time and effort. The choice of whether to work on a group or individual reflection complicated the relations of individuals to groups; if one member opted for an individual portfolio, the other group members felt that they were required to work harder to complete a final collaborative project. But we hoped that the groups would support each other in whatever work occurred.

## INTENSIVE MENTORING

In the spring, Susanmarie initiated another program: intensive mentoring for TAs whose student evaluations from the previous semester had raised serious concerns. We initially reviewed students' comments on the fall course evaluation forms, hoping that students' comments on the curriculum would help us plan workshops that would target timely issues. But our review showed us that a small number of experienced TAs (eight out of fifty) had consistently poor evaluations. Their students were angry, and clear patterns could be observed in each set (one TA spent classes reading the text aloud; several were criticized for being mean-spirited in written comments or in class, for example). These evaluation forms moved us to action, out of concern both for the undergraduates in those classrooms and for the TAs themselves. Such situations are as distressing for students who feel compelled to write vituperative feedback as they are for the TAs who have to read it. We believe that course evaluations must be interpreted by the classroom teacher in order to have meaning, but we could see that the learning environment in these classrooms had been compromised. We decided that individual attention was the best way to approach this situation; confidential, one-on-one mentoring would allow the TAs to interpret the feedback, design a plan for future action, and evaluate their efforts in the next semester.

Realizing that any discussion of teaching evaluations is sensitive, we tried to anticipate problems. We enlisted the support of the Department Chair, Director of Graduate Studies, and Director of Composition. We pitched the program as an extension of the regular workshops and the apprenticeship program. TAs who struggle in the classroom despite these supports had no easy way to ask for structured help. We designed the intensive mentoring to support the TA so that such demoralizing situations could be avoided.

TAs invited to participate in intensive mentoring received a letter, written by Susanmarie, but sent out over the Director of Composition's signature, that outlined the situation:

> The composition staff recently reviewed teaching evaluations from Fall 1998, and noticed some areas of concern in your evaluations. While teaching evaluations provide only a partial evaluation of all your teaching efforts, the forms do suggest that students in your section(s) experienced some frustration with some elements of the course. The student comments need to be evaluated in the context of other factors, such as assignments or levels of student preparation and enthusiasm.
>
> In order to support you as you interpret your students' feedback and use it to guide your teaching practices this semester, I invite you to schedule a meet-

ing with [an assigned mentor]. This meeting will help you analyze your students' feedback, and will allow you to discuss elements of the class that may not have been reflected on the evaluations. It will also help you develop a plan for reducing student dissatisfaction in the future.

Susanmarie and Becky took on most of the mentoring responsibilities; the Director of Composition elected to meet with one TA who had received several student complaints in the past. After the letter was sent and an initial meeting was set up, we tried to work with the TAs to identify why students may have reacted as they did and what might change in their pedagogy. Our assumptions underlying the intensive mentoring and peer collaboration programs were complex. Part of our responsibility, as we see it, is to help TAs understand what it means to be a professional in academia; we find compelling Richard Fulkerson's argument that ethical graduate programs must look beyond research preparation to teacher preparation. Although Fulkerson argues for curricular teacher preparation, our extracurricular program[4] works toward his goals: preparing PhD students for the jobs they are likely to get, in which teaching is the primary role. As Fulkerson notes, teaching "is not a natural activity, and it does not derive naturally from being a superior scholar" (132). Fostering reflective practice in a supportive environment helps prepare TAs for this future and promotes better teaching.

## WHAT HAPPENED: RESISTANCE AND CONFLICT

This utopian vision wasn't quite what unfolded. Tension quickly arose, and we got a crash course in program and departmental politics. Most importantly, there was a perceived lack of trust between TAs and program administrators. Both faculty and TAs seemed to assume that the other group was vaguely dissatisfied with their administration or teaching, respectively—although when we tried to pin down specific instances of problems, we could not. But there was a vague sense among the TAs that workshops existed to spread a "party line" approach to teaching, and there seemed to be a similarly vague fear among faculty of encouraging too much individuation or experimentation. Second, there was the problem of oversight. Given the large numbers of TAs relative to the program administrators, very few TAs had close contact with administrators, outside of conferences to handle large problems. Once the new MA students had finished with the apprentice program, there was little opportunity for formal or informal interaction with administration. While relations in the program were cordial, teaching had been a very private activity (even among tenure-line faculty) before our initiatives were instituted, and making teaching public aroused fears all around. We needed to cultivate trust.

We quickly realized that solving one problem created another. Our priorities were two-fold: to improve the learning/teaching environment for both TAs and undergraduates and to ensure that all TAs felt supported by the program. We surmised, rightly, that teaching was sometimes a frustrating experience even for experienced TAs; it was especially frustrating for those receiving poor teaching evaluations. At the same time, we wanted all TAs, even struggling ones, to feel a part of the writing program—we wanted their concerns, their frustrations, to be part of what the program considered as it worked. We didn't want to marginalize TAs; rather, we wanted to use collaboration, within a structured mentoring program, to help build program cohesion and teaching effectiveness.

That's what we wanted. The problem was that TAs wanted something else entirely. What they wanted, it seemed on the most problematic days, was to compare themselves to the worst teacher they knew and feel OK because they weren't that bad themselves. "I've seen much worse than this," one TA told us, when we asked about his students' complaints that their comments on his evaluations were too harsh. "But plenty of other people have problems with their students," said another. "Why isn't everyone required to be mentored?"[5] In retrospect, these attitudes may harken back to the "maternal" aspect of mentoring that informed parts of our programs, modeled after the supportive relationship between a mother who loves unconditionally and a child who welcomes the nurturing. Yet in these problematic cases, the child seems to have moved into a rebellious adolescent phase. The child no longer welcomes nurturing and wants to think and act alone. No longer satisfied merely to co-opt and integrate the maternal figure's rules and ideals, this person, teetering on the brink of adulthood, automatically rejects what those in authority value. Our experience with mentoring, in this situation, wasn't as fulfilling and enjoyable as it had been previously, and it made us wonder if perhaps we weren't quite ready for motherhood.

As program administrators and mentors, we both muddled on through a series of meetings with TAs, some more productive than others. We offered workshops to help groups develop their portfolios. We visited classes, we reviewed lesson plans, we looked at TAs' work reflectively with them as they created collaborative portfolios. We also, although it's embarrassing to admit, had some of the worst conferences we've ever had in the course of this program. Susanmarie remembers one conference in which she and a TA were practically yelling at each other, he saying, "Just tell me what you want me to do, and I'll do it" and she responding, "What I want you to do is look at your responses to the students and describe what kind of teacher you are." That conference resulted in bad feelings all around. Others, we hasten to add, were more productive. Susanmarie focused on the use of classroom assessment techniques as a way for TAs to collect information about what their students were learning during class and as a way to let the undergraduates know their feedback was valued and useful during the term. Becky focused on careful analysis of assignment sequences and structured reflection about students' work. At the end of the term, evaluations for these eight TAs generally improved, and some improved substantially; one TA has become an active member of the program and has participated in workshops on assessment. More importantly, only two TAs were identified to participate in intensive mentoring the next semester.

In the end, the mentoring program was a struggle—yes, TAs' evaluations had improved, but at quite a cost in terms of time and emotional energy in the intensive mentoring program. Peer collaboration groups had formed, one or two had even met regularly and successfully, but while all had completed the requirements, few had produced portfolios that looked as if they would get future use. Looking to see what went wrong, we started to evaluate the conditions necessary for a feminist approach to successful mentoring.

## LOOKING AHEAD

It's long been a commonplace in feminist theory that "the personal is political," and feminist studies have pushed the academy to consider the role of the personal in the professional for some time. While it seems obvious now, in hindsight, we see that we had neglected to look at TAs' personal concerns. We assumed that TAs would welcome the chance to discuss their teaching and reflect on their professional development. While this was the case for some, others were deeply suspicious. We were new to the department (one of the TAs assigned to intensive mentoring went to the Director of Composition to complain about "those new women" and their meddling in his classroom), and the TAs didn't know us. Furthermore, improving their composition teaching was simply not the focus of TAs' professional work. TAs were juggling demanding course loads; they were thinking about seminar papers, exams, and dissertations. Only those actually on the job market could see the practical benefit of having a course or teaching portfolio or documentation of efforts to improve teaching. For many of the TAs, the mentoring program was an intrusion into their busy lives.

Similarly, we failed to look critically at our own concerns. While our different views of mentoring complemented one another, we were unaware of the extent of our theoretical differences until we started drafting this chapter. Earlier awareness of our differences might have helped us think through our programs more fully. In retrospect, it's clear that we didn't fully prepare for how collaborative mentoring programs might affect us as individuals and how much resistance it might generate. We brought to the TTU program recent administrative experience from two institutions, and we wanted to re-create the successes we had, perhaps without thoroughly examining the differences in context. We had experienced successful scholarly collaboration, and we assumed TAs would find the same value in collaboration and peer mentoring. Too, by creating new programs, we hoped to grow as feminists, as administrators, and as professionals, in the same way we hoped our students would grow. Finally, as visiting professors, we wanted to make positive impressions on our department, and our initiatives were due, at least in part, to our efforts to be active participants—team players—in an already established composition program. We also wanted a way to make parts of the program our own.

On a larger scale, we found that our emphasis on improving TAs' teaching through collaborative and intensive mentoring was not always shared by their graduate advisors, another problem we'd neglected to examine. We had assumed that having the administrative support up through the hierarchy to the Department Chair meant that the program would be smoothly implemented. We didn't anticipate that some colleagues (who didn't know us well, either) would misunderstand our work and worry that it was either targeted at particular TAs or would take time that "properly" belonged to a TA's scholarship. Our model of program building, we now realize, makes all department members responsible for some level of change. Only after we experienced resistance to the mentoring programs did we realize what great personal demands such a vision places on all participants, TAs and faculty alike. As Phelps explores in detail, change agents are asked to take risks, to reinvent their teaching and relationships to others, and to change with a program (310). This change requires trust, optimism, and shared power. In retrospect, our notion that setting up collaborative groups would automatically empower TAs seems naïve. In setting up groups, we did, in fact, promote conversation, but that conversation needed to be part of wider conversations and collaborations about what it means to diffuse power among TAs. Rather than culminating the experience in a static portfolio, we needed to find ways for TAs to represent their reflection and dialogue that would continue to be of use. We needed to discuss what kinds of power and authority were inherent in our positions as Associate Directors of Composition and what kinds of power and authority were inherent—and could be inherent— in TAs' positions, particularly as they began to observe each other's teaching. Links need to be formed between the composition committee and the graduate studies committee and between WPAs and dissertation advisors in other areas of the department. New lines of communication need to be opened.

After a year of experimenting with mentoring, we have not lost our commitment to it. Although Susanmarie has returned to her position in a program staffed by part-time faculty rather than TAs (a very different political and professional setting), we continue to make collaboration among teachers an important element of teacher preparation. But we are more sensitive to the politics involved and more sensitive to teachers' personal considerations. We see a broader audience for our educational efforts, and we see the value of dialogue. Mentors need to understand what it's like to be a TA, juggling so many concerns. At the same time, we need to see that good administration—and, more particularly, good teacher preparation programs—uses power wisely, encouraging all faculty to become collaborative and reflective change agents. This is not a comfortable position; indeed, it is one in which we can never rest. We can only reflect, identify, and acknowledge the conflict and move forward, hopeful that groups of teachers, talking together, will do good work for the students they teach and the program they inhabit.

## NOTES

1. Universities such as TTU often fill vacancies at the advanced assistant/associate level by asking a candidate to come for a year as a Visiting Assistant Professor. These positions are often precursors to tenure-track offers/employment. Additionally, at TTU every composition and rhetoric faculty member participates in the administration of the writing program. This collaborative administration is historically based, and TAs expected it. At the time, we had one director (Dr. Fred Kemp) and three Associate Directors (Susanmarie, Becky, and Dr. Linda Myers-Breslin). While our status as new faculty might have influenced the events we describe, the fact that we were visiting faculty probably did not, since most TAs assumed we would be staying.

2. The Southern Association of Colleges and Schools (SACs) has instituted the "18-hour rule" which stipulates that graduate students must have taken eighteen hours of graduate course work before they can be the teacher of record in a classroom. If a TA at the master's level has taken sufficient graduate work, it is conceivable that he/she might be exempt from the apprenticeship.

3. The MA students participating in the apprenticeship program did not participate in peer collaboration teams during the fall; however, they did participate during the spring, as they taught their first composition course. Ideally, we would ask all writing faculty to participate in this kind of professional development, but our program dictated that we could only require participation among TAs.

4. Becky has designed a course, "Professional Politics: Situating Composition Studies," to prepare students for life as assistant professors. See http://english.ttu.edu/rickly/5365/s99.html.

5. This is a good question, and in an ideal program, we'd make time for every teacher to have a more experienced partner to review evaluations and teaching.

## WORKS CITED

Bizzell, Patricia. "Foreword: On Good Administrators." *Kitchen Cooks, Plate Twirlers, and Troubadours: Writing Program Administrators Tell Their Stories.* Ed. Diana George. Portsmouth, NH: Boynton/Cook, 1999. vii–ix.

Cain, Mary Ann. "Mentoring as Identity Exchange: Conflicts and Connections." *Feminist Teacher* 8.3 (1994): 112–8.

Caywood, Cynthia L., and Gillian R. Overing, eds. *Teaching Writing: Pedagogy, Gender, and Equity.* Albany: SUNY P, 1987.

Dickson, Marcia. "Directing Without Power: Adventures in Constructing a Model of Feminist Writing Program Administration." *Writing Ourselves into the Story: Unheard Voices from Composition Studies.* Ed. Sheryl Fontaine and Susan Hunter. Carbondale, IL: Southern Illinois UP, 1993. 140–53.

Enos, Theresa. *Gender Roles and Faculty Lives in Rhetoric and Composition.* Carbondale, IL: Southern Illinois UP, 1996.

———. "Mentoring—and (Wo)mentoring—in Composition Studies." *Academic Advancement in Composition Studies: Scholarship, Publication, Promotion, Tenure.* Ed. Richard C. Gebhardt and Barbara Genelle Smith Gebhardt. Mahwah, NJ: Lawrence Erlbaum, 1997. 129–45.

Fulkerson, Richard. "The English Doctoral Metacurriculum: An Issue of Ethics." *Foregrounding Ethical Awareness in Composition Studies.* Ed. Sheryl I. Fontaine and Susan M. Hunter. Portsmouth, NH: Boynton/Cook, 1998. 121–43.

Gilligan, Carol. *In a Different Voice: Psychological Theory and Women's Development.* Cambridge, MA: Harvard UP, 1982.

Hesse, Doug. "The WPA as Father, Husband, Ex." *Kitchen Cooks, Plate Twirlers, and Troubadours: Writing Program Administrators Tell Their Stories.* Ed. Diana George. Portsmouth, NH: Boynton/Cook, 1999. 44–55.

Jarratt, Susan. "Feminisms and Composition: The Case for Conflict." *Contending with Words: Composition and Rhetoric in a Postmodern Age.* Ed. Patricia Harkin and John Schilb. New York: MLA, 1991. 103–23.

Jessup, Emily, and Marion Lardner. "Teaching Other People's Children." *Feminine Principles and Women's Experience in American Composition and Rhetoric.* Ed. Louise Wetherbee Phelps and Janet Emig. Pittsburgh: U of Pittsburgh P, 1995. 191–209.

Myers-Breslin, Linda. *Administrative Problem-Solving for Writing Programs and Writing Centers: Scenarios in Effective Program Management.* Urbana, IL: NCTE, 1999.

Phelps, Louise Wetherbee. "Becoming a Warrior: Lessons of the Feminist Workplace." *Feminine Principles and Women's Experience in American Composition and Rhetoric.* Ed. Louise Wetherbee Phelps and Janet Emig. Pittsburgh: U of Pittsburgh P, 1995. 289–339.

Ruddick, Sara. "Maternal Thinking." *Feminist Studies* 6.2 (1980): 342–67.

Stranger, Carol. "The Sexual Politics of the One-to-One Tutorial Approach and Collaborative Learning." *Teaching Writing: Pedagogy, Gender, and Equity.* Ed. Cynthia L. Caywood and Gillian R. Overing. Albany: SUNY P, 1987. 31–44.

# 11. Negotiating Resistance and Change: One Composition Program's Struggle Not to Convert

KATRINA M. POWELL, PEGGY O'NEILL,
CASSANDRA MACH PHILLIPS, AND BRIAN HUOT

> *By continually having graduate students reflect on the theories that would explain their teaching and on the theories that would explain their students' practices—and their own practices as students—we help develop habits of learning and teaching that will serve both them and the profession. This reflection invites dissonance and thus always has a cost. It denies smugly rejecting what doesn't neatly fit our worldviews (231).*
> —Douglas Hesse, "Teachers as Students, Reflecting Resistance"

In examining the ways teachers come to understand and learn their professional work and create their professional identities, scholars have considered issues of resistance and negotiation within discourse communities (Berkenkotter et al.; Prior; George and Shoos; Herndl). One specific discourse community, teachers of writing, has been discussed in terms of graduate student preparation and collaboration and the ways that writing programs prepare graduate students for teaching careers (Barr Ebest; Miller et al.; Taylor and Holberg). These discussions focus on graduate student satisfaction with preparation, on resistance to and negotiation of the process of preparation, and on ways writing programs can improve preparation. This chapter discusses resistance and negotiation in preparing teachers in a specific writing program to examine the complex and sometimes controversial ways that teachers with varying degrees of experience (theoretical and/or practical) work within a program and how their experience influences them as teachers.

This project examines the acceptance, resistance, and rejection of the theories and practices espoused by the particular composition program in which we taught collaboratively. We examine the program structurally, explaining the ways that the primary training course has been taught and the programmatic changes resulting from student/teacher and teacher/administrator input. Although there is a structured attempt not to "convert" writing teachers to a specific instructional approach or curriculum, it is clear that the instructors of the class—the director (a tenured faculty member) and three assistant positions held by nine individuals (all doctoral graduate students) over four years—hold particular values about language and teaching (Bishop; Welch). This chapter, then, examines the complex issues that arise in such a system of program administration and teacher education and the ways that this course influences classroom practice and teacher attitudes. In addition, this discussion examines the program's underlying assumptions in an attempt to engage in "doubting, debating, questioning, and revising" (Welch 400), a practice that should not only profit this specific program but also contribute to our understanding of how programs create identities for themselves and contribute to the identities of the teachers within them.

## PRACTICAL DIMENSIONS OF THE UNIVERSITY OF LOUISVILLE COMPOSITION PROGRAM

The Composition Program at the University of Louisville, a large, urban university, is staffed and administered through the English Department. Its seventy-five teachers teach more than 100 sections of first-year composition each semester; class size averages twenty-six. In addition, there are four to five sections each of business writing, technical writing, and advanced composition. Approximately 10 percent of the courses are taught in two large computer labs. For the last two years, English professorial faculty have taught one semester of first-year composition each year, and the remaining sections are taught by graduate students and lecturers. All graduate students and lecturers (who only teach part-time) must take English 602: "Teaching College Composition" the summer before they teach in the program. This course, offered only during the summer, is a requirement for TAs and a condition for employment for lecturers. Only TAs are paid a summer stipend of $500 to attend the course. While TAs receive immediate tuition remission (through their assistantships funded by the department), lecturers receive retroactive tuition remission once they teach full time (two courses) for U of L (through the university's benefits package). There are typically fifteen to eighteen teachers in the course and generally an equal representation of doctoral TAs, master's TAs, and lecturers.

Administrators of the Composition Program have designed a two-tiered preparation program: one focused on teaching for teachers new to the profession or to the U of L Composition Program and one focused on writing program administration for rhetoric and composition doctoral students. (See Powell et al. for an in-depth description of theoretical and practical implications of graduate student involvement in collaboratively administered writing programs.) Mark Long, Jennifer Holberg, and Marcy Taylor suggest that writing programs provide a "multi-tiered professional development program which utilizes the experience of upper level instructors in all levels of the administrative structure" (73), which is the approach taken at U of L where experienced doctoral students participate in program administration and teacher preparation. Three doctoral student TAs are selected as assistant directors of the writing program. Assistant directors can be at different points in their graduate careers and serve two-year terms, which are staggered so that at least one experienced assistant director returns to help mentor the new ones. The Composition Program assumes that the graduate student assistant directors are what Chris Anson and Carol Rutz call "developing professionals" (107). During the academic year, the assistant directors carry out a number of duties including mentoring new teachers, designing professional development workshops for all writing teachers, writing teacher evaluations, observing instructors, addressing grievances, and scheduling teachers for all writing courses. The assistant directors largely work independently, consulting mostly with each other and the director periodically when questions arise and when planning certain activities. While the four program administrators meet regularly during the academic year, the director provides initial training and support and then assumes the graduate student administrators are competent to perform assigned duties.

Although the assistant directors begin their terms during the first summer term, the main preparation for their positions occurs through the summer seminar for all new teachers. The graduate student assistant directors and the WPA, a tenured faculty member, collaborate to plan and teach the course sharing the responsibilities for deciding on readings, planning daily activities, and leading the class. In return, the assistant directors gain excellent professional experience.

After taking the required course, beginning teachers participate in several programmatic requirements: mentoring, observations, teaching portfolios, and professional development workshops. Several of these requirements have changed over the years to better meet the needs of both teachers and the program. For instance, teachers used to be observed by a faculty member once a semester. Now, teachers can either be observed or participate in a teaching group that meets biweekly throughout the semester. Group members observe each other's classes and discuss their teaching. These and other programmatic changes have occurred based on feedback from teachers in the program. Professional development workshops are offered but not required. As changes have been made, program administrators have tried to adhere to specific state accreditation guidelines while also letting teachers choose ways to improve their teaching.

Since 1997, TAs and lecturers must also maintain a teaching portfolio with documents like vitae, syllabi, observations, reflective narratives, and optional items such as teaching materials and workshop reflections. While teaching portfolios are required, they are not individually assessed. Like classroom observations, they are part of the program assessment for state accreditation. Teachers have also used these materials to apply for other teaching positions and graduate programs.

## THEORETICAL DIMENSIONS OF THE UNIVERSITY OF LOUISVILLE COMPOSITION PROGRAM

U of L's current Composition Program is based on several theoretical stances. Part of the program's commitment echoes recommendations for TA preparation made by Nancy Welch, who wrote about her TA preparation at two universities. Building on the conversion metaphor that Wendy Bishop identifies in her ethnographic study of a teacher preparation program, Welch criticizes University B for attempting to "convert" her and her TA colleagues to a certain epistemolog-ical and pedagogical approach. Welch concludes that a teacher training pro-gram should not seek conversion but convergence: "bringing opposing view-points into contact so that richer, fuller, more provocative viewpoints might be imagined" (400). Welch argues that this latter approach can encourage more active, reflective participation through reading, questioning, critiquing, and active engagement by the graduate students. However, as Hesse points out, introduction to new and sometimes difficult theories inevitably means resis-tance from teachers. He urges teachers of teachers, however, to realize that resis-tance to new discourses is a valuable part of the learning process (229). Even so, learning and resisting new discourses can be daunting or intimidating to grad-uate students (or lecturers) who are (or will be shortly) new teachers, to those preparing the new teachers, and to the WPA responsible for writing instruction.

Our theoretical approach to the teacher preparation course attempts to fos-ter the "reflexive position" that Hesse recommends (225) by asking teachers to develop individual "theories of language" as they read about theories of lan-guage acquisition, literacy, and teaching. We purposely ask teachers to learn social theories of language that will inform practical decisions they will make about their teaching. We believe this theory is important, yet inevitably teachers will resist that theory (Hesse 229).

## PREPARING TEACHERS IN ENGLISH 602: "TEACHING COLLEGE COMPOSITION"

The Composition Program at U of L is theoretically "open" to any method of teaching. Administrators do not specify textbooks: Some teachers do not require one at all, some require a reader, some a rhetoric, some a handbook, and others some combination of the three. The purpose behind an open approach is to encourage teachers to "own" their classes by asking them to design their own curriculum and instructional materials. That is, different teachers have different approaches to teaching writing, and administrators value various approaches. This valuing of various approaches carries over into the writing classes as teach-ers work with the multiple literacies of a diverse student body in an urban setting.

However, despite this "openness," new teachers must take English 602. Indeed, it is because of the extensive theoretical and practical training offered in the course that program administrators feel comfortable in allowing even inex-perienced teachers to design curricula and choose texts. The course, however, is laden with certain theoretical values—in part because of the readings chosen by the program administrators and in part because of their theoretical stances. One purpose of the course is to introduce teachers (whether experienced or not) to current theories in composition studies. New teachers read several texts which have over the years included George Hillocks's *Teaching Writing as Reflective Practice,* Joseph Harris's *A Teaching Subject: Composition Since 1966,* Gary Tate and Edward P. J. Corbett's *A Writing Teacher's Sourcebook,* Erika Lindemann's *A Rhetoric for Writing Teachers,* Mike Rose's *Lives on the Boundary,* and Russell Durst's *Collision Course: Conflict, Negotiation, and Learning in College Composition* (see Appendix for sample required readings). Participation is a large portion of teachers' grades as they develop questions for each reading and lead class discussions. Participation is factored into the portfolio grade, which counts for 60 percent; group presentations count for 20 percent; and discussions on the class listserv count for 20 percent. The portfolio also includes a reflection on the teacher observation experience, a course outline and syllabus for first-year composition, writing assignments for that course, sample listserv postings, a final exam explaining the teacher's theory of language, and a reflective letter that details the function of each piece in the portfolio. Many in-class activities are designed to give students/teachers examples of the activities for their own classes.

The teacher preparation program at U of L attempts to prepare new teachers of writing in ways consistent with Catherine Latterell's suggestions while also addressing the professional development of doctoral students in composition and rhetoric. That is, Latterell suggests that TA preparation programs strike a better balance between practical and theoretical approaches, develop teaching communities, and involve more teachers in the preparation program. This approach, argues Latterell, will encourage reflective practice as writing instructors—both new and experienced—continue to discuss theory and practice so that they think "about what's happening in their classrooms and [arrive] at their own solutions to problems" (20); at the same time, writing instruction adheres to programmatic standards. The theoretical portion of U of L's English 602 prepares both doctoral and master's students to address issues in composition studies. In addition, because the course was designed with the belief that a foundation in teaching theories would then inform teaching practices and vice versa, teachers are encouraged to develop their theories of language and pedagogy throughout the course. During the year that the four authors taught together, the course focused mainly on theory for the first three weeks (the class meets five days a week for five weeks), established foundations, then moved to practical issues for the last two weeks as teachers designed syllabi.

However, we noticed that many teachers resisted our emphasis on theory during the first part of the course—not because they didn't think teaching theories are useful but because they wanted practical classroom strategies from the beginning. The instructors, however, when asked practical questions such as, "Should I use portfolios?" responded to the teachers by asking, "But what's your theory of language? And how will you address portfolios based on your theory?" Our goal by responding this way was to get students to articulate a theory behind the practice. For instance, as teachers consider using portfolios, we ask them to reflect on the theories of literacy that Pat Belanoff explains. But we also ask them to consider the cautions that Kathleen Blake Yancey explains. We want teachers to read and reflect on the scholarship and the theories driving them, and then make their own practical decisions. We emphasize to teachers that it doesn't matter so much whether they use portfolios (or any other practice), but that they are able to reflect on the theory behind that practice.

By this response we meant to get teachers to think about not only their theories of language learning and acquisition but also the social, political, and cultural values surrounding language learning and the ways that individuals come to know language and subsequently learn to write. We felt that if teachers could begin to articulate some of these theories, then they could answer their own practical questions. However, new teachers often became frustrated with our response. In a short, intense summer course, practical issues such as designing syllabi seem much more pertinent as teachers (some for the first time) face their first-year composition classes within six weeks. In fact, because some teachers resent not having more practical preparation before they teach, they resist our question, "What's your theory of language?"

We ask this question frequently to encourage new teachers to design their own pedagogy. The program is committed to a foundation in theory that informs practice; therefore, we believe that once teachers have articulated their theories about language and learning, they can answer their own questions about course design. Like James Zebroski, we believe that "Theory is not the opposite of practice; theory is not even a supplement to practice. Theory *is* practice, a practice of a particular kind, and practice is always theoretical. The question then is not whether we have a theory of composition, that is, a view, or better, a vision of our selves and our activity, but whether we are going to become conscious of our theory" (15). Our focus, then, is not to push one theory or another but to advocate that teachers realize the theoretical positions and implications of their actions. Further, we respond to teachers' practical questions through theory as a way to avoid the quick fix, skills-based course that Latterell warns against (7). In addition, we don't want to dictate what practices teachers use in the classroom—we avoid "converting" teachers to one practice or another. Thus, our focus on theory. We realize, however, that the teachers' resistance to theory reveals a resistance to a "conversion" to theory. We must point out here, however, that many of the teachers' practical questions stem not from a resistance to theory but from a lack of practice on which to ground a particular theory. At the same time, many teachers resist theory, whether they are experienced or not. While we avoid answering practical questions with "quick fixes" at the beginning of the semester, as the semester progresses, we share our own teaching practices and the theories that inform them.

For example, in the graduate course we taught together, teachers resisted our listserv assignment. The use of an electronic listserv discussion in this course was informed by our own social constructionist stance that listservs can provide an alternative to participating in class discussions. As part of the course grade, teachers had to participate in the class listserv with a minimum of two postings a week. A week or two into the course, teachers expressed concern about meeting this course requirement. They wanted to know what kinds of "posts" were considered adequate, noting that some teachers posted several short posts, while others posted only one that was longer and more thoughtful. They wanted to know how we would assess the posts and what we meant in the syllabus when we said that the posts should demonstrate teachers' engagement with the topic. To address teachers' concerns, we first directed students toward scholarship on computers and composition (e.g., Selfe and Hilligoss; Hawisher and Selfe) to explain theoretically why we included such a practice in the writing classroom and how the listserv could be an alternative space for knowledge-making. Teachers, however, insisted that they needed to know more "practically" what we meant by engaged participation. We responded by providing teachers with several examples from the list that we had found particularly "engaging."

Several teachers reacted against these "samples" online within the listserv discussion. One teacher commented that he felt as though he were "doing a little jig for the gatekeeper." For a couple of days, this resistance was the topic on the listserv, varying from annoyance to heated debate about the appropriateness of our giving teachers "models" of posts that were engaged. Some teachers were clearly upset but used the listserv as a way to articulate their frustrations with it as a course requirement. As one teacher summarized:

> If the purpose of the listserv was to create a space for conversation and interaction to foster meaning-making (I may be wrong in this assumption, which is why I asked for clarification of the theory behind it in my earlier post) it seems to me at odds with the structure surrounding it which yields a certain number of posts which conform to an ideal pattern, guidelines, which, I think, leave little room for conversation, interaction, or meaning-making.

This resistance to our practices and stated theories is indicative of the resistance to some other practices in the course. Teachers told us that their concern over the "modeling" of "engaged" postings was a questioning of pedagogical theory: In other words, if a model did not work for them, perhaps modeling for their students would not work either. In addition, teachers were critical of voices that could "shut down" conversation on the listserv, which in turn led them to reflect on the potential use (and misuse) of a listserv in their classes. After several days of discussion about the theoretical implications of our model, we tried to explain that we were responding to their "practical" questions as they had asked. This response only further complicated the issue as teachers continued to critique our "giving" them what they wanted.

Our perceptions were clearly different from those of the teachers, and the use of a model or the listserv itself continues to spark debate not only for us but also for the field. However, the subsequent discussions, in which students grappled with issues of practice and theory together, were valuable (we think) to them *and to us* as teachers. In response to resistance to the "theory of language" behind a listserv in a composition classroom, the program administrators have revisited the requirement. In fact, the listserv assignment has undergone several changes over the years to address concerns that teachers have raised (in course evaluations, for instance) about requiring the assignment, assessing it, and finding alternative ways to use listservs in a writing class.

## REVIEWING THE COURSE

The resistance to "theory" by many teachers led the program administrators to reflect on the course readings themselves and the way they are presented during the summer semester. To obtain the teachers' opinions about the course, we surveyed all English 602 teachers from 1996 to 1999, asking them to explain their responses to the following questions:

- What was your initial reaction to 602 and how has it changed since you've been teaching?
- After taking 602, in what ways, if any, did your teaching methods/theories change?
- Have you decided not to use any theories/practices espoused in 602?
- Did you ever feel pressure to adhere to certain theories and/or methods?
- Did you experience any difficult emotions during 602, i.e., anger, sadness, frustration?

The theoretical and practical issues raised about the listserv assignment mirror some of the considerations teachers raised in a survey we conducted in 1999 to learn what teachers thought about the graduate course. To the question, "What were the most negative aspects of 602?" several respondents commented about the listserv. One teacher in the graduate course described above said that "the listserv/computer discussion was not a productive enterprise . . . there were complaints that it was being abused." Another student from the same class said, "The email discussion angered me a lot. I couldn't think the way those people [those frustrated about the course] thought." Some other teachers commented that the listserv assignment was too time consuming. Again, while these comments are rich sources of discussion about the theoretical and practical implications of using listservs in writing classes, for purposes of teacher preparation, we see their analysis of the course and the online discussions as places where teachers engaged in reflective and critical thought about teaching. Their learning about teaching practices and theories was directly implicated in this classroom practice. As instructors, we resisted "convincing" teachers of our pedagogy and let them work on those theoretical and practical questions on their own—even at the risk of dissent.

The surveys also indicated that teachers had some difficulty managing the reading. In such a short class, teachers are expected to read fifty to seventy-five pages a day, an appropriate amount of reading for a graduate seminar. However, as one respondent pointed out, there was "too much material to cover in too little time, especially with teaching [composition] for the first time." When teachers are faced with teaching in a few short weeks, learning new theory *and* the prospect of teaching are overwhelming, a response true of experienced teachers as well, several of whom were changing their methods drastically based on theories learned in the course.

As those who prepare teachers, we are concerned when teachers feel disconcerted. How do we help them deal with their discomfort yet at the same time maintain a syllabus that challenges them practically and theoretically? One teacher described his initial reaction to English 602 as "suffocation": "I was drowning in words, terms, and ideas I had never seen or heard. I was literally overwhelmed. Four days a week I felt like an alien in our class. But it was also exciting and the idea of teaching—alone with a class of students—was equally exciting." This student, a new master's student with no teaching experience, also expresses the excitement the graduate course created in him. Several respondents reported that the course was overwhelming but in retrospect appreciated. The survey showed us that administrators and teachers of teacher preparation courses must acknowledge the anxiety that "theory" can precipitate.

In the survey, teachers suggested ways to make English 602 more useful to them. One student said, "More [discussion of] practice. It seemed to always be something we were 'going to get to' but we never really did. I felt this left me hanging." But later, this same student said, "I learned more about teaching in 602 than in a full year of MAT [Master's in Teaching] courses." Several experienced teachers expressed similar sentiments. As teachers look back on the course, they value and appreciate how it was taught. But they responded that during the course, anxieties about not having enough practical suggestions for their teaching seemed to have been ignored.

Over the years, recurring comments on course evaluations, the listserv, and the portfolio reflections could not be ignored, so in 1999, we significantly changed the course. According to Assistant Director Susan Popham, who taught the course in 1998 and 1999, the syllabus changed to incorporate more practice throughout the course, so that the theory would not be so abstract for new teachers. While program administrators remain committed to the amount and kind of theory offered through the training course, based on teachers' concerns, they have restructured English 602 to help teachers see the relevance of theory earlier on.

Some survey respondents expressed concern about pressure to adhere to particular methods or prescribed theories. For example, several teachers felt pressured to adopt the portfolio system of grading, a method clearly valued by course instructors as endorsed by our own use of them in our classes, including English 602. And no matter how many times we told teachers to choose their own methods, some felt pressured to use the system because we did. One respondent said, "I have to admit that I did feel some pressure to adopt certain beliefs proposed in class. It was more peer pressure than grade pressure. . . . I don't think I was coerced in any way."

What we have done as a program is to listen to teacher concerns and to understand the source of them, and then to restructure our teaching and program requirements to meet those concerns. One teacher said about 602 and the program: "Looking back, that class produced some pretty excellent teaching, and those teachers are various and conflicting with one another in an appreciative manner. That is, I can think of at least 10 people in that class whom I've seen teach or talked to about teaching since 602, and their approaches are all different from mine and from each other's." As we continue to avoid "converting" teachers while training them, we will try to help teachers gain this perspective about teaching: There are many approaches to teaching, all of which we try to accept if a teacher has a sound theoretical basis for her practices. We want to see, however, that our teachers are able to articulate theoretically why they choose the methods they do.

## CONVERSION AVOIDANCE THROUGH
## ATTENTION TO TEACHERS' CONCERNS

Finally, the Composition Program at U of L tries to prepare graduate students for teaching (and for administration) by making them responsible for their own learning. This kind of professionalization, we believe, creates reflective practitioners who have a theoretical basis for their decisions, both in classrooms and in programs. U of L's "collaborative workshop model" (Johannessen qtd. in Hillocks 136) allows teacher educators to model different approaches and teaching styles in one course, thereby working against "conversion." Although the administrators in the writing program and the TA preparation course attempt to be theoretically consistent—and do acknowledge some theories of language, teaching, and writing to be more legitimate than others—their approach to TA preparation allows for various theories and practices. In fact, even if TAs gravitate toward pedagogies that seem out of sync with programmatic values, the program's strategy is to ask teachers to discuss their theoretical rationale for such a pedagogy instead of merely demanding compliance to certain practices. We've seriously considered the concerns of teachers and changed the program accordingly. The very writing of this chapter collaboratively suggests a continuing of the preparation and professionalization of graduate students in composition studies and an articulation of our own theories and practices for preparing college teachers of writing.

## APPENDIX: ENGLISH 602 BIBLIOGRAPHY
## SAMPLING OF THE ORIGINAL READING LIST

Heath, Shirley Brice. "Protean Shapes in Literacy Events: Ever-Shifting Oral and Literate Tradition." *Spoken and Written Language: Exploring Orality and Literacy.* Ed. Deborah Tannen. Norwood, NJ: Ablex, 1982. 91–117.

Horner, Bruce. "Rethinking the 'Sociality' of Error: Teaching Editing as Negotiation." *Rhetoric Review* 11 (1992): 172–99.

Hull, Glynda, Mike Rose, Kay Losey Fraser, and Marisa Castellano. "Remediation as Social Construct: Perspectives from an Analysis of Classroom Discourse." *College Composition and Communication* 42 (1991): 299–329.

Mayher, John. "Chapter 5: Language I: Nature of the System and How We Acquire It." *Uncommon Sense: Theoretical Practice in Language Education.* Portsmouth, NH: Boynton/Cook, 1990. 107–35.

Nelson, Jennie. "Reading Classrooms as Text: Exploring Student Writers' Interpretive Practices." *College Composition and Communication* 46 (1995): 411–29.

Shuy, Roger W. "A Holistic View of Language." *Research in the Teaching of English* 15 (1981): 101–11.

Yancey, Kathleen Blake. "Make Haste Slowly: Graduate Teaching Assistants and Portfolios." *New Directions in Portfolio Assessment.* Ed. Laurel Black et al. Portsmouth, NH: Boynton/Cook, 1994. 210–18.

Zebroski, James. "Introduction: Composing Theory: How Theory Can (and Can't) Help the Writing Teacher." *Thinking through Theory: Vygotskian Perspectives on the Teaching of Writing.* Portsmouth, NH: Boynton/Cook, 1994. 1–30.

# Works Cited

Anson, Chris, and Carol Rutz. "Graduate Students, Writing Programs, and Consensus-Based Management: Collaboration in the Face of Disciplinary Ideology." *WPA* 21 (1998): 106–20.

Barr Ebest, Sally. "The Next Generation of WPAs: A Study of Graduate Students in Composition/Rhetoric." *WPA* 22.3 (1999): 65–84.

Belanoff, Pat. "Portfolios and Literacy: Why?" *New Directions in Portfolio Assessment: Reflective Practice, Critical Theory, and Large-Scale Scoring.* Ed. Laurel Black, Donald A. Daiker, Jeffrey Sommers, and Gail Stygall. Portsmouth, NH: Boynton/Cook, 1994. 13–24.

Berkenkotter, Carol, Thomas N. Huckin, and John Ackerman. "Conventions, Conversations, and the Writer: Case Study of a Student in a Rhetoric and Composition Program" *Research in the Teaching of English* 11 (1988): 9–43.

Bishop, Wendy. *Something Old, Something New.* Carbondale, IL: Southern Illinois UP, 1990.

Durst, Russell K. *Collision Course: Conflict, Negotiation, and Learning in College Composition.* Urbana, IL: NCTE, 1999.

George, Diana, and Diana Shoos. "Issues of Subjectivity and Resistance: Cultural Studies in the Composition Classroom." *Cultural Studies in the English Classroom.* Ed. James A. Berlin and Michael J. Vivion. Portsmouth, NH: Boynton/Cook Heinemann, 1992. 200–10.

Harris, Joseph. *A Teaching Subject: Composition Since 1966.* New York: Prentice Hall, 1996.

Hawisher, Gail E., and Cynthia L. Selfe, eds. *Critical Perspectives on Computers and Composition Instruction.* New York: Teachers College P, 1989.

Herndl, Carl G. "Tactics and the Quotidian: Resistance and Professional Discourse." *Journal of Advanced Composition* 16 (1996): 455–70.

Hesse, Douglas. "Teachers as Students, Reflecting Resistance." *College Composition and Communication* 44 (1993): 224–31.

Hillocks, George. *Teaching Writing as Reflective Practice.* New York: Teachers College P, 1995.

Latterell, Catherine G. "Training the Workforce: An Overview of GTA Education Curricula." *WPA* 19.3 (1996): 7–23.

Lindemann, Erika. *A Rhetoric for Writing Teachers.* 2nd ed. New York: Oxford UP, 1987.

Long, Mark C., Jennifer H. Holberg, and Marcy M. Taylor. "Beyond Apprenticeship: Graduate Students, Professional Development Programs and the Future(s) of English Studies." *WPA* 20.1/2 (1996): 20–32.

Miller, Scott L., Brenda Jo Brueggeman, Bennis Blue, and Deneen M. Shepherd. "Present Perfect and Future Imperfect: Results of a National Survey of Graduate Students in Rhetoric and Composition Programs." *College Composition and Communication* 48 (1997): 392–409.

Powell, Katrina M., Cassandra Mach, Peggy O'Neill, and Brian Huot. "Graduate Students Negotiating Multiple Literacies as Writing Program Administrators: An Example of Collaborative Reflection." *Dialogue* 6.2 (2000): 82–110.

Prior, Paul. "Response, Revision, Disciplinarity: A Microhistory of a Dissertation Prospectus in Sociology." *Written Communication* 11 (1994): 483–533.

Rose, Mike. *Lives on the Boundary: A Moving Account of the Struggles and Achievements of America's Educational Underclass.* New York: Penguin, 1989.

Selfe, Cynthia L., and Susan Hilligoss, eds. *Literacy and Computers: The Complications of Teaching and Learning with Technology.* New York: MLA, 1994.

Tate, Gary, and Edward P. J. Corbett, eds. *A Writing Teacher's Sourcebook.* 2nd ed. New York: Oxford UP, 1988.

Taylor, Marcy, and Jennifer L. Holberg. "'Tales of Neglect and Sadism': Disciplinarity and the Figuring of the Graduate Student in Composition." *College Composition and Communication* 50 (1999): 607–25.

Welch, Nancy. "Resisting the Faith: Conversion, Resistance, and the Training of Teachers." *College English* 55 (1993): 387–401.

Yancey, Kathleen Blake. "Make Haste Slowly: Graduate Teaching Assistants and Portfolios." *New Directions in Portfolio Assessment.* Ed. Laurel Black, Donald A. Daiker, Jeffrey Summers, Gail Stygall. Portsmouth, NH: Boynton/Cook, 1994. 210–218.

Zebroski, James T. *Thinking through Theory: Vygotskian Perspectives on the Teaching of Writing.* Portsmouth, NH: Boynton/Cook, 1994.

# PART 3

## Programs

# 12. Preparing Graduate Students across the Curriculum to Teach Writing

## KATHERINE K. GOTTSCHALK

Cornell University specializes in diversity. With seven colleges, hundreds of programs, and 1,000 acres sending students in as many directions, it can be surprising to find that each year 3,000 first-year students share two experiences: All must pass the 100-yard swim test; all must take first-year writing seminars. But while students can prove they already know how to swim, they cannot prove they already know how to write, for Cornell has long operated on the conviction that writing is a central part of academic life. In fact, in 1966 it decided that first-year writing should be taught by many departments, not just by English, setting into motion a writing-in-the-disciplines program that continues even more strongly today, with over 120 topics in seminars offered by faculty and graduate students in over thirty departments and programs.

Such diversity of choice is wonderful for students, and for the faculty and graduate students who teach the courses. Administratively, however, such diversity presents challenges, challenges that make some institutions reluctant to involve "non-writing" faculty in the teaching of writing or to let instructors teach seminars of their own design. Certainly, preparing graduate student instructors located in up to thirty disciplines to teach writing seminars presents a major challenge, especially given that they always teach seminars in their own disciplines, often in fact designing their own courses.

While describing how Writing Program TAs are prepared, then, I will therefore necessarily address the following questions: What kinds of preparation can help TAs in the disciplines to become effective teachers of writing, not just of their subjects? What kinds of preparation might they value, not just for their work in the writing program, but for later careers, perhaps as anthropologists or literary scholars? And what is the value in investing in the preparation of graduate students who may never teach writing, per se, again?

## THE HISTORICAL AND INSTITUTIONAL CONTEXT FOR TA PREPARATION AT CORNELL[1]

In past years, dissatisfaction with TAs' teaching caused serious upheavals in the Writing Program and indeed led to the present administrative form of the Writing Program and of its TA programs. Experience has taught us that an entire program can be negatively affected by problematic TA preparation and administrative supervision.

Originally, writing at Cornell was long taught—as it still is at many places—as an English Department course firmly rooted in the study of literature. While "Freshman English" was taught only by the English Department, itself located in the College of Arts and Sciences, the course nevertheless served students in all seven of Cornell's colleges, whose interests and needs ranged widely, from agriculture to hotel administration. In the 1960s faculty concern about the emphasis on writing *skills* grew: They believed the courses should focus on writing that emphasized *thinking.* Students disliked the lack of choice, and instructors were bored, even antagonistic toward the course. In addition, too many TAs were teaching seminars without adequate faculty supervision.

This dissatisfaction with a literature-based, English-department approach to teaching writing led to the 1966 institution of a Freshman Humanities Program, administered by a faculty member from the English Department, but with seminars in thirty subjects offered by nine departments: Comparative Literature, English, German Studies, Government, History, History of Art, Philosophy, Romance Studies, and Speech and Drama. The widespread departmental contributions were intended to revitalize the content of the seminars, provide additional faculty-taught seminars, and also increase the number of TAs who would teach their own writing seminars, supervised by faculty from their departments.

In this new program TAs indeed benefited from working closely with faculty, and in 1975 a summer TA apprenticeship program was initiated. Nevertheless, by 1976 a crisis once again was underway. Communication and collaboration were problematic among teachers, administrators (even within the writing program), and colleges. The lack of collaboration was particularly harmful for TA preparation. Little attempt was made to ensure preparation of TAs, and some were trained but never taught. One investigative study did not, therefore, find it surprising that seminars often barely taught writing: "[S]tudents are sometimes asked for only three or four large papers; they are seldom given the opportunity to rewrite their papers, and grading is often inadequate or untimely. These conditions are the result of administrative weakness, due to the departments' independence and the lack of supervision of the graduate students teaching the courses" (*Report of the Provost's Commission* 3).

Such were the results of a program run by one member of the English department, of a program having too little contact with its clientele, its contributing departments, its teachers, and most especially with its graduate instructors—in sum, the results of a program not attending to the interdisciplinarity that was at its core.

One solution to the situation might have been to go back to an English department writing program. Fortunately, the chosen solution was to give the Writing Program independent status. The Writing Program gained authority and perspective by being disengaged from allegiance to one department and its courses; it became an independently situated program that reports to the dean of the college and that consults regularly with a university-wide committee. It also was given its own substantial financial base.

## THE NEW CONTEXT FOR THE PREPARATION OF TAs

The new writing program administration (now the John S. Knight Institute for Writing in the Disciplines[2]) began, then, in 1982. Six features loom prominently in the 1982–2000 context for the preparation of TAs: (1) In the fall of 1982, twenty-four departments and programs contributed seminars to the First-Year Writing Seminars; in the spring of 2000, thirty-two contributed; recently, as many as thirty-eight in one semester have been involved. (2) Now, as in 1982, the Writing Program coordinates registration and other administrative details of the First-Year Writing Seminars. Departments select possible graduate student instructors, subject to Writing Program approval; design courses, again, subject to Writing Program approval; and are in charge of room and time assignments, subject to Writing Program negotiation. (3) A major financial policy, quickly instituted in 1983, is that while departments fund some TA-taught seminars, the Writing Program controls further TA funding for those departments. Writing Program distribution of funding can vary, depending on factors such as a department's offering additional faculty-taught seminars, which generally elicits increased TA support from the Writing Program. Fewer faculty-taught seminars result in decreased funding from the Writing Program. (4) Starting in 1982, class size, initially not having a firm cap, was steadily decreased until in a few years it was fixed at seventeen students. Class sizes are not increased in response to increased numbers of students; rather, the program receives money to add more seminars. (5) Throughout 1982–2000, members of the faculty have taught about one-third of the seminars (about 150–170 seminars are offered each semester); TAs teach the remaining sections; there are no adjuncts. (6) Again, throughout this time, TAs have been assigned faculty mentors from their departments, an excellent legacy of the earlier system, and they have continued to teach only one course per term. TAs begin teaching after at least one year of graduate school; many have even more years of graduate school experience.

## DEVELOPMENTAL PROGRAMS FOR TAs

Clearly, the new Writing Program was planted in rich soil: full and willing involvement of many departments, including tenured faculty; reasonable teaching loads and class sizes; a firm financial basis. Preparation and guidance for TAs were, however, only tentatively in place. Chief among the program's new responsibilities, therefore, were that guidelines be established for all seminars, that a handbook be written for the guidance of instructors, and that a preparatory program be developed that would be required of all TAs. These areas were, accordingly, among the first in which the new director (Fredric Bogel) and the then associate director (the author) took action.

To establish guidelines was a straightforward task. The guidelines drew on preferences expressed when the Writing Program was under review; over the years these have been modified and used to ensure basic uniformity in numbers of papers and attention to writing throughout the seminars. The current guidelines are (here in somewhat abbreviated form) as follows:

- Seminars require at least six—and at most ten—formal essays on new topics. While these assignments should total about thirty pages, some of the page total may include preparatory drafts.
- At least three of the six to ten required essays are developed through several stages of revised drafts. Guidance may include, in addition to commentary on drafts, individual conferences, in-class group work, peer commentary, and reading responses.
- All seminars spend ample classroom time (about half) on work directly related to writing.
- Reading assignments in the course subject are kept under seventy-five pages per week to permit regular, concentrated work on writing.
- All students meet in at least two individual conferences with the instructor.

For the handbook, Cornell faculty contributed chapters, and in 1988 it was published as *Teaching Prose: A Guide for Writing Instructors* (Bogel and Gottschalk). As the years have passed, the Writing Program has produced new teaching materials, and reliance on the handbook is fading. Significant among the new materials available to instructors are syllabi and assignments developed by instructors in the program. These materials have become available largely because of Writing 700: "Teaching Writing," the course developed as a primary means to prepare TAs for the teaching of writing in their disciplines.

## WRITING 700: "TEACHING WRITING"

The approach followed in Writing 700, as in the program at large, emerges from Cornell's longstanding view of writing as belonging to every discipline, and as best learned and taught as part of the (conscious) immersion in a subject. The Writing Program has never shared the view that members of "other" disciplines may be, if put into a writing classroom, sorry substitutes for "real" teachers of writing. Rather, our approach assumes that faculty and TAs in the disciplines know a great deal about writing, that indeed they may have insights into writing in their own fields that others do not.

### THE ADMINISTRATIVE STRUCTURE OF WRITING 700

Enrollment in Writing 700 is the common preparatory experience guaranteed to, and required of, all TAs who are to teach First-Year Writing Seminars. This six-week course, one-credit, S/U, is offered in the summer, when about fifty TAs enroll, and again in the fall, when some twenty TAs participate. Of the fifty summer participants, about thirty also act as interns in a First-Year Writing Seminar under the guidance of the faculty member teaching the course (see below for further details). TAs who take the fall version of Writing 700 tend to be more experienced in the classroom; about half actually teach their seminars that semester; the remainder will teach in the spring. Writing 700 meets once a week for two-and-a-half hours. Each session has a two-part structure, with a presentation in the first half and discussion sections in the second.

The course is now run primarily by the director of First-Year Writing Seminars (at present the author), but only through collaborative work with other members of the Writing Program, namely with the director of the Knight Writing Program (currently Jonathan Monroe); with the director of the Writing Workshop (Joe Martin); and with James Slevin of Georgetown University, who has long assisted in shaping the seminar.[3] All of those involved may lead discussion sections and give presentations. It has also long been customary to hire experienced graduate student instructors (from five to ten a year) to cofacilitate discussion sections and to make presentations. Presentations from their peers are often the most convincing for TAs, although talks by new members of the faculty are also well received. The experience of working as facilitators for Writing 700 provides TAs with valuable additional experience in working through issues of teaching writing and with additional teaching credentials.

### WRITING 700 READING ASSIGNMENTS

The Writing Program provides all Writing 700 participants with a substantial packet of readings from which assignments are made each week. One group of materials includes professional articles by theorists such as David Bartholomae, Peter Elbow, Toby Fulwiler, Joseph Harris, Mary Louise Pratt, James Slevin, Nancy Sommers, Richard Straub, and Joseph Williams. The other group includes pedagogical guides developed by the author and sample handouts, assignments, and syllabi created by experienced First-Year Writing Seminar instructors. All are coordinated with the topics of the weekly writing assignment.

### WRITING 700 WRITING ASSIGNMENTS

TAs in virtually all disciplines begin Writing 700 with the questions, "How do I teach writing as well as my subject? How do I teach grammar?" We consequently design the writing assignments to help instructors discover that teaching writing well is a means to teaching their subjects well. This approach is, we believe, key to helping TAs find Writing 700 appropriate to their knowledge and their interests; it is how we hope to help them become good teachers of writing and eventually of their disciplines.

The writing assignments for participants of Writing 700 must, then, be very carefully thought out: Rethinking them is a yearly job. When we began the seminar in 1983, TAs were asked to read a great deal but to write only two or three general essays. This approach did the reputation of the course no good, for it did not mesh with the starting point of the participants. When TAs face their first independent teaching assignments, they want practical, immediate advice: They don't want to read the manual—they want to press the start-up switch as quickly as possible. What should they plan for the first day? Which readings should they select?

It's natural to provide assistance on matters such as class management during presentations and discussion groups. And we know that wild horses couldn't prevent TAs from planning the readings. (We also know that in the second semester of teaching, TAs will discard half of the readings they scheduled the first time around.) What TAs most need to work on at length, and where we can most help them, is on the planning of the essay assignments. Through the sequence of essay assignments and the preparation designed for those assignments, much instruction both in writing and in the intellectual life of the course will occur.

For many years, therefore, Writing 700 has concentrated on having participants design writing assignments for their prospective students. What does a well-written assignment looks like? What writing assignment sequence can be planned in conjunction with the sequence of readings? How might students be prepared to do a good job on an essay, in everything from use of Web site sources to organization? David Bartholomae, who has observed Cornell's Writing 700 for many years, has enthusiastically described the developmental process TAs undergo as they come to grips with being responsible for these matters in a writing seminar:

> Let's say there were going to be two books at the center of the course; then the problem is how you organize the engagement with those books in such a way that you're not only covering the material but students are learning to write. . . . And you watch these graduate students suddenly think through the reading of these two books of anthropology not as learning the field or covering the field, but as taking you into a way of reading, a way of writing, that marks somebody's young professional entrée into a community. . . . The sequences are brilliant, really wonderful! (qtd. in Boe and Schroeder 13)

Four of the six Writing 700 assignments therefore focus TAs' attention on developing particular kinds of writing assignments (the remaining two have focused on various topics including response to student essays). Three assignments ask for the development of preparatory, individual, and sequenced writing assignments, with accompanying rationales in which TAs reflect on what they are trying to do and why. A fourth writing assignment asks TAs to direct students' attention to sentence-level language. (See the Appendix for a sample assignment sequence, with rationale, designed by a first-time graduate student instructor in music.)

By the end of Writing 700, TAs are worrying less about grammar and coverage of readings and more about what their students will learn. TAs generally are excited about their subjects, and they are eager to help students share their enthusiasm. Wanting to read good student essays, they take earnestly to working on what will help their students become better writers. And surely it is not lost on TAs that, as future professors, they have ahead of them a lifetime of planning good courses, of designing good assignments, and of reading the results.[4]

## WRITING 700 ADMINISTRATIVE DECISIONS AND DILEMMAS

One of the early decisions in regard to Writing 700 was when to offer it. Summer has been a good choice because TAs are not taking classes; further, we can coordinate their taking Writing 700 with internships (more on that below). Summer preparation offers inexperienced teachers time to prepare and to develop their confidence. The fall version of Writing 700 makes sense for experienced TAs or those who will not teach until the spring semester. A six-week, once-a-week format (compared to a three-day or one-week marathon) provides time for TAs to assimilate their work in Writing 700 and in the mentorship: They are not overloaded with material before they can take it in; they have ample time in which to write and revise.

An ongoing issue for Writing 700 is whom to select to make presentations or act as facilitators. In the summer, presentations tend to be more varied, with invited speakers such as David Bartholomae, James Slevin, and Nancy Sommers. We consider it helpful to include faculty from other campuses because they provide a larger context within which TAs can view writing in the disciplines. For similar reasons we involve tenured faculty from various departments at Cornell as discussion leaders or participants. In the past, full professors from fields such as anthropology and government have assumed facilitating roles. Such participation makes clear to TAs that teaching writing is viewed seriously by faculty in their own departments, not just by "The Writing Program"; it brings faculty and TAs together to consider the teaching of writing within their own disciplines, emphasizing the (inter)disciplinary nature of the project.

## OTHER PROGRAMS FOR PEDAGOGICAL DEVELOPMENT

After completion of Writing 700, graduate students are provided with a number of further opportunities for pedagogical development. Only the assignment of a faculty mentor during their teaching is mandatory; all other programs are voluntary. As most writing programs no doubt have experienced, offering rewards is an easy way to encourage the development of good work and ideas that will benefit students, instructors, and future instructors. The Writing Program therefore offers not just awards for student essays (and, as of 2000, portfolios) but also substantial prizes for instructors' assignment sequences and development of new courses.

## THE SUMMER INTERN/MENTOR PROGRAM

A more intensive feature of Cornell's developmental options is the internship/mentor program. Each year about thirty TAs combine taking Writing 700 with interning with a faculty member who is teaching a summer-session First-Year Writing Seminar; they receive financial summer support for doing so. Interns attend all classes and receive guidance in teaching, planning assignments, holding conferences, and responding to essays. Often the faculty member with whom a TA interns is participating in the Faculty Seminar for Writing

Instruction, a program that includes attending the presentations for Writing 700. The learning experience is frequently interdisciplinary, as when a graduate student from English interns with a professor from the Department of Anthropology. This interdisciplinary arrangement of faculty and interns suits the very nature of the seminars, which place undergraduates in disparate writing contexts: It is appropriate that the instructors themselves encounter the teaching of writing in different disciplines.

## PEER COLLABORATION

A popular follow-up program (easily administered) is Peer Collaboration, in which TAs team up to work on such projects as responding to papers, working out a sequence of preparatory assignments, or observing each other's classes. They write up their proposals for collaboration; they write reports on the outcome. Faculty mentors and the Writing Seminar director approve the proposals and reports. The small carrots are two free lunches in the company of the faculty mentor and a $100 stipend to be received when the final reports have come in. The cost is minimal compared to the results, namely better-taught seminars and future professors who have begun their teaching careers by working collaboratively. TAs like the program; they especially appreciate the encouragement to find out how other people do things and to get each other's help.

## ESSAY RESPONSE CONSULTATION

An unusual opportunity, Essay Response Consultation draws on the expertise of undergraduate and graduate tutors who work for the Walk-In Service. In the program the tutor reads a set of papers on which the instructor—whether TA or faculty—has commented and then meets with the instructor for a one-to-one consultation. Working from their knowledge of how students view instructors' comments, tutors can spot which kinds of responses may confuse or discourage students; they notice when perhaps the assignment itself has created the problem. Instructors who use this completely confidential and voluntary service are uniformly enthusiastic about it because the tutors have a thorough expertise developed from their many personal interactions with students. Again, the program draws on existing strengths—the tutors. An easy program to put in place, it has far-reaching benefits for instructors from any discipline or at any level of expertise.

## IMPLICATIONS

What can be the rewards of investing in developmental programs for TAs in a writing-across-the-curriculum writing program? Nadine Weidman, who took Writing 700 and taught a First-Year Writing Seminar while completing her PhD in science and technology studies, has had additional experience that makes her believe the benefits go beyond preparing teachers of first-year composition. Students throughout their academic years need courses in which teachers attend to writing, not just one or two semesters of freshman composition, for

> [n]o one learns to write that way; the Harvard seniors who show up in my classes and who routinely have trouble putting together a paragraph, never mind an essay, attest to that fact. Given this situation, every teacher . . . must be a teacher of writing, and every course must be a writing-intensive course. Inasmuch, then, as graduate students are teachers in training, they must be trained to teach writing, which should involve actually teaching it. ("Response" 75)

Recently, Richard E. Miller, also arguing for preparing graduate students across the curriculum to teach writing, noted the intellectual limitations in an English/Writing department–only approach. "[R]estricting access to teaching undergraduate writing . . . to people with training in English, rhetoric, or composition" has meant, he argues, that the courses

> have tended to reflect the intellectual preoccupations of this labor force. The result is a situation where first-year students, who come from all the disciplines, frequently find themselves in classes devoted to the study of literary texts, cultural criticism, or rhetorical analysis. And upon completion of these courses . . . they quickly circulate to other areas of the university, where the instruction they've received proves—at best—to be of limited value. (101)

Miller has found that at Rutgers the practice of training graduate students from across the curriculum to teach writing "has not only improved the overall quality of instruction in the first-year course" (102) but has also helped to institute writing across the curriculum institutionally, for "these teachers [of writing] take this knowledge back to their home departments, where they are integrating it into traditionally content-based courses" (102).

Cornell does not face Rutgers's problem of getting faculty to teach first-year writing seminars or participate in writing-across-the-curriculum: Many faculty enthusiastically take part in Writing in the Majors, a program designed explicitly for upper-level courses, primarily in the sciences and social sciences. (In these courses faculty who wish to improve the teaching of a course focus on ways in which uses of writing can be directed to that end.) Nevertheless, it is undoubtedly true that the presence of a large-scale across-the-curriculum first-year writing program and especially of the many TAs trained to teach in that program means that departments regularly encounter fresh ideas about the role of writing in the teaching of a discipline. More importantly, the graduate student instructors do not go back just to their departments; they eventually go on to other institutions, fortified with the unusual experience of having taught a course in their own disciplines in which student writing was a primary means and subject.

Ultimately, students at Cornell, Rutgers, or anywhere else should view writing as integral to all of their academic life. As Weidman ("Response") points out, they will be more likely to do so if instructors of all their courses also view writing as a normal part of instruction. It's worth considering, then, that when a writing program takes on the challenges of diversity and helps graduate students in disciplines across the curriculum to become teachers of writing, it is not taking up a needlessly complicated project that will weaken the instruction of writing. Rather, it is investing in increased diversity and richness of instruction, in the present and in the future.

## APPENDIX: A SEQUENCE OF ASSIGNMENTS DESIGNED FOR A FIRST-YEAR WRITING SEMINAR—*MUSIC 111: FAMOUS FIRST PERFORMANCES*

*Sarah Day-O'Connell, Instructor*
*Program Music and Absolute Music: Opening Sequence on Berlioz*

### Berlioz Assignment 1

- *Listen* to Berlioz *Symphonie fantastique*. If you read music, follow the score. The goal of this first listening is to concentrate on your own reaction to the music. Do not read about the piece in the CD liner notes or any other source.
- *Write:* In one to two pages, take one of the following approaches (each is valid and potentially interesting):
  1. "This music evokes various abstract images and emotions, such as . . ."
  2. "This music seems to tell a story about . . ."
  3. "This music doesn't really suggest anything outside itself; rather, it is a collection of artfully arranged pitches, timbres, and rhythms. I especially noticed . . ."

### Berlioz Assignment 2: The "Programmists"

- *Read* the article excerpts by Jonathan Kramer, Robert Winter, and Joseph Kerman.
- *Listen* to the *Symphonie fantastique* again, this time with the program.
- *Write:* In one to two pages, describe your "before and after" listening experiences. Organize your paper around a single idea; for example, try agreeing or disagreeing with this comment: "Knowing Berlioz's program helped (did not help) me appreciate his symphony." (You will later edit this essay using techniques we are studying in Joseph Williams, *Style: Ten Lessons in Clarity and Grace*.)

### Berlioz Assignment 3: The "Absolutists"

- *Read* (a) the entries "absolute music" and "program music" in *The New Harvard Dictionary of Music* (ed. Don Randel) and (b) the article excerpts by David Cairns and W. J. Turner.

### Berlioz Assignment 4 (in-class writing)

As you begin, consider the following questions: What is the difference between absolute music and program music? Can music "mean" something outside itself . . . or can it ever not? Is familiarity with the program necessary for understanding the music . . . or is it actually detrimental to the musical experience? Where do the various authors stand on this question? Where do you stand?

## Berlioz Assignment 5

In this unit we have

- Compared hearing *Symphonie fantastique* with and without its program
- Read about and discussed musical devices and features, including the *idee fixe* and *Dies Irae*
- Read and compared various authors' views on the importance of the program
- Weighed the usefulness of the terms "absolute music" and "program music"
- Observed two tools for organizing an essay: controlling ideas and counterarguments

You should now write a three- or four-page paper taking a position in the ongoing historical debate over absolute and program music. For support use (improved) material from your Assignments 1–4. (You'll later revise this essay, concentrating especially on your first and last paragraphs.)

## Rationale

At the first performance of *Symphonie fantastique,* Berlioz astonished the audience by providing a written program, which explained in detail the "story" of his semi-autobiographical symphony. For centuries before and since, musicians have argued for the superiority either of program music (which invokes something extra-musical) or of absolute music (supposedly free from any extra-musical associations).

Rather than first outlining the merits of the various arguments and then asking students to choose their own stances, I immediately try to give students "authority" from their own experience. In class discussion after the first assignment, students are already taking positions in the debate, before they even become aware of its existence outside our classroom. (My job in this discussion is to move students from relatively subjective comments about the music ["it sounds scary"] to the use of specific musical terminology ["the change from thin to thick texture," "the string tremolo"].)

We then build up to the last paper in which students take an informed position in the debate by adding arguments from opposing sides for support or refutation. As we engage the "programmist" side of the debate, the thrust is twofold: to uncover the covert agenda of the three commentaries (namely, that knowing the program is imperative for a worthy listening experience) and to observe the readings' organization around a single controlling idea. Likewise, we address the "absolutists" stance (that a program is a crutch for the lazy or weak listener), while also taking note of how these particular authors strengthen their assertions by addressing counterarguments. After both sets of assignments, students are asked to respond by rewriting their own previous work, incorporating the new perspectives and mimicking the new organizational methods.

## NOTES

1. For much fuller accounts of the material in this section, see "An Historical Perspective on TAs and the Teaching of Writing at Cornell," my chapter in *Local Knowledges, Local Practices: Cultures of Writing at Cornell,* ed. Jonathan Monroe (under review at the U of Pittsburgh P), and my article "Putting—and Keeping—the Cornell Writing Program in Its Place: Writing in the Disciplines."
2. The Writing Program became the John S. Knight Institute for Writing in the Disciplines in 1986 when it received a major endowment from the John S. Knight Foundation, much of

which is used for TA and faculty development. In 2000 the James L. and John S. Knight Foundation provided further major endowment, designated primarily for expansion of Writing in the Majors courses, and for Sophomore Seminars, the latter being a new program designed to fill the gap between First-Year Writing Seminars and Writing in the Majors courses. With the further endowment and the expansion of the program, its name has been modified to The Knight Institute for Writing in the Disciplines.

3. The Director of Writing in the Majors, Keith Hjortshoj, also co-taught Writing 700 when TAs took it in preparation for participating in Writing in the Majors (a program for improving instruction in upper-level courses by intensifying attention to language). As Writing in the Majors grew, a separate course became necessary, which Hjortshoj now teaches.

4. For a full description of a seminar taught by a then graduate student in science and technology studies, see Nadine Weidman's "Gender Issues in Biology: An Approach to Teaching Writing," written while Weidman was teaching in Harvard's Expository Writing Program.

## WORKS CITED

Boe, John, and Eric Schroeder. "Stop Being So Coherent: An Interview with David Bartholomae." *Writing on the Edge* 10.1 (1998–99): 9–28.

Bogel, Fredric V., and Katherine K. Gottschalk, eds. *Teaching Prose: A Guide for Writing Instructors.* New York and London: Norton, 1988.

Gottschalk, Katherine K. "Putting—and Keeping—the Cornell Writing Program in Its Place: Writing in the Disciplines." *Language and Learning Across the Disciplines* 2.1 (1997): 22–45.

Miller, Richard E. "'Let's Do the Numbers': Comp Droids and the Prophets of Doom." *Profession* (1999): 97–105.

*Report of the Provost's Commission on Writing,* November 1981 minutes of the Holmes commission. Chair, Clive Holmes, Department of History. Cornell University, Oct. 1981.

Weidman, Nadine. "Gender Issues in Biology: An Approach to Teaching Writing." *Language and Learning Across the Disciplines* 2.3 (1998): 61–8.

———— "Response to Criticism." *Language and Learning Across the Disciplines* 2.3 (1998): 75–6.

# 13. Creating a Culture of Reflective Practice: A Program for Continuing TA Preparation after the Practicum

BETTY BAMBERG

In the not-too-distant past, thousands of TAs endured a frustrating initiation into teaching college composition similar to that described by David Foster, who recalls that he "had no training in teaching writing" and "no familiarity with any classroom strategies" (n. p.). Today, however, new TAs are likely to receive extensive preparation through orientations, practica, mentoring, and a variety of other activities as described throughout this collection. Once this initial preparation has been completed, the emphasis shifts from preparing TAs to supervising them. Although the goals of supervision may be to help all TAs expand their repertoire of pedagogical strategies, in practice supervision often focuses on improving the teaching of less effective TAs rather than on raising the program's overall level of instruction. The relatively limited role of supervision is hardly surprising. Faced with a group of inexperienced graduate students who will soon have full responsibility for teaching composition courses, WPAs understandably make initial preparation their top priority. Moreover, preparing TAs is truly the labor of Sisyphus: One year's cadre of new TAs has no sooner completed its initial preparation than WPAs must begin gearing up for next year's group. Given the limited resources available in most programs, relatively little time or energy is likely to remain for supervising experienced TAs and for continuing staff development. Nevertheless, continuing the preparation of TAs after the practicum is essential if they are to become more effective writing teachers. In their article "TA Supervision," Jo Sprague and Jody Nyquist describe the beginning TA as a "*senior learner* who is more sophisticated and motivated than most undergraduate students but whose primary academic success so far has been in the role of learner" (43). TAs later become "colleagues in training" after they have begun to internalize their teaching role and develop a sense of professional identity. When they have "developed substantial instructional skills and demonstrated sound judgment" (44) and "their primary concerns involve discovering ways to help students learn" (45), they have reached the stage of "junior colleague." Because TAs do not necessarily move steadily along this developmental continuum, supervision can play a critical role in helping them evolve from a senior learner into a junior colleague. This chapter describes a program at the University of Southern California (USC) for continuing the preparation of TAs after the practicum. Although developed for the particular context at USC, the model can be adapted to quite different institutional settings.[1]

## BACKGROUND AND INSTITUTIONAL CONTEXT

When I became director of the USC Freshman Writing Program, it was in crisis. At the beginning of the 1984 fall semester, the Student Senate surveyed student opinion on the university's general education program, and the *Daily Trojan's* front page headline reported "Freshman Writing Worst GE Course." Although admittedly unscientific, the survey results indicated serious instructional problems, confirmed widespread student dissatisfaction, and created a mandate for change.

The Freshman Writing Program had begun in 1978 as part of a major revision in USC's general education curriculum. At that time, the freshman composition requirement was expanded to two semesters, and a traditional, product approach to writing instruction was replaced with one based on rhetorical principles and the emerging process paradigm. W. Ross Winterowd—founding director of USC's graduate program in rhetoric, linguistics, and literature—created the conceptual and theoretical framework for the new program; and Sylvia Manning, the first director, devised the administrative structures to implement it.[2] At that time, it was removed from English Department administration to become a separate instructional program within the College of Letters, Arts, and Sciences. Under the previous set of general education requirements, more than a dozen departments had supported graduate students by offering sections of freshman composition or by teaching courses that met a distribution requirement, both of which were eliminated by the new writing program. Their continued support for the new program was contingent upon a guarantee of continued assistance for their graduate students. From its inception, therefore, the program had an interdisciplinary instructional staff that consisted initially of about eighty TAs from fourteen departments and programs with roughly half of the positions held by graduate students from the English Department. As a result, the program for preparing TAs not only had to demonstrate how to teach writing within an innovative curriculum but also needed to consider the TAs' varied disciplinary backgrounds and accommodate their conflicting departmental schedules and requirements.

Although the problems within the program were partly attributable to its complex curricular structure, the primary difficulty was that the TAs were not being adequately prepared for the complexities of teaching writing within a process paradigm. The original TA preparation program consisted of a two-week orientation before the fall semester and a weekly practicum during the first semester of teaching. The first year's program in 1979 took a heavily theoretical approach that mistakenly assumed that inexperienced instructors could move effortlessly from theory to practice. The two-week orientation consisted almost entirely of lectures on rhetorical and linguistic theory; the planned practicum was optional. Not surprisingly, this approach failed disastrously, and in response the following year's program consisted of an atheoretical approach of ad hoc mentoring where experienced TAs passed on their expertise or "lore." Although the mentoring gave new TAs some practical classroom strategies, their preparation was inconsistent and uneven, and it left them with a collection of disconnected techniques and little guidance in ways to use them effectively. In the third year of the program, Michael Holzman, the new director, revised the orientation and instituted a required one-unit practicum, changes that attempted to balance theory and practice. He also encouraged the TAs to develop individual syllabi for the "writing workshop" that drew on their own academic interests and expertise. However, these modifications also failed to prepare TAs adequately. By the time I became director in 1984, TAs were using widely divergent approaches to teaching writing, and even many experienced instructors remained confused and unsure about how to teach writing within the program's curriculum.

The institutional context—particularly the program's size and its location in Los Angeles—posed other problems. During my tenure as director, the writing program offered about 140 sections of composition every fall semester and 120 every spring. These sections translated into enrollments of 2,600–3,000 students, who were taught by 110–120 TAs. In addition, there were practical problems of geography and time schedules. TAs lived all over the sprawling Los Angeles metropolitan area, often a considerable distance from campus, and as a result, many tried to minimize the number of days they came to the university. When they were on campus, they usually had one eye on the clock, estimating the additional freeway traffic they were likely to encounter if their departure were delayed by fifteen minutes. These commuting constraints, along with the graduate course work schedules of more than a dozen different academic departments, made it extremely difficult and sometimes impossible to find meeting times when all TAs could attend once the semester had begun.

## THE ROLE OF INQUIRY AND REFLECTION

In addition to resolving the context-specific problems described above, I needed a theoretical framework that would unify the components of the preparation program into a coherent whole and facilitate learning. As the program evolved, I built that framework using the concepts of reflection and inquiry. In recent years, the process of reflection has been recognized as an important tool in learning, one that is particularly valuable for practitioners, who regularly encounter nonroutine or unique problems that need new solutions. Donald Schön's description of reflective practitioners, who conduct "frame experiments in which they impose a kind of coherence on messy situations" (157), can be contrasted with Stephen North's account of practitioners who rely on lore, "the accumulated body of traditions, practices, and beliefs . . . about how writing is done, learned, and taught" (22). To move beyond lore, practitioners must engage in the kind of inquiry that characterizes Schön's reflective practitioner.

However, North claims that "practice qualifies as inquiry less than ten percent of the time" (34) because the overwhelming demands of teaching a full load of composition courses leave the teacher with little time or energy for inquiry. As a result, teachers fall back on "ritual and routine" (34), a practice that uses a limited number of strategies, simplifies complex bodies of knowledge, and fails to respond adequately to new situations. In arguing for the importance of increased reflection, George Hillocks claims that reflection allows teachers to "learn *through* practice" [emphasis added], which allows for "the building of knowledge," rather than through trial and error, which does not (28–9). In *Reflection in the Writing Classroom,* Kathleen Blake Yancey demonstrates how the mental acts of reflection—reviewing, projecting, and revising—positively affect all aspects of the writing classroom, and ethnographies by Christine Farris and by Elizabeth Rankin document the powerful insights that TAs can gain through reflection. Thus, opportunities for reflection and the inquiry that is central to the process of reflection need to be an integral part of any program designed to prepare TAs to teach writing.

However, creating conditions that promote reflective practice among TAs is no easy task. For their studies, Farris and Rankin both met weekly with a small number of TAs (four and five respectively), and all participants committed substantial time to reflective activities during the respective studies. Although such a time- and labor-intensive approach is characteristic of research, it is not usually feasible when supervising TAs, especially in large programs where there may be more than 100 TAs to supervise. Unless a program's practices and conditions foster reflection, little is likely to occur. Beginning TAs, struggling to cope with the demands of both teaching and graduate course work, are likely to see the ritual and routine of lore as offering easily accessible solutions to the challenges of teaching composition. More experienced TAs are also unlikely to engage in substantive reflection, as the tight job market increasingly pushes them into an early professionalism. Told that it is no longer enough for them to do well in their graduate courses and to complete a publishable dissertation, many TAs feel pressured to deliver conference papers and publish articles early in their graduate careers (Leverenz and Goodburn 9), a pressure that directs their energy and attention away from the classroom and toward research and professional activities. However, these opposing forces can be countered if there is a program "culture" that supports inquiry and reflection. For a culture of reflective practice to exist, it must first be built into the TAs' initial preparation and then sustained through programmatic structures and practices that occur after the practicum.

## INTRODUCING REFLECTIVE PRACTICE: THE ORIENTATION AND PRACTICUM

Although this chapter focuses on encouraging inquiry and supporting reflection *after* the practicum, the groundwork for reflection must begin in TAs' initial preparation. Given the problematic history of USC's initial program for preparing TAs, creating a functional, effective orientation and practicum was my top priority. To resolve the theory/practice conflict that had frustrated previous efforts, I redesigned the orientation and practicum to create an "instructional scaffold" (Applebee 176), an approach that provides learners with an initial support structure, then gradually withdraws that structure as they internalize concepts and can apply them independently.

The scaffold consists of a six-week outline of activities and lessons for our first-semester writing course. To embed theory within practice, it introduces TAs to the rhetorical principles and theory underlying the program's curriculum through a day-by-day schedule of activities that includes the first two writing assignments; lessons on topics such as prewriting, revision, and peer evaluation; and various teaching materials to carry out the activities. These materials as well as the theoretical rationales for the various approaches are assembled in a loose-leaf notebook that TAs receive at the beginning of the orientation. During most orientation and practicum sessions, new TAs are organized into small instructional groups of six to eight, each group led by a team of two mentor teachers who guide TAs through the repertoire of "good practices" for teaching writing contained in the course outline.[3]

During the orientation, mentor teachers and the new TAs review the schedule for the first few weeks of the semester with the mentors relating practice to theory and research. Once the semester begins, weekly practicum sessions guide TAs through the remainder of the course outline while at the same time the mentor teachers help them plan assignments and lessons for the second half of the semester. Initially, there were formal practicum meetings for the entire semester with later sessions focused on preparing TAs to teach the second semester course. However, this format was unsuccessful because TAs were too concerned with teaching their first semester course and completing their first semester's graduate course work to focus on the second semester. Therefore, we ended the first-semester practicum after the seventh week and created a second-semester practicum modeled on the first, but with somewhat less scaffolding required—the course outline covered one assignment and three weeks of lessons. Second-semester practicum meetings also ended after the seventh week, as we gradually withdrew support as the TAs became more self-sufficient in the classroom. However, mentor teachers remained available to review TAs' assignments and lesson plans and to help them resolve classroom problems that arise later in the term.

Although a highly structured day-by-day course outline might seem antithetical to promoting reflective practice, such is not the case. Because new TAs do not have to worry about planning their initial assignments and class activities, they can focus instead on solving classroom problems and issues that arise as they teach. Having met with their mentor teachers and the same small group of TAs for most orientation and practicum sessions, they feel comfortable acknowledging classroom problems and issues. During the practicum, the mentors model reflective practice by encouraging TAs first to reflect orally on their experience by identifying problems and then to project possible solutions as they discuss classroom interactions and collaboratively plan the remaining weeks of instruction.

Although this program worked very effectively, a major revision of USC's general education program in 1997 necessitated making changes in its structure and content. In the new general education program, all first-year writing courses are linked to courses in the social issues category. The eighteen to twenty social issues courses offered each semester cover a wide range of topics (e.g., "War and the American Experience," "Changing Family Forms," "Environmental Issues in Society," "Poverty and Welfare in America"). All are taught by regular tenure-track faculty, and most are large lectures, so each course has between four to eight linked writing sections. Writing instructors grade assignments written for the linked writing class, while social issues faculty and TAs grade papers written for those classes.

The new curriculum has greatly increased the complexity of preparing new TAs as well as supervising experienced TAs. Prior to 1997, the program directors developed a common first assignment for the six-week course outline, and each pair of mentor teachers designed the second assignment for their instructional group, a total of five assignments. In the new program, however, these assignments must be tailored to fit the issues and content of the social issues courses, so as many as forty different assignments (two for each writing link) may be needed. As a result, the program directors cannot provide close oversight over the writing assignments that existed under the previous general education program.

Mentor teachers continue to conduct the orientation and practicum sessions, but an additional mentor—the course coordinator—has been added. The course coordinator serves as the liaison between social issues faculty and the writing instructors for each group of linked writing sections, and they, rather than the mentor teachers, are now responsible for designing the first two writing assignments, based on topics, readings, and issues from the social issues course. They also assist both new and experienced TAs throughout the term in developing subsequent assignments and in linking the two courses. With the increased complexity of the program's curriculum and links between social issues and writing classes, the instructional scaffolding provided by the six-week course outlines prepared for the new TAs has become a valuable resource for all TAs.[4]

The practicum too has been modified and now consists of a ten-week program during the fall semester. Because the new TAs are teaching many different links, it no longer deals with assignment development and cannot address problems related to the content and issues of the linked social issues classes. However, the practicum continues to focus on rhetorical principles, to introduce the new TAs to practical strategies (e.g., guiding students through the writing process, helping them read texts assigned in their writing and social issues classes more critically), and to assist the TAs in resolving instructional problems.

## AFTER THE PRACTICUM: STRATEGIES AND STRUCTURES FOR SUSTAINING REFLECTION

Introducing TAs to reflection and modeling it during the practicum are not enough to ensure that it will continue; structures must be created to sustain and support reflection. Within the USC context, the model that gradually developed consisted of multiple sites: advanced workshops, student evaluations, staff development projects, and teaching portfolios. Although the original impetus for a multisite model was pragmatic, it proved to be a serendipitous choice. Once fully implemented, multiple sites encouraged systematic and ongoing reflection and created a synergy that infused reflective practice throughout the program. The remainder of this chapter describes the various sites of the USC postpracticum preparation program.

## ADVANCED WORKSHOPS FOR EXPERIENCED TAs

When I became director, continuing staff development was conducted through one-hour meetings of small groups of TAs that were scheduled biweekly throughout the academic year and led by mentor teachers known as Instructional Coordinators. Their purpose was to "coordinate" instruction within the program through a discussion of instructional practices and problems. Even though meetings were held at eight to ten different times in an effort to accommodate the TAs' diverse schedules, attendance was irregular. In addition, the meetings were generally ineffective because the group discussions lacked focus and direction.

After several unsuccessful attempts to enforce an attendance requirement[5] and to make the biweekly meetings more productive, the program's assistant directors and I replaced them with two longer "advanced" workshops, one each semester. Scheduled on the day before the semester begins, these workshops continue the small group discussion format and are conducted by the mentor teachers but follow a carefully planned agenda. These advanced workshops enable the program both to require attendance and to address instructional issues systematically. Prior to the institution of the new general education program, we selected topics and issues suggested by TAs or mentor teachers, sometimes having a general discussion on broad topics such as evaluation and feedback strategies and sometimes focusing on program-specific concerns, e.g., relating specific class activities to the program's writing competencies. We also adapted materials developed for the most recent orientation, thereby presenting new perspectives and strategies to the experienced TAs and introducing them to changes made to improve the program's curriculum and pedagogy.

After the writing courses were linked to the social issues courses, the content and role of the advanced workshops changed. Now they are organized according to course groups and focus on strategies to strengthen the links between the two courses. In addition, TAs must also attend three additional workshops during the semester, organized by course and focusing on assignment design (Blum).

## STUDENT EVALUATIONS AS A CATALYST FOR REFLECTION

Too often student evaluations are used primarily by WPAs and higher level administrators as a means of surveillance. They scan them to identify TAs whose ratings and student comments indicate instructional problems, and these TAs are then given warnings and/or additional training. While evaluations can serve as a catalyst for reflection if instructors learn to use them productively, research shows that most faculty typically do not use student evaluations to improve their teaching unless they consult with a skilled peer or professional consultant (Marincovich 46–7). When used to initiate reflection on classroom practices, evaluations can help TAs improve their instructional effectiveness. The first step in turning student evaluations into an opportunity for reflection is to revise the standard university evaluation form so that it asks questions specifically about writing instruction. For example, we added questions on a range of topics: evaluation ("Feedback on essays/other graded assignments was valuable"), course design ("Assigned readings contributed to an understanding and investigation of essay topics and issues"; "Encouraged students to participate in their learning, e.g. through discussion, projects, study groups and other appropriate activities"), and student-teacher interaction ("Instructor was open to points of view other than his/her own"; "Was accessible to students") as well as an overall assessment of progress ("Your writing skills improved as a result of this course"). By focusing students' and TAs' attention on the classroom interaction and activities involved in teaching writing, questions such as these help instructors identify their strengths and weaknesses. TAs receive a summary of students' responses to all questions with results reported both as an individual average and a program average. They also receive a typed copy of students' open-ended comments with all positive comments organized in one group and all suggestions for improvements in another group.

TAs are usually anxious about their evaluations, as they worry that low ratings or unfavorable comments might affect their continued employment or future letters of recommendation. However, most are uncertain as to how to respond to negative student responses. To allay their anxieties, new TAs are told that additional, individualized training will be provided for any instructors who have difficulty during their first semester of teaching, and they are assured that experience and further training resolve most problems. To help new TAs interpret their evaluations and to model ways to reflect on student responses, their first evaluations are returned in the small instructional groups established during orientation and continued during the practicum, as they provide a safe, supportive context for discussion. Prior to the discussion, mentor teachers review the evaluations of new TAs so they can identify issues raised by the evaluations and plan the discussion. The mentors begin by discussing their own evaluations; usually they select one question that had mixed student responses and then relate those responses to open-ended comments. Whenever possible, they point out successful changes that they have made in response to previous student evaluations and conclude by indicating how they might respond to current suggestions. Mentors then invite the TAs to discuss their evaluations, facilitating the discussions by commending TAs for positive ratings and comments, encouraging them to reflect on less positive or negative responses, and helping them identify how to modify their classroom practices based on the evaluations.

The program encourages further reflection on classroom practices by offering TAs a special midsemester evaluation that enables them to receive feedback on their instruction early enough to make adjustments. Offered initially as an option during the second semester, midsemester evaluations proved so successful that they are now required of all new TAs during their first semester of teaching. The mentor teachers, who are trained as facilitators, conduct these evaluations as part of their mentoring responsibilities.

The midsemester evaluations use the small group instructional diagnosis (SGID) format (Weimer, Svinicki, and Bauer), a model in which a facilitator conducts a discussion during the last twenty minutes of a class. After the instructor leaves the room, the facilitator places students into small discussion groups and asks the groups to identify two or three aspects of the class that are helping them learn and anything that is not helping them learn. Following the small group discussions, the facilitator conducts a whole class discussion to clarify their comments and determine areas of consensus among the groups. Afterwards, the facilitator meets with the TAs to reflect on the comments and to strategize appropriate responses to the students' feedback. Because the SGID is a time- and labor-intensive process, this type of midterm evaluation is limited to new TAs; experienced TAs use a required university form to receive written feedback from their students at midterm.

## ENCOURAGING INSTRUCTIONAL EXPERIMENTATION— STAFF DEVELOPMENT PROJECTS

Central to reflective practice is the "frame experiment" where practitioners identify a problem, then design and assess a response to that problem (Schön). Throughout the practicum and during advanced workshops, TAs are encouraged to develop their own lessons and assignments to achieve their instructional objectives, then to evaluate their success and make any needed changes. This expectation has been formalized to require all TAs to submit a yearly "staff development project," which can be any successful assignment, lesson, or activity that they developed and used during the previous year and that demonstrates their continuing growth as an instructor. In addition to asking them to describe their project and procedures so that another instructor can adapt and use their ideas, the format encourages reflection by asking them to explain why they developed the lesson or assignment and to evaluate its effectiveness. To disseminate these projects to other TAs, the Writing Program maintains a "Rhetorical Resources File," a compilation of projects stored in a filing cabinet located in the TA work room, where TAs can browse and copy any they wish to use. Jack Blum, Associate Director of the USC Writing Program, initiated this project and continues to oversee it. He has created an index, cross-listed by topic, activity, and course link, that enables TAs to find useful materials easily and plans to place the file online.

## RETROSPECTIVE REFLECTION—THE TEACHING PORTFOLIO

Teaching portfolios, an increasingly popular means of evaluating instructional performance and encouraging continuing faculty development (Zubizaretta), are also an excellent way to engage TAs in sustained reflection. TAs must submit two teaching portfolios, which are reviewed by and discussed with the program's directors, during their first four years of teaching: the first during their second year, after completing three semesters as a TA, and the second during their fourth year, after completing seven semesters as a TA.[6] For their portfolios, TAs write a reflective statement that explains their philosophy of teaching composition, then select sample syllabi, assignments, instructional materials, student papers, and teaching evaluations to demonstrate that philosophy and show their development as an instructor. They conclude the process by meeting with one of the program's directors to review and discuss their portfolios. The portfolio review held during the TAs' second year is particularly crucial in their continuing development as teachers because TAs set goals for improving their instruction during the review and discussion. The fourth-year review provides a capstone experience for TAs as they trace their growth over almost four years and construct a product that they can use when applying for academic positions.

## TRANSFORMING A PROGRAM'S CULTURE: STRATEGIES FOR CHANGE

The program of continued TA preparation and training that I have described was developed over a number of years and continues to evolve as conditions within the program change. Managing change is rarely easy, as there is usually resistance, even when change is clearly needed. In addition, WPAs must work within constraints of limited time and resources as well as contend with academic practices and attitudes that may officially support good teaching but neglect it in practice. As a result, WPAs need to find relatively low cost, low effort approaches that will be supported by powerful faculty constituencies and higher administration. Although this program is situated within the institutional context at USC, several of the underlying principles and strategies that contribute to its success can be generalized to other settings.

First, good communication with all constituencies is essential. Particularly in the early stages, I was careful to explain our overall strategy to administrators and to report regularly on the improvements we were making to the TA preparation program and their positive effect on classroom instruction. I also consulted with academic departments regarding their requirements and scheduled the practicum and other requirements to minimize scheduling conflicts. Second, I avoided making too many changes at once. Adopting an incremental approach not only reduced resistance to change but also allowed time to evaluate the effectiveness of any changes made and to modify them. Third, I set priorities and addressed the most important ones first. Initial efforts, for example, focused on the preparation program for new TAs, but once that foundation was in place, activities and requirements were added to continue preparation after the practicum. Fourth, I began by modifying existing procedures and structures, as these are usually easier to change than the process of instituting new ones. Once early changes proved successful, I built on them and added new requirements. For example, changing the student evaluation forms and modeling new ways of interpreting the ratings and comments was a fairly easy change and one that we made relatively early. When new requirements such as the advanced work-shops and teaching portfolios were added later, they had a clear rationale so that TAs could see their value. New requirements should be presented, whenever possible, as replacements rather than additions. The staff development project and the teaching portfolio, for example, were introduced as alternatives to the biweekly meetings that had been reduced to two advanced workshops.

Transforming a program's culture so that it leads TAs to become reflective practitioners takes time, imagination, and insight into an institution's culture and context. Despite the relative lack of attention to continuing TA preparation after the practicum, such a program is essential if TAs are to continue their development as writing teachers. When programs, such as the one described in this chapter, succeed in creating a culture of reflective practice, they raise the overall level of instructional effectiveness, the ultimate goal of all TA preparation.

## NOTES

1. Developing the TA preparation program at USC is an ongoing, collaborative effort that is still underway. Between 1984–1996 when I directed the program, the program's assistant directors—John Holland and Jack Blum, now Director and Associate Director of the USC Writing Program, respectively, and Irene Clark, now Director of Composition at CSU, Northridge—assumed responsibility for different parts of the process. Many of our mentor teachers, known as Instructional Coordinators, also made significant contributions. John Holland and Jack Blum are primarily responsible for changes since 1997, which respond to the curriculum required by USC's new general education program.
2. For a full description of the initial program, see Manning (79–83).
3. Mentor teachers, who are chosen from among the most experienced and effective instructors teaching in the program, are predominantly graduate students in English but include some instructors from other departments. They receive additional compensation for their assistance in planning and conducting the summer orientation and release time for conducting practicum sessions and mentoring new TAs during the academic year.
4. Jack Blum reports that a recent program survey shows that these course outlines are widely used by experienced TAs. Because many TAs teach different linked courses each semester, they rely heavily on the course outlines to help them plan and develop their new courses.
5. The TAs' academic departments support required attendance at the orientation and practicum because it is a condition of appointment. However, they are less supportive of continued staff development when it involves meetings during the semester, as the time required is seen as infringing on TAs' work as graduate students.
6. When the portfolio review was initially instituted, university policy limited TA support to four years. Although TAs often received extensions of support, these were not guaranteed, so the second review occurs during their last official semester of teaching.

## WORKS CITED

Applebee, Arthur. *Contexts for Learning to Write.* Norwood, NJ: Ablex, 1984.

Blum, Jack. Personal communication. June 7, 2000.

Farris, Christine. *Subject to Change: New Composition Instructors' Theory and Practice.* Cresskill, NJ: Hampton, 1996.

Foster, David. *A Primer for Writing Teachers: Theories, Theorists, Issues, Problems.* Upper Montclair, NJ: Boynton/Cook, 1983.

Hillocks, George. *Teaching Writing as Reflective Practice.* New York: Teachers College Press, 1995.

Leverenz, Carrie, and Amy Goodburn. "Professionalizing TA Training: Commitment to Teaching or Rhetorical Response to Market Crisis?" *WPA* 22. 1/2 (1998): 9–32.

Manning, Sylvia. "The Freshman Writing Program at the University of Southern California." *Options for the Teaching of English: Freshman Composition.* Ed. Jasper P. Neel. New York: MLA, 1978. 79–83.

Marincovich, Michelle. "Using Student Feedback to Improve Teaching." *Changing Practices in Evaluating Teaching.* Ed. Peter Seldin and Associates. Bolton, MA: Anker, 1999. 45–69.

North, Stephen. *The Making of Knowledge in Composition: Portrait of an Emerging Field.* Portsmouth, NH: Heinemann Boynton/Cook, 1987.

Rankin, Elizabeth. *Seeing Yourself as a Teacher: Conversations with Five New Teachers in a University Writing Program.* Urbana, IL: NCTE, 1994.

Schön, Donald A. *Educating the Reflective Practitioner.* San Francisco: Jossey-Bass, 1987.

Sprague, Jo, and Jody D. Nyquist. "TA Supervision." *Teaching Assistant Training in the 1990s.* Ed. Jody D. Nyquist, Robert D. Abbot, and Donald H. Wulff. San Francisco: Jossey-Bass, 1989. 37–56.

Weimer, Maryellen, Marilla D. Svinicki, and Gabriele Bauer. "Designing Programs to Prepare TAs to Teach." *Teaching Assistant Training in the 1990s.* Ed. Jody D. Nyquist, Robert D. Abbot, and Donald H. Wulff. San Francisco: Jossey-Bass, 1989. 57–70.

Yancey, Kathleen Blake. *Reflection in the Writing Classroom.* Logan: Utah State UP, 1998.

Zubizaretta, John. "Evaluating Teaching through Portfolios." *Changing Practices in Evaluating Teaching.* Ed. Peter Seldin and Associates. Bolton, MA: Anker, 1999. 162–82.

# 14. Experience and Reflection in Multiple Contexts: Preparing TAs for the Artistry of Professional Practice

CHRIS BURNHAM AND REBECCA JACKSON

*[E]xperiences in order to be educative must lead out into an expanding world of subject-matter, a subject matter of facts or information and of ideas. This condition is satisfied only as the educator views teaching and learning as a continuous process of reconstruction of experience.*
—Dewey (*Experience and Education,* 87)

*Experience . . . when reflected upon . . . solves more problems which have troubled philosophers and resolves more hard and fast dualisms than any other theme of thought.*
—Dewey (*Experience and Nature,* 393)

Dewey reminds us that learning and growth reside in reflection, in our attempts to make meaning from various, often competing, theories, practices, experiences, and perspectives. This process is complicated and enriched as we bring ourselves to multiple contexts and play radically different roles. A professor, TA educator, or administrator in one instant might shift from being a self-assured professional following a familiar plan to solve a well-defined problem to being a vulnerable improvisor, an artist, responding to the surprise of the moment, pursuing the opportunity to reconcile various experiences and perspectives, ultimately devising new moves to address the situation at hand. Reflecting on this action after it has occurred, this same professional may reinterpret and reframe the situation once again, theorizing her own practices in the process and laying the foundation for future action and reflection.

Drawing on Dewey, Donald Schön argues that professionals "reflect in and on action," actively and recursively engaging the tensions between theory and experience in local contexts in order to solve problems, uncover and evaluate tacit knowledge, make and remake theory. While a novice may respond to the unexpected with confusion and fear, a professional welcomes the unexpected as an opportunity in Dewey's sense to "stop and think," to join "observation and memory," and enter the "heart of reflection" (*Experience and Education* 64). Recognizing an anomaly in the routine, she focuses her attention, reflects to frame a new question to guide her performance, and, in an analytical or critical act, devises a new plan. The professional carefully attends to outcomes to evaluate whether the problem is solved, or further complicated. This experience is then assimilated into the tacit theory-of-practice that will guide her subsequent actions; it becomes part of the knowledge and experience base she invokes once another problem is encountered.

Reflection in and on action, the "artistry" of practice (Schön 13), is what we strive to teach our TAs, though the art resists direct teaching (17). Schön argues that such reflection can be modeled and encouraged through a reflective practicum that places professionals and novices in relation to one another under circumstances closely resembling the architect's or musician's studio, the psychoanalyst's or counselor's office, or the encounter between consultant and client—all loci where professional problems are posed, analyzed, reflected upon, and eventually solved. Working with the professional as coach, consultant, and supervisor, novices can begin to learn the artistry of practice in the profession.

We believe our teacher preparation program at New Mexico State resembles and, in many respects, actually improves upon Schön's reflective practicum. Yearly we support approximately sixty TAs working on PhDs in rhetoric and professional communication or MAs in rhetoric, literature, or creative writing. Each semester our TAs teach as many as 2,500 students in more than 100 sections from a menu of five courses ranging from first-year writing through junior-level advanced composition and technical and professional communication. To capture the complexities inherent in our profession, the program (1) places TAs in *real* contexts that require different modes of being and communicating—as novices in pre-semester orientation, students in a composition theory course, teachers in the classroom, consultants in the Writing Center, growing professionals in advanced course work in composition, writing program, and writing center studies, and eventually as mentors to less experienced TAs; (2) encourages them to reflect upon the similarities and differences among the contexts and through reflection to discriminate exemplary practices from acceptable practices; (3) urges them to use reflection to theorize their own practices; and (4) supports reflective practice through modeling and discussion of options for dealing with problems in context.

When it works best, our preparation program creates a supersaturated solution of experience designed finally to yield the perfect crystal of professional identity, interweaving teaching and being taught, writing and reading about the teaching of writing, interacting with professors, peers, and students in formal and informal circumstances, mixing all these in the solution of life, and finally achieving the worldview of the professional—thinking, acting, *being* the work to be done. Ours is a holistic preparation program, one that depends upon a coherence among parts. We have come to call this interrelatedness of parts "program-ness." Although an awkward term, "program-ness" invokes a gestalt that parallels the phenomena elaborated and valued by Schön.

In the following sections, we sketch twenty years of program growth in a way that reinforces our theme of professional practice and elaborates the schema by which we facilitate complex and exemplary professional practice—working with TAs in multiple modes and contexts, modeling professional and reflective practices, and creating formal and informal spaces for TA reflection.

## 1981–1984: ESTABLISHING GOALS AND OBJECTIVES

Our experience of coming to "program-ness" began in 1981 when six TAs taught six sections of a skill- and drill-based basic writing course and six sections of traditional freshman composition. They worked independently, without common objectives or course materials for either course, and with very little preparation and support. To address this problem, Chris convened a group of TAs who were interested in writing pedagogy and who were particularly impressed by his own approach to writing courses, a collaborative model supported by Kenneth Bruffee's *A Short Course in Writing.* As the semester progressed, several adjuncts who also taught basic and freshman writing courses joined the working group. In weekly meetings, the group discussed using peer evaluation and developed guidelines and supporting materials for small writing groups. The group was also quite curious about the evaluation practices Chris used to measure and encourage student success, including a pre/post common writing sample in the remedial course and portfolios in the first-year course. Near the end of that semester, the members of the subgroup agreed to use Bruffee's text the following semester, to work through the text as a group—writing in collaborative peer groups just as their students would—and to use this semester-long experience to rough out a common syllabus for the first-year course. The TAs also decided to adopt the pre/post common writing sample in the basic writing course and portfolios in the first-year course. Thus, Chris's initial effort at staff development established the pattern for subsequent training. Training was collaborative, interactive, and, at this point, voluntary. The group strove to identify, improve, and facilitate exemplary practice as it was available either in professional literature or in their own teaching. This working group, in which training met teachers' real and specific needs, marked the first step toward developing a program identity.

By the end of Chris's second year, the working group had recommended the Bruffee text for course-wide adoption and had roughed out a set of first-year course objectives emphasizing writing as a complex and recursive process that enabled writers to accomplish various academic, civic, and personal purposes. They had also designed a set of argumentative assignments and recommended a collaborative, workshop-based pedagogy. They identified evaluation standards for existing courses as major concerns and adopted the pre/post common writing sample and portfolio evaluation systems Chris had transported from his previous work on large-scale program and student assessment. During the semester, they participated in holistic evaluations of the common writing sample completed by all students in the basic writing courses and associated benchmarking and other staff training to make the evaluation valid and reliable. In addition, they collaborated when evaluating first-year writing portfolios with an eye toward adjusting their teaching in response to student performance. In sum, the group developed a tradition of openness, curiosity, evaluation, innovation, and collaborative reflection among the TAs and other writing teachers. Stated course objectives and recommended pedagogies addressed not only what students should learn through the course but also how the course might be taught. These moves marked the first of several steps toward "program-ness."

## 1984–1988: DEVELOPING A PRE-SEMESTER PREPARATION PROGRAM AND A COURSE IN THEORY AND PEDAGOGY

In the mid-1980s, the program began to develop a stronger identity. Chris and others worked to solve the longstanding problem of course availability, one that resulted in the first-year course enrolling large numbers of upper-division students who had been unable to take the course earlier and who deemed it—the only required course in the university—a bureaucratic nuisance. The department received resources to guarantee new students access to the first-year course if not in their initial semester, at least during their first year. The resources came, in large, because the program had gained credibility by instituting internal quality controls, including the holistically scored pre/post essay in basic writing classes. Originally designed to demonstrate that writers had improved and were ready for the first-year course, its real value turned out to be staff development. TAs were involved from top to bottom of the process, from test development to scoring. Understanding the value of establishing standards through common evaluation, we developed a parallel evaluation activity for the first-year course. Near the end of the semester, all students completed an exit essay that staff read holistically. Writing on the exit essay showed TAs the range of actual student accomplishment in the course, and thus encouraged them to develop reasonable and appropriate expectations for their students' writing portfolios. The last weeks of the semester were devoted to reviewing "ideal" exit standards in light of concrete performance and helping students complete revisions and reflective essays for their course portfolios.

Another credibility- and identity-building program activity was instituted during this period. Again following the suggestion of TAs, Chris and others initiated a pre-semester preparation program designed to familiarize them with a newly articulated course structure, new evaluation practices, and current writing pedagogies. This preparation program—modified and extended over the years—continues today. All new TAs are required to attend the pre-semester session, which spans five full days during the week before classes begin. Until 1997, pre-semester orientation was devoted exclusively to preparing new TAs to teach our first-year writing course.

Creating community among new TAs was and still is a primary objective of teacher preparation. During the first day of the pre-semester orientation, new TAs are asked to introduce themselves to the group by explaining who they are, why they have enrolled in graduate school, and what they expect from the week of training. Participants use freewriting to explore these questions and to tell the group enough about themselves to establish an identity. Program leaders—the WPA and experienced TAs working as writing program assistants—then explain that scheduled activities are systematically designed to address their concerns, including the objectives and set of assignments for the first-year course, the university's demographics, and how the structure and substance of the course prepares students to do these things. TA preparation moves from global conceptual concerns—what role writing could play in a student's life, how writing is effectively taught, how the program aims at multiple purposes of writing, especially writing for civic purposes, political action, and personal human development—to concrete and specific issues such as what to do during the first weeks of class.

Leaders invite conversation and critique as they discuss teaching writing as a process, using collaboration and peer groups effectively, responding to and evaluating writing, and using the portfolio evaluation system. Using frequent formal, informal, and collaborative writing activities, teacher educators model how writing might be taught and give TAs the opportunity to practice these approaches. During the orientation, TAs complete many of the same assignments their students will complete and participate in peer-evaluation sessions of writing they produce. In addition, TAs write an exit essay similar to the one their students will write and participate in a benchmarking session on exit essays to introduce them to the level of work our students produce.

From the beginning, leaders stress that the pre-semester work will not provide a recipe to be followed. Instead, pre-semester work helps TAs become familiar enough with the program that they and their students can work with rather than against the program requirements. Actually teaching the class is the only way to become adept at recommended program practices. TAs learn how the course is structured—as a series of loops modeling the recursive process of writing, with sufficient time for students and teachers to practice their way toward mastery. Just as students don't have to get everything right from the beginning, so new TAs can become more competent as the semester progresses. Pre-semester preparation and additional support—forums for readings, discussing, and reflecting—are needed to make experiences rich and productive for TAs and students. Our goal is to provide enough support so that cognitive dissonance does not overwhelm and so that TAs can develop sufficient self- and professional awareness, even the first time they teach a course. Developing intensive pre-semester orientation has been a substantial step in defining ourselves as a program.

Shortly after Chris established pre-semester training, he began to implement a full-semester course to investigate, support, even challenge the pedagogy of the program. Designed originally at the request of TAs as a one-time graduate seminar, "The Composing Process" eventually became "Problems in Teaching Freshman Composition" and, as the purpose and scope of the course was further developed, "Composition Theory and Pedagogy." This course, required of all new TAs unless they have substantial teaching experience and/or a comparable theory/pedagogy course, carries full academic credit. It is not a practicum in teaching writing devoted exclusively to day-to-day classroom issues, although these are certainly discussed. Rather, the course elaborates the theoretical and practical basis of the first-year course that can only be suggested in pre-semester training. TAs explore current scholarship in composition studies, especially writing processes, effective peer collaboration and teacher response, reflection, revision, portfolio evaluation, computers and writing, and effective approaches to grammar instruction. Our goal is twofold: We want to engage TAs in current conversations about teaching writing while cultivating their critical capacity to construct useful knowledge from conflicting frames of reference.

Course assignments support this objective: TAs keep a reflective teaching journal, observe and reflect upon a class taught by one of their peers, and submit an elaborated situation or "case study" from the class they are currently teaching for their peers' comments and reflections. They also develop a teaching portfolio, including a collection of teaching materials and resources as well as a teaching philosophy. Crucial to developing professional identities, the portfolio showcases the products of TAs' reflections on action, their reconstructions of multiple experiences. In another central project for the course, TAs conduct formal research either to challenge and replace current practice or to confirm and further elaborate that practice. While some TAs resist this project, arguing that they are novices and unable to critique or challenge institutionalized professional practice, many complete the assignment successfully, provoking significant changes in our/their writing program. This semester, for example, several TAs focused this assignment on our first-year writing course guide and argued for altering the sequence of writing assignments. Their rationale was strong, grounded in composition theory, surveys of and interviews with their fellow TAs, and their own experiences as teachers of the course and Writing Center consultants. They are currently revising both the sequence of assignments in the guide and accompanying readings. As mentioned earlier, this particular assignment is more successful for some TAs than others, especially those who need more teaching experience, more exposure to theory and application, and more reflection to interrogate existing practice. In these cases, the assignment begins critical conversations that TAs will flesh out later as they read, discuss, gain more experience, and reflect. For us—as professors and administrators—TAs' varying responses to this assignment have confirmed our belief that a multimode and multicontext training program that extends throughout a TA's entire term is the best way to develop the self-confident professional identity needed for productive critique and reflection. Individual activities, either presemester preparation or semester-length course work, need to be embedded in a fully articulated training program.

## 1993–1997: ALTERING TA WORK LOADS AND RECONFIGURING THE WRITING CENTER

Despite advances in training and professional development, TAs continued to labor under a strenuous work load. To address the problem, we redefined the graduate assistant work load, assigning each TA four credit hours of teaching—at that time, either one first-year writing course or two basic developmental classes. An ill-advised legislative mandate that research universities in New Mexico would not be funded to offer non-college credit courses resulted in shifting developmental work to our local branch community college, so we could no longer, to the detriment of our students and TAs, offer basic writing. However, within a year the university expanded the writing program and writing requirement to include two courses—first-year writing and an advanced course later in a student's career. Our TAs teach only one of these classes each semester. Additional working hours needed to total the twenty hours per week required by the TA contract are made up with what we call "nonclassroom assignments," including work in the Writing Center.

Changes in TA work load and institutional policy meant significant changes for the Writing Center itself. Formally staffed by a combination of paid peer tutors, adjunct faculty, and TAs, the Writing Center was now staffed exclusively by TAs from graduate programs in creative writing, literature, and rhetoric and professional communication. In fact, during their first semester of teaching, all new TAs were required to complete their four hours a week of nonclassroom duty as consultants in the Writing Center, a requirement still in effect today. The Writing Center also became an informal locus of TA training, a place TAs met to discuss both their experiences as new teachers of writing and the reading they were doing in composition theory and pedagogy and a place for experienced TAs working as Writing Center Assistant Coordinators to add administrative work to their experiences as students of composition theory and pedagogy and teachers/consultants of writing.

## 1997–PRESENT: REARTICULATING THE ROLE OF THE WRITING CENTER IN TA TRAINING

In 1997, after several years of hiring non-tenure track faculty to oversee the Writing Center, the department hired Rebecca as an assistant professor and Director of the Writing Center. Like most new Writing Center directors, Rebecca spent her first semester trying to learn as much as possible about consultant attitudes, needs, and objectives; the center's history, mission, policies and procedures; its working relations with faculty and departments; its role in TA training; and its relationship to the Writing Program. Through her research, Rebecca identified several pressing needs. First, separate pre-semester preparation programs for Writing Center consulting and teaching first-year writing needed to be meaningfully combined to reflect the program's stated philosophy that TAs learn to teach by working with students in multiple settings, and the Writing Center pre-semester preparation program itself needed to be more extensive and fully theorized. TAs also needed multiple opportunities for continued conversation and reflection—professional development—during the semester. Ongoing Writing Center education would be vital to all TAs' success in their work with students, but it would be especially important to TAs struggling to find connections between their consulting responsibilities and their future careers as creative writers or teachers of literature.

Revised procedures were in place by the spring of 1998. Today, our week-long pre-semester orientation program fully integrates preparation for teaching first-year writing with preparation for Writing Center consulting. Writing Center pre-semester orientation and ongoing professional development activities have been extended, incorporating reading and discussion, modeling, guided practice, and formal and informal reflection to accomplish several large objectives: improve consultant commitment to Writing Center work; help consultants recognize and reconcile their overlapping and competing roles in multiple contexts; and facilitate professional practices, including the ability to construct working knowledge from the intersection of theory and practice.

In pre-semester preparation, for example, new TAs/Writing Center consultants explore the theoretical underpinnings of Writing Center work and the often conflicting practices that arise from these theories (Should tutoring *always* be nondirective? What's the best way to help ESL writers?). For our last training session, new TAs read Stephen North's "The Idea of a Writing Center" and Jeff Brooks's "Minimalist Tutoring" alongside Linda K. Shamoon and Deborah H. Burns's "A Critique of Pure Tutoring" and Judith Powers's "Rethinking Writing Center Conferencing Strategies for the ESL Writer," readings that speak to and against one another in provocative ways. We then discuss readings in small groups, record our thoughts on overhead transparencies, and present these ideas to the larger group for continued discussion. The goal here is threefold: to help consultants acquire a knowledge base; to explore differences (and similarities) between the Writing Center and the composition classroom, the consultant and the teacher, and consultants in different local settings; and to open up a dialogue about the dialectical nature of theory and practice. Last, consultants pull these conversations together by constructing metaphors for Writing Center work. A forum for reflection, this activity brings us full circle—from understanding of multiple perspectives, to evaluation, to reconciliation and reconstruction.

New consultants also observe mock tutorials between senior practitioners and engage in their own "practice consultations" with the help of experienced consultants. In mock tutorials, the senior practitioner who has agreed to play the role of Writing Center consultant works with another senior practitioner on a real piece of writing (usually a journal entry) that the "student" senior practitioner has just completed and the "consultant" senior practitioner has never seen. This element of surprise is key, lending the mock consultation an authenticity often missing in staged consultations. As twenty or more new consultants watch, consultant and writer work together in a thirty-five to forty-minute-long conference, engaging in the back and forth, collaborative construction of meaning that characterizes Writing Center consultations. We then use the observers' notes and questions as springboards for large group discussion, asking the senior practitioner who played the role of consultant to verbalize her thoughts at key moments in the consultation, to try to articulate both her knowing in action and her reflection in action, what Schön describes as a "rethink[ing] of knowing in action in ways that go beyond available rules, facts, theories and operations" (36). In making their thinking visible, senior consultants attempt to capture and convey the artistry of consulting for new, less experienced consultants; they make explicit both *what* and *how,* in much the same way we, as consultants, help writers understand readers' thoughts through methods like Peter Elbow's "movies of the mind."

Next, new consultants work with each other in mock tutorial sessions with senior practitioners as guides. Using journal and learning log work completed for their teaching composition orientation sessions and "case studies" Rebecca has developed over the years, new consultants practice the art of tutoring, receive feedback from their peers and experienced consultants, practice some more, and then reflect on their practice. Robert Tremmel's idea for encouraging reflective practice works well in this situation: Rebecca often asks consultants to describe a specific moment in their mock consultation, to reflect on this moment, to explore what they were thinking during the moment, what they think now, and how the moment might be reframed, viewed from another perspective. The object, as Tremmel says, is to create a space for consultants' voices and introduce them to the value of reflective practice.

Clearly, TAs learn the most about consulting by tutoring with writers from across the disciplines and at various stages in their academic careers, from first-year undergraduates to graduate students working on MA and PhD degrees. Most who visit the Writing Center, however, are students enrolled in English 111, the same course new TAs teach during their first year in the program. Thus, new consultants are engaged in a triangulation of sorts—teacher, consultant, graduate student—that invites them to consider the teaching of writing, the coaching of writing, and *writing,* from multiple perspectives. Consulting with writers individually works to extend and complicate TAs' evolving under-standing of what it means to write and to teach writing; it demands that teach-ers "interrogate, reflect on, and transform the theoretical, personal, and institu-tional voices that inform their teaching" (Jacobs et al. 2). One-to-one consulting in the Writing Center, for example, may clarify a TA's understanding of the complexities of individual writing processes and further develop her ability to "reflect in action," to successfully negotiate unique situations in practice by reframing, experimenting, and improvising. At the same time, collaboration with writers may complicate a TA's belief in the individual nature of writing or in the value of delivering lectures in writing courses, prompting her to rethink her classroom practices.

Perhaps more important than the actual experience of consulting with indi-vidual writers is the time new TAs spend observing, working side by side with, discussing, even arguing with their fellow consultants. During, between, and after tutoring sessions, consultants *consult* with each other—about questions writers have, about particular consulting experiences, about classroom situa-tions, about problems, triumphs, strategies, feelings, epiphanies. Consultants practice, but they also *talk* about practice, trying on the metalanguage that sig-nals professional understanding.

Ongoing professional development is encouraged through regular Writing Center meetings, a Writing Center listserv, and a two-tiered system of evalua-tion: Each enables TAs to further discuss and reflect upon the multiple contexts and roles they occupy. Staff meetings, for example, work to build community and encourage critical conversation among consultants with different program-matic allegiances. Twice a month during the fall semester and once a month dur-ing the spring semester, Writing Center staff convene to discuss issues and strategies, solve problems, listen to a talk, commiserate, tell stories, seek advice. One week, a professor from the biology department might speak with us about working effectively with students writing papers in the sciences; our next meeting may involve something more informal, a troubleshooting session, for example. Listening to each other, consultants realize that they have all encountered puzzling situations, that even the most experienced consultants lack confidence sometimes. In at least one meeting during the semester, Rebecca asks TAs to reflect aloud on the connections and tensions they are finding among their roles as teachers, graduate students, and consultants.

The Writing Center listserv provides yet another forum for reflection on action and goal setting, one that doesn't require a special meeting time or place. Instead, consultants can log on, ask questions, and respond to queries and comments at their leisure. The advantage of this forum is that it encourages discussion from those who might otherwise remain silent. Furthermore, they are recorded thoughts that can be archived, returned to, and used in ways that we can't use spoken discourse. More to the point of this chapter, our Writing Center listserv stimulates the kind of reflection that leads to reconstruction of experience. Excerpts from a listserv discussion on "authority" illustrate this well:

> . . . how the heck are we supposed to balance teaching and consulting, the two positions seems so antithetical. . . . I have to literally slap myself on the wrist to stop being the teacher. It's incredibly difficult to sit back and let the student direct the session when you know the assignment . . . and already have preconceived notions about what students find difficult. . . . (Duhamel)

*   *   *

> My experience is that [students] are expecting something like direction from us. And I believe it is our obligation to provide the direction they are looking for. Sometimes . . . that means assuming authority and modeling productive behaviors for students and then divesting yourself of that authority and investing it with the student. (England)

Like Writing Center meetings and the listserv, evaluation of consultants' work in the Writing Center is grounded in conversation and reflection among Rebecca, Writing Center Assistant Coordinators, and the consultant. In their first semester, consultants are asked to list their consulting expectations and goals. At mid-semester, Assistant Coordinators observe consultants in at least two sessions and record their observations, while consultants complete a self-evaluation of their work in the Writing Center using items from our Consultant Evaluation form to guide their responses. Assistant Coordinators and consultants then discuss their respective observations and reflections and write a collaborative evaluation of the consultant's best practices. The collaborative, highly negotiable nature of the evaluation system seems to diffuse any tensions that might arise when TAs, however experienced, evaluate their fellow TAs.

Consultants then meet with Rebecca to discuss their evaluation in relation to their expectations and goals. This process gets them ready for the second stage of evaluation, writing the goal statement. After consultants have tutored in the Writing Center for at least a semester, they draft a goal statement for the following semester discussing their perceived strengths and weaknesses, goals for the semester, and ways to achieve those goals. Consultants then tape and listen to at least one of their sessions that semester, evaluating the session against their semester goals. Evaluation at this point is self evaluation, an invitation, as Kathleen Blake Yancey puts it, to "tell our [own] stories of learning" (53). This kind of reflection is vital; without it we "live the stories others have scripted for us: in a *most* unreflective, unhealthy way" (53). Goal statements are founded upon reflection; reflection generates connections; connections generate interest and motivation, learning and growth. One new TA put it this way:

> You asked us to write goals for ourselves this semester and I'll admit that 1) I wasn't sure what I was doing wrong that needed improvement and 2) I thought it was a waste of time. BUT I have to say that it has really gotten me thinking about my own practices in the WC. Every consultation I think about whether I'm meeting my own evaluation of myself and how I can do it better. And I'm always thinking of new goals that I should set for myself. I wasn't conscious of some things until you asked that we become so—to formalize our self-reflection. (Omar)

In her recent overview of TA education curricula, Catherine Latterell observes that the best, most impressive preparation programs immerse TAs in "multiple forums and conversations about teaching" that extend "well beyond" TAs' first semester or first year of teaching" (21). Our preparation program, which takes places in multiple contexts throughout TAs' careers, exemplifies the "teaching community" approach to TA education. We encourage our TAs to see tensions among their roles as graduate students, writing teachers, and Writing Center consultants as opportunities for growth rather than conflict and to understand that the confusion brought on by competing perspectives and experiences is often an occasion for achieving clarity. Observing, discussing, and practicing, our TAs learn to reflect and reconcile: They learn the artistry of professional practice.

## WORKS CITED

Brooks, Jeff. "Minimalist Tutoring: Making the Student Do All the Work." *The St. Martin's Sourcebook for Writing Tutors.* Ed. Christina Murphy and Steve Sherwood. New York: St. Martin's, 1995. 83–7.

Bruffee, Kenneth. *A Short Course in Writing.* 2nd ed. New York: Little, Brown & Company, 1980.

Dewey, John. *Experience and Education.* 1938. New York: Touchstone Books, 1997.

———. *Experience and Nature.* 1925. New York: Dover Publications, 1958.

Duhamel, Katherine. "Re: digression, dissensus, and doughnuts." Online posting. 22 Jan. 1998. NMSU Writing Center Listserv. <rebjacks@nmsu.edu>.

Elbow, Peter, and Patricia Belanoff. *A Community of Writers: A Workshop Course in Writing.* New York: McGraw Hill, 1994.

England, Stephen. "Re: digression, dissensus, and doughnuts." Online posting. 23 Jan. 1998. NMSU Writing Center Listserv. <rebjacks@nmsu.edu>.

Jacobs, Dale, et al. "Evolving Pedagogies: Four Voices on Teacher Change and the Writing Center." *The Writing Lab Newsletter* 22.10 (1998): 1–9.

Latterell, Catherine G. "Training the Workforce: An Overview of GTA Education Curricula." *WPA* 19.3 (1996): 7–23.

North, Stephen. "The Idea of a Writing Center." *The St. Martin's Sourcebook for Writing Tutors.* Ed. Christina Murphy and Steve Sherwood. New York: St. Martin's, 1995. 22–35.

Omar, Jamili. "Re: Resistance to Writing Center Work." E-mail to Rebecca Jackson. 24 Sept. 1998.

Powers, Judith. "Rethinking Writing Center Conferencing Strategies for the ESL Writer." *The St. Martin's Sourcebook for Writing Tutors.* Ed. Christina Murphy and Steve Sherwood. New York: St. Martin's, 1995. 96–102.

Schön, Donald. *Educating the Reflective Practitioner.* San Francisco: Jossey-Bass, 1987.

Shamoon, Linda K., and Deborah H. Burns. "A Critique of Pure Tutoring." *Writing Center Journal* 15.2 (1995): 134–51.

Tremmel, Robert. "Beyond Self-Criticism: Reflecting on Teacher Research and TA Education." *Composition Studies* 22.1 (1994): 44–64.

Yancey, Kathleen Blake. *Reflection in the Writing Classroom.* Logan: Utah State UP, 1998.

# 15. The Three-Part Program for Preparing TAs to Lead Professional Communication Courses at Miami University (Ohio)

PAUL ANDERSON, TODD DELUCA, AND
LISA ROSENBERGER

In the early 1980s, when the English department at Miami University (Ohio) planned its new master's degree program in technical and scientific communication, it needed to design a novel strategy for preparing the program's teaching assistants to teach the technical or business communication courses they would be assigned to lead. The department's existing TA preparation program simply would not work. Directed at preparing graduate students in literature and creative writing to teach first-year composition, it assumed that these new TAs would already know a great deal about such a course. Even if they had not taken one themselves, they would have earned undergraduate degrees in English and hence gained years of experience writing many of the forms of discourse that composition classes teach. In contrast, most of the TAs in the department's new technical and scientific communication program would come from majors outside of English. Also, these new TAs would be teaching courses at the 300 level, not the first-year courses taught by new TAs in the department's other graduate programs. Moreover, many would be coming directly from their undergraduate studies. Consequently, they would not have experience as writers in the professional, nonacademic settings for which they would need to prepare their students to communicate successfully, settings where the audiences, purposes, genre, conventions, and standards of discourse are much different than those that apply to the writing students generally do in college.

In this chapter, we describe the three-part strategy the department devised to prepare these new TAs to teach a subject about which they knew little or nothing when beginning their graduate studies. To illustrate, we'll draw on our work together in fall semester 1997, when Lisa and Todd were new TAs and Paul was beginning his fifteenth year helping TAs prepare for their teaching.

An essential feature of this strategy is that Miami devotes a full semester to preparing TAs for the courses they will lead, postponing their assignment to their own classes until the second term. During the first semester, the TAs engage in the following carefully coordinated activities designed to provide them with preparation that is both broad and deep:

- A teaching partnership in which each TA assists a faculty member who is conducting a technical or business communication course
- A seminar on teaching technical and business communication
- Participation in the other seminars required for all first-semester students in the master's program in technical and scientific communication; these cover the topics that fill out the knowledge the TAs will find most useful when they teach solo in the second term

Taken together, the first two activities require an average of fifteen to twenty hours per week beyond the TAs' regular course work, which is the amount of time Miami expects TAs to devote to their teaching responsibilities. Usually, five or six master's students out of an incoming class of twelve to fifteen are prepared in this manner. Others find other assistantships in our program (for instance, as supervisors of our computer lab) or elsewhere on campus. Students who are not TAs may enroll in the teaching seminar, but they do not work as teaching partners or conduct their own courses. (Although some students eventually pursue PhDs, none come intending to follow an academic career.)

Our experience with Miami's three-part strategy for preparing TAs suggests that it might work equally well not only for other professional communication programs but also for graduate programs in literature and other areas of English studies. Where it is not feasible to keep new TAs out of their own classrooms for a full semester, there may still be ways to adapt the most beneficial features of our program. We'll return to this point at the end of our chapter.

## CHARACTERISTICS OF THE PROFESSIONAL COMMUNICATION COURSES OUR TAs TEACH

Miami's strategy for preparing TAs to teach technical and business communication classes is directly linked to the goals of these courses. The hallmark of workplace writing is that it is a form of action that is intended to precipitate, guide, or inspire action. Reports, for instance, are intended to provide managers with the information they require when making practical decisions. Instructions are written to enable lab technicians to perform tasks they do not at present know how to perform. Complicating every on-the-job writing situation are contextual factors such as the attitudes the readers bring to their reading, the readers' understanding of their responsibilities and the constraints upon their options, and ethical concerns about how the action initiated or aided by the communication will affect people other than the writer and readers. Generally, introductory professional communication courses teach students to analyze these complex communication situations, paying particular attention to the needs and characteristics of the target readers and to the communication's purposes from the perspectives of the writer, the readers, and the organization(s) that employ them; to plan a communication whose contents, organization, tone, page layout, and visual aids (where appropriate) will achieve these objectives;

and to execute that plan in an easy-to-use, attractive, error-free, and ethical communication.

In our courses, every assignment requires students to address a rhetorical situation they are likely to encounter in their careers. We specify the type of document (instructions, unsolicited recommendation, etc.) and ask the students to pick their own topics and readers (usually real ones), which we must approve. Our courses teach a process approach involving situational analysis, planning, drafting, peer reviewing, and revising. Topics include the nature of workplace communication—its functions, conventions, and genre—and the communication strategies that distinguish successful from unsuccessful instances. Visual aids, layout, and sometimes the creation of informational Web sites are also covered. Always, the emphasis is on presenting information and arguments in an effective manner—the heart of rhetoric. All sections of technical communication and some of business communication are taught in a computer classroom. Instructors and students often use email to communicate outside of class.

To prepare the TAs for their courses, the English department must ensure that they know not only the subject matter they will teach but also how to present it effectively in a course students will find challenging, educational, and fun. The goals, then, are to prepare the TAs to do the following:

- Understand and teach effectively about the goals of the course
- Understand and teach effectively the rhetorical principles, the action steps, the genre, and the theoretical and ethical considerations that are central to the course
- Present the projects and guide students through the process of creating them
- Write helpful, informative comments on student projects and assign fair grades
- Treat students fairly and respectfully in all situations, while also maintaining high expectations for student performance
- Interact effectively with students in class, during office hours, and in meetings with groups of students working on team-written assignments
- Motivate students to devote attention to the course and approach their projects thoughtfully and creatively

## TEACHING PARTNERSHIP WITH A FACULTY MEMBER

The first element of Miami's first-semester strategy for preparing the TAs is the teaching partnership in which one or two TAs work with a faculty member who is conducting a section of the professional writing course that the TAs are likely to teach alone in the second term, either "Introduction to Technical and Scientific Communication" (English 313) or "Introduction to Business Communication" (English 315). Generally, the faculty members who work with TA teaching partners are specialists in technical or business communication, although there have been some exceptions over the years. In these partnerships, the TAs are partly observers, partly apprentices, and partly co-teachers. The three of us

(Lisa, Todd, and Paul) were partners for a section of the introductory course in technical and scientific communication. Our ways of working together toward the twin goals of preparing Lisa and Todd for their spring-semester courses and presenting a high-quality course to our current students bear all the features shared by the other teaching partnerships in this master's program. Lisa and Todd attended all class sessions, assisting where they felt ready to do so (generally more toward the end of the semester); completed all of the readings assigned to the undergraduates; attended some of the conferences in which Paul met with students; and held three office hours per week. Paul usually presented lessons, led class discussions and exercises, and explained assignments, following a syllabus he had developed before the semester began. This arrangement enabled Lisa and Todd to see how Paul explained assignments to students, discussed topics, and tied readings and class discussions to the students' work on their course projects. But Todd and Lisa did more than watch. They also contributed substantially to class discussions, based on their own experiences before attending graduate school: Lisa was an education major with one year of teaching experience in a public high school, and Todd was an economics major with two years of experience in business. Often students asked them questions during in-class workshops, peer review sessions, and office hours. If they were asked questions about assignments or other matters that they could not answer, Lisa and Todd told students they would check with Paul. Generally, however, they provided information and advice on their own.

The three of us usually met before each class and also at other times to discuss upcoming course activities and review past events. At times, we brainstormed together about how to focus a class session or respond to difficulties we perceived a particular student to be having. Our time together grew considerably after students turned in projects. The evaluation of student work (including the comments provided to the student and the grade assigned) provides a focal point around which many issues central to teaching professional communication are arrayed. At Miami, we view our comments on student projects to be a critically important part of our teaching. TAs must learn how to frame comments that are clear, instructive, and supportive. It is equally important, and sometimes more difficult for students to learn what to emphasize in their comments. To comment effectively, they must learn which aspects of a student's project contributes most to its success and which would be most important for the student to revise. These judgments require knowledge of what readers look for in workplace settings and how they use the communications they receive—knowledge that TAs who lack workplace experience can gain only gradually. When working together to evaluate student projects, the three of us always followed the same general cycle. As each project was turned in, we first met to discuss assessment criteria and go over two or three papers together. Then, Todd and Lisa commented on several papers and passed them to Paul, who reviewed their comments and the grade, sometimes suggesting and explaining possible changes we would then discuss together. With this guidance, Todd and Lisa completed their grading and commenting on the entire set of papers, all of which Paul reviewed before we returned them to our students. We always told the students whether Todd or Lisa had lead responsibility for evaluating a project, and we asked them to approach that person with questions about the evaluation.

By the end of our semester's partnership, Todd and Lisa had seen every detail of the course they would teach on their own, and they had gained substantial experience in the critically important activities of interacting with students and of evaluating and commenting on student work. The same outcome is achieved in the teaching partnerships for all other TAs in the master's program.

## TEACHING SEMINAR

To supplement the knowledge and experience gained through the teaching partnerships, TAs take a seminar in teaching technical and business communication. In fall 1997, Paul taught the seminar. It included Todd, Lisa, and three other TAs who were partners with three other faculty. In many respects, this seminar resembles those for TAs at other universities. Our syllabus included readings and discussions of articles and chapters on theory and practice. Specific topics included goals for professional communication courses, differences between technical and business communication courses, motivating students, evaluation of student work, conferencing, the teaching of specific course topics (e.g., defining objectives for writing, using visual dimensions of communication, reviewing other people's drafts, and revising), use of the Web for teaching, collaborative learning, ethics, and gender in the classroom. For several sessions, TAs brought copies of interim and final drafts of student work from the sections in which the TAs were partners. We individually read, commented on, and graded the student work, and then we discussed our results. In addition, each TA created and delivered a lesson employing PowerPoint and appropriate handouts; during the lesson the rest of us played the role of undergraduates in the TA's class. Afterward, we gave detailed, supportive critiques. Because the other three TAs each worked in partnership with a different professor, our group had a rich variety of events and perspectives to discuss. We also invited the second-year TAs to an open discussion that addressed the questions the new TAs had and the advice the advanced TAs wanted to give. Also, during the first two-thirds of the semester, the TAs kept teaching journals in which they wrote for one hour each week, reflecting on something about teaching, whether an event in the class where they were teaching partners, an idea encountered in the seminar readings, or some other teaching-related topic. Paul responded to the journals twice.

In two important respects, however, our seminar differed from other teaching seminars with which we are familiar. First, we devoted most of our time to discussing effective teaching practices, not the content of the undergraduate courses the TAs would teach. We were able to achieve this focus because the teaching partnerships enabled the TAs to observe the presentation of every lesson and project in the undergraduate course. Also, in the other seminars the TAs were taking during their first semester, they were gaining much additional knowledge related to the content of the courses they would be teaching (see below).

Second, we followed a very flexible agenda in order to respond quickly and thoroughly to the specific concerns and questions of the TAs. Individual class sessions often began with the question, "What's happened this week in the class where you are a teaching partner?" or its more generic variant, "What do you want to talk about this week?" Sometimes, the TAs would describe an exemplary lesson or student interaction by their faculty partners. Sometimes, they would talk about the challenge of motivating an indifferent student, their perplexity when challenged publicly by a student about a grade on a project, or ways of talking about rough drafts with students who want the TA to make their writing decisions for them. Sometimes, they would express their anxieties concerning the next semester, when they would be teaching on their own: How could they maintain the respect of students who (in many cases) were only one year younger than the TA and who knew much more than the TA about the subjects they would write about? What should TAs do when they don't know the answer to a student's question and no faculty member is present to help them out? We explored all these questions together, and several times we adjusted the initial seminar schedule so we could discuss topics when they were most salient to the TAs' concerns.

## TEACHING-RELATED MATERIAL IN OTHER FIRST-SEMESTER SEMINARS

The third element of Miami's strategy for preparing TAs to teach technical and business communication consists of four seminars taken by all first-semester students in the master's program. These seminars are for master's students only (we have an undergraduate program in technical and scientific communication but the two programs do not share courses). They include an intensive, graduate-level introduction to technical and scientific communication. In it, the students read some of the theoretical work that would otherwise go in the TA seminar, and they undertake (at a much more advanced level) projects that resemble some the TAs will assign their undergraduates the next term. The TAs also take a seminar in "Organizational Communication." In it they study the settings where the undergraduates will write in their careers. Finally, the students take a half-semester "Introduction to Rhetoric" designed specifically for technical and scientific communication students and a half-semester seminar in "Technical and Scientific Editing." In the latter course, they learn how to work effectively with authors (a skill eminently transferable to working with students on their drafts), how to undertake substantive editing (a skill that increases their ability to give helpful suggestions in conferences and in comments on graded assignments), and how to identify and discuss lapses in usage (a skill that enables them to talk knowledgeably on such problems in student papers).

## TRANSITION TO THE SECOND SEMESTER

By the end of their first semester, the TAs have seen—and helped—a faculty member teach all aspects of the undergraduate course. They have read, reflected on, and discussed a wide variety of a teacher's tasks and responsibilities as well as all aspects of the material they will teach in the second semester. And they have developed a group of TA and faculty colleagues with whom they can share the excitement, triumphs, questions, and problems that will arise in their own classes.

In the second semester, the program continues its intensive support for the TAs. First, it provides them with a detailed syllabus that includes a lesson plan for each class. Although the syllabus is not identical to the one used by their faculty partner, it incorporates the same teaching strategies and types of assignments. Also, the TAs continue to meet in a weekly seminar, taught by a second professor. It focuses on the day-to-day work of the TAs, such as preparing for specific class sessions, handling issues that didn't come up during their partnerships, and (again) commenting on and grading student projects. The TAs also take seminars in technical and scientific writing and in graphic design through which they gain additional knowledge related to the courses they teach. After the second semester, the TAs are free to revise their syllabi in ways consistent with the goals of the course, although they must consult with faculty about major changes.

## JOINT REFLECTIONS ON THE THREE-PART PROGRAM BY TODD AND LISA

In fall 1997, we (Lisa and Todd) helped Paul teach "Introduction to Technical and Scientific Communication," an undergraduate course required for engineering and applied science majors. Our sections included mainly juniors and seniors in systems analysis, manufacturing engineering, and dietetics. The fact that our students were experienced college learners with advanced knowledge in specialties very different from ours added to the apprehension we felt as neophyte TAs. During the first semester, three other TAs were also partnering with faculty members, but ours was the only section with two TAs. Our team approach allowed us to draw on one another's experiences and ideas, as well as on Paul's thoughts and observations. It also allowed the three of us to provide much individualized attention to each student. In the weekly TA seminar, we developed teaching skills, discussed issues and trends in college instruction, and formed a kinship that carried over to the next semester, when we TAs each taught our own section. The regular graduate seminars we took in the first semester provided intense study of technical communication's theoretical foundations and practical applications. We modified the concepts and strategies learned in these seminars for presentation to our undergraduate students, but, interestingly, it was only in the next semester that the connection between our work as instructors and our study as graduate students became readily evident to us.

While the program provided us with the tools we needed to become effective teachers, it did not fully address our individual needs. Each TA comes to Miami's program with a unique background and set of experiences. Each must synthesize what she learned in the first semester and apply it to her own class the second semester. The level of success varies from TA to TA. For some, being a TA is enjoyable and comes naturally; for others, it is more challenging and difficult.

Our experiences as TAs helped us improve our skills in a vast spectrum of professional areas, including information gathering, interviewing, editing, and diplomacy. We honed these skills while instructing our classes, and now we are extrapolating them to our "real-world" jobs. Below, we discuss some thoughts about being TAs in Miami's program.

## A CONVERSATION BETWEEN LISA AND TODD

**TODD:** I graduated from Miami University in 1992 with a B.S. degree in economics and worked as a computer professional in graphic arts, marketing, and technical writing before entering the master's program in 1997. I also wrote procedural manuals and edited documentation.

**LISA:** When I entered the program in 1997, I had less "real-world" working experience. Eighteen months earlier, I had earned undergraduate degrees in English and secondary education but decided not to teach in a high school. Instead, I tutored college students in developmental writing. I also worked as a receptionist for a technical writing company, where I observed how writing functions in business settings but did not participate in the process.

**TODD:** In the first semester, an important issue for me was nervousness about instructing students in a subject I was just going back to school to learn myself. The semester of guided preparation and sharing experiences with peers helped to relieve much of this anxiety for all of us. It seemed that most of our early concerns were with the types of unfamiliar situations we would have to deal with in the second semester. The teaching seminar and our teaching partnership gave us a lot of exposure to the majority of issues we would face when teaching on our own. Helping Paul conduct the actual course I would be instructing was the most beneficial and confidence-boosting aspect of Miami's program. Although each TA could make minor changes to her individual sections in the second semester, having a framework to start with and build upon was very important. Also very useful, especially in Paul's class, were the supporting materials, particularly the syllabus. These materials made things clear to both the instructor and the students. For a beginning TA, they were an excellent source for support and guidance.

**LISA:** The structure and content of our first semester provided me with practical and theoretical foundations for improving my teaching skills. The most important lessons I learned, however, took place on the micro-level, involving my daily interactions with students and my routine responsibilities as a TA. I learned these lessons through my observations and interactions with you and Paul and through class discussions with other professors and TAs.

Gender was a particularly important topic for me. I was encouraged that the women in our technical communication class (about half the students) volunteered to speak as much as the men did. Most were pursuing degrees in traditionally male-dominated professions, such as engineering, systems analysis, and information systems management. Perhaps they had learned earlier that being vocal is a requirement for success in these competitive fields. However, gender often shaped students' interactions with me. When talking with students in class and conferences, I ensured that we addressed all questions and concerns about class material, and I also engaged students in casual conversation to nurture the student/instructor alliance. Our male students were more willing to initiate the casual part of our discussions than were our female students. Often, my discussions with the men began with casual conversation and ended with their questions about the subject matter. With the women, the pattern usually was inverted: Only after we had exhausted the course-related issues did they steer the conversation to other topics. Another example involved our students' six-week collaborative projects. You, Paul, and I divided up conferencing responsibilities so that we each met weekly with the same student teams. When the members (all men) of one of your groups received a lower grade than they had expected, they wanted to schedule a meeting with me, even though they had met entirely with you up to that point. Whether I was perceived as an easier grader or a more willing listener, these male students apparently felt the best chance for an overturned grade rested in their female TA.

Paul actively addressed gender issues in our teaching seminar by asking all TAs to read and discuss gender-related articles[1] and by inviting feminist guest speakers to share their views with us. We also considered gender in other seminars, grappling, for example, with ways to integrate gender in our understanding of our readers and the design of our communications. I began to discern that in progressive settings, such as a liberal arts college, gender bias goes underground, revealing itself in subconscious or seemingly innocuous action. By relating our readings and discussions to my observations as a TA, I discovered that nuances of gender were present in every classroom interaction. My gender-related observations and experiences as a TA revolved around perceptions of power, specifically how our students viewed authority in our classroom and how you and I defined power for ourselves. I adopted a hands-on, informal approach to teaching, which I deemed powerful because it allowed me to form strong connections with students. However, your group of male students recognized a more traditional view of power that equates nurturing with gullibility, weakness, and relaxed expectations.

Equipped with the knowledge I acquired throughout the semester and supported by our teaching partnership with Paul, I combated such misconceptions with practical tools. For example, I often used my conversations with students to recognize and support women in positions of local, national, and international power. When you and I taught lessons together, we helped to thwart bias in our classroom by demonstrating mixed-gender professional cooperation. It was essential for our students to witness and participate in these interactions because as the corporate workforce grows larger and more diverse, it increasingly will demand that conventional ideas of power be reevaluated and expanded to include the wider demographic spectrum.

**TODD:** It wasn't until our first teaching seminars and assigned readings that I realized how important gender was to the majority of the TAs in our class (three of the five were women). Understanding the concerns of my colleagues became an important aspect of learning the roles that instructors are placed in and how instructors handle these roles. We discussed situations in which gender becomes important in teaching, and we talked about the different attitudes that students have toward instructors depending on the gender of the students and the instructors. Although issues related to gender were not as prominent a concern for me as for you and some others in the seminar, our discussions helped me recognize them in my teaching the next term.

For me, grading and commenting on student assignments were among the most important activities we shared with Paul. This work was both time-consuming and difficult, especially during the first few assignments. Initially, we both graded each student's assignment and then made changes based on Paul's suggestions. Surprisingly, the three of us were often very close in our initial comments and grades. When we weren't, we quickly came to a mutually agreeable decision after a short debate. Having the three of us compare comments and grades helped me see things in the students' writing that I might have overlooked. As the semester progressed, I was pleased that we improved to the point where we were able to confidently grade and comment on student assignments in a more manageable time frame—and with less feedback from Paul.

The biggest lesson Paul taught me about commenting was always to give constructive and specific comments to the students. I also benefited from the general pattern we followed: Assign a letter grade (with plus or minus, based on a twelve-point scale); write both marginal comments and a summary note (usually a memo); begin the summary with comments on areas where the students had successfully completed the assignment (at least a couple of examples, regardless of grade); and finish the summary with areas needing improvement. Using this formula, we were able to justify our letter grades, encourage students, and give them helpful feedback. Based on the few instances of student complaints, I considered this means of evaluating successful.

LISA: The time devoted to examining the role of the instructor—and its implications—was perhaps the most beneficial part of our teaching seminar for me. I decided to cast myself as a facilitator rather than an authoritarian. Pedagogically, I wanted our students to gain insight into how they might apply the course material in their careers. With the trend toward teaming in business and industry, students preparing for technical careers need to be well-versed with the team approach to project work. By acting as facilitator instead of authoritarian, I hoped to encourage students in their group work to take the lead in finding answers, devising solutions, and resolving conflict. Also, I believe solid interpersonal relationships are imperative for a classroom atmosphere conducive to learning. By presenting myself as a facilitator, I could more easily convey my wish to learn from our students (whose specialties were different from mine) and establish easy rapport with them. In such a learning environment, students were more willing to accept that I believed their work had value and that my top priority was helping them to grow as writers.

Of the three female and two male TAs in our group, most, if not all, viewed themselves as facilitators. The TA seminar sessions in which we discussed our work as facilitators were so valuable not merely because they allowed us to gather feedback on our efforts, but, more importantly, because they provided concrete points of contrast between male and female facilitation experiences. While we all had stories about how students reacted to and, in some cases, abused this interactive teaching style, we female TAs usually experienced the most notable repercussions. Some were subtle, such as the different ways male and female students structured their conversations with me, and served as interesting material for discussion in our teaching seminar and other graduate courses. In other instances, the conflicts were more severe and required the professor's intervention for resolution. In examining my own experiences and those of my colleagues, I find the implications of gender to be an inherent complexity in the facilitation approach to teaching, a complexity that merits frank discussion in any TA program.

## PAUL'S REFLECTIONS ON THE THREE-PART PROGRAM

In my view, the most important element of our three-part program is the teaching partnership. As Lisa and Todd indicate, many of the most valuable lessons that TAs learn derive from participating in and observing the detailed conduct of the course they will teach and from their daily contact with students. Also through the partnerships, TAs develop a close relationship with a faculty member who is deeply committed to their success in the classroom. In addition, the partnerships enable faculty partners to work closely with remarkable students like Lisa and Todd. Invariably, the TAs improve the classes with which they assist us.

A critical feature of our program is the amount of attention devoted in the partnerships and TA seminar to helping TAs learn to evaluate and comment effectively on student projects. The TAs benefit enormously from guided experience in assessing organization, tone, tables, illustrations, page layout, and all other elements of student work from the perspective of its workplace (nonacademic) target audience. Once TAs have learned how to *evaluate* writing from the perspective of a workplace audience, they have a solid foundation for *teaching* students to write to such readers.

As Todd and Lisa point out, a substantial challenge for the program is figuring out how to meet the needs and build on the strengths of each individual TA. The differences between the concerns that Lisa and Todd emphasize in their conversation above merely hint at the vast diversity of concerns among all our new TAs. I believe the teaching partnerships and flexible design for the TA seminar are largely successful in achieving this goal. However, the seminar's flexibility also means that occasionally some topics are treated more briefly than seems desirable, as least from an academician's perspective. A special advantage of the partnerships is that they enable each TA to receive intensive and extended support in whatever areas the TA or faculty partner believes are important to address, whether this involves issues around recognizing grammatical problems in student work, working effectively with students in conferences, articulating principles of good communication, or any other aspect of course content or teaching technique. In some instances, providing this kind of support and guidance can become very time consuming for the faculty member (it was not so with Lisa and Todd), but the return in what the TA learns in our program and in the quality of teaching the TA can provide undergraduates more than compensates.

Our decision to require TAs to follow a detailed, standard syllabus during their first semester of solo teaching reflects our sense of the enormity of the challenge faced by our TAs, whom we ask to teach an upper-level course in a subject most of them don't know much about before coming to us. The majority express gratitude for the standard syllabus because it relieves them of the time-consuming and risky task of devising their own syllabi. Yet, this policy is not ideally suited to every TA. Although we allow TAs to make minor adjustments during their first term of teaching with advance approval, the standard syllabus probably curtails the creativity of some TAs that would allow them to reach their full effectiveness in the first section they teach on their own. On the other hand, on rare occasions in subsequent semesters when the TAs have more freedom, a TA has modified the course in ways that prevented it from achieving some of its fundamental goals.

Since our master's program opened in 1983, our three-part strategy for preparing TAs has remained basically unchanged, a sign that the faculty believe that, even if not perfect, it is the most effective one we can devise. I concur. Our TAs are delightful colleagues for their teaching partners and wonderful students in the TA seminar. They develop mutually supportive peer relationships, teach their undergraduate sections well, and seem to gain a sense of fulfillment from their teaching.

## IMPLICATIONS FOR OTHER TA PREPARATION PROGRAMS

What might other TA preparation programs—including those in literature, creative writing, or other areas of English studies—be able to adapt from Miami's three-part design? We have three suggestions, each keyed to programs that must assign TAs to their own classes in the first term.

First, programs might benefit from devising ways to provide TAs with *extensive* preparation before they teach solo. For example, Miami requires new TAs for its composition courses to arrive before the fall term for a three-week seminar that consists of day-long sessions about teaching these classes. The TAs' enrollment in the seminar generates enough state subsidy to pay the instructors and provide a stipend for the TAs (Miami is a state-assisted university).

Second, programs might benefit from devising ways to provide new TAs with *intensive* teaching partnerships with regular faculty who are invested in the course the TAs are teaching. For example, each new TA might be assigned a mentor who will teach the same course and syllabus as the TA. TAs and their faculty partners might meet weekly, visit one another's classes biweekly, and talk over selected student papers when commenting on and grading student work.

Third, programs might consider ways of making their seminars more responsive to the needs of individual TAs and groups of TAs. For instance, to increase time to discuss TA-initiated topics they might determine whether some planned topics could be dropped, abbreviated, or moved to another seminar taken by the TAs in the first term. For TAs who will teach composition, this other seminar might be in contemporary controversies in composition, recent composition theory, or rhetoric and argument. Also, in the teaching seminar the TAs might be asked periodically which of the remaining planned topics they would find it most helpful to address next. To respond to the variety of individual needs, leaders of TA seminars with large enrollments might set aside time for small-group discussions and invite additional faculty to interact with these groups.

Overall, we believe that the keys to creating a highly successful TA preparation program are to recognize the enormous task new TAs face—the wide range of things they must learn, the depth of their concerns, and the substantial differences among individual TAs—and then to think creatively about ways to help each individual prepare for his or her teaching responsibilities.[2]

## NOTES

1. Some helpful readings were Peggy Orenstein, "Introduction" and "Anita Hill Is a Boy: Tales from a Gender Fair Classroom," *School Girls* (New York: Doubleday, 1994), xi–xxv and 245–274; Bernice Resnic Sandler, "Women Faculty at Work in the Classroom, or, Why It Still Hurts to Be a Woman in Labor," *Communication Education* 40 (1991): 6–15; and Elizabeth Grauerholz, "Sexual Harassment of Women Professors by Students," *Sex Roles* 21 (1989): 789–801.
2. We thank Jean A. Lutz for her helpful comments. Jean was the faculty partner for another TA in fall 1997, and she led the TA seminar in which Lisa and Todd enrolled in spring 1998.

# 16. Preparing College Teachers of Writing to Teach in a Web-Based Classroom: History, Theoretical Base, Web Base, and Current Practices

CHRISTINE HULT AND LYNN MEEKS

Kenneth Green in "The Coming Ubiquity of Information Technology" points out that the use of technology in academia can be measured by how long it took the overhead projector to move from the bowling alley to the classroom—a mere forty years (24). In contrast to the generally conservative approach to technology in academia, computer experimentation in the English Department at Utah State University began twenty years ago, and our attempt to prepare college teachers of writing to teach distance learning courses via the Web has been a five-year journey through cyberspace. Boldly going where we did not dream to go before, we have learned with and from the writing instructors, developing pedagogy, practice, and Web-based technology at the same time.

Looking back on our journey, it is hard for us to separate our preparation of teachers of writing to teach in a Web-based classroom from the development of the Web-based classroom itself (SyllaBase™). Rather than a journey, perhaps a better metaphor is a braid in which the separate strands of writing pedagogy, teacher preparation, and the development of a Web-based classroom constantly interweave to create a learning environment as effective and student-centered as a face-to-face classroom. To best describe our teacher preparation, we will start with a brief history of our institution, then describe the theory undergirding the writing program and the preparation of new teachers for both online and face-to-face teaching. We will show how the development of a Web-based classroom interacted with our teacher preparation, and finally how we continue to use and refine our notion of a Web-based classroom.

## INSTITUTIONAL CONTEXT

Utah State University is a land grant research university, designated Carnegie Type I, with 780 faculty members, a School of Graduate Studies, 4,000 graduate students, 44 departments, and approximately 20,000 undergraduates in both on-campus and extension programs. The English Department is one of the larger departments on campus—as well as one of the fastest growing. During the last twenty years, the English Department's Writing Program has undergone several changes that reflect the changing mission of institutions in this country (McLeod). In 1985, tenure-track faculty taught all forty-three sections of first-year English—two required quarters of writing (English 101 and 201). Gradually the Writing Program moved away from using tenure-track faculty as the English Department's graduate programs in literary studies, American studies, folklore, technical writing, and theory and practice of writing grew and the student population increased from 10,000 to 20,000 in approximately fourteen years. The Writing Program now offers approximately eighty first-and second-year English courses each semester, some taught entirely face-to-face, some taught entirely on-line, and some a combination of both face-to-face and online instruction taught by teaching assistants (TAs) and instructors.

## EARLY MAINFRAME BEGINNINGS

The USU English Department has a long history of using computers to teach writing. In 1983, we opened a Writing Center computer lab with terminals connected to the university mainframe. Since then, the English Department computer facilities have grown and changed to keep up with the needs of our various student clientele. In 1990, Professor Hult received a state grant to fund a computer lab, primarily meant to serve English majors who were prospective teachers and technical writers. From then on, the department has supported two computer facilities for students in English courses: a thirty-station drop-in lab (still connected with the Writing Center) and a twenty-station computer classroom. These facilities are staffed by two full-time computer technicians and several student lab assistants.

## THE DEVELOPMENT OF SYLLABASE—AN ENGLISH DEPARTMENT WEB-BASED CLASSROOM

The preparation of teachers to work in a Web-based classroom cannot be separated from the development of the classroom itself. Following the coresearcher model, English Department computer programmers, faculty members, graduate students, and instructors worked together to design an on-line classroom that would provide a learning community for students and teachers. The 3GB Group, the English Department's research and development team of computer technicians and faculty, then developed the SyllaBase Online Classroom.[1] That software now delivers over 100 distance education courses in a variety of disciplines, including a master's degree in technical writing taught completely online.[2]

SyllaBase does not provide prefabricated courses-in-a-box (that tend to confine the teacher), nor does it use templates to build course pages individually (and expensively). Rather, SyllaBase is a dynamic, database-driven system that uses active server pages to create, deliver, and manage a complete Web site for each of as many courses as are requested. The content, features, and appearance of a particular course's site are determined individually and exclusively by that course's teacher. Because the system is driven by server-side rather than client software, teachers and students can access and use their site through any standard Web browser on any desktop computer with an Internet connection. Using a set of simple Web forms, the teacher provides content to the site: syllabus, lecture materials, class notes, writing assignments, and announcements. The teacher may also use these forms to enable, disable, and modify the major communication tools of the site: threaded discussion groups, real-time chat rooms, file sharing, homework upload, and electronic mail. At any time the teacher can easily change the links from the other online resources, the appearance of the site, and all its content and features.

The flexibility of SyllaBase still allows teachers to use their "critical awareness . . . to think primarily about learning and secondarily about the technologies that support it," a concern expressed by Bertram Bruce (227). Teachers using such a system therefore do not need specialized technical knowledge or technicians to update and administer the site; instead, the server and the database manage the site, leaving the teacher free to concentrate on pedagogical rather than technological issues. In developing on-line courses and programs, we have learned a great deal about the "best practices" for teaching and learning at a distance and how to modify our preparation of TAs to help them succeed in the Web-based classroom.

## THE PEDAGOGICAL BASIS OF THE "WRITING PRACTICUM": HOW WE PREPARE TEACHERS; HOW WE PREPARE TEACHERS TO TEACH IN A WEB-BASED CLASSROOM

We prepare new TAs to teach English 1010 (formerly 101) through a course called the "Writing Practicum." The Writing Practicum starts a week before fall classes begin and continues to meet twice a week during fall semester. Taught by the WPA and two assistants, the curriculum of the Writing Practicum is designed both to teach the new TAs the content of English 1010 and to demonstrate the pedagogy that research on staff development and learning theory shows will most benefit the students. Informed by the research of Brian Cambourne ("Toward"), Jan Turbill, James Gee, Lauren Resnick, and Turbill et al., the curriculum of the Writing Practicum (and therefore the Writing Program) is based on collaborative learning, literacy learning, social linguistics, and discourse theory. TAs learn to create student-centered classrooms based on what Cambourne calls "Conditions of Learning" and what Resnick calls "Principles of Learning." Adapting these conditions and principles for the Writing Program means the TAs are taught to nurture their students' academic success through (1) demonstrations (providing models), (2) making expectations explicit, (3) allowing students to be responsible for their own learning, (4) allowing students time to practice new skills, (5) responding positively but honestly to students' attempts to master academic discourse, (6) giving students opportunities for critical thinking, (7) helping students understand cultural frameworks for writing, (8) making explicit the skills and strategies used by successful academic writers, (9) setting up opportunities for students to participate in "accountable talk," and (10) setting up situations in which students view learning to write as an apprenticeship. Just as we educate the TAs to use the above pedagogy in their regular classrooms, we also educate them to apply these principles when teaching in a Web-based classroom. Thus over the years, the principles of learning that underscore the entire program have been adapted to a Web-based environment. The following sections describe the additional factors we deem essential for successful teaching and learning in a Web-based environment.[3]

## ENSURING INSTITUTIONAL-LEVEL SUPPORT FOR TECHNOLOGY

A crucial ingredient to on-line instruction is institutional and departmental support. It is impossible to prepare teachers without first establishing the context in which such instruction can flourish. Our experience with Web-based instruction confirms the research of David Kumar and James Altschuld who identified the following features (in italics) found in successful technology-based teacher education programs:

1. *The Department's environment must support and encourage the development of the technology and encourage continuing innovation.* USU English Department administrators are committed to technological support and innovation. Every faculty member has an up-to-date office computer with a direct Internet connection. All instructors have access to an office computer, which they share with two to four other instructors.

A portion of the budget each year is set aside for upgrading department computers. Faculty and instructors request computer funding from a department committee. Computers in TA offices are replaced every three years, and TAs also have twenty-four-hour access to the English Department's computer labs, which contain more extensive software than office computers. All of our departmental business is now conducted on-line via our department's Intranet Web site. Faculty and instructors who need help in becoming proficient with the department's Intranet receive one-on-one guidance. Those who wish to use the SyllaBase classroom are taught how to use the Web environment.

2. *Faculty who use the technology must be committed to using the technology both in their classrooms and for their personal purposes.* Our ongoing education of all our teaching staff encourages the use of technology both in classrooms and for personal research. Each semester, workshops on particular topics of interest are provided, e.g., using the library's Internet resources, grading and responding to writing on-line, setting up a SyllaBase classroom. The university Faculty Assistance Center for Teaching (FACT) also provides regular workshops to help teachers wishing to make better use of technology in their classrooms (e.g., Photoshop and writing HTML).

3. *The departmental administration must find ways to encourage and support the use of technology.* Each year, the faculty succeed in securing grants to help stretch the meager operating funds allocated to technology. Nearly a million dollars in

operating funds have been raised in the past five years to support technology in the department; a portion of that amount goes to upgrading equipment for faculty and labs and supporting faculty, instructors, and technicians.

**4.** *There must be strong technical support which will respond immediately to the inevitable technical breakdowns and glitches.* When we began developing our online programs, we also hired two computer technicians to oversee and maintain department computer facilities. These two technicians are the founders of the 3GB Group, the think-tank that spearheads research and development in Web-based teaching and learning. They also maintain all the computers in the department, including those in offices and those in the computer facilities. Extremely knowledgeable and quick to respond to all technical needs, they are funded through lab fees paid by students who use the English Department facilities, although we are working to secure permanent funding.

## SUPPORTING TEACHERS VIA SPECIALIZED PREPARATION FOR WEB-BASED TEACHING

New TAs arrive on campus with little experience in on-line instruction. Because they have so much to learn about face-to-face writing instruction, we don't immediately provide specific instruction in teaching online. Instead, we quickly immerse them in an on-line environment (Cambourne, "Breaking"; Turbill et al.) for their own course work and create what Resnick refers to as a learning apprenticeship. We expect the new TAs to set up their own computer accounts so they can send and receive email immediately. Meanwhile, the TAs are also immersed in doing their own Web-based work for the Writing Practicum such as posting and responding to teaching and reading journals and participating in collaborative writing projects. Thus, as in any good apprenticeship, they learn by doing (Gee 138).

Taking to heart one principle for brain-compatible learning, "Complex learning is enhanced by challenge and inhibited by threat associated with a sense of helplessness or fatigue" (Caine et al. 195), we ease the new TAs into the notion of teaching in a Web-based classroom. Toward the end of the first semester, when the TAs are not feeling so overwhelmed with learning and teaching a new curriculum, we introduce them to the idea of using a Web site to supplement their own classes for the following semester. Again, we don't mandate, but give TAs the information they need to set up a Web site.

Most TAs inevitably work some use of SyllaBase into their second-semester course. For example, they have experienced the benefits of an on-line discussion group in the Writing Practicum, so they do not need to be convinced of the ways in which a threaded discussion can contribute to the overall feeling of comradery within the class as well as allow for the exchange of important information. This is another excellent example of what Gee refers to as learning by acquisition (138).

To further immerse new TAs in the computer culture of the department, we also take advantage of department experts through demonstrations. We have found that in addition to learning to use the Web via their own graduate classes, the models or demonstrations (Cambourne, *The Whole Story*; Resnick and Hall) provided by experienced instructors are very persuasive. When the new instructors see the innovative use of the Web in others' classrooms, they become even more convinced of both the pedagogical and practical reasons to use computers.

The teaching demonstrations are supported by weekly meetings, led by a WPA, for the TAs who are teaching on-line for the first time. At first, the discussions serve to answer basic questions that range from "What do I do when no one is posting the assignments?" to "How do I handle a student who expects me to answer her questions within the hour?" These weekly support groups are very helpful to the new on-line instructors because, as they teach in an on-line environment, questions arise for which no amount of traditional classroom experience can prepare them. However, over time we have developed some basic rules which guide our preparation of our on-line writing instructors:

1. *Develop a classroom presence.* To develop a classroom presence in the same way that face-to-face instructors do, instructors need to have almost daily interactions with students. Our most successful on-line instructor checks her email two or three times a day to make sure students know that she is "listening." Others find that posting to their bulletin boards daily gives the students the sense that the instructor is in the classroom. However, to keep from being inundated with urgent requests from students, on-line teachers do need to learn to set boundaries (e.g., I don't answer email on weekends).

2. *Monitor homework carefully.* Holding students strictly to deadlines and letting them know immediately if they did not meet a deadline are most effective in on-line courses. Once students understand that there is no negotiation on missed homework deadlines, even though they can work at their own pace and in their own time, classes usually function smoothly. Those who never understand this concept are likely to fail the course.

3. *Employ threaded discussion forums to best advantage.* Threaded discussion forums can be very important to giving students a sense of belonging and group identity. We encourage teachers to open and close forums frequently to keep them fresh and current. SyllaBase makes it very easy to label forums according to topic and to divide students into groups to join specific forums. It is also good in the spirit of group-building, to allow one ongoing forum for discussions that are "off-beat" and of the students' choice.

4. *Keep class sizes small.* Because on-line instruction is so labor-intensive for the instructor, especially with first-year composition students, we hold the maximum class size to twenty, while counting on three or four students to drop each class. More than about fifteen students in an on-line composition class make overwhelming work for the instructor.

5. *"Lurk" on each other's Web sites.* The on-line environment is an alien landscape for instructors new to it. There is no innate sense of what is "normal" in a successful learning environment because few instructors have taken on-line classes themselves. Therefore, we encourage new instructors to "lurk" on the sites of experienced instructors to get used to the lay of the land.

## MEETING SPECIAL NEEDS OF STUDENTS AND
## INSTRUCTORS WITH WEB-BASED CLASSROOMS

The sheer practicality of Web-based instruction for both the teacher and the student becomes an overwhelming argument for its use. For example, early on we discovered that the Web-based classroom provided hearing-impaired students with the chance to participate fully in class. Furthermore, taking a course on-line eliminates the need for and expense of an interpreter who translates the classroom language. Similarly, we have found that SyllaBase facilitates learning for visually impaired students who are unable to negotiate taking courses on a regular campus. In fact, one of our first students to complete the Web-based technical writing master's program was visually impaired. She took the entire sequence of courses in three semesters from her home by using specially designed hardware and software.

Just as the Web-based classroom has helped students with disabilities, it has also helped teachers with physical challenges. Our teachers experience accidents or illnesses, from broken legs to pneumonia, or emergencies such as caring for a sick child or parent. Ordinarily these teachers have been replaced by substitutes. Because the SyllaBase system is available to all teachers from anywhere they can access the Internet, we now are able to move such courses on-line until the teacher is able to resume the face-to-face meetings. In one case, a teacher took two weeks away from the classroom to have her baby but taught the class on-line during that time. When she came back to class, the students unanimously requested to continue in the Web-based environment. With the permission of the WPA, that course continued to the end of the semester on-line.


## THE MEDIUM IS NOT THE PEDAGOGY—PREPARING
## INSTRUCTORS TO UNDERSTAND THE DIFFERENCE

In his article "Academic Technology and the Future of Higher Education: Strategic Paths Taken and Not Taken," Paul Privateer argues that, all too often, when "learning migrates to a computer screen—with students memorizing information and then taking on-screen exams," educators fail to take the appropriate learning path that technology can provide. In fact, he states that, if American colleges and universities are to be effective, their "technology agenda should be focused on the production of intelligence rather than on the storage and recall of random and quickly outmoded information" (60). We couldn't agree more.

Too frequently, on-line classrooms have been designed by large corporations with outmoded learning paradigms. Such classrooms are simply a replacement for a lecture or a textbook to disseminate information and a testing mechanism to find out if the students can recall that information. In contrast, the SyllaBase discussion forums and chat rooms provide places for intellectually stimulating dialogue. Teachers who use Web-based discussion forums to supplement classroom instruction invariably find their in-class discussions are richer and deeper because the on-line discussions have preceded them. The file sharing and homework upload features in SyllaBase allow students to work together on projects, to peer review each other's work, to submit early drafts to their teacher for guidance, and to revise their works-in-progress. Thus, the pedagogy of the Writing Program is strengthened by the use of the Web-based elements available to TAs, instructors, and faculty. The Web-based classroom becomes not a place to lecture but a place to continue a student-centered, interactive, face-to-face classroom. Furthermore, the many links to other resources on the Internet, including libraries, on-line textbooks, and the Writing Center, also extend the traditional classroom in pedagogically appropriate ways.

## MAKING RECORD-KEEPING ACCESSIBLE FOR BOTH INSTRUCTORS AND STUDENTS

For beginning TAs the paperwork in a face-to-face class can be overwhelming, but it is even more so in an on-line class because all interactions take place online. The homework upload feature of the SyllaBase classroom is helpful to both new and experienced TAs as well as to students because it provides a course management tool that facilitates record-keeping. The homework upload keeps careful track of assignments and students' responses. It logs when the assignment was uploaded as well as keeps track of revisions and subsequent drafts. Instructors can keep in a sorted fashion a record of each student's homework for the class. This is a vast improvement over the first on-line classes we taught wherein hundreds of email messages came to instructors, including discussions, questions, assignments, in an unsorted and random fashion. The importance of the course management features of a Web-based classroom cannot be underestimated. In fact, without this capability, it would be much more difficult to educate teachers to be effective in the on-line environment and to support the Writing Program's philosophy about on-line teaching. Finally, we stress that, throughout the research and development efforts, we have consciously striven to provide students and teachers with a classroom environment using a single interface. That is, to participate in the class, students need no special computer software or hardware other than a standard Internet browser. Dorm rooms are hardwired for Internet access. English Department and campus computer labs, for which students pay access fees, are available nearly twenty-four hours a day.

## REASSURING THE CYBERPHOBES—ON-LINE TEACHING IS OK

Many TAs come to Web-based teaching with great and justifiable skepticism. Furthermore, the experience and background in technology vary widely among our teaching staff. Some have considerable experience already (a new hire in medieval studies began using SyllaBase to supplement her classes her first semester on campus) while others are novices. It is not always easy to overcome "Cyberphobia." George Gerard et al. suggest that technology aversion is not uncommon. The authors suggest that we should reach out to specific groups, especially the novice, the skeptic, and the optimist, to channel their efforts toward greater use of technology in classrooms (604).

An essential factor for success is finding ways to reassure the skeptics—persuading them that Web-based teaching can be as effective, and perhaps at times even more effective, than face-to-face teaching. In our assessment, we have found that the English 1010 courses, the courses we have taught the most consistently and researched the most completely over the past five years, are rated very highly by students who take them. For example, in the spring term of 1997, we evaluated twenty-three sections of English 1010: thirteen traditional and ten online. The average student assessments of course and instructor effectiveness were the same for both groups (5.2 on a 6-point scale). Teachers are far more likely to engage in on-line instruction once they have been reassured that their teaching will not suffer and that their students will like their classes just as well. One skeptical graduate student was converted to on-line instruction, once she had tried it: "I was very much against the idea of on-line instruction and felt there was no way it could match personal interaction between student and teacher. But . . . I've been converted."

Many cyberphobic TAs learn quickly that being prepared to teach in a Web-based classroom demonstrably increases their marketability. One experienced Web-based teacher, who teaches her courses for us from her home miles from the USU campus, was hired by the Continuing Education division at USU to educate extension teachers around the state in Web-based teaching techniques. It also helps the cyberphobic to see that award-winning faculty from other departments are using Web-based teaching successfully.

## ASSESSMENT DETERMINES THE PREPARATION OF ALL WRITING PROGRAM INSTRUCTORS

We assess our Web-based classrooms each semester. Ongoing assessment efforts take place on several levels. Before widely offering a course online, we establish test classes. Portfolios and student evaluation forms from traditional and Web-based courses are compared. From these investigations, we are determining (1) how best to adjust the Web-based classes for better instruction and (2) how best to instruct the future on-line instructors. Only through assessment, evaluation, and rigorous TA preparation will be we able to improve the teaching and learning occurring in Web-based classrooms.

## NOTES

1. The authors wish to thank both the 3GB Group and the USU English Department's Writing Group, Family Home Evening (FHE), for their assistance with this chapter.
2. For more about SyllaBase and 3GB Group, visit the following Web site: http://english. usu.edu/3gb.
3. The National Education Association and Blackboard, Inc., recently commissioned a study on Internet-based distance learning by the Institute for Higher Education Policy. The study lists twenty-four measures of quality (benchmarks) that are "important guideposts as our nation navigates the future of online higher education." Although broader than the six factors we identified because they are intended as institutional guidelines, the benchmarks listed by the study parallel ours. Similar factors were also identified in an earlier study by Susanmarie Harrington and William Condon: (1) Institutional support is crucial. (2) Technical expertise should be readily available. (3) Students need to be able to use the software.

(4) Listen well and ask good questions. (5) Be willing to talk. (6) When you think the software is finished, test it—and test it and test it and test it again.

## WORKS CITED

Bruce, Bertram C. "Speaking the Unspeakable about 21st Century Technology." *Passions, Pedagogies, and 21st Century Technologies.* Ed. Gail E. Hawisher and Cynthia L. Selfe. Logan: Utah State UP, 1999. 221–8.

Caine, Geoffrey, Renate Nummela Caine, and Sam Crowell. *Mind Shifts.* 2nd ed. Tucson, AZ: Zephyr, 1999.

Cambourne, Brian. "Breaking the Lore: An Alternate View of Learning." *Theory of Others.* Ed. Jan Turbill, Andrea Butler, Brian Cambourne, with Gail Langton. Stanley, NY: Wayne Finger Lakes Board of Cooperative Educational Services, 1994. 10–20.

———. "Toward an Educationally Relevant Theory of Literacy Learning: Twenty Years of Inquiry." *The Reading Teacher* 49.3 (1995): 182–7.

———. *The Whole Story: Natural Learning and the Acquisition of Literacy in the Classroom.* Penrose, Auckland, New Zealand: Ashton Scholastic, 1988.

Gee, James Paul. *Social Linguistics and Literacies: Ideology in Discourses.* London: Falmer, 1996.

Gerard, George, Randall G. Sleeth, and C. Glenn Pearce. "Technology-Assisted Instruction and Instructor Cyberphobia: Recognizing the Ways to Effect Change." *Education* 116 (1996): 604–8.

Green, Kenneth C. "The Coming Ubiquity of Information Technology." *Change* 28 (1996). 20 Dec. 1999. http://webbetaC.hwwilsonweb.com/cgi.

Harrington, Susanmarie, and William Condon. "Don't Lower the River, Raise the Bridge: Preserving Standards by Improving Students' Performances." *The Dialogic Classroom.* Ed. Jeffrey R. Galin and Joan Latchaw. Urbana, IL: NCTE, 1998. 92–105.

Kumar, David, and James Altschuld. "Contextual Variables in a Technology-Based Teacher Education Project." *Journal of Technology and Teacher Education* 7.1 (1999): 75–81.

McLeod, Susan. "The Ethics of Hiring in a Time of Change: A Response to the Final Report: MLA Committee on Professional Employment and to the 'Statement from the Conference on the Growing Use of Part-Time and Adjunct Faculty.'" *ADE Bulletin* 122 (1999): 31–4.

National Education Association and Blackboard, Inc. "NEA and Blackboard, Inc. Study Finds 24 Measures of Quality in Internet-Based Distance Learning." News Release, Institute for Higher Education Policy, March 22, 2000. http://www.ihep.com/PR17.html.

Privateer, Paul Michael. "Academic Technology and the Future of Higher Education: Strategic Paths Taken and Not Taken." *The Journal of Higher Education* 70.1 (1999): 60–79.

Resnick, Lauren B. "Making American Smarter." *Education Week on the Web* 16 June 1999. 15 Nov. 1999. sysiwyg://190http://www.edweek.org/ew/1999/40resnick.

Resnick, Lauren B., and Megan W. Hall. "Learning Organizations and Sustainable Education Reform." *Daedalus* 127.4 (1998): 89–118.

Turbill, Jan. "Changing Our View of Staff Development: A Focus on Language and the Role that Language Plays in Learning." NCTE Convention, Detroit. 21 Nov. 1997.

Turbill, Jan, Andrea Butler, Brian Cambourne, with Gail Langton. *Literacy and Learning.* 4th Rev. ed. Newark, NJ: Wayne Finger Lakes Board of Cooperative Educational Services, 1999.

# 17. "What Would You Like to Work on Today?" The Writing Center as a Site for Teacher Training

MURIEL HARRIS

When TAs reflect on the many benefits of being writing tutors, they frequently include in their lists—often with great enthusiasm—an affirmation that their writing center experience also makes them better classroom teachers. Alan Jackson emphatically states that "working in a writing center prepared me for teaching more than any methods course or composition theory book" (1). Lynnea Chapman King et al. agree that "working face-to-face and one-to-one in the writing center forever alters the way we interact with students in our own classes" (4). Adding to the list of endorsements from tutors, James Anderson et al. describe tutoring as "the best possible training for future teachers of writing" (37). And Christina Van Dyke extends this affirmation of what is gained from tutoring to recommend that all teaching assistants equip themselves with the skills they need to teach composition by tutoring in a writing center before they enter the classroom. For Irene Lurkis Clark, the numerous advantages of using the writing center to train composition teachers "seem almost self-evident" (348). In short, that writing center down the hall or across the campus, a place often crowded to overflowing with students who find it valuable, can be equally useful for training college composition teachers.

Why these panegyrics to one-to-one tutoring as a road to better classroom teaching? For those of us who tutor and are personally and professionally enriched by the experience, tutoring is the most effective form of teaching we have encountered. And we welcome the opportunity to share our approaches and methods with those who teach in classrooms because we know that tutoring also has much to offer classroom teachers. An examination of what is gained from tutor training and the accompanying experience of meeting students in the tutorial setting will help illustrate why writing centers can be a particularly effective—and unique—training ground for graduate teaching assistants, a place where they can learn approaches and insights that can be carried over into their own interactions with students.

To contextualize the goals and methods of tutor training, I offer first a brief overview of the two tutoring staffs in our Writing Lab at Purdue University—

one staff with classroom experience and the other novices—because different goals and training methods are needed for people with different prior experience. This overview will allow others to select and choose from what is offered here, according to what is appropriate for other settings and contexts. Then, I offer an analysis of what tutors learn through training and tutoring experiences, and finally I describe activities and projects we use for tutor training at Purdue to meet these goals. My hope is these can also be incorporated into teacher training to provide insights, strategies, experiences, and understanding that can—and do—improve teaching.

## TRAINING STAFFS WITH DIFFERENT ENTERING LEVELS OF SKILLS AND EXPERIENCES

The training goals and methods to be described here are an amalgam of two training programs in our Writing Lab, one for graduate TAs who have already taught composition in classrooms for at least one year and are joining the Writing Lab's tutoring staff and a second for undergraduates who will then tutor in our developmental writing program.

### TRAINING EXPERIENCED GRADUATE STUDENTS

Our Writing Lab, a part of the English Department, funds our graduate tutoring staff, thus limiting us to hiring only English Department TAs as tutors. All of our graduate tutors have prior experience in teaching before applying to our Writing Lab staff for two reasons: (1) The English Department requires all new graduate students to start their careers at Purdue by teaching only in the first-year writing program and to be trained in a mentoring course for that teaching, and (2) we have found that training in the theories and pedagogies of our first-year writing program provides useful background for tutors who work with many of these students and the diverse group of other students from various corners of the campus who also come to the Lab. When graduate students join the Lab, therefore, they have already completed a credit-bearing mentoring seminar that focuses on teaching first-year composition (a program discussed in Irwin Weiser's chapter in this collection). In that seminar they were introduced to theories of writing instruction, classroom matters such as how to structure and write a syllabus, grading techniques, and classroom management strategies. Thus, when they move on to other teaching assignments after their first year as TAs, they have had a year of classroom experience and mentoring in teaching writing.

Beginning in their second year, when TAs can branch out and opt to teach in other programs, such as professional writing, developmental writing, writing with computers, ESL courses, the Writing Lab, and so on, they enroll in other credit-bearing mentoring seminars designed to train them as instructors in these programs. These seminars evolved from non-credit staff meetings to credit-bearing courses as the content for each began to demand more time and more training than could be accomplished in orientation or staff meetings. Historically, then, from the Writing Lab's beginnings in the 1970s (when the graduate program was already in place, though with a more informally structured training seminar for first-year composition), TAs have joined the Lab's staff already having taught at least one year in composition classrooms.

For the Writing Lab's graduate seminar in tutoring writing, which I teach, this means that TAs new to the Writing Lab have already taught, read, discussed, and been observed and evaluated as classroom teachers of composition. Those who are working on advanced degrees in our rhetoric/composition program are also taking courses in rhetorical theory. My role in the Writing Lab training seminar is to acclimate them to tutoring as it differs from teaching, to introduce them to writing center theory and practice as it differs from or is related to composition theory and practice, to help them acquire tutoring strategies, to introduce them to the varieties of documents students will be working on, and to provide a forum for discussion and reflection on their tutoring experiences. Because TAs are enrolled in the seminar when they begin tutoring, they can draw on their daily experiences and raise questions about concerns or problems they may have had in tutorials.

## TRAINING INEXPERIENCED UNDERGRADUATES

The other tutor training course I teach is for undergraduates who are majoring in a variety of fields within the School of Liberal Arts. The course trains them to work as paid tutors (with funding provided by the English Department) in the developmental composition program, a program that integrates tutoring by having a peer tutor assigned to each classroom section. These tutors, whom we call undergraduate teaching assistants (UTAs), join the composition class one day a week and also meet every student from that class in the Writing Lab, every week. The training course is taught in the semester before the undergraduates begin tutoring, and students selected to be in the course come with little or no background in theories or practices in teaching writing and a great deal of misinformation about tutoring as primarily error correction. In addition to helping these students move past these misconceptions to a more appropriate appreciation of tutoring theory and practice, the credit-bearing undergraduate training course covers basics that aren't included—or only touched on—in the graduate course for TAs who have come to the Lab with classroom experience and knowledge of composition theory and writing processes.

## TRAINING TO WORK WITH DIFFERENT POPULATIONS OF STUDENTS

Different training courses are also needed for our two staffs because the students whom they work with will differ. The UTAs will meet only students who are writing papers in the developmental course, while the graduate students will be meeting with students from across the university who are composing a variety of documents. This diversity mirrors the nature of Purdue's student body. Purdue University is a land-grant university enrolling over 37,000 students, about 5,000 of whom are speakers of other languages who have journeyed to Purdue primarily to study engineering, computer science, the natural and physical sciences, agriculture, and business. Many other students are traditional undergraduates or traditional graduate students who begin graduate studies immediately after completing undergraduate degrees. Others, in both the undergraduate and graduate programs, are nontraditional students who have returned after a hiatus or are retooling for new careers. Because the Writing Lab serves this mix of students, members of all of these groups are likely to appear for tutorials with graduate tutors, bringing essays from first-year composition classes, documents from business writing courses, engineering reports, grant or conference proposals, research papers for upper-level undergraduate courses, applications to professional schools, resumés, doctoral dissertation chapters, and so on. This means that TAs selected to be tutors in our Writing Lab (and not all applicants are accepted as staff members) are trained to work with a great diversity of writers and to meet them both in one-to-one tutorials and online via our OWL (Online Writing Lab).

## WHAT DO TUTORS LEARN ABOUT TEACHING?

### WRITING PROCESSES

Reading about writing processes provides a background for understanding how we write, but that knowledge is one step removed from observing writers at work and seeing the messiness and reality of actual composing. In a writing center, students come in at all stages of a paper's development. Sometimes it's to think about the paper they're going to write, or as Clark notes, "simply to talk about a topic in order to clarify their own thinking" (347). The watching, listening, and question-asking the tutor engages in is a vivid demonstration of the convoluted paths writers take to find out what they want that illusive main point to be, of the ways in which outlines can assist or inhibit that exploration, and of the directions early drafts slowly take, often in zigzag fashion, as the paper moves toward coherence. As they work with students, tutors learn more about when and why writers get stuck and can't proceed to work on a draft that is not yet successful. For example, one problem tutors learn to recognize is that often at this blocked stage of writing, students wander in, asking for assistance in some vague way (e.g., "Could you look at this paper?" or "I need some help with this.") because they don't know how to talk about their writing and, therefore, can't begin to identify what they want to work on. Lacking any metalanguage to talk about writing, the writer can't identify what to do next (that is, from the perspective of problem solving, we can't think about how to solve a problem if we can't even articulate it). With more first-hand understanding of how composing works, how students think about writing, and what kinds of difficulties they are prone to, teachers are more aware of how to help writers. Clark's emphasis on tutoring as a way to learn about writing processes is based on her premise that while process approaches are presented in teacher training courses, novices don't really understand what is actually meant by process teaching and how it can be implemented in the classroom (347). As tutors, however, they sit with writers at work and gain a close understanding of when and how to intervene and what classroom activities help develop students' understanding of their own writing processes.

## INDIVIDUAL DIFFERENCES AMONG WRITERS

Preparation for classroom instruction often considers student writers as an almost homogeneous group, acknowledging perhaps categories such as different levels of abilities or English-as-a-second language problems. Entering the classroom, then, the teacher is inclined to respond to a sea of indistinguishable faces, focusing instruction on what the majority of students should know. But in the tutorial, those faceless students become very distinct individuals, each with his or her own concerns, questions, background, cultural differences, writing habits, literacy history, modes of learning, and levels of motivation. Tutors must learn how to find out who that person is and what he or she wants to work on in order to proceed effectively, and tutor training incorporates numerous ways to assess or diagnose concerns not just with the paper but with the writer as a whole person. The writing center mantra here is Stephen North's oft-repeated statement that a tutor's goal "is to produce better writers, not better writing" (438). And that means attending closely to who that particular writer is. As a result, tutors recognize that just as no two tutorials are alike, no two writers are the same. One of the rationales for the success of tutorial instruction is the ability of the session to focus tightly on that individual writer, and much has been written on the effectiveness of individualized instruction. Tutor training and tutoring experience, then, hone a teacher's ability to move beyond generic instruction to acknowledging differences and to learning how to work with those differences. Having spent "up close and personal" time with writers, classroom teachers who are or have been tutors see beyond the prose on the page to considerations of who that writer is and how to assess and respond to the paper in terms of that writer, not just the disembodied words on a page.

## RESPONSE TO STUDENT WRITING

Just as tutors learn to look beyond the page for clues as to how to help the writer, they also learn how to respond to the writer in ways other than giving back comments such as those written on the margins of student papers. And they learn to prioritize in terms of what to work on first. One of the early books to articulate a hierarchy of concerns and thereby affirm the nature of a useful agenda for tutoring was Thomas Reigstad and Donald McAndrew's *Training Tutors for Writing Conferences* (1984). Among the basics articulated by Reigstad and McAndrew was that higher-order concerns (HOCs, the larger rhetorical issues in creating effective writing) should be dealt with before lower-order concerns (LOCs, the sentence-level concerns of grammar, spelling, and mechanics, although I suggest we think of LOCs as an acronym for "later order concerns" to indicate not that sentence-level concerns are unimportant but that they should be dealt with after the HOCs). This emphasis on HOCs and LOCs is repeated throughout the literature on tutor training and in training manuals because prospective tutors, like new teachers, are prone to coming to their work thinking they are error spotters. They envision their first job to be catching all the grammatical errors and misspellings before attending to focus, audience, organization, development, and the other HOCs.

The concern for ridding student papers of errors as the first priority is an inclination that dies hard. Novices usually come to tutoring and teaching with mindsets created by what happened to them in their English classes and what their friends expect of them when they are asked to proofread papers. Training helps to undermine the rock-hard inclination to error hunt. But the real death knell for this inclination is the tutor's experience as she works with the writer to revise. As she does so, she watches those corrected comma splices and fragments they labored over disappear from the page as the writer's ideas come into focus and the arguments are reformulated into other phrases and sentences. Kate Gadbow, in "Teachers as Writing Center Tutors: Release from the Red Pen," notes that this shift away from error correction also "develops respect for the student. It's easy to lose it when all we see of students' thinking is hastily-written, error-riddled essays and assignments. In talking with them, we learn what they know and start looking for ways to help them say it" (15).

From a slightly different perspective, tutors also see how little students absorb or understand some teacher comments, and tutors learn why one of their roles is to serve as a translator, someone who is situated somewhere between the teacher and student, helping the student interpret the teacher's comments. When tutors move into classroom instruction, they are not likely to write those extensive and jargon-laden notes with which some teachers so carefully (and with the best of intentions) annotate student papers, a lesson I learned early on from my own tutoring (Harris, "The Overgraded Paper"). Lost in a sea of suggestions, questions in the margins, directives, check marks, alternate word choices, and long summary comments at the end of the paper, some students simply shove the paper across the table to the tutor and offer their interpretation as "she didn't like my paper." Moreover, when tutors perceive how downcast and disheartened some students are by negative comments, they understand the tutoring principle of starting a session on a positive note and the students' smiles that follow when the tutor notes what is good or effective in the students' writing. Such experiences, once embedded in a tutor's consciousness, dramatically change how he or she will comment when responding in writing to a set of class papers.

## DIFFICULTIES WITH ASSIGNMENTS

Early on in a tutorial, to set goals for the session and to define the student-tutor context, tutors often ask students to explain the assignment they are working on. Here tutors learn how much students understand—or fail to understand—or misunderstand—the assignment. All too often they hear students struggle to restate the assignment, going around in verbal circles until they give up, dive into their backpacks, and shuffle the assignment sheet over to the tutor, hoping the tutor can figure it out. Tutors observe first-hand why students write papers that fail to accomplish the task because as writers, students may perceive that task in ways quite different from the instructor's conceptualization. Such difficulties can range from the student's assuming that the event she is supposed to interpret or analyze should include every last detail she can remember about it (resulting perhaps in a dazzling array of specific sensory detail, but embedded in rambling discourse with little point or focus) to the student's assuming that writing an interpretation of a short story is supposed to be, primarily, a plot summary extensively peppered with quotations. Anyone who tutors for any length of time becomes aware of how often student writing goes awry because the writer never quite perceives the appropriate elements of the task at hand. And tutors see assignments that border on impenetrable, that are far too complex for the class, that require the writer to address so many concerns that a well-focused essay is impossible, or that give no hint of who the audience is.

Training sessions that help the tutor learn how to assist students in these situations also result in tutors' defining for themselves how to write assignments that work. (In our Writing Lab, we discuss how to handle what we call "AFH's," or "Assignments from Hell." Occasionally, a grad tutor groans as she recognizes something in the assignment similar to one of hers.) This sensitizing to effective elements of assignments is something that Lisa Johnson-Shull affirms after her tutor training: "TAs are better prepared to create assignments that challenge and interest students after seeing what assignments work and don't work from a myriad of other sources" (13).

## INSTRUCTIONAL STRATEGIES

A basic principle of tutoring is to avoid lecturing and presentation of information and, instead, to ask writers questions that help them verbalize their ideas, identify what their papers might lack, realize what revisions they will make, or correct awkwardly phrased sentences. The goal is to help writers learn to take active control of their own writing and not to wait passively for instructions for what to do. This entails learning how to ask questions that encourage appropriate responses and that help students think about what they want to write. It also involves listening rather than talking, collaborating with the writer rather than providing information, but learning when the student does need information and how to present that information in ways the student will understand. Tutors also need to learn how to talk with the student about setting goals for what they will accomplish together during their session. Because their time together is limited, tutors learn how to become efficient users of time and how to end a discussion in ways that help the student see where to go next or what to do with the paper after leaving the tutorial. For on-line interaction with writers, where tutors are unable to draw on tone of voice or nonverbal language to encourage students to respond, tutors must learn to ask—in writing—questions that invite responses from students rather than silence them, to build a working relationship via text on a computer monitor that invites interaction, and to refrain from responding in writing with directive comments or statements that convey too much authority or ownership of the student's text.

To accomplish all this, tutors learn question-asking strategies and techniques for establishing rapport so that collaboration can take place, for assessing who that writer is and what she needs (rather than what the paper needs), and how to motivate the student to write or revise the paper. All of these strategies can be transferred to teacher conferences, on-line conferences or discussions of drafts, and workshop classrooms.[1] Teachers who have had tutor training and tutoring experience learn how to use these strategies to talk effectively with their students and learn why they need to conference with their students rather than meet solely via written comments on paper. Moreover, they learn powerful lessons about collaborating with their students in relationships that aim to reduce the power dynamic. As Johnson-Shull explains, "The Writing Lab's practice of conversational, non-authoritarian tutoring exposes teachers to the educational impact they can have as peers rather than as distanced professionals" (13).

## WHAT ACTIVITIES CAN A TUTOR TRAINING PROGRAM INCLUDE?

The list presented above of what tutors learn is also a detailed agenda for tutor training, but tutors also acquire this knowledge in part through actual experience sitting and talking with students. Tutor training becomes a mix of (1) on-the-job experience, (2) reflection on and discussion of that experience, and (3) class activities that promote effective tutoring strategies. The programmatic suggestions offered below are a combination of these elements and what is covered in the two different training courses I teach, one for graduate tutors and another for undergraduates. The practices and activities described here, then, bring together what happens in the graduate and undergraduate training courses, and I offer these activities with the assumption that others can pick and choose among them, to select which might be appropriate for their institutional context and their TAs.

### OBSERVATION AND REFLECTION

While reading about tutoring provides a background for understanding this type of teaching (and I have coursepacks of readings for both training classes), the reality of watching tutors at work is far more useful. In lengthy end-of-the-semester evaluation essays that future UTAs write, they frequently rate their hours of sitting in and observing tutorials as one of the major factors that contribute to learning how to tutor. Watching, listening, and observing, they soak in the reality that makes the principles come alive, and they see the various ways that generalized theories can be enacted. They begin to understand what is meant by helping the writer become an active participant in her own learning, and they learn, simultaneously, how that is done and—equally important—what doesn't work. Tutorials where future UTAs sit quietly at the tutoring table as observers and hear tutors answer their own questions so quickly that the student is silenced, sessions where future UTAs hear a student first voice a question that is ignored and then retreat when the concern isn't addressed, or tutorials that end with minimal or no learning because the student's obvious hostility to being there is not dealt with illustrate what to avoid in helping students take control of their own learning and writing processes. Seeing successes and failures as they happen has a stronger impact than reading about them.

While observations are useful, the experience can be so data-rich with possible factors to contemplate that for initial observations I prepare a note-taking sheet with questions to guide the observer in deciding what to look for. The questions help focus attention on important aspects of tutoring in the welter of sensory input with which the observer is being overwhelmed. Questions on the note-taking sheet include prompts such as the following:

- What did the tutor do or say to establish rapport at the beginning of the tutorial? What body language or verbal cues from the student did you observe that indicated the success of what the tutor did?
- What were particularly effective questions the tutor asked, and how did you know they were effective?
- What did the tutor do or say to help him/her assess the student's learning?
- What are some comments made by the student that indicated he/she had learned something in the tutorial?

After a few observation sessions, such note-taking sheets are not necessary as observers begin to recognize aspects of the tutorial they want to think about. Writing papers on three or four of the observation sessions helps to organize their thoughts and provide a way to reflect on what they've learned. Even for those who do not go on to tutor, the experience is valuable in that, as they repeatedly affirm in their end-of-semester evaluations, their own writing improves, their understanding of writing processes is enriched, and their interpersonal skills are honed.


## ROLE PLAYING

Particularly for our undergraduates who have not worked closely with students yet, practicing to be a tutor helps to defuse very real anxieties about their abilities and gives them some experience beforehand. In such sessions, they can try out tutoring strategies, gain some modicum of confidence in their abilities, and move beyond initial hesitation about their own skills. In our setting, for some mock tutorials the students in the training course role-play with each other, and for other mock tutorials, experienced UTAs take the student role. We introduce into each mock tutorial a role for the "student"—the hostile student, the shy student who is difficult to engage in conversation, the defensive student who is intent on warding off any suggestion that the paper is less than perfect (because his or her high school English grades were excellent), the hand-wringing student who is convinced she's hopeless and will never write a good paper, the student who wants the tutor to tell him what to write, and so on. The pedagogical premise here is that having stared down such difficult situations in practice, the future tutor does not have to confront similar difficulties for the first time in a real tutorial. And, in the feedback session after the mock tutorial, suggestions and options for more effective strategies can also be discussed.

## INTERVIEWS WITH OTHER WRITERS

As noted above, reading about writing processes helps newcomers grasp some of the complexities of writing, and observing or talking with writers in some stages of composing provides additional dimensions of understanding and often dissipates a lingering and perhaps unconscious assumption that everyone else writes in ways fairly similar to our own. Individual differences in writing processes are, too often, not dealt with in teacher training.[2] Thus, tutors and teachers are prone to recommending their own writing practices to writers for whom such writing strategies can be inhibiting. One way to illustrate the differences among writers is to initiate, in a training session, a discussion about how each person writes. How do they start? By planning in their head? Sitting at the computer? Making an outline? Reading or talking to friends? How does a draft proceed? Does the writer block out the general organization mentally or write and write and write and then go back and cut and paste? Who has to find the perfect first sentence (or paragraph) before proceeding? Who begins in the middle of the paper, and then, later on, when the thesis has emerged, goes back and writes the introduction? Such conversations help future tutors and TAs begin to see that their writing processes are not universal.

To add depth to this understanding, future tutors in our undergraduate training classes are asked to write a paper interviewing another writer and then comparing similarities and differences between that writer and the tutor. In the coursepack, I list some suggestions for interview questions, although after the class discussion in which the tutors have talked about themselves it is easier to envision how they might question another person about how he or she writes. In addition to the questions already raised in the discussion, other suggestions for the interview are as follows:

- What kinds of writing do you typically do? Which are most enjoyable?
- Tell me something about where and when you usually write and what you usually use: e.g., pencil or computer. Do you think any of this makes a difference in your writing?
- When do you usually start a paper, soon after the assignment is given or close to the deadline? Why? How much time do you allow for revision? Or do you revise as you proceed?
- What happens in the days or hours before you write? What are your first words on paper? notes? outlines? random jottings?
- What helps you most when you're stuck?
- Tell me a story about a time when you were really pleased/disappointed with your writing.
- Do you show your writing to others as you are working on it? What kind of feedback do you prefer?

The papers that analyze these interviews are filled with musings about how startled the author is to learn that the friend composes differently from the way the author does. Such an exercise also sensitizes tutors to the fact that some writers fear feedback, that other writers use the computer only as a last stage typewriter, that procrastinators tend to use looming deadlines as their motivation, that some people never outline, that others need an outline to start the paper, that while some people love the freedom of an assignment that is somewhat open-ended or not closely structured, others are lost or uncomfortable without structure. While this is critical information for tutors, it is equally important when TAs consider what deadlines to impose, what kinds of assignments work best, what kinds of response and feedback to offer—and when to offer it.

## TAKING A PERSONALITY PREFERENCE TEST

Much has been written about the use of the Myers-Briggs Type Indicator (MBTI) and its relationship to writing, teaching, and tutor training.[3] By taking the test themselves or discussing the various personality preference continua that are identified by the MBTI (e.g., the spectrum that identifies the degree to which some people prefer to work in spontaneous, less well-defined situations vs. those who are more comfortable with structure; the spectrum along which people divide themselves in preferring to talk over their ideas with others vs. those who prefer to think quietly by themselves, etc.), tutors become more aware of differences in the composing process and differences in how and when writers benefit most from assistance. There are, as well, implications for designing assignments, for understanding why some students grasp the concept of audience more easily than others, for why some students rely more on sensory data than on abstractions in developing main points and supporting arguments, and so on.

## COLLABORATIVE REPORTS

When new tutors first confront the responsibility of assessing a student paper, many worry about their evaluative abilities—that is, whether they will be able to spot areas for the student to work on. Others are less aware of possible responses other than their own. To give them practice in hearing how others might respond to a paper and how to collaborate, our tutors meet in small groups to read a paper together and come to some consensus about matters such as whether the paper met the assignment, what its main point is, what its strengths are, what positive comments the tutor might make to the student, what needs revision, and what the tutorial might focus on. These discussions are meant to help novices gain confidence in their own ability to assess the writing of others and to hear a wider range of responses. With prior cautioning about the lack of absolutes in responding to student writing, tutors also gain a deeper insight into the varieties of reader response.

## DISCUSSIONS

While the activities described above are all valuable, discussion time for tutors to reflect on what they have learned and to share their concerns and questions remains an absolutely necessary component of training. Reflection done in tutoring logs or journals is helpful—and a valuable way for each tutor to analyze in depth some of what he or she has learned or tried. Using writing to push these thoughts into more permanent records also allows the tutor and the person doing the training to communicate personally when the trainer reads the log or journal and responds. (I have found that some undergraduates training to be tutors will write about, but not openly discuss, some of their concerns, so I find this written interaction very important and a good way to get to know each person more closely.) But, finally, it is the open discussion among the trainer and those being trained to tutor (or already tutoring) that brings to the surface the concerns and questions that new tutors have. Often a question prompts another tutor to offer a different tutoring strategy that might help or to suggest a different analysis of the situation. A description of a failed attempt with a student may cause another member of the group to see his experience in a new light.

For on-line tutoring, a service in which we answer questions about writing via email to our OWL, we often share techniques or review archived copies of each other's responses to learn from each other how to phrase questions, how to pare down written responses so that we do not overwhelm the student with screens filled with text, and how to respond to requests that are either too vague or that indicate the writer's determined inclination to let the tutor find the answers. Sometimes, our group discussions also help us realize that we are stepping into areas where more expertise is needed, and we call upon experts around the university to help us. For example, we've called upon professionals on campus to help us identify and understand learning disabilities and to recognize emotional difficulties that require professional intervention. Such knowledge helps greatly when our tutors also meet up with similar symptoms in their classrooms.

## WHO SHOULD TUTOR?

In sum, tutor training adds a dimension of awareness about writing and writers and experience in working closely with individual writers that is a valuable element in any TA's growth as a teacher. But tutor training may not be appropriate for every TA because some may not be comfortable in the tutorial setting. Those who work best in highly structured situations and prefer a tightly scheduled classroom hour will not profit from being plunged into the fluidity of the tutorial setting, where flexibility and adeptness at using cues from the student to structure the session are critical to a successful outcome.

However, for those instructors who enjoy the give-and-take of tutorial conversation and the nonhierarchical relationship in which the student is invited to consider the tutor as a collaborator who determines neither the assignment nor the student's grade, tutor training offers a context for learning that is unique in terms of the tutor's personal and professional growth. Tutors enhance their interpersonal skills and their knowledge about how to interact effectively with students, and they begin to appreciate the benefits of a student-centered environment that helps students develop as writers. Moreover, as those of us who tutor know, sitting with writers in a one-to-one setting may be exhausting, but it is almost always rewarding. As we watch the student begin to understand how she's going to revise her paper, and as we hear her repeated expressions of thanks for helping her figure out what she wanted to write about, we remember why it is we want to work with writers.

## NOTES

1. Such strategies can be found in the numerous tutor-training manuals on the market. Two excellent new manuals are by Gillespie and Lerner and Ryan.
2. My interest in individualized differences in writing processes has led me to explore this topic in Harris ("Composing").
3. The major contribution to the literature on the MBTI and writing is DiTiberio and Jensen. For uses of the MBTI and classroom teaching, see Thompson and for tutoring, see Harris ("Don't Believe").

## WORKS CITED

Anderson, James E., Ellen M. Bommarito, and Laura Seijas. "Writing-Center Tutors Speak Out: An Argument for Peer Tutoring as Teacher Training." *Improving Writing Skills.* Ed. Thom Hawkins and Phyllis Brooks. *New Directions for College Learning Assistance.* San Francisco: Jossey-Bass, 1981. 35–7.

Clark, Irene Lurkis. "Preparing Future Composition Teachers in the Writing Center." *College Composition and Communication* 39 (1988): 347–50.

DiTiberio, John, and George Jensen. *Writing & Personality: Finding Your Voice, Your Style, Your Way.* Palo Alto, CA: Davies Black, 1995.

Gillespie, Paula, and Neal Lerner. *The Allyn & Bacon Guide to Tutoring.* Needham Heights, MA: Allyn & Bacon, 2000.

Gadbow, Kate. "Teachers as Writing Center Tutors: Release from the Red Pen." *Writing Lab Newsletter* 14.4 (1989): 13–5.

Harris, Muriel. "Composing Behaviors of One-and Multi-Draft Writers." *College English* 51 (1989): 174–91.

———. "Don't Believe Everything You're Taught." *The Subject Is Writing.* Ed. Wendy Bishop. Portsmouth, NH: Boynton/Cook, 1993. 189–201.

———. "The Overgraded Paper: Another Case of More Is Less." *How to Handle the Paper Load: Classroom Practices in Teaching English, 1979–1980.* Ed. Gene Stanford. Urbana, IL: NCTE, 1979. 91–4.

Jackson, Alan. "Writing Centers: A Panorama to Teaching and the Profession." *Writing Lab Newsletter* 18.6 (1994): 1–2, 12.

Johnson-Shull, Lisa. "Teaching Assistants Learn Teaching Tips by Tutoring." *Writing Lab Newsletter* 18.9 (1994): 13.

King, Lynnea Chapman, Jeff Williams, Joanna Castner, Amy Hanson, and Lady Falls Brown. "Writing Center Theory and Practice: Pedagogical Implications for Teacher Training." *Writing Lab Newsletter* 21.8 (1997): 4–8.

North, Stephen. "The Idea of a Writing Center." *College English* 46 (1984): 433–46.

Reigstad, Thomas J., and Donald A. McAndrew. *Training Tutors for Writing Conferences.* Urbana, IL: NCTE, 1984.

Ryan, Leigh. *The Bedford Guide for Writing Tutors.* Boston: Bedford, 1998.

Thompson, Thomas, ed. *Most Excellent Differences: Essays on Using Type Theory in the Composition Classroom.* Gainesville, FL: CAPT, 1996.

Van Dyke, Christina. "From Tutor to TA: Transferring Pedagogy from the Writing Center to the Composition Classroom." *Writing Lab Newsletter* 21.8 (1997): 1–3, 10.

# PART 4

## PRACTICES

# 18. Mentoring: Past, Present, and Future

SALLY BARR EBEST

If readers were to peruse recent books and essays on education, they might get the impression that mentoring was a recent phenomenon. Nothing could be further from the truth, for examples of mentoring can be found as early as the ancient Greeks. But even though the concept is familiar and longstanding, the practice has only recently been recognized as integral to graduate education. To illustrate this progression, in this essay I trace the practice of mentoring. After a brief overview of its historical roots, I focus more specifically on how the traditional conception of mentoring in academia evolved from a preoccupation with graduate students' research skills to include preparation for teaching and administration. This discussion provides the basis for the final section, which suggests new directions for compositionists and WPAs to consider when revising their curricula. Mentoring is neither new nor unproblematic; nevertheless, the variety of approaches existing within graduate composition programs provides models to fit practically any institution's needs.

## MENTORING IN THE PAST

One early reference to mentoring can be traced to the ancient Greeks in the story of Mentor and Telemachus. When Odysseus began his journeys, he asked Mentor to look after his son, Telemachus. In Sharan Merriam's review of the literature on mentoring, she describes this relationship as "father-like" and "loving," one that "set a standard for characterizing future mentoring relationships," noting that at one point, Mentor even saved the life of his protégé (162). This incident is further explained in *The Classic Myths*. In his commentary, Charles Gayley recounts that while searching for Odysseus, Telemachus visited the isle of Calypso. To thwart Calypso's attempts to seduce Telemachus, the goddess Athena "in the shape of Mentor, accompanied him and governed all his movements, made him repel [Calypso's] allurements. Finally, when no other means of escape could be found, the two friends leaped from a cliff into the sea and swam to a vessel which lay becalmed offshore" (532). In this, we find many elements characteristic of mentorship: guidance, supervision, friendship, and protection. Yet this myth also contains a major contradiction to the traditional definition, for Mentor is only a "vessel" for Athena, chosen "so that she herself can oversee Telemachus's upbringing." As Michael Galbraith and Norman Cohen explain,"When Athena speaks through him, Mentor possesses the goddess's glorious qualities. . . . [H]e is wisdom personified" (1).

Various accounts of Mentor's guidance overlook the source of his wisdom. But perhaps this should not be surprising, since within the history of mentoring the female presence has been notably absent. Within academia, mentoring has traditionally referred to a male professor's guidance and cultivation of a male protégé's intellect Hall and Sandler 4. According to a 1979 study by G. M. Philips, in these relationships the faculty member seeks advancement for the student in order to enhance the field and the student's role in it (340). Similarly, J. Schmidt cites three functions—"role model, information provider, door opener"—as characterizing the mentor-student relationship within the university (qtd. in Merriam 167). Eugene Anderson and Anne Shannon expand upon this concept, pointing out that mentoring is generally intentional, nurturing, insightful, and supportive (25–6). Mentors may serve variously as teachers, sponsors, counselors, and friends; they help develop their protégés' professionalism by modeling appropriate practices and behaviors, providing feedback, and willingly offering their time to meet with and support their protégés' endeavors (32). Conversely, Edward Ducharme offers the term *academic conscience*—"a model for excellence in the work one has chosen, an individual who helps evoke the best from others," but who may otherwise possess none of the previous characteristics (72). Such disparity reflects Merriam's findings that the literature on mentoring contains few clear-cut conclusions, a variety of definitions, vague or inconsistent methodologies, and a failure to examine "potential drawbacks" (169–70). However, these problems may also be due to the limitations of Merriam's own study published in 1983. Merriam focused primarily on the research conducted in the previous decade, but mentoring in academia did not become widespread until the 1980s (Anderson and Shannon 26).

Prior to that time, mentoring might be considered more de facto than de jure. Ostensibly, the German model of the research university suggested that faculty would work closely with their graduate students, in effect mentoring them throughout their apprenticeship as junior researchers (Russell 48). As composition historian David Russell puts it, "in theory" graduate students would "receive an intensive form of writing instruction—*mentoring*—to use today's term, as they pursued research" (48). In actuality, these experiences may have been more like those cited by R. McGinnis and J. S. Long: rather than benefiting the protégé, mentoring in the sciences was more likely to "contribute to the research visibility of the mentor" which led in turn to greater salaries and more promotions (qtd. in Merriam 168). A similar focus was evident across the disciplines. Although faculty were "expected to be mentors, guiding the apprentices as they learn the written conventions of the discipline," the pressure to research coupled with fairly simplistic notions regarding the necessity of writing instruction resulted in "little formal supervision" (Russell 242). As research gained importance, interaction and instruction with graduate students diminished to the extent that professors began to prefer students who were so well prepared and smart that faculty were not needed. This state of affairs is best summed up by Cary Nelson and Stephen Watt, who maintain that through "the 1950s and the 1960s dissertation directors were often rarely seen or heard" (162).

If graduate students received little direction in their research, they received even less in preparation for teaching. Jane Tompkins describes the prevailing attitude toward teaching as a "fear of pedagogy" and "antipedagogical indoctrination" (171)—feelings that reflect Cardinal Newman's belief disseminated in *The Idea of the University* that "To discover and to teach are distinct functions" (qtd. in Turner 5). This problem did not pass unnoticed. Jody Nyquist, Robert Abbott, and Donald Wulff point out that complaints about college-level teaching began in the 1930s and continued every decade thereafter (8). Over the years, this attitude resulted in "weak pedagogy, the preoccupation with 'covering the material,' the proliferation of multiple-choice tests, and [a refusal to] accept primary responsibility for graduate and undergraduate education" (Holmes Group 4–5). Nowhere was this attitude more evident than within departments of English.

Betty P. Pytlik reports that in the early 1900s, critics such as Irving Babbitt, Lyle Spencer, and George Miller expressed dissatisfaction with the narrow focus of doctoral programs in English and urged that TAs be prepared to teach writing ("Short History" 2–6; see also Pytlik's chapter in this collection). These calls were answered at Harvard, which instituted an apprenticeship program in which graduate students observed experienced teachers, wrote lectures, and simulated student conferences, but this practice did not spread (Pytlik, "Short History" 6). During the next fifty years, the teaching of writing proceeded without a research base and with no clear sense of pedagogy, a fact best described by Stephen North's reference to the latter as "lore." Teachers were not trained; they merely passed on what had worked for them. Because this approach lacked theoretical and pedagogical bases, teaching writing was considered "an intellectual backwater" (Connors 13–4). Moreover, because of these beliefs, there were few attempts to prepare TAs for their classroom duties. Spurred by the return of GIs from World War II, some efforts were made at major institutions, such as UC–Berkeley, Connecticut, Ohio State, Illinois, Washington, and Kansas, where teacher preparation ranged from apprenticeships, meetings, and methods courses (Pytlik, "Teaching" 7–8). But for the most part, TAs perpetuated the drudgery of composition pedagogy by teaching as they had been taught.

## MOVING TOWARD THE PRESENT

The collapse of the academic job market in the 1970s proved the catalyst for a renewed attention to mentoring (Nelson and Watt 162). With intensified competition for an ever-decreasing number of tenure-track positions came the realization that graduate students would need strong vitae. Consequently, faculty members attuned to the job crisis often began mentoring certain graduate students almost as soon as they embarked on their doctoral studies, continued to do so during their protégés' job searches, and even maintained contact throughout the six-year odyssey toward tenure and promotion (163). This mentoring did not focus on teaching; it maintained the traditional concern with graduate students' ability to research, write, and publish. Faculty who viewed them-selves as mentors began helping their protégés develop research projects that were realistic, manageable contributions to the field, then followed their progress to ensure that they remained on track and became neither discouraged nor overly optimistic. When the research was finished, mentors often read, responded to, and sometimes edited drafts of a student's dissertation. When the dissertation was completed, mentors might discuss publishing options (Nelson and Watt 163–4). In this, the mentor may be said to be not only "friend, guide, [and] counselor, but above all, a teacher" (Merriam 169). But this teaching applied only to research skills. If graduate students learned anything about ped-agogy, it was indirectly, through emulation or assimilation.

Throughout most of the 1980s, mentoring could be defined as relationships dominated by male professors who helped develop their protégés' research skills and fostered their professional egress. Reviews of TA training from 1979–1987 reveal no mention of mentoring across the disciplines (Abbott, Wulff, and Szego 114–5), and only a few within departments of English. (See, for example, Connolly and Vilardi; Lambert and Tice; Pytlik, "Short History"; or Catalano et al.). However, by the end of the 1990s, TA preparation had expanded to include mentoring through service learning, peer mentoring, team-teaching, and administrative assistantships (Barr Ebest, "Successes," "Fighting," "Next Generation"). What brought about these changes? In what may be one of the first positive uses of the term, the growth of mentoring could be partially attrib-uted to "the feminization of composition," for female WPAs constitute 50 per-cent of the membership of the Council of Writing Program Administrators (Barr Ebest, "Next Generation" 67), while females account for 70 percent of the grad-uate students in rhetoric (Enos 70).

## MENTORING IN THE 1990s

Within composition-rhetoric, the history of mentoring parallels that in other fields—up to a point. A 1995 survey of WPAs reported that among administra-tors earning doctorates between 1977 and 1984, men were twice as likely as women to have been mentored. Consequently, WPAs acquired their administra-tive skills primarily through trial and error (Barr Ebest, "Gender" 54). Having experienced the disasterous effects of this lack of knowledge on their profes-sional development, many WPAs began to realize that "To be a WPA is to regard administration as a *teaching* job" (Bruffee 57, emphasis in the original). Recog-nizing the need to enter the job market prepared to administer a writing pro-gram while simultaneously teaching and conducting research led WPAs to incor-porate a variety of mentoring programs into both the graduate curriculum and into what Richard Fulkerson has termed the "meta-curriculum." In so doing, composition-rhetoric has moved to the forefront of educational reform at the graduate level. Indeed, James Slevin argues that the rest of the university would do well to emulate the model of graduate education established in the field (154).

According to a 1996 survey by Catherine Latterell, seventy-two universities offer PhDs in composition-rhetoric, and half of these programs include some sort of mentoring for their graduate TAs (10). Among writing programs in general, 61.3 percent provide students with a mentor (Barr Ebest, "Next Generation" 67–8). The structure of these mentorships ranges from formal to informal and may constitute all or part of a TA's professional training; the focus may include teaching, research, or administration; and mentors may be drawn from WPAs, full- and part-time composition faculty, and experienced TAs. The next paragraphs discuss the variety of mentoring models across the country.

## WPAs AS MENTORS

In smaller programs, WPAs may function as de facto mentors, an approach advocated by David Foster, by Jo Sprague and Jody Nyquist, and by Ron Smith. Regardless of program size, WPAs could be said to mentor their TAs in five overlapping, interrelated areas: in the pre-semester workshop (orientation), in the pedagogy seminar (practicum), by supervising their teaching, during periodic in-service workshops, and in their general availability as counselors and sounding boards. Furthermore, WPAs can be strong role models through the examples they set in their research and publication and by encouraging graduate students to submit papers and conference proposals.

In larger programs, WPAs also mentor when they offer TAs opportunities to serve as administrative assistants. At the University of Oregon, for example, these TAs gain experience in reviewing syllabi, counseling TAs, designing and/or supervising exit exams, reviewing program data, and writing required reports. They also meet with department chairs across campus to discuss large-scale proposals, address pedagogical problems and problem students, find solutions to these problems, or help to organize public events, such as awards ceremonies or luncheons. At Purdue, graduate students assisting WPAs might serve as summer directors of a program or lab, help raise funds, write grants, run the program's Web site, or coordinate the peer tutoring program (Barr Ebest, "Successes").

Participating in these programs yields remarkable results. When TAs finish terms as administrative assistants, they know how to develop a writing program, organize in-services, design curricula, and teach various courses using a range of approaches. If necessary, they could administer a writing program, prepare TAs to teach, and design mentoring programs. Because they have been mentored by faculty and administrators across campus, they have enlarged their views of their department and its role in campus affairs. In sum, such experiences teach graduate students how to balance their teaching and research with administrative work—to organize their time, prioritize, delegate authority, negotiate political minefields, and build bridges between teaching and administration.

## FACULTY MENTORS

Given the demands on WPAs' time and the sizes of some writing programs, they cannot be solely responsible for mentoring. In 1987, Isaiah Simpson discussed the benefits of faculty and TAs team-teaching a course during TAs' first year of graduate study. Similarly, Eugene and Marilyn Smith describe a mentoring program that places TAs from the University of Washington in writing classes at North Seattle Community College, where they observe teaching and serve as teaching assistants. Faculty mentors can also promote professional development by arranging for TAs to team-teach upper division courses. At Brigham Young, for example, TAs observe their mentor's teaching for a semester and then take over the class the following semester (Hayes 227–9). TAs may even play a role in the teaching of graduate seminars. At the University of Louisville, WPA Brian Huot has developed an intensive, four-week pre-semester graduate pedagogy course required for new TAs and adjuncts which he team-teaches with his assistant WPAs—experienced graduate students who have completed their doctoral course work. Huot mentors his assistants by helping them develop teaching strategies; in turn, the assistants serve as mentors to the new class of TAs (Barr Ebest, "Fighting"). (See Katrina Powell et al.'s chapter in this collection for a more detailed discussion.)

## ADJUNCT FACULTY AS MENTORS

Some universities are beginning to build bridges within their own departments by drawing on the expertise of non-tenure track faculty to help prepare new TAs. At Penn State, some senior TAs and lecturers offer practica for TAs teaching a new course for the first time. These practica are one-credit-hour, self-designed courses that introduce TAs to the various facets of a new course via syllabi and directed readings. After teaching three semesters of freshman composition, new TAs may sign up for as many as five different practica in which they learn how to tutor in the Writing Center, teach in the writing-across-the-curriculum program, or teach developmental, business, or technical writing. These courses focus on practical applications. One goal, for example, is to teach TAs how to encourage students to be active learners through collaborative learning and small groups specifically designed for whatever course they will be teaching (Barr Ebest, "Re-designing").

A similar initiative was put into place at Ball State University by Jeff White during his term as assistant WPA. When the university was suddenly given several new computer labs in which to teach composition, new TAs needed more instruction than a single assistant could provide, so White called on the English department's lecturers. Working in pairs, the lecturers mentored the new TAs, sharing not only lesson plans but also technical know-how and practical advice. Such an initiative benefited both parties. The TAs gained knowledge and developed relationships and respect for heretofore unknown colleagues, while the lecturers felt more involved in and appreciated by the department.

## PEER MENTORS

This approach is practiced in writing programs across the country. Future teachers of writing are mentored by their peers at the University of Pittsburgh's Writing Workshop by working in a three-tiered internship program. New TAs learn the basics of teaching by interning with Writing Lab tutors and then working as tutors before they are assigned classes to teach (Smith, "Using" 76–82). At the University of Massachusetts, experienced TAs train "volunteer counselors" at the university's Resource Center, after which they help refine new TAs' teaching styles through videotaping (Puccio). In a 1991 survey, Allene Cooper and D. G. Kehl describe a form of mentoring they term "collaborative coaching," which pairs new and experienced TAs. At the Universities of Oregon and Tennessee-Knoxville, TAs take course work and work with a peer mentor during their first year of graduate school and prior to teaching. For these students, mentoring consists of observing their mentor's classes and meeting periodically to discuss teaching issues. At universities where graduate students begin teaching during their first year, such as Arizona and UMass–Amherst, groups of TAs are assigned a peer mentor with whom they meet individually and in groups (Latterell 11). In turn, the mentor observes the TAs' teaching, confers afterward, and writes teaching evaluations; analyzes their syllabi, assignment sheets, and handouts; and reviews sets of graded papers (Latterell 12).

At Northern Arizona University, mentorship is a privilege. Only a few TAs are chosen, based on their openness, pedagogical skills, and ability to listen. Mentorship is also a serious responsibility, for this work is the equivalent of teaching a course or tutoring in the Writing Center. Good mentors model their behavior for their protégés, who in turn have the opportunity to mentor the following year. Mentoring also provides TAs with the opportunity to reflect on their own teaching and to select the most successful lesson plans and handouts to share with their mentoring group. This combination of reflection and responsibility in turn helps mentors to become better prepared, more self-confident teachers (Barr Ebest, "Fighting").

At Purdue, after TAs teach two semesters of freshman composition, they have the opportunity to teach professional writing, technical writing, developmental writing, science writing, WAC, ESL, or tutor in the Writing Lab, but the first time they do, they must sign up with the appropriate mentoring group. Mentors are advanced PhD candidates who have finished course work. Their position combines mentoring and administration, usually for a two-year term. TAs are introduced to their mentoring duties and responsibilities in the summer by co-mentoring with the WPA in charge of the course. At the end of the summer, the mentors are responsible for leading a pre-semester orientation for TAs teaching the course for the first time. When school begins, the mentoring groups meet for an hour once or twice a week to help TAs apply composition theory to pedagogy, to discuss teaching and technical problems, to explain how to integrate technology with pedagogy, and to report on successful and unsuccessful projects and assignments (Barr Ebest, "Hidden"; see Irwin Weiser's chapter in this collection for a more detailed discussion of Purdue's mentoring program).

What do peer mentors learn? The experience teaches curricular planning and institutional perspectives on staffing and recruiting, as well as how to integrate pedagogy and technology, to collaborate and help new students conceptualize collaboration, to prioritize and manage time, to reflect on the integration of teaching and administration, and to negotiate with people outside the English department. They develop self-confidence, a strong voice that reflects it, and the ability to lead. Equally important, these mentors gain an awareness of the breadth and depth of the knowledge and skills that writing program adminis-tration requires and with it, a respect for the work. As a result, these graduate stu-dents will enter academia with the type of insider knowledge it has taken us years to acquire (Barr Ebest, "Hidden").

## MENTORING IN THE FUTURE

Clearly, participating in one of the many facets of mentoring can be highly ben-eficial for graduate students. Nevertheless, when the mentor is a faculty mem-ber, the power differential holds the potential for abuse. In a 1994 CCCC pres-entation, John Warnock raised the spectre of a mentor's becoming what self-help groups term an "enabler," allowing the protégé to skirt certain rules and requirements. Conversely, cross-gender mentoring opens the possibility for sexual harrassment or abuse, problems well-documented by Myra and David Sadker. In *Modern Sexism*, Nijole Benokraitis and Joe Feagin warn that male mentors may use female protégés to do their "dirty work," such as grading or researching, which may retard the protégé's progress toward a degree. But same-sex mentors can be equally culpable. Sometimes females, emulating their own male mentors, have failed to acknowledge their protégé's contributions when publishing or receiving public recognition for fear of being outshown (128–9). Such behavior exemplifies Gary Olson and Elizabeth Ashton-Jones's reports of cross-gender mentoring resulting in the indoctrination of female pro-tégés into the dominant (male) hierarchy (237). But such behavior is more likely to emerge within traditional research-oriented mentorships, where competition remains fierce, than in relationships focused on teaching, which are generally collaborative.

Nevertheless, such findings suggest that same-sex mentoring is preferable. As a rule, these relationships avoid threats of sexual abuse; they are also more likely to flourish because of shared understandings. Same-sex mentors provide clear-cut role models. Elizabeth Tidball found a strong correlation between the number of female faculty and successful female graduates (qtd. in Olson and Ashton-Jones 235). Similarly, Elyse Goldstein concludes that students in same-sex mentorships "are likely to publish significantly more than others" (qtd. in Olson and Ashton-Jones 235). If these findings hold true, WPAs and composi-tion faculty would do well to heed these trends and encourage same-sex men-torships. This should not be difficult, since females currently comprise 70 per-cent of the graduate students in rhetoric and 50 percent of the WPAs.

Of course, shared gender does not guarantee successful mentoring relation-ships. WPAs should bear in mind that students learn best from teachers they can relate to (Merriam 167). Indeed, "the forced matching of mentors and protégés ignores a characteristic crucial to the more intense mentor relationships—that the two people involved are attracted to each other and wish to work together" (171). These findings suggest that whenever possible, mentoring assignments should be left to individual choice. WPAs can build in opportunities for TAs to meet and interact. In programs where mentoring begins prior to or during a TA's first semester, WPAs or their assistants might initiate contact through a Writing Program listserv; if this is not possible, it is useful to provide occasions for introductions and casual exchanges. In sum, TAs should have a voice in choosing their mentors so that the experience has the potential for friendship because of mutual interests. Needless to say, WPAs should also ensure that those TAs serving as mentors are appropriately trained and rewarded through a reduction in their teaching loads, not only to make mentoring feasible, but also to reinforce its value. Finally, WPAs might consider making each mentoring experience worth one hour's credit to underscore its intellectual importance within the academy.

In his argument for reconceptualizing teaching as scholarship, Ernest Boyer maintains that to achieve this goal, "graduate study must be broadened, encouraging not only research, but integration, application, and teaching, too. It is this vision that will assure . . . a new generation of scholars, one that is more intellectually vibrant and more responsive to society's shifting needs" (74). By developing our own mentoring programs, WPAs have begun to answer that call. Just as we pioneered the extensive preparation of TAs for the classroom, we are clearly the most advanced in our understanding of our graduate students' needs for mentoring—for guidance, support, and protection. In so doing, we are taking the lead in preparing the next generation of professors.

## WORKS CITED

Abbott, Robert D., Donald H. Wulff, and C. Kati Szego. "Review of Research on TA Training." *Teaching Assistant Training in the 1990s.* Ed. Jody D. Nyquist, Robert D. Abbott, and Donald H. Wulff. San Francisco: Jossey-Bass, 1989. 111–21.

Anderson, Eugene, and Anne Lucasse Shannon. "Toward a Conceptualization of Mentoring." *Issues in Mentoring.* Ed. Trevor Kerry and Ann Shelton Mayes. New York: Routledge, 1995. 25–34.

Barr Ebest, Sally. "Fighting the Backlash: Graduate Programs in Composition-Rhetoric." MLA Conference. Chicago. 30 December 1999.

———. "Gender Differences in Writing Program Administration." *WPA* 18.3 (1995): 53–73.

———. "Hidden Successes: Graduate Programs in Composition-Rhetoric." Council of Writing Program Administrators' Conference. West Lafayette. 17 July 1999.

———. "The Next Generation of WPAs: A Study of Graduate Programs in Composition-Rhetoric." *WPA* 22.3 (1999): 65–84.

———. "Re-designing the Metacurriculum: Preparing TAs to be WPAs." Conference on College Composition and Communication. Minnneapolis. 13 April 2000.

Benokraitis, Nijole V., and Joe R. Feagin. *Modern Sexism: Blatant, Subtle, and Covert Discrimination.* 2nd. ed., Englewood Cliffs, NJ: Prentice Hall, 1995.

Boyer, Ernest. *Scholarship Reconsidered.* Princeton, NJ: Carnegie Foundation for the Advancement of Teaching. 1990.

Bruffee, Kenneth. "Thoughts of a Fly on the Wall." *WPA* 22.3 (1999): 55–64.

Catalano, Timothy, Will Clemens, Julia Goodwin, Gary McMillin, Jeff White, and Stephen Wilhoit. "TA Training in English: An Annotated Bibliography." *WPA* 19.3 (1996): 36–54.

Connolly, Paul, and Teresa Vilardi, eds. *New Directions in College Writing Programs.* New York: MLA, 1986.

Connors, Robert. *Composition-Rhetoric: Background, Theory, and Pedagogy.* Pittsburgh: U of Pittsburgh P, 1997.

Cooper, Allene, and D. G. Kehl. "Development of Composition through Peer Coaching." *WPA* 14.3 (1991): 27–39.

Ducharme, Edward R. *The Lives of Teacher Educators.* New York: Teachers College P, 1993.

Enos, Theresa. "Gender and Publishing Scholarship in Rhetoric and Composition." *Publishing in Rhetoric and Composition.* Ed. Gary A. Olson and Todd W. Taylor. Albany: SUNY UP, 1997. 57–74.

Foster, David. "Training Writing Teachers in a Small Program." *WPA* 10.1/2 (1986): 43–9.

Fulkerson, Richard. "The English Doctoral Metacurriculum: An Issue of Ethics." *Foregrounding Ethical Awareness in Composition and English Studies.* Ed. Sheryl I. Fontaine and Susan M. Hunter. Portsmouth, NH: Boynton/Cook, 1998. 121–43.

Galbraith, Michael W., and Norman H. Cohen, eds. *Mentoring: New Strategies and Challenges.* San Francisco: Jossey-Bass, 1995.

Gayley, Charles Mills. *The Classic Myths in English Literature and in Art.* Rev. ed., Waltham, MA: Ginn-Blaisdell, 1939.

Hall, Roberta M., and Bernice R. Sandler. *Academic Mentoring for Women Students and Faculty: A New Look at an Old Way to Get Ahead.* ERIC, 1983. ED 240 891.

Hayes, Darwin L. "Integrating Supervision, Evaluation, and Training: Graduate Student Internships in Teaching Composition." *Institutional Responsibilities and Responses in the Employment and Education of Teaching Assistants.* Ed. Nancy Van Note Chism. Columbus, OH: Ohio State University Center for Teaching Excellence, 1987. 227–9.

Holmes Group. *Tomorrow's Teachers.* East Lansing, MI: The Holmes Group, 1986.

Hulbert, Kathleen Day. "Gender Patterns in Faculty-Student Mentoring Relationships." *Gender and Academe: Feminist Pedagogy and Politics.* Ed. Sara Munson Deats and Lagretta Tallent Lenker. Lanham, MD: Rowman and Littlefield P, 1994. 247–64.

Lambert, Leo M., and Stacey L. Tice, eds. *Preparing Graduate Students to Teach.* Washington, DC: American Assn. of Higher Education, 1993.

Latterell, Catherine G. "Training the Workforce: An Overview of GTA Education Curricula." *WPA* 19.3 (1996): 7–23.

Merriam, Sharan. "Mentors and Protégés: A Critical Review of the Literature." *Adult Education Quarterly* 33.3 (1983): 161–73.

Nelson, Cary, and Stephen Watt. *Academic Keywords: A Devil's Dictionary for Higher Education.* New York: Routledge, 1999.

North, Stephen. *The Making of Knowledge in Composition: Portrait of an Emerging Field.* Upper Montclair, NJ: Boynton/Cook, 1987.

Nyquist, Jody E., Robert D. Abbott, and Donald H. Wulff, eds. "The Challenge of TA Training in the 1990s." *Teaching Assistant Training in the 1990s.* San Francisco: Jossey-Bass, 1989. 7–14.

Olson, Gary A., and Evelyn Ashton-Jones. "The Politics of Gendered Sponsorship: Mentoring in the Academy." *Gender and Academe: Feminist Pedagogy and Politics.* Ed. Sara Munson Deats and Lagretta Tallent Lenker. Lanham, MD: Rowman and Littlefield P, 1994. 231–46.

Philips, G. M. "The Peculiar Intimacy of Graduate Study: A Conservative View." *Communication Education* 28 (1979): 339–45.

Puccio, Paul M. "TAs Help TAs: Peer Counseling and Mentoring." Conference on Employment and Education of Teaching Assistants. Columbus, OH. November 1987. ED 285 502.

Pytlik, Betty P. "A Short History of Graduate Preparation of Writing Teachers." Conference of National Council of Teachers of English. Louisville. November 1992. ED 355 545.

———. "Teaching the Teacher of Writing: Whence and Wither?" Conference on College Composition and Communication. San Diego. March 1993. ED 355 541.

Russell, David. *Writing in the Academic Disciplines, 1870–1990.* Carbondale, IL: Southern Illinois UP, 1991.

Sadker, Myra, and David Sadker. *Failing at Fairness: How America's Schools Cheat Girls.* New York: Scribner's, 1994.

Schmidt, J., and J. Wolfe. "The Mentor Partnership: Discovery of Professionalism." *NASPA Journal* (1980): 45–51.

Simpson, Isaiah. "Training and Evaluating Teaching Assistants through Team Teaching." *Freshman English News* 15.3 (1987): 4, 9–13.

Slevin, James. "Disciplining Students: Whom Should Composition Teach and What Should They Know?" *Composition in the Twenty-First Century.* Ed. Lynn Z. Bloom, Donald Daiker, and Edward White. Carbondale, IL: Southern Illinois UP, 1996. 153–65.

Smith, Eugene, and Marilyn Smith. "A Graduate Internship in Teaching." *Teaching English in the Two-Year College* 17 (1989): 197–200.

Smith, Ron. "The Supervisor of In-Service Training in Small Programs: A Basic Job Description." Conference on College Composition and Communication. Philadelphia, PA. March 1976. ED 128 806.

Smith, William. "Using a College Writing Workshop in Training Future English Teachers." *English Education* 16.2 (1984): 76–82.

Sprague, Jo, and Jody Nyquist. "TA Supervision." *Teaching Assistant Training in the 1990s.* Ed. Jody E. Nyquist, Robert D. Abbott, and Donald H. Wulff. San Francisco: Jossey-Bass, 1989. 37–53.

Tompkins, Jane. "Pedagogy of the Distressed." *Changing Classroom Practices.* Ed. David B. Downing. Urbana, IL: NCTE, 1994. 169–78.

Turner, Frank, ed. *The Idea of a University: Rethinking the Western Tradition.* New Haven, CT: Yale UP, 1996.

Warnock, John. "Critical Mentoring among TAs." Conference on College Composition and Communication. Nashville. 18 March 1994.

White, Jeff. "Re-storing a Community: Mutual Development of TAs and Contract Faculty." Conference on College Composition and Communication, Minneapolis. 13 April 2000.

# 19. Mentors, Models, and Agents of Change: Veteran TAs Preparing Teachers of Writing

WANDA MARTIN AND CHARLES PAINE

Our chapter might be said to describe how we manage an embarrassment of riches. We feel fortunate to have a staff of creative and motivated writing teachers whose backgrounds, styles, and strengths represent a spectacular diversity. On the one hand, we want to give these teachers—experienced as well as new ones—as much free rein as possible to discover and practice what works best for them and their students. And of course we as WPAs often learn from them. On the other hand, we have our own beliefs about what constitutes good writing and good writing instruction, we want to articulate and practice a relatively coherent and stable philosophy of writing, and we are obliged to ensure a degree of consistency across all sections of first-year English. As every WPA knows, this balancing of freedom with control is tricky.

In our experience preparing writing teachers, we have found three particularly productive tensions. Like good dialecticians, we strive not to eliminate them but rather to use them to improve the experience of TAs and undergraduate writing students. The first is between the institutional imperative to control the program—be in charge, know what's going on in the classrooms, make multiple sections consistent in content and grading—and the human necessity of letting go to promote individual responsibility and prevent WPA heart attacks. The impulse to impose coherence can be overwhelming, but such imposition fosters passivity, resentment, and rote performance among writing teachers, who are by nature creative and independent.

The second tension arises between providing information adequate to support teachers in meeting their responsibilities and creating an atmosphere of collegiality and continuous learning. Given limited time to prepare teachers to teach, it's tempting to march them through everything we know about teaching writing. But the ability to absorb information is finite, and no matter how we spend the time during orientation, most teachers won't get all they need. We have learned that some time is better spent in fostering relationships that help teachers learn from peers throughout the year as experience demands.

The third tension is between keeping the program theoretically sound and giving it room to grow and change. WPAs are hired partly because departments use contingent and apprentice labor to reduce the cost of first-year composition, and they are responsible for properly supervising that labor. Yet college writing teachers, even the least experienced, are highly educated professionals or developing professionals whose innovative thinking can help the program stay fresh, lively, and in touch with student sensibilities.

In a workplace full of unpredictable crises, it's difficult to welcome change. But when we muster the courage and energy to embrace these contraries, we create a climate in which the writing program and its teachers can move forward. We believe that by putting TAs substantially in charge of our August Orientation, we have made strides toward creating a composition program whose teachers are prepared to work effectively with our students and a peer education program that enhances our graduate students' future employability. But most importantly, by putting TAs in charge, we foster a participative climate that keeps the writing program in a constant process of reflection and transformation.

## THE SITUATION

The two of us are jointly responsible for the first-year writing program in a large public university—Wanda directed it from 1995–1999; Chuck took the reins in fall 1999 and will direct until handing it over to his successor in three or four years. We share general agreement about the goals of our program. We want students to understand writing as a process of inquiry, to proceed from questions toward answers or claims that they know to be subject to revision. We want students to write from their own base of experience and knowledge while incorporating the new perspectives and techniques they encounter in college. We want them to make arguments that acknowledge and exploit complexity and to explore the significance of their claims. We want students to produce work that is well organized from a reader's perspective and reasonably correct in observing the conventions of written English.

We also share goals for the writing teachers who help students develop these capabilities. We hope they will come to an understanding of "writing as process" that's somewhat similar to ours. We hope they will develop teaching strategies that grow out of that understanding (however much it may differ from ours) rather than engaging in what Ann Berthoff famously labeled "recipe swapping" (4). Most importantly, to make the experience of teaching challenging, satisfying, and enriching for all participants, we hope that each will use his or her unique abilities to the fullest.

Our program offers over 200 sections per year of English 101 and 102, both required of nearly all undergraduate students. In any given year, only three to five sections are taught by tenure-track faculty members, with the remainder staffed primarily by TAs. In recent years, this staffing pattern has undergone changes that affect our curriculum and our teacher preparation. Declining upper division and graduate enrollments in the 1990s have created pressure for tenure-track faculty to teach more lower-division courses, in part to generate a student following for their upper-division offerings. While most older professors in our department have rarely taught first-year composition, new hires are expected to do so regularly. To facilitate increased participation among professors, we have developed (that is, our senior TAs have developed) a curriculum model for 102 that incorporates a literary or other substantial "core" text as a springboard to writing about a broader range of topics.

Tenure-track faculty can be a problematic group to orient to first-year composition. Professors typically see themselves as authorities in the classroom, have strong views about what first-year students should already be able to do, and may doubt their ability to help students write for academic situations other than literature courses. Accustomed to teaching independently, they may resist practices such as collaborative grading that are aimed at assuring consistency across sections. Our professorial colleagues generally cooperate with the program, but we have to attend to their needs, especially as their representation in first-year composition increases.

We hire about sixty TAs each year, of whom eight to sixteen are pre-master's students, about half studying literature and half creative or professional writing. Pre-master's TAs, most of whom come to us without teaching experience, can serve for no more than five semesters. These teachers, like those studied by Elizabeth Rankin in *Seeing Yourself as a Teacher,* often doubt their ability to do the job at all. They are typically unfamiliar with composition theory and have thought little about writing processes. Their ideas about teaching spring largely from memories of their own student experiences. They bring a variety of views, often related to their field of study, about the role of personal experience and the centrality of correctness in successful writing. Many question their authority to teach anything to anyone.

The remainder are doctoral students, whose eligibility stretches to six years. Of the nine or ten who begin the doctoral program each year, two or three come from our master's program already familiar with our teaching practices, while the rest come from other institutions, bringing various experiences and preparation as writing teachers. Each year one or two have substantial professional background in teaching or writing. Some of these TAs are capable and richly educated teachers; others have been trained by what Catherine Latterell calls an "inoculation method" (20) that emphasizes classroom activities and classroom management. They know things to do in the classroom, but these activities are often fragmented and theoretically incoherent. As these TAs have a large task in adjusting to new circumstances as students and teachers, it can be difficult to persuade them to reexamine their tried-and-true teaching strategies.

In the early 1990s, the department shifted funds from part-time instruction to the TA budget to increase support for graduate students and thus increase graduate enrollment. So in 1995 and 1996, the program was staffed entirely by TAs. But since 1997, we have confronted simultaneously a shortage of TA candidates and large increases in the first-year class, from about 1600 in 1996 to about 2600 in 1999. In response, we have established several limited-term lecturer positions and hired a significant number of part-time instructors on a per-course basis. These additions increase the complexity of the mix. For example, in 1999–2000, we had eight lecturers, all but one of whom was a graduate of our master's and doctoral programs. Per-course instructors bring a relevant master's degree and some experience teaching first-year composition. Our pool that year included a retired professor from another state, a woman with a recent doctorate in American literature from a well-regarded university, a brace of technical writers, a poet, a few graduate students from other disciplines, and several people who teach here and at the nearby community college because they prefer the flexibility of part-time teaching or their circumstances limit their mobility.

## ORIENTATION AS A COLLABORATION AMONG PEERS

The university is fortunate to have so many capable people willing to work hard for minimal compensation. But the diversity of this group and the way it comes together suddenly, in the last days of the summer break, significantly influence the kind and quality of instruction we can offer to first-year students. If we hope to make first-year composition coherent for students, a substantial and effective August Orientation to the job and the program is essential.

The August Orientation Week is designed to meet as many as possible of the teaching staff's wide-ranging needs: to provide some confidence and usable teaching material for (often terrified) beginners; to acquaint returning instructors with changes in the program and offer them new ideas, materials, and strategies to advance their teaching; to introduce TAs and adjuncts from other programs, as well as tenure-track faculty, to our program's curriculum and assumptions; and to persuade them to keep an open mind so they can collaborate with a new team.

In fact, orientation is as much an exercise in team-building as in teaching, and participants' needs go beyond acquiring information. New people, whatever their previous experience, need to feel known, supported, and cared for. They require assurance that someone will help them to do a good job. Similarly, people who have been teaching in the program for five years, or elsewhere for twenty, need to feel that their expertise is recognized and valued if they are to be motivated to learn new ways. And all participants need to know that they are responsible for the long-term growth and quality of the program.

We try to answer these needs by offering an orientation that is substantially designed and presented by teachers who are close to the experiences of other participants, who have recently come here as beginners or transferred skills developed elsewhere to our program. Orientation runs from Monday through Friday the week before classes begin, with four days of teaching-related activities and Friday reserved for orienting all students to the graduate program. We generally schedule two two-hour blocks of meeting time on each day, with plenty of time in between for meeting people, settling into offices, and taking care of business around campus.

Late in the spring semester, the director recruits several experienced TAs who want to work on orientation and who will be available during the summer. Consulting with the director and other teachers, this team considers what issues will be most salient in the new year's teaching and plans the week's meetings, seeking ideas and session leaders among their colleagues. Salient issues are different each year as the program and the staff change. When we began using portfolios, we focused on portfolio theory and practice; when we replaced an anthology in 102 with Wallace Stegner's *Angle of Repose,* we designed meetings to address the challenges of working with a long, literary text instead of shorter and more diverse readings. The goal is to make orientation more like a professional conference than like an indoctrination. Teams of TAs conduct nearly all sessions that deal with what to teach and how to teach it; program directors preside mainly at sessions dealing with policies and problem solving. We work closely with the planners and presenters to assure that important issues are addressed and that the program is balanced so that everyone can begin teaching with confidence. But beneath this overt agenda of "getting ready to teach," each orientation in recent years has been designed to push growth and change in the program as well as in its teachers.

## HOW WE STARTED ON THIS PATH

Before 1995, the program had been directed for several years by a succession of caretakers who had invested little in curricular innovation and professional development. Under a stern common syllabus that specified texts, modes of discourse, and the number of words students should write, TAs were left to their own devices in deciding *how* to teach students to write for academic purposes. The TA practicum, a semester-long course required of all first-year TAs, was devoted largely to classroom management. Staff meetings, which usually focused on "correct" standards of grading, were dominated by senior TAs; new people rarely felt comfortable enough to speak, either to pose a question or challenge a doctrine.

Our task in that year's orientation was to initiate change in various relationships that had shaped our program. By expanding the orientation from one-and-a-half days to four, we sought to indicate that teaching composition in our department is an important and intellectually complex job. We wanted to introduce some theoretical grounding to a program that had little capability to reflect upon its practices. And we wanted to create a social climate that would welcome and nourish new ideas.

In this first orientation, with such large changes contemplated, the director took a strong lead, defining its overall shape and recruiting leaders and presenters. We arranged a schedule that alternated policy-oriented meetings for different populations with workshops designed to elicit active participation and to lead participants through a sort of composing process. We intended to provide both new and experienced teachers with an overview of what we regard as good practices in first-year composition—attention to student reading and discussion, the unit of work formulated as a cumulative inquiry process, carefully articulated writing tasks, and the use of formative response to student writing in addition to summative grading.

During that week, we began to see potential in this kind of peer education. By selecting peer teachers as workshop leaders, we validated their practices and opinions, improving their status among colleagues and creating a leadership group. And because they were sensitive to peers' desire for concrete and practical information about ways to teach, including suggestions for conducting participatory workshops rather than making speeches, they modeled a style of teaching we hoped to see in the program's classrooms, letting theory shine through activities rather than preaching abstractions.

This first attempt was not, of course, perfect. We elevated to leadership some people whose practices did not, on closer scrutiny, bear validation. Some senior TAs were incensed that people they regarded as peers were being identified as leaders by the administration. And we made some scheduling mistakes, trying to do too much in too little time. But the evaluations completed (by eighteen respondents from about sixty participants) at the end of the week were overwhelmingly positive. TAs, even the most experienced, were relieved to have clear guidance and a coherent sense of what the program valued. The least experienced TAs were the most enthusiastic and vocal in suggesting improvements: Start earlier and give us more time to develop our ideas; show more samples of student work and help us understand them; offer meetings like these during the semester as we encounter new problems.

What surprised us about those evaluations was that their highest praise was reserved for the social occasions. Using volunteer labor and about $300 from a small budget that supports program activities such as guest speakers and book purchases, we provided coffee, bagels, and fruit every morning. Our administrative assistant organized a breakfast on Friday with homemade local foods, and the graduate student association sponsored a Friday night party. The praise for these events reminded us of the importance of feeling welcomed, or welcomed back, and reflected how much productive conversation took place outside the formal sessions. We resolved to build on that insight even though it meant giving up "instructional time" to what might seem mere socializing.

Each year's orientation differs from the last as we address current issues and incorporate new ideas. Early sessions (some participants think this "scary stuff" should be reserved for later in the week) designed to acquaint participants with university policies and resources often include speakers from such offices as the Dean of Students and the Learning Support program, who help teachers learn to identify and solve problems in their classrooms. Other meetings are divided according to the course that participants will be teaching. Designed to draw attention to course objectives, the characteristics of the student population, and any changes in curriculum, they feature work with relevant texts, small group activities, and "take home" materials that TAs can use or adapt. Here's a sample selected from a recent orientation schedule:

### Tuesday, August 18

| | |
|---|---|
| 8:00 to 9:00 | Coffee, pastries, and fruit in the Lounge |
| 9:00 to 11:00 | 101 Workshop: Helping Students Read Discerningly<br>102 Workshop: Reading *Angle of Repose* |
| 1:00 to 3:00 | 101 Workshop: Helping Students Write about a Text<br>102 Workshop: Helping Students Read *Angle of Repose* |

### Wednesday, August 19

8:00 to 9:00    Coffee in the Lounge

9:00 to 11:00   101 Workshop: Annotating Student Work to Assist Revision
                102 Workshop: "Mining" *Angle of Repose* for Writing Topics

11:00 to 1:00   Lunch for First-Year TAs and Mentors

1:00 to 3:00    101 Workshop: Tools for Teaching Revision
                102 Workshop: Finding and Using Outside Sources

### Thursday, August 20

8:00 to 9:00    Coffee in the Lounge

9:00 to 10:30   Course Portfolios and Grading Standards

11:00 to 1:00   Collaborative grading groups meet over lunch

All TAs are required to attend the meetings relevant to their teaching assignments. Since normally about a third of the TAs are leading meetings, and since
by now everyone expects to come away with useful information, even the most
senior TAs don't grumble much. We cordially invite both new and returning
adjuncts and lecturers, who seem to come because we ask them to and they
want to join the community. Tenure-track faculty attend the meetings selectively, looking for instruction on issues specific to the course or seeking to learn
from TAs with whom they've worked in other capacities. New professors, who
expect to teach first-year composition every year, regard orientation as an
important part of learning their jobs and as an opportunity to get acquainted.
We continue to distribute an evaluation questionnaire at the end of each orientation and receive responses from about 50 percent of participants. We use this
information to assess what works well and what needs rethinking, and we mine
it for ideas when we begin planning the next orientation. But the real measure
of the orientation's value is the quality of TAs' thinking about teaching and the
energy with which they pursue new and better practices.

## A CHAIN OF CONSEQUENCES

In 1996, we moved to formalize the welcome offered to new teachers by recruiting a core of experienced TAs willing, for a small stipend, to mentor new TAs
throughout their first year. In the first year, we invited prospective mentors and
new teachers to have lunch together, hoping that the occasion would encourage
people to identify compatible mentors rather than have them assigned. Some
new teachers found mentors who helped them greatly, but others were shy about
initiating contact. And so, surprisingly, were some of the prospective mentors. In
subsequent years, we've assigned mentors to newcomers, TAs and adjuncts
alike. We use what little information we have about the new teachers—age, gender, field of study, prior experience—to guess at suitable pairings, and we try to
arrange teaching schedules so the pair can visit each other's classes and meet easily. Although this is somewhat antithetical to the spirit of the mentoring rela-

tionship, it has helped new teachers to identify a reliable source of help and advice. We don't provide TA mentors for tenure-track faculty, largely due to lack of personnel and money. But senior TAs do make sure to include professors in their collaborative grading groups, where a graduate student may find herself providing a new kind of education to a professor whose seminar she's taking or who is directing her dissertation. While newcomers rely on mentors for program information, it is perhaps more important for our purposes that mentors some-times give advice with which we don't agree. Thus our new teachers learn early on that senior colleagues have diverse ways of working in the classroom and solving problems, that faculty members respect those differences, and that some things are worth disagreeing about in teaching first-year composition.

Each year has brought additional innovations in teacher preparation, each of which is increasingly driven by TA leadership. Giving TAs significant respon-sibility for orientation has sharpened their attention to program design and encouraged them to articulate their ideas. In 1996, led by TA discontent with a program that emphasized writing process for fourteen weeks and then tested students with an impromptu essay, the director initiated a move to portfolio assessment. She opened that August's orientation with a theoretical introduc-tion to portfolios, and veteran TAs conducted course-specific workshops with examples of student work. The subsequent meetings focused on two issues that would be most salient in the new system: guiding students through revision and grading portfolios collaboratively.

Later in 1996, a TA-led subcommittee charged with selecting a new textbook for English 101 returned with a thoroughgoing critique of the choices and pro-posed that the program develop its own book. All the subcommittee members had been orientation leaders, and their proposal was grounded in careful analy-sis of the cultural and theoretical shortcomings of the commercial books and a vision of the program in which they hoped to teach in the future. With the Fresh-man English Committee's approval, this group organized a staff of eighteen to create *La Puerta,* an anthology of local work exemplifying the kinds of inquiry typical at this university. The director spent the entire academic year learning to let go of this one, but watched, elated, as the manuscript went to press in June 1997. The staff turned its attention to developing orientation materials to address the possibilities and challenges the new book would bring. Like most of our innovations, this book had mixed reviews in its first year. In its second year, a new editorial board organized a new staff, including some of the most vocal critics, to produce a second edition which built on the strengths of its predeces-sor and corrected some of its flaws.

In October 1997, pressed to revamp English 102 so teaching it would feel less alien to tenure-track faculty, the director wondered aloud in a committee meet-ing if there were some way to bring in literary texts without relinquishing the course's focus on writing for diverse academic purposes. The TAs on that com-mittee answered with the "core text" idea and set in motion the process whereby each spring, the staff chooses one new book that six to eight veteran TAs then pilot, creating resources for teaching with it. During the following fall semester, teachers can choose that book or a previously piloted one. Teachers can currently choose from Stegner's *Angle of Repose* and Mary Shelley's *Frankenstein;* we are now piloting Kalle Lasn's *Culture Jam,* our first nonliterary text. We plan to continue piloting new books through the foreseeable future and to maintain a pool of about five books from which to choose. In each cycle, a team of veteran TAs tests and expands its abilities to bring a text alive for first-year students, to connect that text to other disciplines and topics, and to develop materials that they and other teachers can use. Each text-development team presents the new course curriculum to colleagues at the end of the pilot semester and helps the next year's new TAs get ready to teach the text in their second semester.

The director and the Freshman English Committee oversee this work, but the members of the text-development team own the task. Their autonomy gives them the room to be innovative and makes this central activity in developing our curriculum truly collaborative. By extension, because anyone can participate with this team, all members of the teaching staff feel they have a voice in the program's direction. Although as yet no adjuncts or tenure-track faculty have taken a major role in piloting a text, there is no barrier to their doing so. In fact, the adoption of Shelley's *Frankenstein* was sparked by a long and thoughtful memo from a professor who specializes in British Romanticism, who suggested how we could use that novel to provoke the cross-disciplinary inquiry we want our students to pursue.

Yes, by now we're far afield from the August Orientation, but that is the point: While the actual August Orientation ends as the semester begins, the power to do this creative work only begins there. We see this collaborative frame of mind developing during the third week of every August when senior TAs who will soon be professors lead their colleagues in thinking about who this year's students are and what they need to learn. We see it working when a person who has labored here quietly for years finds the courage to lead a workshop on sparking students' inventive processes and gets rave reviews, and when last year's terrified beginner sits at lunch with this year's and makes teaching seem a little less frightening.

## WHAT WE THINK THIS APPROACH ACCOMPLISHES

Looking at this program over the last few years, we see benefits to our first-year students and to the teachers in our program. In 1994, our first-year students were writing seven or eight disparate essays in a semester, getting grades on work written in a single class period, and passing or failing the course based on an impromptu essay. Encouraged to apply what they had been learning in composition theory classes, our TAs have drastically changed the program. Today, first-year students spend their time imagining, researching, and revising their writing. They read longer, more complex and more engaging texts, and they discover ways to connect that reading to issues about which they're concerned. We suggested these directions, but our TAs, in classrooms with the students every day, have made them concrete. Our ongoing portfolio assessment program (described by Martin) reflects a steady increase in the complexity of topics students attempt and in their ability to organize and support arguments.

Our teachers benefit both while they are in this department and when they are ready to move on. We think we've concocted a good mix of theoretical coherence, curricular innovation, and autonomy of practice. We don't hear many arguments about whether the program's approach is a good one, but there's plenty of divergence in the ways that approach is put into practice. Beginning TAs can use the sample syllabi that are offered in orientation and elaborated during the semester-long practicum and thus feel reasonably sure of their ground. But the message is that they're expected to make their courses their own and to begin, as soon as they're able, contributing to the discussion about what we teach and how. When they seek other positions, our TAs, having carried significant responsibility as orientation leaders, as mentors, as administrative interns, as textbook editors and curriculum developers, speak to prospective employers in concrete, practical terms about the work of teaching.

## OPENING UP TO INNOVATION

No matter how much knowledge, enthusiasm, and creativity we have, and no matter how many journals we read, listservs we follow, or conferences we attend, we all get stale. We get conservative, protective of our ideas and projects. Changing the director of a writing program usually causes at least a fleeting bump of energy, but there's nothing like new people with new ideas and experiences to keep the writing program moving forward, fostering new projects, still more new ideas, and new relationships, not only among TAs but also among undergraduates and the faculty. Our collaborative model of teacher preparation takes courage and flexibility. It's not easy to let go of our cherished beliefs, radically opening up our program to those whose ideas are different. (Ask Wanda how she feels about the selection of *Culture Jam.*) We're not talking about unbridled change for the sake of change but rather about creating a context in which new ideas can be heard. And we believe this all starts with the tone of August Orientation, which shows our TAs that they need not be passive consumers of the writing program's line.

Our program's TAs each year spend over 15,000 classroom hours with students and probably another 1000 hours in conferences. While we also teach writing courses, we spend much of our time with high-level administrators who want facts and figures, accurate predictions, and consistency. We live in different worlds, and TAs know things we can't possibly know. They've had countless inspired hunches and have acted on as many leaps of faith and even on crackpot notions. Our job is to see that some of their ideas get heard beyond their own classrooms where other minds can test and develop them.

By encouraging our veteran TAs to innovate, we give up some control, but we open up possibilities. Led by their peers during August Orientation, TAs feel they can legitimately question or add to the philosophy and practices of the writing program. New teachers witness veteran teachers in disagreement and think about their own practice.

Of course, there's the old problem—that tension: Innovate too little and become stale and ineffective; innovate too much and present a disunited front and an inconsistent philosophy. So, of course, we are active (not overactive) managers who weigh in with what we feel and with what we know from research that constitutes sound teaching. We sometimes put the brakes on change. But by putting our TAs in charge of innovation, we manage stability in a dynamic environment.

## Works Cited

Berthoff, Ann E. *The Making of Meaning: Metaphors, Models, and Maxims for Writing Teachers.* Upper Montclair, NJ: Boynton/Cook, 1981.

Latterell, Catherine G. "Training the Workforce: An Overview of GTA Education Curricula." *WPA* 19.3 (1996): 7–23.

Martin, Wanda. "Outcomes Assessment Research as a Teaching Tool." *The Writing Program Administrator as Researcher: Inquiry in Reflection and Action.* Ed. Shirley K Rose and Irwin Weiser. Portsmouth, NH: Boynton/Cook-Heinemann, 1999. 40–51.

Rankin, Elizabeth. *Seeing Yourself as a Teacher: Conversations with Five New Teachers in a University Writing Program.* Urbana, IL: NCTE, 1994.

# 20. Orientation and Mentoring: Collaborative Practices in Teacher Preparation

## GITA DAS BENDER

New York University's Expository Writing Program (EWP) is primarily staffed by doctoral students in the university's English, English Education, and Performance Studies Departments. They receive in-house preparation to teach composition from experienced instructors (also doctoral students) who, under the guidance of program directors, mentor its new and returning instructors. Approximately 130 instructors teach in the EWP. They are given three-year terms to teach in the program but can extend their teaching time to five years or more if the department hires them to mentor. Instructors are allowed to apply for mentor positions after their first year of teaching and are selected based on the strength of their application letter and an interview with the directors and a mentor.

Undergraduate students at NYU take two Writing Workshops (three for international students) in composition writing—Writing Workshop I and II. Class size averages sixteen, and approximately 200 sections are offered each semester. The courses emphasize, as the *Handbook for Instructors* states, the "essential activities associated with process: exploring, reading, thinking and imagining; journal writing; meta-writing; drafting; collaborating; organizing; revising; reconsidering; revising; revising again and again, until this recursive process yields an essay" (7). Smaller classes allow students to workshop their writing frequently in peer response groups and give teachers the opportunity to know the students and their work better.

Instructors and directors openly discuss the theories and pedagogical practices that shape the EWP curriculum. This collaboration takes place well before the semester begins as they plan orientations for new and experienced teachers and throughout the semester as they meet regularly to discuss mentoring in the teacher preparation program. Having been mentored initially by the directors and some senior teachers and then having mentored for three years, I know that effective mentoring happens when the hierarchical structure in place gives way to peer education. Directors, mentors, and instructors work together in orientations and meetings to understand the challenges of teaching composition. And by collaborating and reflecting on our teaching, we learn not only how good writers write but also how good writing teachers teach. This work allows the EWP's community of writing teachers to build what Stephen North has called "lore," experiential knowledge that practitioners in the field of composition rely on as they figure out "what has worked, is working, or might work in teaching, doing, or learning writing" (23). This is not to say that the program builds entirely on lore. In fact, directors strongly encourage instructors to read current literature on composition theory and practice, and research articles on the teaching of writing are often circulated in mentor meetings and become the topics of formal and informal discussions.

Directors and instructors concur that consistent and rigorous preparation in the teaching of writing promotes a common understanding of composition pedagogy and helps maintain high program standards. If the goal of the EWP mentoring program is to promote effective instruction, how is this achieved? In this chapter I discuss the merits of collaboration among instructors and directors in preparing writing teachers and the ongoing collaboration from an orientation through regular mentor meetings to show how preparation to teach in the EWP supports and encourages critical consideration of the process of teaching writing.

## COLLABORATION IN THE TEACHER PREPARATION PROGRAM

Deeply committed to its orientation and mentoring program for new and returning instructors, the EWP at NYU considers preparation and development of writing teachers critical to effective instruction in Writing Workshops. Historically, the program has valued teacher preparation ever since faculty from the School of Education, who believed in the importance of staff development, shaped the current mentoring program. To understand how the present system evolved, we need to go back about a decade when Gordon Pradl, now an NYU senior faculty member in English Education, designed the mentoring program of the EWP from his vision of writing teachers as teacher educators. As the Director of Staff Development, he structured a pilot program in which three or four faculty members from English Education each mentored a group of four or five writing teachers through class visits and informal biweekly meetings. The program was designed to be a pilot arrangement for a select group of teachers interested in mentoring. Although the Director of EWP has always been an English department faculty member, the EWP itself is an autonomous entity, and the program's collaboration with English Education to improve teacher education and teacher performance seemed to happen naturally. Even though the mentors were well informed about the EWP's goals and curriculum, they neither taught in the writing program nor maintained office hours there, contributing instead through regular contact with the teachers.

Gradually, the EWP directors became interested in involving its own teachers in staff development, and the previous arrangement gave way to a system of staff development in which mentor groups were led by instructors who organized the groups by theoretical interest such as queer theory, literary theory, and feminist theory. The mentor groups, though formally organized, lacked the structure they have today, and mentors were not compensated for the service they provided. These mentors were mostly PhD students in English, and although they conducted biweekly meetings with instructors to improve the quality of teaching in the program, the meetings were grounded more in discussions of literary theory than in composition studies. Furthermore, the appointment of program directors who were English department faculty with little experience in teaching writing or developing a writing program compounded the problem. It was not until 1993 that Pat C. Hoy II—a writer, writing teacher, and writing program administrator—was hired as director, and it is his vision that gives the writing program and its mentoring system the distinct structure that it currently has.

Today, the mentoring program is usually comprised of twelve experienced teachers of writing who are supervised by the Director of Staff Development. In addition to a stipend, they receive a reduced courseload, from two courses to one course per semester. While mentoring, all mentors must teach in the program, as do the directors, who also teach one course each semester. Along with the other four directors (i.e., Program Director, Assistant Director, Director of the Writing Center, and Director of International Courses), the mentors coordinate and conduct a two-week intensive orientation for new instructors at the end of the summer followed by a two-day orientation for all instructors at the beginning of the fall and spring semesters. In addition, during the semester mentors conduct seven two-hour meetings every other week with their respective mentor groups, meet weekly with new instructors for the first month of the fall semester, meet biweekly with the other mentors and the Director of Staff Development, attend faculty workshops facilitated by the directors and other instructors, and participate in the hiring of new instructors and mentors.

Mentors who plan, coordinate, and facilitate the first-year orientation program, as well as new instructors, are paid an honorarium. Contracts for all instructors explicitly state that active participation in the first-year orientation, the general orientation, and the mentoring program is required for teaching in the program.

## ORIENTATIONS FOR TEACHERS OF WRITING

It is partly the need to determine what instructors—new and returning—know or should learn and partly the inclination to figure out new, untested yet promising ideas for teaching writing that shape the orientation program the department organizes before the start of classes. The orientation program is based on the kind of preparation new instructors need, on one hand, and what both new and returning instructors need, on the other. An orientation for new instructors is particularly crucial because the program sometimes hires instructors with little or no experience in teaching composition, and preparing these instructors to teach successfully in the two-semester sequence of Writing Workshops is challenging. This challenge is lessened, however, by our beginning to prepare new instructors during the hiring process.

### PRE-ORIENTATION PREPARATION: HIRING INFORMED INSTRUCTORS

Every year as the program directors hire new instructors, they evaluate not only the applicants' experience and potential as writing teachers but also their interest in learning what the EWP offers. Applicants receive the program's *Handbook for Instructors,* application materials, and a sample student essay. To understand the program before applying and interviewing, applicants are instructed to read the handbook, which contains the "important beliefs and expectations" of the program and provides "the beginning of the ongoing conversation about the teaching of writing that constitutes much of the [teacher preparation program] activity" (10). Thus applicants get a clear sense of the program's pedagogical structure, its theoretical and philosophical underpinnings, and its values and goals from the beginning of the process.

Applicant interviews are usually conducted by one director and a mentor and last for approximately thirty minutes. The director and mentor, who participate equally in the interview process, discuss in advance what questions they will ask and in what sequence. While the handbook gives the applicant an idea of the EWP curriculum and the kinds of writing expected of students, the sample essay offers a concrete example of an NYU student's writing. The interviews begin with general, open-ended questions so that applicants can warm up and then move to harder questions such as, "What kind of work do you imagine would be necessary to prepare students to write the sample essay?" As the interviewers assess applicants' concepts of writing instruction, they also try to get a sense of the kinds of teaching activities the applicants practice (or can imagine practicing) and often ask questions about the goals for such activities or what interferes with such goals. Overall, the interviewers aim to get the applicants to think critically and reflectively about their teaching practices and beliefs and to help them reconcile what they already know about writing instruction with what the EWP expects of its writing teachers.

Later, the *Handbook* provides successful applicants with a foundation and a rationale for the kind of teaching they will do in the program. It discusses the essay as a genre, how to teach it, and types of assignments to consider. Yet, newly hired instructors only really begin to understand the teaching requirements once they participate in the first-year orientation program.

## ORIENTATION FOR FIRST-YEAR INSTRUCTORS: TWO WEEKS OF PLANNING AND PRACTICE

Good teaching can be promoted through effective orientation programs that combine a variety of teacher preparation strategies. In 1997, the department instituted an orientation for new (also called first-year) instructors to familiarize them with the content of the writing workshops and to prepare them to teach writing. New and returning mentors meet with the directors during early summer to plan the orientation program. In planning this orientation, they consider effective and interesting ways to introduce new teachers to the type of writing the program values in Writing Workshop I. In my years as a mentor, we focused on teaching the exploratory essay to new teachers. By reading the *Handbook for Instructors,* teachers learn that the program focuses on the entire spectrum of essays—from the exploratory essay to the academic essay—but that it is important for teachers, initially, to understand the basic form of essay-writing in which the writer develops a compelling idea through use of personal experience, reflection, and sometimes external sources as evidence.

During first-year orientation, new instructors come to understand the essay as a genre by writing one of the essays their students will produce in Writing Workshop I. What better way to understand how the essay works than to write one? In two weeks of orientation, new instructors read, write, and reflect in the same way that their students are expected to write in the semester ahead. For the writing exercise, instructors follow an essay "progression," a sequence of writing assignments designed by the Program Director, Pat Hoy, which culminates in a final essay. In particular, instructors fulfill writing requirements for the second writing assignment—called the "Deepening Progression"—that they will assign students in the writing workshop class they will teach in the fall. For this progression writers borrow an idea from an assigned essay and analyze it in light of questions such as these: What are the larger implications of the idea? How do other essays you have read in this course, or in other courses, change the way you think about the idea? How do your own experiences influence your thinking? This assignment helps writers learn to analyze a text and develop their essays by deepening a reader's understanding of the ideas they borrow from the text. The tasks associated with the essay—reading and writing critically, identifying and analyzing ideas, incorporating evidence—make it a challenging piece of writing for new instructors to experiment with so that they can understand its nuances and teach it better.

Instructors also learn about classroom pedagogy as mentors and directors collaboratively model teaching practices endorsed by the EWP. Group work is emphasized; peer review in small group workshops and whole class reading of one writer's text help instructors understand the teaching methods they are encouraged to use.

During orientation, most work—thinking and writing—is done in small groups led by mentors and directors who facilitate discussions and workshops to guide participants and provide opportunities for them to absorb and reflect on the process of learning. Instructors work together, reflecting on the syllabus for the writing workshops and on essays written by former students. They also focus on their own writing to problematize and clarify the specific processes of writing essays. Often instructors study *Encounters,* the required text for Writing Workshop I, edited by Pat Hoy and Robert DiYanni of Pace University.

Reflection on the writing process and finally on the teaching process is integral to the work of orientation, but to reflect critically on the dual experience of being a student/writer and a writing teacher is difficult and complex. Teachers come to realize, for instance, that developing an interesting, universal idea from experiential evidence in a personal essay or analyzing a published essay to build a compelling idea out of it is challenging and time-consuming. This realization, therefore, inevitably raises questions about the pace at which instructors teach and the painstaking task of modeling good writing in the classroom. How can teachers show students ways to develop an idea? How can they help students revise, perhaps over and over again, to refine their ideas? As instructors assume the role of student, they understand the complicated job of teaching writing. Thus, to encourage reflection, facilitators sometimes suspend group work to answer instructors' questions. Although questions may break the flow of the experience, they create a real space for the instructors to reflect on basic, immediate problems. These interruptions prepare them for the reality of the classroom experience since their questions are indicative of the problems and questions students will have.

Through the process of writing the "Deepening Progression" assignment, instructors share their writing with the mentors, the program directors, and each other. To model the teaching instructors will do in Writing Workshops, the facilitators conduct small group workshops in which writers read each other's essays in progress. As instructors work in groups and respond to writing, mentors and directors discuss ways to structure peer response groups so that writers can receive the maximum benefit from the exchange. Such modeling of peer response groups helps teachers understand the process of workshopping as a learning technique by exposing them to ways of responding to writing and to group work. Instructors finish their essays by the end of the two-week orientation, and although they don't necessarily use their own essays to teach the unit to students, some instructors' essays have been used as samples during general orientation.

During the semester (until October), new instructors meet weekly with the director with whom they interviewed to exchange ideas about their own writing in particular and the writing assignment in general. This is the only time new instructors can receive feedback on their own writing since the work of orientation ends with these conferences and directors do not look at any other writing that teachers do. In these one-on-one meetings, instructors get to know their directors better as they learn more about the writing process. More importantly, these conferences build a community of teachers who, although aware of the program's hierarchy, are comfortable interacting with the "elders." As a new instructor in the program, I always looked forward to consulting about teaching problems with the mentors and directors I worked with closely, and I was gratified not only by the knowledge and insights I came away with but also by the sincerity and thoughtfulness with which they addressed even my most inane questions.

Finally, the first-year orientation provides new teachers with a common vocabulary, with language they become familiar with as teachers and writers and that they use with their students with confidence. It is exciting to see new instructors talk about "idea," "evidence," and "movement" in the essay, to see them internalize complex concepts even as they struggle to understand them to teach them better.

## GENERAL ORIENTATION: TWO DAYS OF READING, WRITING, AND REFLECTION

The general orientation is a required faculty development session for all instructors, new and returning. Lasting two days, usually from 9:00 a.m. until 4:00 p.m., it includes training sessions facilitated by directors and mentors for the entire teaching staff, and it also allows time for individual mentor group meetings.

In a planning meeting, directors invite input from mentors, and together they set the agenda for the general orientation by considering several factors: what the program emphasized, in theory and in practice, during the previous academic year; how this emphasis influenced teaching in the program; what teaching strategies worked particularly well based on the quality of student essays; and what teachers are still struggling with both in and out of the classroom. Generally, directors bring to the table ideas that they have discussed amongst themselves, ideas that might suggest a shift in program emphasis or objectives. Yet, it is the collaborative aspect of this exchange and the room for disagreement that make the planning meeting an occasion for mentors' voices to be heard. Even though the directors may already have determined programmatic changes for the academic year, the program depends largely on the feedback and input of its mentors who are encouraged to present new ideas and suggestions.

For example, at one recent planning meeting the Program Director announced his plans for making Writing Workshop I more challenging to students. Although mentors did not immediately question the structure of the course and the guidelines for teaching that he proposed, during the meeting they reflected on why the first semester course was not effective and concluded that maybe the excessive, and perhaps too prescriptive, directions that instructors receive on how to teach the essays give them little leeway in making the assignments more challenging to students. Following step-by-step directions for teaching each essay, they conjectured, may help teachers understand the pedagogy of the Program Director, the creator of the "progression," but it may also prevent teachers from making the assignment their own, and more importantly, from teaching it as their own. Although the director had disseminated the teaching materials to give the program consistency, mentors challenged the control that directors had over the curriculum and how it is taught. As a result of this exchange, in the following fall new instructors received only brief descriptions of the essays to be taught.

Although the orientation agenda varies every year, the goals and format of the meetings generally remain the same. On the first day, all program participants—directors, mentors, new and returning instructors—meet in the morning for introductions and group work. Group work varies depending on the current focus of the program, as determined by the directors and mentors. Often in the past, for this large group session, one director has facilitated a large group reading of a text. Two years ago, for instance, the text was the first draft of a promising student essay that the instructors had received two weeks prior to orientation along with other orientation materials. The goal of the exercise, and indeed the focus of that orientation, was to consider ways of responding to student writing that let students develop their own thinking rather than giving them too many ideas. In the previous semester, mentors had noticed that students latched on too quickly to their teachers' creative suggestions. This dependence affected the originality of their essays. The director guided the reading, asking the group of readers to respond in writing to key questions such as, "Where do you see the writer thinking about an idea?" and "How would you help the writer develop this idea without telling her too much about it?" Then, small groups of four or five instructors led by a mentor shared their writing and ideas, giving everyone an opportunity to meet each other and to participate in the orientation.

Directors and mentors reflect on the structure of the group work in the morning session every year, asking, "Which works better, to continue the work of the large group in small groups or vice versa? How would instructors learn best and participate the most? How can the work that is started in the morning session be continued in the afternoon? How can orientation workshops be more holistic and more connected to the teaching that instructors will do in the days to come?" The questions and concerns change, but the practice of reflecting on how to maximize the effectiveness of these training sessions remains.

## MENTOR GROUPS: A YEAR OF PEER SUPPORT

On the second day of orientation, once the large group work has been done in the morning, mentors meet their individual mentor groups (consisting of new and returning instructors) in the afternoon to continue discussing issues raised in the morning session and to establish a community of teachers who will meet regularly for a year to talk, write, and reflect on their teaching. Thus, the first mentor meeting of the year happens as part of orientation. Mentors usually work with a group of eight to ten instructors who participate for one year and meet about seven times each semester. They also attend faculty development workshops usually facilitated by directors in collaboration with mentors. The meetings generally focus on theory and practice. While the theoretical under-pinnings of composition pedagogy are addressed through discussions of pro-fessional and student essays, the practical elements of teaching writing are explored through sharing syllabi, writing assignments, and classroom tech-niques. In general, according to the *Handbook for Instructors,* for all the meetings they conduct during the semester, mentors have the responsibility to "facilitate conversations about teaching and learning and plan group activities that address any number of teaching matters from "How do we connect reading with writing in the syllabus?" to "How do we help students understand how informal writing can turn into essays?" to "What are good ways to conduct indi-vidual writing conferences with students?" to "How might we more effectively read and assess student portfolios?" (10).

Mentors decide what approach to take in their mentor group meetings. Since mentors meet with the Director of Staff Development every other week during the semester, it is not unusual to collaborate with the director to gener-ate ideas or to chat with fellow mentors about their plans for the mentor meet-ings. In fact, as a mentor I found it impossible to work in a vacuum, not to know what my fellow mentors were planning, not to seek the director's feedback. The important thing, however, is to remember that instructors need support in the first few weeks of classes, not just with their teaching but also with issues such as placement, add/drop, and room assignment. Mentor groups provide this practical support, but mentors also emphasize connections between, for instance, the reading and writing exercises of the orientation and the immediate work of teaching writing in the classroom.

The orientation program models exemplary teaching strategies. In addition, the large group workshop reinforces the teaching strategies the instructors already have and provides insight into as well as problematizes some of their teaching methods. This, however, may not be obvious to teachers, especially the new ones, who are not yet ready to see the complex pedagogical implications of the workshop. The meta-conversations that take place in the mentor groups that meet right after the orientation make it clear to teachers that orientation, like the rest of the teacher preparation program, is *meant to* raise questions, to challenge assumptions, and to reaffirm what teachers know about teaching and writing and their complicated intersections.

NYU's program for preparing new college teachers of writing provides instructors with maximum support in and out of the classroom and encourages instructors to become teacher educators themselves. From the onset, instructors see peer mentors not only as experienced teachers but also as individuals who passionately share their knowledge about and insight into writing instruction. They see the directors as the "elders"who collaborate with mentors. As instructors learn to reflect on their teaching with mentors and directors and among themselves, they understand the collaborative nature of learning. What the teacher learns the teacher teaches somebody else. And the cycle of good teaching continues as a collaborative enterprise.

## WORKS CITED

*Handbook for Instructors.* Expository Writing Program. New York University, 1997.

Hoy, Pat C. II, and Robert DiYanni, eds. *Encounters: Readings and the World.* New York: McGraw-Hill, 1997.

North, Steven M. *The Making of Knowledge in Composition: Portrait of an Emerging Field.* Portsmouth, NH: Boynton/Cook, 1987.

# 21. From Discomfort, Isolation, and Fear to Comfort, Community, and Confidence: Using Reflection, Role-Playing, and Classroom Observation to Prepare New Teachers of College Writing

Michael C. Flanigan

I have taught new college writing teachers for over twenty-five years. Many of these new teaching assistants have never taught, and many, because they were so verbally skillful and such thoughtful readers and analyzers of literature, have never taken a required writing course. These TAs are accepted into our graduate program because of their academic promise—their ability to do research. They are not accepted because of their teaching experience or their teaching potential, although those may have some indirect influence. I suspect our recruitment policies differ little from those of most other graduate programs in English. For these new TAs, preparation is essential. In this chapter, I describe two long-standing major components of the preparation program for TAs at the University of Oklahoma—the pre-service orientation and the class observations.

## PRE-SERVICE WORKSHOP

When TAs arrive at the University of Oklahoma for our ten-day workshop, spread over three weeks in August, just before school starts, they have read a couple of articles about our program that were mailed to them early in the summer (Flanigan, "What Do") along with George Hillocks's *Teaching Writing as Reflective Practice* or something similar on teaching and/or teaching writing. All TAs and all adjuncts must attend the workshop to teach in our program, and usually twelve to twenty new teachers are involved. They are paid a stipend to come to campus early. The daily sessions run from 8:30 a.m. to 3:30 p.m. or 4:30 p.m., although some sessions end at 12:30 p.m. so that participants can prepare plans, policy statements, or syllabi; assess student papers; or prepare to lead discussions. The Director of First-Year Composition, his two assistants, and I conduct most of the workshop, although all rhetoric/composition faculty contribute.

So, with little or no teaching experience, new TAs often come to the summer workshop fearful of what teaching writing has in store for them. In the reflections gathered daily in the workshop, TAs also tell us their fears. The last question of the day, "What is your greatest concern right now as a teacher?" elicits these sample responses: "How to plan fifty minutes and keep students busy." "Today I'm excited, nervous, confident and scared—all at once." "These other participants are way ahead of me. I don't want my classes to be deprived because of my lack of knowledge." "Juggling all the roles of a teacher, leader, guide, counselor, student, creator, etc."

When the Director of First-Year Composition, his two assistants, and I design the workshop, our goals are based on what we have learned from former participants. Our general question is: What can we do to move these new TAs from feeling alone and fearful, and, therefore, uncomfortable and insecure, to being confident and comfortable? Obviously, we need to teach them something about how to teach, what to teach, and the why of what to teach. We need to move them from little or no knowledge of what is involved in writing and teaching, from general ignorance about composition as a field, to being knowledgeable about composition studies. We also need to show them how we have structured and conceived the beginning writing course, how to accomplish the goals of that course, and how they can adapt those goals to fit themselves.

In addition, we need to introduce new TAs to the people and resources that support them as teachers and graduate students. During the workshop, they meet all the composition faculty. They also meet alone with experienced TAs to ask questions they might feel uncomfortable asking faculty. Counselors advise them on how to deal with various student problems/issues, as do the Director of the Writing Center, the head of media services, and the secretarial support staff, people who can help new TAs be more effective in their jobs. These support staff people and departmental administrators usually attend the workshop late in the day and participate over the three weeks. (A condensed sample schedule for the workshop is appended.)

During the workshop, we expect TAs to gain much new knowledge through active engagement with the ideas and resources we share, and if that is all we did, we would probably overwhelm them, creating more anxiety and fear. Therefore, we focus each day of the workshop on four basic goals: (1) making them comfortable with us and one another; (2) creating a sense of community; (3) giving them frequent opportunities to reflect on what we've done in the workshop, on how they feel, and on how we as a group could improve what we are doing together; and (4) creating frequent opportunities to generate course materials and to work actively with ideas, concepts, and strategies. We give them a packet (used over the ten days) that includes materials on versions of the writing process, an overview of the introductory writing courses, strategies for asking questions and using group processes, sample syllabi and lesson plans, whole units of instruction, three drafts of a student paper with various revision guides to serve as the basis for teaching them how to teach revision, sample student papers to grade, classroom scenarios, and a host of readings and guide sheets ("Ways to Guide Reading," "Questions for Argumentative and Position Essays," "Some Possible Collaborative Tasks," etc.).

## ACTIVE REFLECTION

From the beginning of the workshop, TAs are involved in issues that will make them effective composition teachers. After brief staff and faculty introductions, they write a response to the following prompt: "Write about one of the best teachers you have ever had. What made that person the/a best? Give an instance—tell a story—showing something about this teacher that you have not been able to forget." After they finish writing, small groups follow these directions:

1. Introduce yourselves and talk briefly about your background and interests.
2. Then *read* what you wrote. Don't talk about what you wrote; read it.
3. Discuss what your group wrote, noting any patterns.
4. Take notes about what others say and who they are because you will each introduce another person. In your introductions, tell us both about the person and what she had to say about her "best" teacher.

After the introductions and some discussion of the patterns of good teaching and good teachers that had emerged, TAs review the series of events that we just went through. As they recall the events, I outline them on the board:

1. Wrote on a specific topic.
2. Introduced selves.
3. Read what they had written and took notes of their discussion.
4. Looked for patterns of good teaching that may have emerged.
5. Decided at some point whom they would introduce.
6. Introduced each other.
7. Discussed as a whole group the characteristics of good teaching that emerged.

They then reflect on why they think I chose to start the workshop with these activities. What were my objectives? Why would I spend so much time on these activities?

After they reflect and take notes, we discuss the phases of my plan, and usually they see that the approach allowed them to get to know a few other people right away and to feel more relaxed, more part of a friendly, cooperative group. They also see that the approach got them to write and think about how good teaching is based on their own experience and knowledge. It got them working with each other for common goals and gave them a good sense of the whole group. I point out other objectives I had in mind for the activities: to show them how to use short writing assignments as bridges to discussion, to use the richness of small group discussions to focus purposeful whole class discussions, and to use in-class writing to focus on the heart of the workshop and the first-year course—writing.

Using reflection and writing at the end of a series of tasks is one approach we use throughout the two-week workshop. By asking TAs to pause frequently to reflect and write on what has occurred, we demonstrate ways reflection and writing can help them (or their students) make sense of events and give them a chance to assess those events. I stress that assessment is a crucial activity that compares goals with outcomes. Even if I believe an activity is valuable, TAs themselves need to assess it by drawing on their experience with the activity, the effect it had on workshop participants, and the goals I articulated.

## DAILY EVALUATIONS/ASSESSMENTS

A second approach to reflection used at the end of each workshop session is the evaluations/assessments of each day's activities. We ask participants to write in response to the same four questions everyday except the last day, when we ask them to reflect on the whole workshop and its impact. The four questions are (1) "What ideas or strategies do you think will be most useful to you from today's session?" (2) "Was/were the workshop leader/s clear in explaining issues and approaches covered today?" (3) "What suggestions would you make for improving today's session?" (4) "What is your greatest concern right now as a teacher? Why?" These daily writings allow workshop leaders to reflect on what is being learned, what problems may be occurring that we are unaware of, and what worries participants as we move through the three weeks.

As I mentioned earlier, answers to Question 4 ("What is your greatest concern right now as a teacher? Why?") often reinforce our notion that new TAs come in worried and somewhat fearful. Experienced TAs and adjuncts focus on issues that reflect their experiences and backgrounds. However, as the workshop progresses, the new TAs' answers show growing confidence. For example, one participant in last year's workshop wrote, "Although this may sound arrogant or naïve, I must admit that my fears have subsided, and I wholly expect to be ready and prepared by the time my first class comes around. I'm very excited." And another participant wrote, "I'm feeling very confident today. Only concern is butterflies." But concerns continue to be voiced as we introduce different issues into the workshop: ". . . maintaining discipline—I've heard horror stories from other TAs." And another participant, probably an experienced teacher, raised concerns central to the workshop, the whole issue of freedom and discipline:

> One thing that is troubling me more and more is the "descriptions" of the teaching processes that I can't help but take as "prescriptions." I've always felt I was best in dancing on the edge of chaos. I'm scared that I'll get so caught up in technique (doing it the right way according to external criteria) that I'll forget to watch for and use those moments of classroom dynamic that are anything but predictable. I hate paint-by-the-numbers approaches. Course outlines, objectives, etc. are the reflections of good teaching, not the heart of it.

Obviously this participant raises issues that most thoughtful teachers worry about—how to plan and still be open to spontaneity, something workshop leaders reflect on often as we plan.

The daily assessments show us that as confidence grows and knowledge increases in one or more areas more complex concerns arise. On the seventh day of the workshop, one participant wrote, "Feeling better about planning; now I'm concerned about sequencing activities and having enough time in a semester to get through material." On the ninth day, after we had done some role-playing (discussed in detail below) one participant noted, "I'm scared of having to deal with the situations on the tapes [an angry student confronting a teacher about a grade and another in which a student questions the teacher's criteria]! I do, however, feel better equipped to handle them, if they arise." And a quote from the ninth day of the workshop: "Getting started on the right track. I want to set a productive atmosphere for the class and first impressions are important." Obviously, these latter responses are a long way from the concerns that arose in the beginning days of the workshop. After each day, the workshop leaders read the daily reflections, and sometimes, because they are anonymous, we use them in the workshop to kick off discussion or to clarify concepts/issues that participants raise. We have at times read several of the evaluations to participants to show how their comments guide our thinking and planning as the workshop progresses. When we plan the following year, we read through the evaluations again to guide our planning.

## ROLE-PLAYING TEACHING PROBLEMS

Another workshop approach is role-playing to simulate "real-life" problems TAs might encounter in their classes. Role-playing provides opportunities for TAs to practice coping with "real-life" situations, confronting and reflecting on classroom problems before they happen. A few years ago, Diane Menendez and I developed a series of video tapes entitled *Critical Moments in College Teaching*. We realized that teachers face certain problems year after year—a student who believes his final grade was unfairly based on subjective criteria, a student who cries about failing her midterm, a student whose nonstandard dialect has affected his grade, a student who dominates discussion. We created forty-four scenarios with the feel of immediacy that confrontations with real students have. We solicited stories or incidents from our staff of teachers, reviewed them, wrote brief scripts, and got student volunteers—many of whom were drama majors—to play the roles of students. All taped incidents were shot so that viewers see a student talking directly to them. The tapes are designed to be used in the company of an experienced instructor. Although they have been used for self instruction and for discussion, they are most effective when new TAs are asked to role-play in response to the incidents, largely because effective teaching habits are learned by practice, not by talk.

In the workshop, TAs role-play following these ground rules:

1. Each incident should seem possible/real to you.
2. When you talk about the incident, use "I." This is you in the incident, not

some imaginary teacher. Whatever the teacher in the incident is supposed to have done, you did. Whatever the student says is said to you.

3. You can't say, "I wouldn't do that." Consider the possibility that (like all
   human beings) you may have made what you consider a mistake.
4. After the person role-playing the student repeats the last phrase from the
   video, you need to respond in some way.
5. Try thinking of a useful/better way to respond; you want to build the
   relationship from that point—don't burden yourself with trying to find
   the "best" way to respond. That can hamper you.
6. Ask clarifying questions to give yourself time to adjust to what has just
   happened and time to think.

Two TAs volunteer to play the student and the teacher. I ask the "student"
not to cave in too quickly but also not to be too difficult, and for both TA and
"student" to listen to each other. The TA playing the student repeats the last line
or two from the tape, and the pair starts talking. The other workshop members
observe their exchange. When the two role-players are finished, others in the
group may be quick to criticize the way the person playing the teacher handled
the incident. They want to discuss a better response. As session leader, I discourage negative judgments of others' attempts to deal with the incident.
Instead, I ask the new TAs to suggest alternative ways—not necessarily better
ways—of responding. Once someone offers an alternative, I ask her to take the
place of the teacher, and the "student" repeats the last lines, and they go from
there. It is often easier to talk about solutions than to work them out in "real" situations. When several participants have tried to find a solution, we discuss the
incident as a whole group, especially the difficulties involved. We do another
incident using new participants. This activity usually goes on for about two
hours. In a single role-playing session we do four or five incidents, with everyone playing either TA or "student." Scenarios on grading, improper fraterniza-
tion, and racial tensions have proven most useful.

We follow-up on these role-playing sessions with the more complex written
case studies from *Scenarios for Teaching Writing* by Chris Anson et al., and TAs
are not only challenged to think on their feet but are also asked to reflect on the
scenarios in writing, exchange their responses, and then reflect on what others
had to say. We find ourselves in a sea of role-playing, writing, and talking that
prompts more reflection. TAs welcome the focus on classroom problems and
comment on how these sessions gave them experiences that they had not had
before: "As was pointed out in the 'Professional Difficulties' role-playing session, it's easy to say/think, 'This is what I would do and how,' but actual experience, writing, hashing out, presenting, adds a world of confidence and understanding." "The role-playing was invaluable. The difference between speech
and performance is much clearer in my mind, and I have a repertoire of strategies for dealing with student/teacher problems." "The information on dealing
with awkward student situations was helpful. I feel I am less likely to panic."

Throughout the workshop TAs assess each activity, and at the end they
assess the full impact of our ten days together. I suspect these final evaluations
are the best kind of evidence of what they found valuable, so I will close this sec-

tion with some of their written responses to the question asked on the last day: "You came into the workshop expecting something. How were your expectations fulfilled or not fulfilled? Were the ten days worth your time?"

• I didn't expect such [a] thorough and practical approach to teaching. The ten days were well worth the time. Thanks for not thrusting us into the classroom with a book and a syllabus. On a more practical/social note, it is a great thing to have a built-in, already established, support network.

• Truthfully, I wondered what could *possibly* take two weeks worth of work. Here at the end of these two weeks, I feel amazed at how much I've accomplished. I feel that I've done more work and worked more closely with my curriculum than I did in a five-year education degree! So many activities were extremely helpful and practical, and I feel very prepared for my first week. (I did *not* feel prepared for my first day in the classroom two years ago.)

• I honestly had a fairly vague idea about what I would be doing. I was shocked at how helpful and beneficial the experience has been. I was prepared to do all the class set-ups myself, and the level of development along these lines has been *so* stress relieving. As far as classroom strategies go, I encountered policies and tools I never really thought of. . . . I was totally impressed with the methodology taught. Basically, my stress and anxiety have been reduced to a manageable level, but more importantly, my skills/repertoire for being an effective teacher have been expanded. . . . I think/feel that the nice jump provided by being provided an opening unit outline will allow me the cushion needed to maintain my health, both physically and mentally; and to stay "on top" for the rest of the semester rather than starting out in a hole.

• I honestly came *dreading* the workshop. I said, "Why the hell do I have to do this?" Now, I feel prepared. I feel a bond with the group, and I feel excited.

## OBSERVATION OF TEACHING

The reflection TAs do after a sequence of activities, the daily assessments, and the role-playing sessions represents a small part of the activities that foster reflection and critical thinking. TAs are introduced to a variety of teaching methods and recent theory and practice in composition. They explore issues in guiding the writing process, setting objectives, creating criteria for judging assignments, designing lesson plans and full units of writing, holding conferences, grading, and a host of other concerns central to the effective teaching of writing. To ensure that the learning fostered in the workshop has the best chance of continuing and growing, new TAs take a three-hour required course called "Teaching College Composition" their first semester of teaching. Besides creating instructional units, reading more theory, and discussing more practices, TAs also learn to observe other TAs and are observed themselves by both the instructor of the course (the Director of First-Year Composition or the Director of Composition) and other class members. The goal is to give new TAs opportunities to see other teachers, their peers, in practice and to reflect on that teaching and on their own. Often they will learn something from a TA who has taught only one year more readily than they would from an experienced faculty member. Early in the fall semester, I ask two or three experienced TAs to let me bring from a half to a third of the "Teaching College Composition" class (six or fewer students) to their classes to observe. Before the visit TAs read an article ("Observing Teaching") I wrote a few years ago about what is involved in the kind of observation I believe is helpful. They not only observe an experienced TA (guided by their instructor) but also observe three peers from "Teaching College Composition" and write up their notes as one of their class assignments.

The observation procedures TAs learn have three underlying assumptions: (1) Knowing what individual teachers want to accomplish is essential to helping them with their teaching. (2) Teachers need information about their own teaching styles and not about some hypothetical "best" way to teach. (3) Detailed information about teaching is more valuable to teachers than generalized evaluation. With these three assumptions in mind, I then teach the new TAs strategies for the pre-observation interview, the observation, and the post-observation conference.

### PRE-OBSERVATION INTERVIEW

In the pre-observation interview, the observer listens as the teacher discusses goals for the class, feelings about teaching, attitudes toward students, what seems to be going well for the teacher and what isn't, and what her/his special teaching style is. The observer asks questions to elicit a fuller description of the teacher's goals and concerns. But mainly the observer listens to learn what is important to the teacher and what is especially important to attend to when visiting the teacher's class.

### OBSERVATION

During the observation, the observer's principal task is to compile a record of precisely what is seen and heard. Again, as in the pre-observation, the observer notes patterns of behavior that point to the teacher's style and records what the teacher does that helps accomplish the goals discussed in the pre-observation interview and what the teacher does that interferes with these goals. Throughout the observation, the observer's primary task is to describe what happens in the class, avoiding generalizations, analysis, evaluation, imposing a structure, or drawing conclusions too early. To take detailed notes, the observer devises a shorthand system to record observations quickly, thoroughly, and legibly. Detailed, accurate, descriptive notes require the observer to focus on specific, observable behaviors. Here is a sample from a log recording of a large lecture class:

> People talking to T before class in front of class. BELL. T keeps talking, 4 seconds. T walks in front of class up side aisle, right. T explains where class left off last time. Refers to S remark from last class. 4ss come in late, chairs bang. T: "look at p117" (pause). All ss I see find page. 2ss come in, bang desktops. 1 more

late s. T looks at class, then at one s while talking, smiles. T: "energy in story"—
refers to one s remark from last time. T: "Sharon, what happened to . . . ?" s Q.
T: "anyone?" s. s. s.

Nothing in this record is analytical or evaluative. It is entirely as objective, descriptive, and detailed as the circumstances allow. The accumulated details reveal patterns and show both the observer and the teacher exactly how something happened from the observer's point of view. For example, in this brief sample, we can see that the teacher remembers students' names despite the large class and the lecture format, refers to previous student comments, and gives students enough time to find a passage in the text, which she later talked about briefly. Any behavior in the class may turn out to be significant, but since the observer cannot know in advance what will prove important (in this case the teacher was not concerned about the late students), everything possible should be recorded. For a fuller description of what observers can note in classes, see "Observing Teaching" (Flanigan 18–21).

## POST-OBSERVATION FOLLOW-UP CONFERENCE

The third stage of the observation program is a private discussion between the observer and teacher, in which the observer helps the teacher analyze what went on in the class and how what happened relates to the teacher's objectives. In this segment, the teacher outlines once again the specific objectives for the class, so that the observer understands how the teacher now perceives those plans, how clearly the objectives were tied to the original goals, and what is important in the plan and its execution. Then the teacher describes in detail the events of the class as best he/she remembers them and compares this account with what had been planned. Next, the observer reads the log aloud, reinforcing points the teacher has made and allowing new patterns of behavior to emerge. As the observer reads through the log, he/she stops to discuss behavior with the teacher when the evidence warrants it or when the teacher wants to explore the meaning of recorded events. How the observer and teacher go through the log depends on the patterns that emerge, the concerns of the teacher, or the class (beginning, end, group work, etc.) that need most attention. Sometimes what happens in the class takes the lesson in directions the teacher had not planned, and many times these detours turn out to be more effective and useful than what was planned. Taking advantage of the unexpected moment is encouraged, but how to do it is difficult to teach. Teachers are encouraged to tap their special talents and to take chances. Whether these unexpected moments are successful or not, they still serve as opportunities for teachers to learn as they reflect on them. After the teacher and observer have discussed the class and areas that might be improved, they plan together. The observer offers several suggestions that fit the teacher's style and goals. They then often plan the next observation, which will focus on issues they determine together.

Under the supervision of the faculty member teaching the "Teaching College Composition" seminar, all TAs learn these procedures before observing someone else's class. All participate in the pre-observation interview of an experienced TA, although the faculty member conducts most of it. They then attend the TA's class, and in the post-observation, the faculty member and the new TAs read from and discuss their individual logs. Next, TAs record their reflections, which are then read and discussed. The goals for TAs are to discuss what was learned from each part of the procedure, to ask questions, and to understand the value of the process in helping them become effective observers and teachers. Not all nervousness or insecurity is erased by introducing the observation program in this way, but it does decrease the fear often associated with being observed. The faculty member then schedules a day to visit individual TAs' classes. Such visits do not take place until the third or fourth week of the semester in order to introduce the process and to give the new TAs time to run their classes on their own. We do go in earlier if someone requests a visit.

## CONCLUSION

All the activities described above, done cooperatively, emphasize that planning and reflection are central to effective teaching. They introduce new teachers to the how and why of planning, to role-playing teaching problems, to observing how others teach so they can reflect on their own teaching, and to learning how an observer can serve them in accomplishing their teaching goals. By the end of the summer workshop and the "Teaching College Composition" course, new TAs have gained considerable experience. As a result, the discomfort, isolation, and fear they felt initially disappear, or at least diminish considerably. These solid pre-service and in-service programs allow us to limit the number of times a new person is observed, because from the beginning of their entrance into our program they have been taught how to plan, formulate objectives, and use a variety of pedagogical techniques long before they are observed. TAs also feel they have support when they need it, and they have frequent opportunities to reflect alone and with others both on the quality of their own teaching and on the program designed to enhance their work as teachers. The theories and research that undergird workshop activities unfold in a context of ongoing experience. They surface as participants engage teaching problems and issues, read others' approaches to those same problems and issues, and use the written and human resources available to them on campus and in the scholarly community of composition studies and teaching.

### APPENDIX: SAMPLE SUMMER WORKSHOP SCHEDULE

Here are agendas for four days of the Pre-Service Workshop. I offer them to give a sense of the purpose, pace, and sequencing of the activities. I've left out breaks and lunch, also important for building a comfortable community.

### Thursday, August 5

8:30 a.m.    Introduction to English Department Staff and Workshop: Setting Goals.

10:45 a.m.    Discussion of George Hillocks's *Teaching Writing as Reflective Practice.* Start discussion of writing processes and inquiry: How Do Writers Write? What Is Inquiry?

1:30 p.m.    Setting and Accomplishing Objectives: Group work using excerpts from *The Life and Times of Frederick Douglass.* (A sample lesson is used to illustrate how goals and class activities mesh.)

3:30 p.m.    Evaluation/Day's End: *Assignments:* Read "English 1113 Core Curriculum," "Asking Questions," "Some Hints for Collaborative Tasks," and "Literacy for the Information Age." (All materials, except books and mailed articles, for the workshop are in a packet distributed on the first day. Most are in-house materials.)

### Friday, August 6

8:30 a.m.    Overview of 1113 (focus on number and kinds of papers for first writing course).

8:45 a.m.    Discussion of responses to Hillocks.

11:30 a.m.    Invention—its meaning in composition and use in workshop.

1:30 p.m.    Leading discussions and asking questions.

2:45 p.m.    Myrna Carney, Director of Institutional Research/Assistant Dean of University College—Profiles of First-Year Students.

3:15 p.m.    Using groups to teach writing.

4:30 p.m.    Evaluation/Day's End: *Assignment:* Design a class plan—applications of setting objectives, leading discussions, asking questions, and using groups to teach writing.

### Monday, August 9

8:30 a.m.    Sharing your day's class plans.

12:00 p.m.    Evaluation/Day's End: *Assignments:* Read "Possible Ways to Guide Reading" and "Reading Questions for Position and Argument Essays."

### Tuesday, August 10

8:30 a.m.    Teaching students to revise their own and others' papers.

11:15 a.m.    Using the campus Writing Center to help your students.

11:30 a.m.    Constructing and using reading guides.

12:30 p.m.    Evaluation/Day's End: *Assignment:* Read "Essay Exam Unit" including the six articles: "Literacy and the Politics of Education" (Knoblauch)—used to model process of how to prepare students to lead discussions; TAs lead discussions on the five other essays; "Literacy in Three Metaphors" (Scribner); "Life on the Mississippi: East St. Louis, Illinois" (Kozol); "Perspectives on the Intellectual Tradition of Black Women Writers" (Royster); "From *Social Class and the Hidden Curriculum*" (Anyon); "Becoming Literate: A Lesson from the Amish" (Fishman).

During the last six days, participants lead discussions on the essays used in the "Essay Exam Unit," discuss and apply criteria for grading, participate in role-playing, construct policy statements and syllabi, and meet with experienced TAs and support personnel from Student Services.

## WORKS CITED

Anson, Chris, et al. *Scenarios for Teaching Writing: Contexts for Discussion and Reflective Practice*. Urbana, IL: NCTE, 1993.

Anyon, Jean. "From *Social Class and the Hidden Curriculum*." *Rereading America: Cultural Contexts for Critical Thinking and Writing*. Ed. Gary Columbo et al. Boston: St. Martin's, 1992. 524–40.

*Critical Moments in College Teaching*. Co-Dir. Diane Menendez and Michael C. Flanigan. Indiana Audio-Visual Center, 1976.

Douglass, Frederick. *Life and Times of Frederick Douglass*. Boston: Dewolfe Fiske & Co., 1892.

Fishman, Andrea R. "Becoming Literate: A Lesson from the Amish." *The Right to Literacy*. Ed. Andrea A. Lunsford et al. New York: MLA, 1990. 29–38.

Flanigan, Michael C. "Observing Teaching: Discovering the Individual's Teaching Style." *WPA* 3 (1979): 21–5, 25–8.

———. "What Do Writers Do? Part I." *Sooner Magazine*. 2 (1992): 21–5.

———. "What Do Writers Do? Part II." *Sooner Magazine*. 3 (1992): 25–8.

Hillocks, George. *Teaching Writing as Reflective Practice*. New York: Teachers College P, 1995.

Knoblauch, C. H. "Literacy and the Politics of Education." *The Right to Literacy*. Ed. Andrea A. Lunsford et al. New York: MLA, 1990. 74–80.

Kozol, J. *Savage Inequalities: Children in American Schools*. New York: Crown, 1991.

Royster, Jacqueline Jones. "Perspectives on the Intellectual Tradition of Black Women Writers." *The Right to Literacy*. Ed. Andrea A. Lunsford et al. New York: MLA, 1990. 103–12.

Scribner, Sylvia. "Literacy in Three Metaphors." *Perspectives on Literacy*. Ed. Eugene R. Kintgen et al. Carbondale, IL: Southern Illinois UP, 1988. 71–81.

# 22. Essaying TA Training

## THOMAS E. RECCHIO

> *Teaching is even more difficult than learning. We know that; but we rarely think about it. And why is teaching more difficult than learning? Not because the teacher must have a larger store of information, and have it always ready. Teaching is more difficult than learning because what teaching calls for is this: to let learn.*
>
> —Martin Heidegger (15)

Since the fall of 1989, I have been directing the Freshman English Program at the University of Connecticut. In my work in developing graduate courses and teaching orientations for teaching assistants, I have had to think about the following question over and over again: How possible is it to create conditions in TA training programs that enable teaching assistants to learn about teaching? In Heidegger's formulation, can a TA training program let teaching assistants learn? That question, of course, is not the same as asking whether teaching assistants can be trained. In fact, despite my title, "Essaying TA Training," part of my purpose in this essay is to argue against the notion of training, and, following Heidegger's lead, to focus on the question of learning, for there is an important distinction between the two. Training, it seems to me, emphasizes external forces that act upon us, whose directions and energies we conform to as we are "trained" to do certain things in certain ways; learning, in contrast, emphasizes the organization and actuation of our capacities to understand and to act, configuring part of our selves in a way that orients us not only to our tasks as such but also to the human relationships that enable and mediate those tasks. Training, then, implies the application of a method; learning implies the orientation of one who begins to see the dynamic and multiple relations between human work and human being. Conditions that encourage, develop, and sustain working relationships are conditions that enable us to learn. For it is the learning that takes place in relationships that moves teachers toward the acquisition of what Aristotle calls *phronesis*, or practical wisdom.[1]

One of the things that I have learned and continue to learn to see (which is also one of the things that I hope TAs in our program will also begin to see) is that the value of questions such as the one raised above is not in the possibility of answering them once and for all but in their capacity to be renewed in such a way that we are, to vary a formulation from Hans-Georg Gadamer, made ready for further experience. Gadamer distinguishes between real questions and false questions primarily on the basis of the extent to which a question brings its object into a state of indeterminacy, thereby opening the object up for deepened understanding and, perhaps, creative development (see *Truth and Method* 325 ff.). If we place that insight in the context of teaching (and learning about teaching), we might say that what both animates and focuses teaching is the continual renewal of questions whose answers we are never completely satisfied with. Consequently, the uncertainty felt by new teachers about such basic questions as how we learn, what reading and writing are, how to verify understanding, what makes writing effective, and so on is an enabling condition for learning and teaching.

The concept of uncertainty as an enabling condition for anything—much less for teaching and learning—is not exactly what new TAs expect or want to hear when they begin their tenure as graduate students and teachers of writing. (By "new TAs" I refer to those who bring no previous teaching experience of any sort to their graduate program.) Most want to be shown only what to teach and how to teach: what texts to use, what assignments to give, how to work with both in class, how to respond to papers, how to grade, how to run workshops, how to establish one's authority in class, how to address questions of rhetoric, of grammar, of style, and so on. And any responsible TA orientation and support program addresses such questions. But those questions are really epiphenomena of the broader question: What is it to learn for teachers and for students? Such a question can be raised, and the effects of raising the question can be experienced, but the question itself, because experience always modifies whatever tentative answers one might propose for it, remains a question.

I would characterize the frame of mind that we try to encourage among TAs in our Freshman English Program as essayistic: open, receptive, adaptable, curious, responsive, and self-aware. These qualities, too, are prerequisite, it seems to me, for one to participate fully in a conversation. The idea of the essay, with particular reference to Montaigne, whose prose has been characterized countless times as tentative, open, and spontaneous (Hall 79), and the metaphor of conversation used in reference to academic writing, have permeated scholarly and academic discussions of the teaching of writing for more than a decade. Consider, for example, Paul Heilker's NCTE publication, *The Essay: Theory and Practice for an Active Form,* to pin the former point and Mike Rose's characterization in *Lives on the Boundary* of academic discourse as an ongoing conversation to pin the latter. The idea of the essay and the metaphor of conversation reflect a resistance to the perceived impersonality of discipline-specific discourses and a skepticism about the adequacy of purely personal writing as the only alternative to those discourses, for both the essay and conversation are relational. As Graham Good puts it in *The Observing Self,* "The essay is at once the *in*scription of a self and the *de*scription of an object" (23). That mutual illumination of the self and the object of understanding in the essay is echoed in the process through which partners in conversation try to understand each other's positions (and thus each other). "Reaching an understanding in conversation presupposes," according to Gadamer, "that both partners are ready for it and are trying to recognize the full value of what is alien and opposed to them" (348). Both the idea of the essay and the actuality of conversation emphasize relationships, the former of self to subject of inquiry and the latter of self to others.

The essayistic frame of mind I am trying to describe is an orientation toward knowledge and thus toward learning that finds expression in our writing pedagogy for freshmen and that we try to foster through ongoing conversations among TAs in the program. In the remainder of this essay, I will examine what might be called "sites for conversation" for TAs in our writing program. Specifically, I will describe the essayistic principles that define our freshman writing courses in order to establish the ground upon which our teacher preparation is based. Then I will trace the contours of the "Theory and the Teaching of Writing" course required for new TAs in order to think through how and why readings have changed in relation to the unpredictable dynamics between theory and experience and to suggest through a discussion of the writing assignments in the course how central writing itself is for the development of writing teachers. I will close by briefly sketching out how we extend the conversations begun in the classroom and in summer orientation throughout the academic year, demonstrating how a commitment to bettering the conditions of learning for TAs can powerfully determine the shape and moral center of a freshman English program. At every level we struggle to foster relationships that make the uncertainties and frustrations inherent in teaching and learning to teach not obstacles to be overcome but the inevitable precondition for seizing control of one's own learning and sustaining that learning through conversation.[2]

## AN ESSAYISTIC ACADEMIC WRITING COURSE

The Freshman English Program at the University of Connecticut offers three courses: a course for underprepared students, a course in academic writing required of everyone, and a literature and composition course also required of everyone. Since the program's pedagogical values are most clearly articulated in the academic writing course, my discussion will focus on that course. All of our courses approach writing as a complex, intertextual activity. In that context, we argue in our course description that "it is [therefore] useful to think of writing as a kind of conversation." The course description elaborates that point as follows:

> Rather than promoting an adversarial or evaluative model of writing, with such questions as "What are the weaknesses of the author's argument?" or "Do you agree or disagree with the author's position?" (although such questions could be a part of a larger sequence of questions), we should encourage students to imagine themselves as participants in a collaborative process of questioning with the goal of new or deeper understanding, at times working with and at other times working against the voices they will encounter in the texts and in the class. A conversational model of writing projects the class as a kind of community, not necessarily of like-minded peers, that includes the authors of the assigned texts, the teacher, and all the students in the class. And it is within that and similar communities throughout the university that student writers must navigate to represent those other voices as they work simultaneously to carve

out space for their own voices to be heard. One goal of [our academic writing course], then, is to establish a context within which students work with academic texts, texts that represent the voices and thus the work of the university, and extend the conversation that is that work.

The "conversation model" sketched out above has a double emphasis: the careful and receptive representation of the textual voices and points of view that have preceded the students in the ongoing academic conversation and the establishment of the students' own voices and points of view through their engagement with those texts. That work implies also a double effort: the impersonal, open responsiveness to and representation of other voices and points of view in the effort to understand them, and the personal response to that understanding through the effort of critical interpretation/application. It is in the interplay between the personal and what we might call the documentary that the essayistic work of academic writing can be realized.

The language of the course description and my gloss on that language are both abstract and idealistic, as they should be, but let me illustrate, by looking at some work from the course I taught in the fall of 1999, how the ideas of the course description can play out in a classroom. The main text in my course is David Bartholomae and Anthony Petrosky's *Ways of Reading* (5th ed.), the same text that we require all new TAs to use their first semester. We require *Ways of Reading* because it balances so beautifully the demands of rigorous academic reading and the varied and rich possibilities of individual response to those readings. (By response I do not mean what one might think in reaction to the general ideas in a text, the student idea of response; I mean an exploration of the ways in which a text may present new possibilities for understanding.) The final writing assignment was an extended (ten page or so) essay on something that my students have always wanted to understand but previously had not had the time, sources of knowledge, and/or opportunity to pursue. In preparation for that assignment, we did three others. The first asked for an analysis, using terms and ideas from Paulo Freire's "The 'Banking' Concept of Education," of specific classroom practices the students had experienced. The second asked for a reading of Freire by way of Richard Rodriguez's "The Achievement of Desire" (a chapter from his autobiography *The Hunger of Memory*), or a reading of "The Achievement of Desire" by way of Freire's "'Banking' Concept," the students' task being to imagine how Freire might understand and interpret Rodriguez's story of his education or to imagine how Rodriguez might respond to Freire's condemnation of the banking concept of education. The third assignment asked the students to lay out the basic structure of Michel Foucault's description of and argument about Jeremy Bentham's "panopticon" (based on the "Panopticism" chapter from *Discipline and Punish*) and to test the explanatory power of Foucault's work by analyzing an institution the students know well by way of Foucault's point of view. The last part of this assignment also asked for a discussion of the limits of the Foucault-inspired analysis, emphasizing those aspects of the institution for which such an analysis could not account. Taken together, all three assignments ask students to construct a frame of reference or point of view from the reading and apply that point of view to something in public life that we all have subjective experience of as a way to deepen understanding. To dramatize the critical component of understanding, the three assignments (the third especially) ask students to exploit their subjective experience of an aspect of public life (educational or other institutions) as a way to resist the frames of reference from the reading and to add their own understanding to that offered in the reading, extending the conversation.

We prepared for the final assignment by reading Paul Auster's "Portrait of an Invisible Man" (from his memoir *The Invention of Solitude*) and Susan Griffin's "Our Secret" (from *A Chorus of Stones: The Private Life of War*). In each of those readings Auster and Griffin weave pieces of documentary research—newspaper accounts, historical documents, journals of historical figures, legal documents, paintings, photographs, and so on—with personal narrative, anecdote, and reflection in order to understand something (as opposed to making a case for something), in Auster's case his father, and in Griffin's the human capacity to brutalize others (perhaps?). We spent time puzzling over those essays, looking at the use of documentary material and the relation between that material and the personal elements in the writing. We contrasted the style and "feel" of those essays to the argumentative edge in Freire and analytical rigor in Foucault, and we talked about the different approaches to knowledge in each, the presentation of a position held independently of the writing that argues for that position (Freire), the careful construction of a series of historical facts presented relationally to make a case for the development of institutional structures and social practices (Foucault), and the use of writing to begin to think through something. We could not help but to stumble on the paradox that students writing in the university usually have to write in a style that reflects the point of view of someone who knows and already has a position as opposed to someone who is learning. (See Bartholomae's "Inventing the University" on the necessary bluff involved in academic student writing.) I hoped that through this final assignment that the students would seize the opportunity to write in a way that takes advantage of academic resources (documentary evidence) in order to begin to learn about something that matters to them and to communicate that learning in a voice and from a point of view that not only is but feels like theirs. The point was to write an essay, not a "research paper."

While a couple of students wrote personal reflections with no documentary material and one student wrote a conventional research paper, taken as a whole, the class's work was genuinely essayistic. I don't have the time or space for a full analysis, so I will list some of the topics and make a few observations about the work. One student wrote about her grandfather who had left a journal about his experiences in World War II. She read the journal in the context of Paul Fussell's work on World War II and of her own experience of her grandfather's warmth; she puzzled over but could not answer why the war seemed buried for him. Another student, drawing on material ranging from her psychology textbook to John Bradshaw, explored parenting patterns in three generations of her family in an effort to come to terms with the peculiarities of her own upbringing. Another worked with material from the National Cancer Institute and a poetry anthology in order to begin to think through her mother's recent breast cancer diagnosis. Another student wrote about stalking based on a recent experience that may or may not fit the definition of stalking based on Connecticut Stalking Legislation, Section 53a-181e. In each case (and in others on such topics as smoking, alcoholism, and friendship), the students drew on enough documentary material to provide a context and basis for the personal reflection while the personal reflection grounded the documentary material in an immediate, ongoing, developing life. (I should note that this essayistic, personalizing of "research" goes a long way to discourage plagiarism as well.)

I've written at some length on our freshman English course because the academic and essayistic pedagogy of that course, a pedagogy that strives to place academic knowledge and personal perception and experience in conversation to tease out aspects of relationship between the personal and the academic, letting the students, therefore, learn, reflects the pedagogical ideals of the required TA graduate course I teach. Or perhaps I should put that the other way round: In the graduate course I teach, I try to enact the ideals of the course that anchors the Freshman English Program.

## THE CONVERSATION BETWEEN THEORY AND EXPERIENCE

The required graduate course for new teaching assistants, "Theory and the Teaching of Writing" (enrollment limit of fourteen, meeting once a week for two and one-half hours) sets out explicitly to bring literary, critical, and composition theory into dialogue with classroom experience through the readings, the structure of assignments, and the conduct of the class.[3] When I first taught the course in 1989, the emphasis was on the relationship between literary and critical theory and writing. The syllabus was structured under headings such as "From Rhetoric to Discourse," "Textual Construction," "Reading," "Understanding," "Interpretation," and "Thinking," and we read theorists ranging from Aristotle and Plato to Bakhtin, Culler, Foucault, Gadamer, and Heidegger in order to, in the words of an old syllabus, "explore the impact of critical theory on the changing conceptualizations of writing and writing/reading relations today." The readings were contained in two very fat Xeroxed packets, which the TAs found overwhelming. After a year or two, when it became clear to me, because of the TAs' hesitance to talk about their own teaching experience in relation to the readings in my graduate course, that my intellectual agenda and the "practical" pressures on new teachers were at odds, I shifted emphasis from reading theory and discussing its implications for the classroom to discussing the classroom and turning to theory as needed to address issues as they arose. (I should point out that at all times there were and are two other course goals: to introduce TAs to current writing pedagogies and to assist them week by week in their first semester of teaching freshman English. Those goals tended to be obscured in the early years of the course.) I also began to find some books that bring insights from literary, critical, and composition theory into direct relation to the experience of the classroom and student writers. The titles that I have used consistently over the past four or five years are Mike Rose's *Lives on the Boundary*,

Joseph Harris's *A Teaching Subject,* Mikhail Bakhtin's *The Dialogic Imagination,* Judith Goleman's *Working Theory,* and Robert Scholes's *Textual Power.*

Rose, Harris, and Goleman in particular pay careful and respectful attention to the work of teaching writing and to the work of student writing. All three books exploit the resources of theory, of reflection, and of experience as they examine the possibilities of student writing. We begin with Rose for the historical background in conceptions of literacy that he provides and for the way he shows how an understanding of teaching emerges from experience. We read Harris for his overview of the key terms and texts that have defined the work of composition teaching since 1966, and for the way he demonstrates how an understanding of composition as a subject defined by teaching helps teachers read student writing and shape the work they ask students to do. We read Goleman because she provides a rich and rigorous theoretical base, developed from the work of Foucault, Louis Althusser, and Bakhtin primarily, for understanding what she calls "critical effectivity," and especially for her powerful and sensitive reading of student writing. In her reading of student work, she illustrates the problems and possibilities of student writing dedicated to what I would call essayistic academic writing, writing that is characterized by the simultaneous development of a critical understanding of culture and of self, in relation, of course, to each other. We read Bakhtin's "Discourse in the Novel" for his dialogic theory of language with an emphasis on how that theory might inform the way we read student writing. And we read Scholes for the ways in which he shows how an understanding of certain structuralist and poststructuralist strategies of reading can provide a way to reconnect our reading of literary texts to our understanding of the world and how doing so can shape a writing pedagogy whose central texts are literary. (We read Scholes at the end of the course because most of our TAs teach "Literature and Composition" the next semester.)

We extend the dialogue between theory and experience that we try to establish through our reading through two aspects of the class's procedure: open discussion and conferences. We begin each class with the floor open for anyone to raise any point of immediate teaching concern for that week. Assignments that students resisted, student papers (most of the time strong ones) that present problems of response, failed class discussions, uncertainty about appropriate readings, readings that sparked an enthusiastic response, peer activities that worked, and the like usually come up. Members of the class may talk about what they would do or raise questions about related matters. I offer my own responses as well, trying in each case to connect those responses to past readings or projected readings. When discussion goes well, we usually find what feels like a natural transition to that week's readings, but sometimes the class simply has two parts: the teaching discussion and the reading discussion.

Our midterm conferences provide the most intimate and at times difficult venue to deepen classroom discussion. At least one day before the conference, each new TA gives me at least three folders of student work. The folders should represent strong, average, and weak work, and they should contain all assignments, papers (with comments and grades), in-class writing, and hand-outs— the complete written record for the class. Scheduled for at least one hour, although some go much longer than that, the point of the conferences is not to evaluate the TAs; to be reassuring on that point I take no notes, and I ask each TA to set the agenda specifically by bringing a list of concerns or questions. If the TA has no agenda, I begin simply by asking for a description of the course being taught that term, and through that description questions emerge in what feels like a natural way. The idea is to talk as specifically as possible about each TA's class in the hope that the TA will understand the dynamics of her/his teaching, will have some suggestions to strengthen the teaching, and will feel validated and supported in the effort. The conferences also set a pattern of conversation about teaching between the TAs and me, a pattern that in most cases extends well beyond the first year of teaching both in more conversations with me and in the TAs' participation in a series of activities designed to support teaching throughout the year.

The dialogue between the idealizations of theory and the unpredictability of experience not only focuses our reading, discussion, and conferences but also focuses the writing in the course. There are three assignments, each designed to explore the relation between theory and experience. The first asks that the TAs do the first or second assignment they gave to their classes, to compare what they did to their students' work, and to assess the value of the assignment. The point of the assignment is to give the TAs a concrete sense of the work they are asking their students to do and to encourage them to think about the implications for them of the gap between what they may have projected for the assignment and what their students actually did. Most TAs do more with the assignment than that, however. Many use it as an occasion to work collaboratively with their students by sharing their own drafts and discussing the development of the paper in progress. Some do not tell their students that the draft the class is working on is the TA's until after the discussion; TAs report that their students are both embarrassed and delighted to discover that their own problems as writers—the uncertainties, false starts, forced transitions, awkward phrasing, and so on—are problems common to writers, not just student writers. Others use it as an occasion to think through rhetorical issues, such as audience, as one student, Stephanie Roach, does here: "Writing my own assignment in the context of this assignment, my anxieties as a student and anxieties over writing are complicated by my position as a grad student and teaching assistant. Should I be writing as a grad student who needs to make a name for herself? Should I be writing as a teacher trying to illustrate with my composition why I'm qualified to teach others to write such compositions? Should I be writing like one of my students, following their lead on this assignment?" Such questions are really about much more than audience; they raise questions about power and authority, suggesting how all those questions are at play in all writing.

The second assignment asks the TAs to keep a journal throughout the semester in which they record their responses, thoughts, uncertainties and so on about class readings, experiences in the classroom, and student writing, behavior, and development. The journal is graded according to contract (thirty pages equals "A," twenty-five "A-," and so on), and it can be submitted in parts throughout the term or all at once in the end. Also, because it is a journal, the form inviting at times highly personal reflections and revelations, each teacher may choose that I will not read it, although only two teachers have taken that option. The point is to provide a free, unpressured space (insofar as that is possible), removed from the performative expectations of graduate student writing, for TAs to begin to reflect fully and honestly on their experiences as teachers. And the journal often functions as a seed-field of ideas for the final paper of the term.

The third assignment asks the TAs to focus on a couple of specific theoretical texts and read those texts through their experience while also reading their experience through the texts. The emphasis could be positive, with a consideration of how that text may provide a way to see and understand aspects of the teaching that otherwise would have been perplexing or invisible, or negative, with a consideration of how the theoretical text may distract from matters that seem more essential to the TA. The point of this last assignment is for the TAs to explore the emergent relationship between their intellectual lives and their teaching experiences, shifting emphasis away from what I was trying to teach them to what they, in fact, are learning. There must be trust between the TAs and me for this assignment to be meaningful. As I hope the following example illustrates, there usually is.

Stephanie Roach, whom I quoted above, wrote her third paper on what might be characterized as her schizophrenic response to "Theory." "When I first started teaching," she writes, " . . . I was too scared to listen to theory." Some three pages later, she notes, "[Now] I [am] afraid *not* to listen to theory." And what happens when Roach listens to theory? Is her teaching enriched as I hoped it would be? Does she achieve a depth of understanding that she otherwise might not have? Does she feel better prepared for her teaching the next semester? I'm not sure. According to her paper, she feels mostly judged. "Somehow in the middle of seeking answers and generating more and better questions through theory, I became a failure." The three paragraphs following that assertion offer an intimidating list of all the possible ways to fail that theory had shown her. Here is a sample:

> According to Bartholomae, I have "failed to involve students in scholarly projects." Worse, according to Lazere, I have failed to involve students in aspects of composition that would develop their "critical civic literacy." Bizzell has accused me of not fostering the "responsible inspection of the politically loaded hidden curriculum" in my classroom; Hairston has accused me of the opposite—seeing "writing courses as vehicles for social reform rather than as student-centered workshops designed to build students' confidence and competence as writers." Fulkerson has lectured me on "mindlessness"; Sommers has lectured me on the inherent dangers in sanctioned sources of power. Perl reminded me that I've failed to take into account a writer's "felt sense"; Reither has reminded me that I've failed to take into account the "writer's relationship to the world." Hartwell has warned me that for one reason or another I may have fallen into "'magic thinking': the assumption that students will learn only what [I] teach and only because [I] teach." [Because I am quoting to illustrate the rhetoric of the paragraph, I have omitted page references. All texts referred to are from Tate, Corbett, and Myers.]

Daunting as that list is—and it goes on for another page—Roach does not remain content with her discontentment because, she writes, "I'm a better thinker when I'm listening to [theory]." Roach does not conclude by asserting a direction for her teaching or claiming a clearer understanding of herself as a teacher or her students as students. She does not assert that next year, the third time around, she will have found a nice middle ground between a rejection and acceptance of theory. "The third time is merely and only the third time," she writes before this final sentence: "And that is all the magic it needs." Although she does not use these terms in her paper, her orientation toward her teaching and her learning about teaching is essayistic, a continual exploration and testing, a process of adaptation, disappointment, some success, frustration, and joy. What remains constant is the depth of engagement and the willingness to listen and to change.

## EXTENDING THE CONVERSATION AND SHAPING A PROGRAM

The conversations on teaching, begun in summer orientation, deepened in course work, and enriched by teaching itself, are extended in many other ways throughout the academic year. The TAs have organized two discussion groups, one via email and the other in the flesh. The latter group schedules one or two workshops during the semester in which they share assignments, discuss readings, and hold open discussions on teaching. The email discussion list tends to be dominated by concerns about the hidden curriculum—conditions of employment mainly—which have a clear impact on general morale. Eight or nine TAs participate in our annual teaching award selection process, which involves two class observations, the submission of a teaching portfolio, and the writing of a statement of teaching philosophy. While only one TA "wins" the award, all participants are recognized at our celebration of teaching. That day we invite a speaker (last year, Peter Elbow) who meets informally with TAs for discussion in the morning. In the afternoon after the talk, the award ceremony involves the winners reading their "Philosophy of Teaching" statements, which usually serve as records of the current state of the award winners' thinking about teaching, and there is some form of TA-run roundtable on teaching. We also sponsor a statewide conference for high school English teachers each year in which TAs participate. Finally, every semester we run a book fair that involves textbook representatives from the major presses and some small local presses such as Curbstone. Fragmented as these activities are, they provide multiple if intermittent opportunities for the Freshman English Program to foster an essayistic stance toward learning and writing through conversation.

Such conversations are so essential to the morale of teachers, who are, after all, the life of the program, that we are working to restructure the Freshman English requirement to enable more contact between students and teachers, among teachers, and between teachers and administrators. This is not the venue to spell out the details, but the restructuring involves in fall 2001 reducing the number of courses TAs teach per term from two to one without any reduction in pay or benefits. Anyone involved in a research university Freshman English program can recognize the qualitative implications of that for letting TAs and their first-year students learn.

## NOTES

1. For a discussion of *phronesis* in the context of the teaching of writing see Phelps, especially pp. 215–8.
2. The issue that shadows my discussion throughout is teacher authority. While this chapter does not provide the scope to address that issue fully, I'd like to make a few observations. First, authority must be distinguished from power. Second, the point of fostering conversation is to try to avoid circumstances where authority gets in the way of learning, in other words, to try to demarcate authority itself as learning. Third, if authority is learning, the role TAs have in a graduate course calls for their assertion of authority over their own learning while the role they are called on to play in their teaching is to enable their students to assert their authority to learn. The tensions implicit in these changing roles may not be fully resolved by way of "conversation," but they are also not avoided.
3. See *Composition Studies/Freshman English News* 23.2 (1995), a special issue on doctoral education, for examples of syllabi and reading lists from seventeen universities that offer courses in the teaching of composition.

## WORKS CITED

Auster, Paul. "Portrait of an Invisible Man." Bartholomae and Petrosky. 49–103.

Bakhtin, M. M. *The Dialogic Imagination.* Trans. Caryl Emerson and Michael Holguist. Austin: U of Texas P, 1981.

Bartholomae, David. "Inventing the University." *When a Writer Can't Write: Studies in Writer's Block and other Composing Process Problems.* New York: Guilford P, 1985. 134–65.

Bartholomae, David, and Anthony Petrosky, Ed. *Ways of Reading,* 5th ed. Boston: Bedford, 1999.

Foucault, Michel. "Panopticism." Bartholomae and Petrosky. 314–46.

Freire, Paulo. "The 'Banking' Concept of Education." Bartholomae and Petrosky. 347–362.

Gadamer, Hans-Georg. *Truth and Method,* no trans. New York: Crossroad, 1986.

Goleman, Judith. *Working Theory: Critical Composition Studies for Students and Teachers.* Westport, CT: Bergin & Garvey, 1995.

Good, Graham. *The Observing Self: Rediscovering the Essay.* London: Routledge, 1988.

Griffin, Susan. "Our Secret." Bartholomae and Petrosky. 402–56.

Hall, Michael L. "The Emergence of the Essay and the Idea of Discovery." *Essays on the Essay: Redefining the Genre.* Ed. Alexander Butrym. Athens: U of Georgia P, 1989. 73–91.

Harris, Joseph. *A Teaching Subject: Composition Since 1966.* Upper Saddle River, NJ: Prentice Hall, 1997.

Heidegger, Martin. *What Is Called Thinking?* New York: Harper and Row, 1968.

Heilker, Paul. *The Essay: Theory and Pedagogy for an Active Form.* Urbana, IL: NCTE, 1996.

Phelps, Louise Wetherbee. *Composition as a Human Science.* New York: Oxford UP, 1988.

Recchio, Thomas. "A Dialogic Approach to the Essay." *Essays on the Essay: Redefining the Genre.* Ed. Alexander Butrym. Athens: U of Georgia P, 1989. 271–88.

———. "The Politics of the Classroom." *Issues in Writing* 5.1 (1992): 37–53.

———. "Parallel Academic Lives: Affinities of Teaching Assistants and Freshman Writers." *WPA* 15.3 (1992): 57–61.

————. "On the Critical Necessity of 'Essaying.'" *Taking Stock: The Writing Process Movement in the 90s.* Ed. Lad Tobin and Thomas Newkirk. Portsmouth, NH: Boynton/ Cook, 1994. 219–235.

————. "The University of Connecticut: English 300: Theory and the Teaching of Writing." *Composition Studies/Freshman English News* 23.2 (1995): 10–5.

————. "Writing Program Administration as Conversation." *WPA* 21.2/3 (1998): 150–61.

Rodriguez, Richard. "The Achievement of Desire." Bartholomae and Petrosky. 621–42.

Rose, Mike. *Lives on the Boundary.* New York: Penguin, 1989.

Scholes, Robert. *Textual Power: Literary Theory and the Teaching of English.* New Haven, CT: Yale UP, 1985.

Tate, Gary, Edward P. J. Corbett, and Nancy Myers. *The Writing Teacher's Sourcebook.* 3rd ed., New York: Oxford UP, 1994.

# 23. Orientation for Teachers of Technical Writing

English 305j, "Technical Writing," is the most popular junior composition course at Ohio University, with over thirty-five sections offered each quarter and thirty during the summer. Originally designed for engineering students in the late 1970s, the course now enrolls students from almost every academic discipline on campus, including journalism, health sciences, social sciences, engineering, natural sciences, education, and the humanities.

About two-thirds of the technical writing sections are taught by MA and PhD graduate students from Ohio University's Department of English. Most of these TAs are literary studies or creative writing majors, although a few students specialize in rhetoric and composition. All the TAs receive preparation to teach first-year composition either at Ohio University or at previous graduate programs, but few TAs have nonacademic work experience. The high demand for English 305j and the TAs' backgrounds and lack of workplace experience create complex constraints and preparation needs that are addressed in a summer orientation and a fall methods course.

## BACKGROUNDS OF TAs AND FIRST-YEAR COMPOSITION PREPARATION

Only TAs who have taken the first-year composition methods course and have taught first-year composition are eligible to take the technical writing methods course and teach technical writing. The transition, however, from first-year, academic composition to technical writing is often difficult for several reasons.

First, the faculty members who prepare the TAs to teach first-year composition generally do not consult with the faculty members who train TAs to teach technical writing, a situation that is quite common in the field (Sullivan and Porter, "Remapping"). Historically, first-year composition preparation at Ohio University has focused on expressivist-social theories of composition, emphasizing collaboration, voice, individual growth, and some broader discussion of politics, ideology, and the social element of writing. First-year composition preparation, however, does not usually cover nonacademic discourse, audience or organizational analysis, visual design, information technologies, or workplace discourse contexts. Since these elements are critical to most professional and technical writing curricula (Sullivan and Porter, "Remapping"), they become the major theoretical and practical points of transition for graduate instructors preparing to teach technical writing.

Second, most TAs preparing to teach technical writing have very little experience in the workplace. Thus, unlike their experience in teaching first-year composition courses, almost all the instructors are teaching assignments in their professional writing courses that they themselves have never written, nor do they usually have experience with the kinds of rhetorical situations, literacy norms, and organizational cultures of professional writing. This lack of workplace experience is a problem for TAs. Although their graduate work in English prepares them with a broad and thorough knowledge of English, so they understand the issues of style, coherence, and grammar, most TAs are inadequately prepared to understand the rhetorical situations of workplace writing, how to immerse their students into these situations, and how to help them intervene at key moments. As a result, they face a problem of teacher ethos: Can they effectively teach writing for situations with which they are not familiar?

In addition to their limited workplace experience, some TAs feel ambivalent or sometimes hostile about the goals of technical writing. In particular, they ask: Is preparing competent communicators in the workplace a "capitulation to the worst, capitalistic demands for docile and cooperative workers?" (Meyer and Bernhardt 91). Paul Meyer and Stephen Bernhardt argue "maybe," but this question should be explicitly considered throughout the preparation of technical writing instructors. Some TAs are suspicious of anything related to capitalism and believe technical writing should teach students to understand and resist the power structures of corporations and organizations, and writing and rhetorical abilities should be secondary. Other TAs feel that improving students' rhetorical skills and writing abilities in organizational contexts empowers the students to achieve the goals they will develop in the workplace.

Nonetheless, technical writing is such a popular course at Ohio University that many TAs choose to teach it because it can guarantee them extra courses during the summer and overloads during the school year. Further, many Ohio University graduates find jobs at smaller colleges where teaching flexibility is an attractive qualification. Thus, despite the lack of real-world experience and ambivalence to the goals of technical writing, many TAs choose to teach technical writing. Obviously, preparing them to do so is challenging, as the next sections demonstrate.

## TEACHING PHILOSOPHY OF TECHNICAL WRITING

A lack of workplace experience, a literary disposition, and first-year composition preparation cause many TAs to conclude that technical writing is simply a vocational or skills-based course with no base in theories and pedagogies of discourse, creativity, and knowledge-making. To dissuade TAs of this belief, I introduce in the methods course discourse theories of Mikhail Bakhtin to underpin the teaching philosophy of technical writing. Most TAs have read Bakhtin in their literature, creative writing, or rhetoric courses, where he is widely respected.

In his early theories of aesthetics and discourse, Bakhtin argues that the rhetorical act involves three mutually constitutive dimensions: the material/physical, cognitive/ethical, and emotional/volitional ("Content"; "Speech Genres"). Using aspects of this discourse theory as a frame, I integrate into the teaching philosophy of technical writing contemporary theories and pedagogies of workplace literacy, rhetoric and composition, professional writing, organizational behavior, technology studies, and intercultural and second language studies.

From the material/physical dimension, TAs need to help their students understand both the material and economic conditions that surround, for example, the writing of a proposal and the physical conditions in which the document is read. This inquiry also involves the availability and structures of technology, especially information technology. Much of this pedagogy is influenced by the Marxist theories of James Berlin and by the workplace literacy and technology studies of James Porter, Jennie Dautermann and Patricia Sullivan, and Andrew Feenberg. Further, I draw on work from sociology, intercultural relations, and organizational behavior to help writers understand the global physical and economic contexts.

Second, arising from the material/physical configuration are the cognitive/ethical possibilities and structures. For this dimension, the course relies on theories from workplace literacy and professional writing (Spilka; Thralls and Blyer), technology studies (Dautermann and Sullivan), and organizational behavior (Driskill et al.) to explore how prevailing writing processes and information technologies encode cognitive and ethical structures. TAs need to help their students understand how cognitive structures such as decision-making processes or policy (at the individual, cultural, or corporate level) imply ethical relationships among authors, audiences, the topic, and the context. For almost all the writing assignments, TAs will need to help their undergraduate students empirically investigate the role of their writing in these processes and how their writing should address the prevailing cognitive-ethical structures. This conversation almost always evaluates the ethics of how audiences, authors, or topics are related or are being represented, especially as they are mediated through information technologies.

Third, the physical and cognitive-ethical structures provide certain rhetorical spaces, possibilities, and constraints for the writer's individual expression and agency (Bakhtin, "Content"; "Speech Genres"). Thus, TAs need to understand how the decision-making patterns and physical constraints of the workplace situation structure a student's ability for personal expression and for carrying out change or intervention. Much of this emotional-volitional pedagogy draws on socio-cognitive theories of genres (see, for example, Berkenkotter and Huckin). Here, the constant change in information technologies makes the question about voice, agency, and personal expression both compelling and problematic.

This Bakhtinian frame provides a good lens for exploring and solving rhetorical situations in the workplace. It satisfies many TAs' desire to engage their students in political and ethical discussions of workplace situations. Yet at the same time, it also forces TAs to move beyond the political and social critique and help their students envision creative and context-sensitive ways to adapt to or change the workplace situation. As many TAs discover, they can draw on their creative writing, composition, and literary strategies to teach this adaptation.

## ORIENTATION

The TA preparation begins with a three-day orientation before the quarter starts, followed by a methods course that the TAs take while teaching their first technical writing course. In the orientation, the TAs are immersed in the same workplace rhetorical situations that they will immerse their students in and write generally the same four documents that they will be teaching, following the same pedagogy, although in the orientation we move faster, cutting some steps in the process. The orientation covers the following four assignments: resumés/cover letters, proposals, instructional manuals, and a Web assignment. Figure 1 shows the schedule of the course introduction, the four assignments, and preparation of the TAs' syllabi. The orientation meets for six hours in the computer lab where TAs can see online sample documents, assignment sheets, and writing heuristics. Since the TAs begin teaching the resumé and cover letter assignment in less than a week after the orientation, I cover this assignment just as I expect TAs to teach it. I progressively reduce the specificity of the coverage of the other assignments in the orientation because we have more time to cover these during the methods course.

| Day 1 (8 hrs) | Day 2 (8 hrs) | Day 3 (8 hrs) |
| --- | --- | --- |
| **Course Introduction** | **Resumé/Cover Letter** | **Instructional Manual** |
| **Resumé/Cover Letter** | •Review of TAs' resumés | •Visual design |
| •Resumé introduction | **Proposal** | •Mockup |
| •Context/audience | •Problem analysis | •Drafting manual |
| •Visual design | •Context/audience | •Usability test |
| •Drafting resumés | •Solution | **Web Assignment** |
| •Review of resumés | •Drafting proposal | •Introduction |
| •Cover letter introduction | **Instructional Manual** | •Hypertext rhetoric |
| **Proposal** | •Introduction | **Syllabus Preparation** |
| •Introduction | •PRIOS | |

**Figure 1** Orientation Schedule

## RESUMÉ/COVER LETTERS

The first step in the resumé/cover letter assignment is to introduce—or review—for the TAs the economic and physical reality of writing a c.v. and cover letter for academic positions and to explore how the academic situation is similar to the nonacademic situation. The economic reality is competition; employers (universities or corporations) are usually bombarded with hundreds of applications for one position, the number so great in some situations that physically handling the applications is too burdensome for humans, so computer scanners have taken over. Thus, the scanner takes only a few seconds to review basic criteria for the job, weeding out the unqualified candidates.

Next, the TAs explore the "matching" scenario, where the reader is most interested in how well the candidate can actually do the job. There is, in essence, a comparing of the candidate, point by point, with the job qualifications. Preparing TAs for this reading situation focuses on content and ethics—how well can the candidate meet the job requirements, and how ethical are the descriptions used to exemplify that matching? In the orientation, I often list job qualifications for a tenure-track position in English on one side of a blackboard and qualifications of one TA (once he or she graduates) on the other side.

It is interesting to note that the TAs—like undergraduates—find it difficult to assess their own strengths and weaknesses in relation to the requirements of a certain job. We discuss this meta-analysis or self-awareness, exploring how to draw out ethically the self-awareness from our undergraduates. This discussion, of course, helps the TAs understand the real situated relations among ethics and professional writing. We discuss the ethical dimensions associated with the genre of resumés and cover letters. That is, there is an expectation that applicants will make the most out of their experience without downright lying, a rhetorical strategy that seems dishonest in other rhetorical situations, such as in developing a user manual.

We then discuss the next reading scenario, that of the image analysis. From the most qualified candidates, the reader usually selects a reduced number for closer attention, noting how well the candidate can do the job and how well the candidate fits the organization in terms of image, personality, and other non-job specific characteristics. Theoretically, this last section fits Bakhtin's discussion of emotion and volition, the personal elements that could arise in response to the physical situation and job requirements. We discuss the rhetorical features that tend to invoke image: page design, font type, word choice, correctness, and some content decisions such as extracurricular activities.

Discussing with the TAs the three reading scenarios (scan, match, and image) helps them understand why the resumé and cover letter call for specific visual, textual, and content designs. Demonstrating the pedagogy we will use in the undergraduate course, we now critique sample resumés of previous 305j students on the overhead projector. First, the scanning step requires great clarity in visual design so that the scanner (whether human or computer) can evaluate in just a few seconds the candidate's qualifications. Here, we focus on the elements of page and visual design: how to make the prominent information readily accessible to the scanner. I ask the TAs how quickly they can read the scannable information from the various resumé designs.

After placing various resumés through the scan test, we discuss the same resumés in light of the matching situation. Here we look at the specific content categories, examining how specific, job-related information is made accessible and organized into logical chunks. Again, using the transparency examples, we discuss designing the qualifications to make them coherent and fit the organization's expectations. We talk about the "stretching" ethics of the resumé genre, that is, making the most out of every characteristic relevant to the situation.

Next we focus on the image that the rhetorical design entails. We first discuss page balance, white space, font type and size, and various organizational patterns. Then we discuss content, word choice, and textual organization. It is interesting to have the instructors flesh out the "personality" of the resumé and decide how the personality that is evoked by the rhetorical features of the resumé actually fits the personality of the 305j student who wrote the resumes.

When the TAs have practiced the rhetorical analysis on three or four examples, they actually grade one resumé, using an analytical grading system based on the acronym PRIOS (Halpern et al.), which stands for purpose, reader, information, organization, and style.

After this discussion, TAs create at home their own resumés for a specific academic or nonacademic position. When the TAs return with their resumés, we place them on the overhead projector and evaluate them rhetorically, following the three stages already discussed. The TAs like this transparency method and usually follow it in their own classes.

I introduce the cover letter assignment, but I do not require the TAs to write their own cover letters because of time limits, because they are usually much more familiar with this genre, and because the skills required to teach it are usually more expository-based. Many TAs are pleased that this resumé and cover letter orientation prepares them to teach the assignment to their undergraduates and prepares them for their own job search.

## PROPOSAL WRITING

The second assignment is a proposal, recommendation report, or feasibility study, which I introduce by having TAs browse through student examples copied to the computer lab servers and professional samples from the textbook. TAs find it essential to study these proposals to understand the assignment. Unlike the resumé/cover letter assignment, TAs have rarely written proposals. They do, however, understand argumentation and persuasion, so they need to transfer their general knowledge to the specific area of proposal writing.

In the orientation, it is critical for TAs to understand the logical relationships among problem exploration, audience analysis, and solutions. For the problem exploration, I use dissonance theory (Olsen and Huckin) and topic selection (adapted from Lauer et al., "Starting Guide"). In fall 1999, the TAs expressed concerns about problems related to their poverty, and through problem exploration, they decided to develop a proposal to increase TA stipend pay. We discussed the art of developing a good proposal objective and how it is easy to do in the classroom but difficult for their students to do on their own. Once the TAs had developed the compelling dissonance, or contradiction, between the emotional and social ramifications of their poverty and the ability to be effective teachers, they broke the problem into causes and effects, using the treeing methods described in various composition textbooks.

With the problem explored, we moved to audience and organizational analysis, following the same pedagogy as in the undergraduate course. I prompted TAs to use this proposal topic because they would understand the sociological analysis of organizational structures and decision-making patterns in English departments. In other words, although they lack experience in the workplace, they are familiar with the organizational culture, power structures, and decision-making patterns of the OU English Department. My goal was to have them transfer their organizational analysis ability from academic contexts to workplace contexts. This part worked well for the 1999 group.

This audience analysis is modeled after the Bakhtinian three-dimensional literacy discussed earlier: the physical, cognitive/ethical, and emotional/volitional elements of the proposal. In 1999, the TAs came to understand the larger economic and political constraints within which an increase in stipend would be situated. They also explored the decision-making patterns that would have to be involved in this type of decision at OU and the ethics of these patterns for those involved. Here, it was helpful to distinguish the department chair as primary audience from university administrators as secondary audiences.

From this physical and cognitive/ethical analysis, the TAs chose the appropriate emotional/volitional appeals for the primary and secondary audiences, focusing on the power the department chair and upper-level administrators would have to enact their proposal. This was a very effective assignment for them because they came to understand the real restraints imposed by the rhetorical situation.

In the morning of the third day, the TAs discuss solutions to their proposal problem. As is the case with the undergraduates, the TAs in 1999 were most perplexed about how to lay out the solution in linear prose that would make the most sense to the audience. Together, we laid out a viable solution and structures to discuss it. Because of the orientation's time constraints, we composed a detailed outline rather than the proposal.

Even with this orientation session, however, the proposal is generally the most difficult assignment for the TAs to teach in their classrooms. First, TAs have a difficult time helping students in the topic selection. Even with the help of the starting guide, many TAs have remarked that it simply takes experience to help students select good topics. Second, the proposal involves a number of complexly related parts, and understanding how these parts work together depends on workplace experience, which the TAs generally don't have. TAs who have taught the course repeatedly learn to rely on former students' proposals to educate them about how workplace writing actually works.

## INSTRUCTIONAL MANUAL

For the instructional manual, we cover all the basic stages in the process, but we produce a handwritten, not camera-ready, manual and conduct a usability test. Thus, we can focus on integrating graphic, text, and page design and understanding usability testing. On the second day of orientation, I show the TAs about twenty samples of previous students' work and ask the TAs to come to day three of the orientation with an idea for a manual. The criteria for the manual are (1) the manual teaches someone how to physically manipulate something, (2) no manual on that topic exists, (3) the manual contains graphics and texts, and (4) the topic is short enough to do in three to ten pages but complex enough to warrant the work. Further, once the first version of the manual is in good shape, the TAs have to do usability tests on it to prepare the final version.

On day three, all TAs bring ideas for their instructional manuals. Using the previously discussed criteria, we evaluate which topic would work best. In the fall of 1999, several topics would have worked, but one was so technical that the TAs would have needed extra time to learn about the technology to do the manual. In the undergraduate course, I assign more complex manuals so that the students learn the technology. But given the time constraints of the orientation, we decided to write a manual on an unusual paper airplane design. All the TAs had made paper airplanes, but only one instructor knew this design.

Having chosen the topic, TAs focus on how to promote successful collaboration. We work from a collaborative model that I adapted from Peter Drucker, who characterizes the different types of teamwork by using sports models: baseball, football, and tennis doubles. The TAs analyze the rhetorical task in conjunction with their own collaborative preferences, time constraints, and talents and build a collaborative model that would be most effective for this situation.

In the morning of the third day, the TAs create the manual and run one usability test. Since the grading criteria for the instructional manual is based on PRIOS (purpose, reader, information, organization, and style), we use these criteria to guide our writing process. Deciding on *purpose* is usually difficult because the TAs try to define the manual's purpose quite broadly, but after some prompting, I show them how important a precise purpose definition is. Next, the TAs analyze the *readers*, using a Bakhtinian frame: the actual physical situation in which the manual would be used, the standardized cognitive assumptions that would be brought to the reading of the manual by the readers, and the purposes and motivation for reading the manual. From this audience analysis, the TAs generate the *information* needed in the manual: steps, graphics, notes, warnings, etc. We generate all of this discussion as a group and list key points on the chalkboard.

After understanding purpose, readers, and information, the TAs explore *organization* and *style*, focusing on the many page-design possibilities to find one suitable for this situation. Having student samples is critical in all phases, especially the page design. When teaching their own courses, the TAs routinely borrow from my stock of examples and are impatient to have their own. The TAs decide the page size, the column layout, the graphic-text interaction, the graphical presentation of steps, notes, and other textual information, and the need for warnings and cautions.

With the page design decided, TAs develop a mockup of the manual on the chalkboard and then break into groups. In the fall of 1999, one group wrote the specific instructions, one group created the graphics, and the third group developed the pages and manual itself, cutting the pages to size, developing margins, etc. The groups then convened to assemble the manual.

With this first draft finished, we talk about our rhetorical assumptions in making the manual and devise a usability test for it. We find a suitable tester based on our reader definitions, and I help the TAs prepare the test, the tester, and the test scenario. The test usually goes well, with only a few errors. As with undergraduate technical writing students, TAs are usually quite satisfied with their accomplishments.

TAs usually like the instructional manual assignment the best, perhaps because it seems most creative, it can be tested, and the undergraduates embrace it as well. Several TAs have won teaching awards based on their technical writing classes, and usually the instructional manual projects figure most heavily in their receiving an award.

### WEB PROJECT

On the afternoon of the third day, I introduce the TAs to the Web assignment, which requires the development of a Web page with a specific purpose and audience. Students develop various links, work with graphics, and explore hypertext design. This Web page assignment is new to many TAs, and I have time only to introduce the assignment, discuss briefly hypertext design, and familiarize the TAs with the hypertext editor. Throughout the following quarter, we cover fully the rhetorics of hypertext design, the computer software needed for Web pages, and uploading pages onto Ohio University's server.

### SYLLABUS PREPARATION

At the end of the orientation, the TAs develop their syllabus, based on a common syllabus for all new instructors. The TAs determine their own attendance policies, office hours, and grading policies. They also fit the teaching schedule to their needs but are encouraged not to vary more than a few days from the model syllabus.

By the end of the third day of the orientation, the TAs have experienced to some degree four writing assignments. They are prepared to talk about the assignments, pedagogy, and expectations of the undergraduate course they are about to teach the next week. The TAs in fall 1999 commented that the three-day orientation was "critical," "essential," and "absolutely necessary" for preparing them to teach their first technical writing class.

## ENGLISH 575, "TEACHING TECHNICAL WRITING"

After the orientation, the TAs begin the methods course and teach their first section of technical writing simultaneously. The methods course, a five-credit course that meets twice a week for a quarter term, combines practical methods of how to teach the assignments with theoretical discussions about the theory and practice of teaching technical writing. The major goal of the course is to critically put into practice the teaching of the assignments developed during the orientation.

The first texts we discuss in the methods course are selections from Bakhtin ("Content"; "Speech Genres"). Unusually difficult, these selections set the stage for TAs' understanding the basic frame for the course. Next is *Foundations for Teaching Technical Communication: Theory, Practice, and Program Design* (Staples and Ornatowski). With a foundation in academic composition, this text helps TAs to understand the pedagogical rationale, methods, and resources for technical writing. It discusses technical communication theory, organizational analysis, cognitive psychology, workplace literacies, ethics and technical communication, collaboration in the workplace, and visual design. When read in the context of Bakhtin's frame, it provides an essential grounding for TAs.

The third text, Rachel Spilka's edited collection *Writing in the Workplace: New Research Perspectives,* provides a vast array of studies of workplace writing situations, workplace writing theory, and theoretical issues in workplace communication. Since many TAs lack workplace experience, this book provides them with situations and examples to draw on to explain the issues they are teaching to their students.

The final text is Stephen Covey's *The 7 Habits of Highly Effective People,* a text that might seem odd in a technical writing methods course but whose purpose it is to help TAs understand various leadership, interpersonal, and instructional theories and explore how they can help TAs improve student-teacher relationships, the overall dynamics of the classroom, and the students' involvement in their own professional growth.

In the methods course, each two-hour class is split between scripting the next technical writing assignment and understanding the rationale and pedagogy of the assignment. This scripting involves reviewing the assignment, its purposes, the teaching methods, the available materials, and processes. The graduate methods course usually stays a week ahead of the undergraduate technical writing class.

After reviewing the assignments, TAs explore how the readings help them understand the rationale behind the assignments and pedagogies, an approach that helps TAs critically examine the methods and materials used in English 305j and put them into practice.

The TAs complete three major assignments in the methods course. The first assignment is a literature review on a topic of their choosing in professional and technical communication, which immerses the TAs into the important conversations in the field. In fall 1999, TAs reviewed the literature on ethics, ESL professional writing, collaboration, the relation between technical and creative writing, electronic literacies, and gender and professional writing. The TAs gave oral reviews to the class and then turned in fifteen-page written reviews.

In the second assignment, based on Covey's *7 Habits,* the TAs pair up and choose one habit to evaluate critically and apply to technical writing instruction. They create a Web site on this habit and post it for all technical writing instructors. In fall 1999, students worked on developing synergy among classmates, encouraging student initiative and creativity in their work, and understanding the purpose of fun in the classroom.

The third assignment is the TAs' observation of a peer teaching technical writing. TAs write up an observation report and orally report on what they found. Done at the end of the quarter, the reports are meant to be positive, focusing on the skills and classroom pedagogies that worked and would be useful to share.

## CONCLUDING THOUGHTS

It is interesting to watch the progress of the TAs, from the orientation through their first quarter and thereafter. The beginning of the first quarter is close to chaos—from the TAs' perspectives. They are teaching a new course in rhetorical situations that are mostly strange to them. This instability inspires some TAs to want scripted, day-by-day guidelines for teaching the course, rather than a practical introduction during the orientation and careful, reflective analysis during the methods course. However, amidst this perceived chaos, interesting things happen by the end of the first quarter. TAs begin to revise the teaching approaches, changing assignments, even inventing new assignments. It is not uncommon for the TAs to revamp much of the course by the time they teach it the third or fourth time.

To me, their revamping of the course signals that what I am doing is effective. Instructors know enough about the rhetorical theory and pedagogy to rework the course. The combination of the orientation and graduate methods course gives TAs a reliable theoretical and practical base for teaching technical and professional writing.

## WORKS CITED

Bakhtin, Mikhail. "The Problem of Content, Material, and Form in Verbal Art." *Art and Answerability.* Trans. Vadim Liapunov. Austin: U of Texas P, 1990.

———. "The Problem of Speech Genres." *Speech Genres and Other Late Essays.* Trans. Vern W. McGee. Austin: U of Texas P, 1986.

Berkenkotter, Carol, and Thomas Huckin. *Genre Knowledge in Disciplinary Communication: Cognition/Culture/Power.* Hillsdale, NJ: Lawrence Erlbaum, 1995.

Berlin, James. *Rhetoric and Reality: Writing Instruction in American Colleges, 1900–1985.* Carbondale, IL: Southern Illinois UP, 1987.

Covey, Stephen R. *The 7 Habits of Highly Effective People.* New York: Fireside P, 1990.

Dautermann, Jennie, and Patricia Sullivan. "Issues of Written Literacy and Electronic Literacy in Workplace Settings." *Electronic Literacies in the Workplace: Technologies of Writing.* Ed. Jennie Dautermann and Patricia Sullivan. Urbana, IL: NCTE, 1996.

Driskill, Linda, Judith U. Ferrill, and Marda N. Steffey. *Business and Managerial Communication.* Fort Worth, TX: The Dryden P, 1992.

Drucker, Peter Ferdinand. *Managing for the Future: The 1990s and Beyond.* New York: Dutton, 1997.

Feenberg, Andrew. "Subversive Rationalization: Technology, Power, and Democracy." *The Politics of Knowledge.* Ed. Andrew Feenberg and Alastair Hannay. Bloomington, IN: Indiana UP, 1995.

Halpern, Jeanne, Judith M. Kilborn, and Agnes M. Lokke. *Business Writing: Strategies and Samples.* New York: Macmillan, 1987.

Lauer, Janice, Gene Montague, Andrea Lunsford, and Janet Emig. *The Four Worlds of Writing.* 3rd ed., New York: Harper and Row, 1991.

Meyer, Paul R., and Stephen A. Bernhardt. "Workplace Realities and the Technical Communication Curriculum: A Call for Change." *Foundations for Teaching Technical Communication: Theory, Practice, and Program Design.* Ed. Katherine Staples and Cezar Ornatowski. Greenwich, CT: Ablex, 1997. 85–98.

Olsen, Leslie A, and Thomas Huckin. *Technical Writing and Professional Communication.* 2nd ed., New York: McGraw-Hill, 1991.

Porter, James E. *Rhetorical Ethics and Internetworked Writing.* Greenwich, CT: Ablex, 1998.

Spilka, Rachel, ed. *Writing in the Workplace: New Research Perspectives.* Carbondale, IL: Southern Illinois UP, 1993.

Staples, Katherine, and Cezar Ornatowski, eds. *Foundations for Teaching Technical Communications: Theory, Practice, and Program Design.* Greenwich, CT: Ablex, 1997.

Sullivan, Patricia, and James Porter. *Opening Spaces: Writing Technologies and Critical Research Practices.* Greenwich, CT: Ablex, 1997.

———. "Remapping Curricular Geography: Professional Writing in/and English." *Journal of Business and Technical Communication* 7 (1993): 389–422.

Thralls, Charlotte, and Nancy Blyer. "The Social Perspective and Professional Communication: Diversity and Directions in Research." *Professional Communication: The Social Perspective.* Ed. Nancy Blyler and Charlotte Thralls. Newbury Park, CA: Sage, 1993. 3–34.

# 24. Learning to Evaluate and Grade Student Writing: An Ongoing Conversation

## DONNA QUALLEY

> [G]rades remind us and our students that there is always a bottom line. . . . And although most of us have reconciled ourselves to this in a general sense, each time we confront a specific decision—each time we need to decide between an A– and a B+, each time we have to give a C to an essay about a grandparent's death—most of us suffer and wince.
>
> —Lad Tobin

No other aspect of learning to teach composition is fraught with as much anxiety and concern as the assigning of grades. Grading, of course, is only the tail end of an evaluation and feedback process that includes teacher comments, conferences, peer response, and self-reflective commentary. In this chapter, I focus on the culminating part of this process precisely because grading does generate so much tension and doubt for new and experienced instructors alike. If anything, experience simply exacerbates matters by introducing more complexity into the process. The bottom line begins to seem more arbitrary, the distinctions of quality less easily categorized and defined. Nevertheless, while it does not necessarily dispel this tension, experience can help us articulate it more clearly. As WPAs, we can learn to use our tension and doubt about assigning grades to advantage when we work with students or when we prepare TAs. My own ambivalence about grading is at least partially responsible for my persistence in making evaluation an ongoing topic of conversation, inquiry, and experimentation with both teachers and students in our first-year writing program. Sometimes I cringe to think my lasting achievement as a WPA may be the creation of a collective uncertainty among teachers in our program about how and why we (should) grade. Nonetheless, I realize that learning to evaluate student writing is an ongoing process, and it is important to build multiple opportunities for the community to revisit its assumptions and policies in light of its actual practices. Over the five years I have directed the first-year writing program, our attitudes, our methods, and our understanding about grading have evolved, and they continue to evolve. Evaluation can serve as a mechanism for pedagogical and programmatic change, but only if it is approached as an ongoing, dialectical process.

As Director of Composition at Western Washington University, I find my circumstances are somewhat different from many other programs where composition courses are typically taught by a combination of tenure-track faculty;

experienced, non-tenure track instructors; and TAs. Except for the class I teach, all of the twenty-eight sections of "Writing and Critical Inquiry" that we offer each quarter to first-year students are taught by master's degree students in literature or creative writing. They teach one course each quarter for five or six quarters and then graduate. Because over half of my thirty-person staff is completely new each year, I find myself engaged in a perpetual cycle of teacher preparation. Interestingly, what might have become a Sisyphisian nightmare for the WPA turns out to be the occasion that ensures our program remains dynamic. We begin our conversation about grading each year during our week-long summer orientation for new and experienced TAs. It continues for new TAs in their graduate teaching seminar during the fall and for everyone in our weekly staff meetings and end-of-quarter portfolio readings. Guiding my work with TAs are two key assumptions.

## STARTING ASSUMPTIONS

### ASSUMPTION ONE: EVALUATION AND GRADING ARE NECESSARILY SUBJECTIVE PROCESSES, AND TAs NEED TO LEARN TO USE THEIR SUBJECTIVITY CONSCIOUSLY

A teacher's subjectivity is a tool for observation, interpretation, and judgment. As with any tool, we have to learn how to wield it effectively by knowing what it is and how it works. Therefore, much of my work as a WPA is designed to help TAs attend to the way their subjectivities operate in the classroom. TAs are particularly sensitive to the effects of grading and evaluation on the human relationships they are establishing with their students, especially when they have worked closely with them over several drafts or in one-on-one conferences. In most cases, TAs have been granted institutional authority long before they have had a chance to earn it or own it. While they may desire having this authority, often, it is easier for them to identify with the undergraduate students in their classrooms than with the institution they supposedly now represent. For one thing, their students are likely to be a far more immediate and physical presence in their lives than are other faculty. Their own recent memories of being undergraduate students and their desire to be "liked" by those persons with whom they have the most contact can compromise any obligation they have to abstract standards. As they learn to negotiate between their dual roles of teacher and student, new TAs may unintentionally misuse their subjectivity: by attempting to bracket, ignore, or dismiss it; by applying their assumptions unconsciously; by imposing their subjectivity arrogantly on the situation at hand. Having to grade students' writing can simply make the slipperiness of their own positions more apparent.

### ASSUMPTION TWO: ANY PROGRAM-WIDE SYSTEM OF EVALUATION NEEDS TO BE DYNAMIC AND OPEN TO CONTINUAL ADJUSTMENT AND MODIFICATION BY THE MEMBERS OF THE COMMUNITY

Grades are based on criteria that will change according to the writing assignment and the writing class. Also, the significance and weight TAs wish to grant specific criteria will shift as they become more experienced and knowledgeable about the forms of writing they are teaching. Initially, for example, TAs may place more significance on the presence of a "personal" voice than on the development of a strong thesis. As TAs become more adept at identifying and understanding different criteria for effective writing, they naturally begin to look for ways to help their students achieve it. Thus, evaluation can serve as the impetus for pedagogical development and educational change, but only if we provide opportunities to involve teachers in the conversation about evaluation. In the rest of this chapter, I describe a few of the activities I use to bring TAs into the conversation about grading and, once there, to keep them talking.[1]

## RANKING STUDENT PAPERS

I begin the conversation about evaluation and grading during orientation by asking TAs to read and rank-order several student papers (a practice that TAs also do with their own students each quarter). The intent of this exercise, which is spread over several days, is to demonstrate why evaluating writing is a subjective process, to complicate TAs' understanding of what constitutes effective writing, and to construct (or introduce) the descriptive criteria we will use to evaluate writing in our program. I vary the specifics of this activity every time I do it according to how much time I want to spend and what I want to focus on. When I have more time, I have TAs construct the evaluation criteria; when I have less time or when I want to introduce a new system of evaluation, I provide them with specific criteria. If I purposely want to complicate matters and demonstrate that there is no one-size-fits-all measure for effective writing, I use different genres of writing. If I want to show how evaluation is tied to assignment requirements, I include the teachers' assignments with the students' papers. However, during orientation when half of the TAs are new, I generally do not mix genres or include assignments. Instead, I select less specialized assignments such as open-topic personal essays because I want to see what kinds of subjective judgments TAs bring with them to the program. Personal essays are also useful because TAs are generally more familiar with this form than they are with critical essays. Later in the year, I might repeat a brief version of this exercise using the more specialized genres of critical and analytical writing that we teach.[2]

To prepare for the exercise, I select four to six personal essays that I expect will elicit a range of responses. I might include a paper that is all narrative; a paper that reiterates common wisdom but does so cleanly and clearly; a paper that has great language and style or "voice"; a paper that has interesting, thoughtful reflection, but tangles its sentences; a paper that will strike TAs as racist or sexist, and so on. In Version One, below, I describe a process a community might use to collaboratively determine its own grading criteria. Version Two explains how the process works when the evaluation criteria are already in place.

### VERSION ONE: DEVELOPING GRADING CRITERIA
### WITHIN A TEACHING COMMUNITY

Our orientation program begins a week and a half before the first day of fall classes and runs from eight to five each day for six or seven days. Much of our time is spent getting acquainted with the computer lab, making our syllabi, and doing the same kinds of reading, writing, response, and evaluation activities TAs will be doing with their students during the first few weeks of the course. On the first or second day of orientation, I distribute sets of student essays with the following directions:

> As you read each student essay, jot down your observations and responses about strengths and weaknesses on a separate piece of paper. When you are finished, rank the essays according to effectiveness, with 1 being the most effective and 5 being the least effective. For each paper, note the qualities of the essay that were most responsible for contributing to your ranking.

Over the next couple of days, I engage TAs in a series of small and large group workshops and discussions that typically follow these steps:

**1.** To get a sense of how each person has ranked the essays, I draw a table on the board and count how many TAs ranked each essay first, second, third, etc. Depending on the spread of the ranking, I might ask TAs to hypothesize about what the distribution means, and if the ranking is widespread, how we can presume to grade student writing fairly with so much disagreement.

**2.** TAs form small groups of five or six people and repeat the process we have just done so they can see the spread of agreement and disagreement within their group.

**3.** Each group selects one essay in which there is substantial agreement and one essay in which there is significant disagreement to discuss further. TAs soon discover that even when people agree on the quality, they may do so for different reasons. And when a great deal of disagreement exists about quality, it is often because people are evaluating the essay using different criteria. When teachers do not consciously articulate their criteria, students may infer that the grades they receive are simply based on the "teacher's opinion." When students complain about grades, it is often because they have applied different standards than their teachers. "But I worked so hard on this essay" is one criterion that students often use, but that teachers, who focus more on products than processes, rarely use! In fact, most grade disputes arise when individuals privilege different criteria, but are unaware they are doing so. After each group determines how their criteria influenced their overall rankings, they compile a list of those criteria they consider to be the most important for an effective personal essay. (Of course, talking about criteria for evaluating personal essays necessitates us also having to articulate our understanding of what a personal essay is.)

**4.** Small groups reconvene as a large group to compare their findings. I compile the lists each group has produced, and then we order the criteria according to which ones the majority believes to be the most important. As we consider our list, I ask TAs if they want to make any further adjustments. Are the criteria themselves explicit and clear enough for everyone? Does the order of importance need to be modified? Are important criteria missing?

**5.** We may not reach complete consensus about which criteria are most important. When there continues to be disagreement, I make a second list of criteria and bracket it for the time being. We will return to that list later in the quarter.

**6.** Even when TAs work collaboratively to develop evaluation criteria themselves, they still need my guidance and expertise. For instance, new TAs often rank more highly papers whose subjects move or interest them. They may be drawn to style over substance. They may not notice a lack of reflection or analysis in the personal essay. Exactly how I go about complicating TAs' thinking is determined by what is on the board. I may question their criteria, or I may introduce additional criteria by sharing my own rank-orderings of the essays and the reasons for my decisions. So that it doesn't appear that I am giving them the correct answer or imposing the voice of authority, I focus on my reading and thinking processes rather than my actual rankings. I note my own subjective biases and discuss how I try to prevent these preferences and tastes from becoming unfairly prejudicial in my evaluation. I reveal my lingering questions and show where I am still having difficulty weighing the strengths and weaknesses of particular papers. To demonstrate the need for teachers to continually evaluate their evaluations, sometimes I intentionally alter my rankings as I speak. Exposing my uncertainties can initially unsettle TAs, but in the long run, I believe it helps them to become more comfortable with their own doubts about grading.

**7.** We now have a list of tentative criteria, although we have not yet discussed how the criteria relate to what grade a paper should receive. I distribute two or three more personal essays for each TA to evaluate, this time using the criteria we have generated. TAs also assign a tentative letter grade. Each person enters our program with a specific sense of what different letter grades mean, and it is necessary to uncover their assumptions. For instance, if they come straight from their undergraduate education, they often apply personal standards to their students' work. If they consider a B a low grade, they are likely to consider it an average grade for their students. If they have been working in the public schools or assisting in writing centers, they may underestimate our students' abilities or unconsciously set their expectations too low. If TAs have been working in the public sector, and they haven't been writing much themselves, their standard for determining grades may be limited to correctness.

**8.** We regroup to see where we stand with our grade assessments. This part of the exercise reveals that even when teachers agree on which criteria are important, they won't always agree on the overall grades. People can weigh the same criteria differently in different papers, even when the papers are in response to the same assignment. (For one paper, "organization" might be a more critical factor in terms of the overall grade than in another paper.) People might agree on the overall grade, but base their assessment on different criteria. (Readers X and Y agree that an essay represents C work, but Reader X bases his judgment on the poor presentation of information, and Reader Y bases her judgment on the lack of analysis.) I often draw an analogy to the movies to explain why the quality of the final product cannot be determined by the sum quality of the individual parts. Sometimes outstanding acting can compensate for a poor script in one movie but not in another. And movies that contain good scripts, acting, and editing can still fail as a coherent product.

We have now covered about as much as we can about evaluation in the abstract. We have drafted a list of evaluation criteria that need to be further tested—not on papers written by nameless students—on papers written by the living, breathing students in our own classrooms. Hopefully, I have complicated TAs' assumptions about grading. We will continue to elaborate and modify our understanding of the criteria we have generated as the quarter progresses.

## VERSION TWO: TEACHING THE COMMUNITY TO EVALUATE STUDENT WRITING USING ESTABLISHED TERMS AND GRADING CRITERIA

With a few adjustments, the ranking activity described above works just as well in programs in which evaluation criteria are already in place. Instead of articulating the criteria, the goal in this version is to help new members of the community claim ownership of existing criteria. In other words, it is designed to enable TAs to saturate, in Bakhtin-like fashion, the program's terms and categories with their sense. Version Two proceeds in the same way as the prior version except that I give TAs a list of specific criteria to use in their initial ranking of the four to six student essays. TAs read the papers and return the next day with the results of their ranking along with a written explanation of which criteria were most instrumental in helping them arrive at their rankings. Later in the process, when I finally divulge how I ranked the essays, I take the opportunity to share what the criteria mean to me using the essays as illustrations.

When I first became the composition director, I failed to remember what I have long understood as a teacher: People don't learn well if you give them only the results of your thinking and experience. (Kathe Taylor of Evergreen College in Washington calls the tendency to see teaching as the giving of information "the academic field of dreams: if you tell them, they will know.") It doesn't work to devise a set of criteria yourself and hand it over for others to apply. The people using the instruments need to become part of the process at some point, for they will be the ones who operationalize the meanings of the terms and criteria for the program. The criteria take hold only after they have been discussed, used, and further modified by our community. (And since our particular teaching community is always in flux, our rubrics are continually being modified.) The criteria we currently use in first-year composition to describe different features of student papers and portfolios are listed below with brief explanations. The terms "responsiveness," "fullness," and "power" are terms I first saw used in some handouts by John Webster at the University of Washington. I liked the suggestiveness of these terms and added my own explanations.

- *Responsiveness:* The writer's attentiveness to the needs of the subject and audience and to the requirements of the assignment and form.

- *Organization:* The effectiveness in which the writer has "composed" (put together and connected) the information and details; the extent to which the individual parts connect to the whole.
- *Fullness:* The depth and amount of detail, research, or thinking about the subject.
- *Power:* The extent to which the writing moves readers to think deeply, visualize freshly, ask hard questions, or examine their own assumptions.
- *Risk:* The "degree of difficulty" associated with the writing task. (The more challenging the subject, form, or approach, the more "risk" involved.)
- *Presentation:* The textual features of writing, including craft, tone, correctness, and layout.

I also develop specific subquestions for each category depending on the kind of writing we are evaluating. For a critical essay, under the category of "Responsiveness" I might ask: To what extent does the writer demonstrate she or he understands the purpose and format of the critical essay? To what extent does the writer demonstrate that she or he has seriously read and understands the ideas in the texts under discussion? How engaged does the writer seem to be in writing about the topic? Although all TAs use the same broad categories, individuals are free to modify these subquestions or construct new ones for their students. In fact, I encourage them to do so, because the act of thinking up their own questions and reworking my language helps develop their understanding of the criteria and enhances their ability to explain these criteria to their students.

## THE LANGUAGE OF GRADES

After observing how TAs naturally seemed to conceptualize grade boundaries, we began defining quality using the following grade groupings: A/A–, B+/B, B–/C+, C/C–, below C–. (In our university, students must earn a C– to get general education credit for this writing course.) Because we didn't want to write a split-grade on student papers, we then played with language to describe each of these groupings. Table 1 shows three examples of different kinds of language (product, process, and task-specific) that we have used at one time or another in our first-year writing program. Although grading remains difficult no matter what words we use, language makes a difference in both TAs' and students' responses to grades. For instance, we came up with the idea to replace product language with process terminology when we noticed that low grades were often the result of papers having been turned in for evaluation prematurely; they were underdeveloped rather than unacceptable. Using verbs instead of nouns was also a psychological strategy designed to encourage revision and to make self-conscious TAs feel less awkward when they finally had to move from responding to evaluating the paper. It was less traumatic to tell students that the ideas in their papers were "emerging" than it was to put a C on the papers. "Emerging" also supports the notion that "writing is never finished, only abandoned."

**TABLE I**

Examples of Descriptive Grade Terminology

| Grade | A/A– | B+/B | B–/C+ | C/C– | Below C– |
|---|---|---|---|---|---|
| Product | Strong | Competent | Acceptable | Weak | Unacceptable |
| Process | Keep Pushing to This Level and Beyond | Maturing | Developing | Emerging | Not Yet |
| Task-specific | Exceeds Requirements | Really Meets Requirements | Meets Requirements | Just Meets Requirements | Doesn't Meet Requirements |

The task-specific language in Table 1 represents a later manifestation that grew out of modifications we made to practices for determining grades described in John Bean's book, *Engaging Ideas*. For each writing assignment, we began to specify approximately five requirements a paper would need to fulfill to meet the basic standard for acceptability (defined as the B–/C+ range). If any one of these requirements was not met, the paper automatically earned the next lower grade (C/C– range). If two or more requirements were not met, the paper was deemed unacceptable. To be considered acceptable, a critical essay, for example, would have to demonstrate that it recognizes and contributes to an ongoing conversation, shows familiarity with the texts under discussion, has a clear center or thesis, poses no serious organizational stumbling blocks for the reader, and contains complete sentences and is relatively free of errors in basic grammar, punctuation, and spelling. This process helped TAs begin to articulate a bottom line of acceptability for every assignment they made. Only after a paper was determined to have met the basic standard of acceptability did we consider the extent to which the paper demonstrated the qualities of responsiveness, fullness, power, etc. At that point, a paper would stay at the acceptable level or move to the competent or strong level. I developed the task-specific language to reflect these practices and to help both TAs and students understand that meeting the requirements for an assignment does not guarantee an A.

Now I offer all of the examples in Table 1 to TAs and invite them to develop their own language for the five grade groupings as another way to help them develop ownership of our grading process. Some TAs have gone a step further by adding a layer to the ranking exercise in which their class works collaboratively to develop their own language for grades. Our syllabi explain the grade-language equivalents (with blanks if TAs plan to have their class develop its own language), but we do not use letter grades until the final portfolio.

A few of us are currently experimenting with subdividing the task-specific language further by talking about whether a paper "meets" or "exceeds" requirements in thought and/or execution. This practice has grown out of ongoing conversations in our program about how to weigh the thinking and analysis features of writing with the performance, language, and fluency features. We continually puzzle over how to evaluate writing that exhibits thoughtful analysis but falls down in performance or writing that exhibits a lively style and voice but lacks explicit analysis. My own bias leans toward privileging the former, whereas the creative writers in the program find the latter kind of paper more compelling. We have come to a tentative compromise by adding specifications to our grade groupings. For example, an A paper would "exceed requirements in thought *and* execution," and an A– paper would "exceed requirements in thought *or* execution." A B– would meet requirements in thought *and* execution, and a C+ would meet requirements in thought *or* execution. This continual language play has not only reduced grading tension and helped us more accurately evaluate student writing but has also improved instruction. We are beginning to articulate the specific criteria students will need to satisfy to meet or exceed requirements for every assignment we give. For instance we might differentiate a performance requirement by stipulating that a paper must show evidence of proofreading to meet the requirement, reveal evidence of editing for clarity and conciseness to really meet the requirements, and show conscious attention to the style and crafting of language and sentence structure to exceed the requirements.

I have also fiddled with schemes to balance and systemize TAs' tendencies to want to reward student effort at the expense of actual performance. One year, we worked out a system to cross-tabulate engagement, development, and risk-taking with performance. Often, TAs are tempted to reward any sign of progress—no matter what—with an A. Under the new scheme, a student who produced C+/B– quality work but challenged herself and showed some development through her drafting process could earn a B. A student who entered the course already a strong writer would need to continue to challenge herself to earn an A. If that student avoided taking intellectual risks, did not seriously engage in the drafting process, or simply attempted to recycle what she already comfortably knew how to do, the highest grade she could earn would be a B+. This cumbersome system was short-lived, but it did alert us to our tendency to succumb to the glow effect and reward signs of development or intellectual breakthroughs with an overly generous grade. All these experiments with criteria and language have helped us articulate what we value as writing teachers, positioning us to complicate and change both our students' and our colleagues' ideas about what is valuable in student writing.

## WEEKLY STAFF MEETINGS

Throughout the year, TAs (who, remember, make up the entire staff for the English 101 program) meet with me for weekly staff meetings. These meetings, which are not a credit-bearing requirement but rather a professional obligation, serve a variety of purposes. A TA can bring copies of a student paper that is difficult to evaluate and enlist the aid of the community. Having a safe forum in which to share uncertainties helps all TAs negotiate the often conflicting roles of coach and critical judge that they must eventually learn to play as writing teachers. In the first role, they work side-by-side with their students, supporting and encouraging them through the complex processes of formulating, composing, organizing, and presenting their ideas in writing; in the second role, teachers don the mantle of authority, finally distancing themselves from their flesh-and-blood charges to evaluate their written performances. Meeting regularly with a teaching community can make the shift between roles less daunting.

## END-OF-QUARTER PORTFOLIO READINGS

During my first year directing the program, we attempted to do a full-scale, holistic assessment of portfolios using a four-point scoring guide I developed. The time involved in doing this work was great and the results questionable. I also realized that I wasn't allowing TAs to develop their own critical judgments of student writing. Our time seemed much better used talking about fewer papers and portfolios than silently trying to score them all according to a pre-determined scale. Now at the end of every quarter, new and experienced TAs spend a day together reading, evaluating, and discussing sample portfolios in small groups. This approach allows for some measure of accountability and encourages all of us to reexamine and calibrate our grading efforts. These end-of-quarter readings also invite us to reflect on our pedagogy. By reading the portfolios of other teachers' students, we gain ideas for new assignments and discover different ways to view our own assignments. We continue to deepen our understanding of the program goals and the purposes of the different genres included in the portfolio: reflective essay, personal essay, critical essay. The purpose of portfolio readings, then, is not to check up on TAs or make them feel incompetent; rather, these sessions are intended to reinvigorate our practice.

I design portfolio reading days differently each quarter. In the fall, when half of the staff are new and we may be implementing newly revised grading criteria, it is important for TAs to receive feedback on as many portfolios as possible so they can gauge their own judgments. During winter and spring quarters, we focus on articulating and defining more precisely the qualities that distinguish different levels of work. Because portfolios represent a body of work, determining what meets and what exceeds the requirements is more difficult, especially when there is some unevenness among the individual papers. Recently, we experimented with the following method for reading fewer portfolios, but examining them more deeply by writing about them in the computer lab. In the morning, we looked at potentially A/A− quality portfolios, and in the afternoon we repeated the process with portfolios thought to be at the B−/C+ level.

### PART ONE: TAs RESPOND TO THEIR OWN STUDENTS' PORTFOLIOS

TAs spend an hour examining and writing about the A/A− portfolio they brought to the reading using the following questions as a guide. When they are finished, they save their responses on the computer. (We examine A/A− portfolios because of our tendencies to be smitten with our own students' intellectual breakthroughs at the end of the quarter. We all need to be reminded of what really constitutes strong work.)

1. Discuss in specific terms what qualities/features you look for or empha- size in your students' portfolios. Briefly describe any specific assignment or directions you gave students for constructing their portfolios or the essays in their portfolios.
2. After reading the student's portfolio, what is your overall (holistic) impression of the quality and range of writing and critical analysis? What grade would you give this portfolio?
3. Discuss the specific strengths of each of the three pieces in terms of our program language and criteria. (By doing so, you will more clearly define what these terms mean to you).
4. Considering the criteria and specifics you discussed above, which ones were most influential or significant in determining your overall assess- ment of the portfolio?

## PART TWO: TAs RESPOND TO OTHER STUDENTS' PORTFOLIOS

Next, I divide TAs into pairs. Pairs exchange their two potentially A/A– portfolios with another pair. Each person in the pair reads and responds to both portfolios using questions 2, 3, and 4 above. TAs spend an hour and a half read- ing the portfolios and writing their responses before saving them on the com- puter. When pairs finish writing, they compare their responses to the two port- folios and read what the student's teacher has written about the portfolio.

## PART THREE: TAs DISCUSS THEIR RESPONSES AND CREATE CRITERIA LIST

TA pairs meet in groups of four for forty-five minutes to discuss their responses to the portfolios. Based on their discussion, they collaboratively con- struct a list of the qualities they all agree are necessary features of A/A– portfo- lios. They save their lists on the computer.

## PART FOUR: TAs REFLECT ON THE EXPERIENCE

After their discussion, each person writes a brief, final observation based on the following prompt and saves it on the computer: "Considering your group discussion and the qualities your group listed, what thoughts, observations, and/or ideas do you now have about portfolios that exceed requirements, the evaluation criteria we're using, and/or your understanding of these evaluation criteria?"

The information saved on the computer is available for TAs and me to read at any time. I use the insights they have generated as a starting point for the next quarter's reading. What follows is a random selection of final observations from our last portfolio reading. I believe these responses reveal why spending lots of time examining and discussing evaluation criteria can help TAs—who only have six quarters to practice—approach grading with authority and confidence.

> Strong portfolios provided evidence of fullness in sustaining an effectively detailed analysis of how they were using the rhetorical tools they spoke of in their reflective essays.

*    *    *

> A strong portfolio demonstrates a sophisticated negotiation between risk (complexity and personal investment) and analysis. I think I am now using the risk category in a more encompassing relationship to power and fullness. In some ways, this equates risk with personal engagement. Risk also involves complexity, an essential component of a powerful argument and a full argument.

*    *    *

> Consistency also seems to be a tricky consideration. A strong reflective essay that acknowledges and predicts problems with the other included essays can perhaps compensate for a somewhat inconsistent portfolio. [The writer's] carefully considered subjectivity [or subject position] would seem to be a key attribute of an effective portfolio.

*    *    *

> I realize that I'm quite a picky bastard but with good reason. . . . Lots of times I see essays that are engaged, tackle some powerful ideas, but they are poorly stuck together. So nowadays I really emphasize organization and center. I guess my hierarchy looks something like this:
>
> 1. Are you raising interesting ideas?
> 2. Are these interesting ideas well-rendered?
> 3. Are these interesting, well-rendered ideas fully analyzed?
> 4. Are these interesting, well-rendered, fully analyzed ideas well-structured?
> 5. Are these interesting, well-rendered, fully analyzed, well-structured ideas properly presented?

It takes time and experience for TAs to articulate what distinguishes strong work from competent work. Just when they begin to feel confident that they can explain the difference, class is over; one group of students leaves; a new group enters. Any understanding that TAs have formed about the meaning of our criteria or about what constitutes effective student writing begins to shift and blur all over again. Each quarter, the portfolio readings provide all of us with the compass we need to get our bearings once again.

One of my favorite educators, Parker Palmer, talks about teaching as a process of getting the subject inside the student and the student inside the subject. Both processes are needed for genuine learning to occur, learning that involves qualitative changes in the ways people approach, interpret, and talk about their subjects. If we truly want to see qualitative changes in the ways

TAs—or any teacher or professor for that matter—think about and practice evaluation, we will need to continue to find ways to get the subject of evaluation inside them and to get (and keep) them inside the subject of evaluation. I have been able to keep the grading discussion alive in our first-year writing program simply because only graduate students teach in the program, and I can ask them to participate as students, people acknowledged to be learners. Just as I can make out-of-class conferences a requirement for my writing students by putting it on the syllabus, I can make attendance at staff meetings and end-of-quarter portfolio readings a requirement of TAs' ongoing professional training. Faculty, on the other hand, are acknowledged to be knowers. Because they are supposed to have the subject inside of them already, they—the assumption seems to be— have no need to continue to get inside the subject. The supreme irony, of course, is that ongoing, critical conversation, so vital to our scholarly inquiry, is considered unnecessary by most universities for our continued development and understanding of our teaching. Fortunately, my work with TAs not only ensures my own active and ongoing participation in the conversation on teaching and evaluation but also reminds me that my status as knower is conditional on my continued status as learner.

## Notes

1. Teaching TAs how to respond and make marginal and end comments on student papers is a large part of our evaluation conversation. However, because of space requirements, I confine my discussion in this essay to grading, criteria, and language. In addition to the material I write for TAs (or "steal" from other teachers) on response, evaluation, and portfolio assessment, I have found these three essays as referenced in Works Cited to be the most useful for my purposes: Chris Anson, "Response Styles and Ways of Knowing"; Peter Elbow, "Ranking, Evaluating and Liking: Sorting Out Three Forms of Judgment"; Lad Tobin, "Responding to Student Writing (II): What We Really Think About What We Think About Grades" in *Writing Relationships*.

2. Students in "Writing and Critical Inquiry" write three papers during the term: an in-class rhetorical analysis, a personal essay, and a critical essay. With the exception of the in-class essay, students compose three or four drafts for each essay. TAs have some choice within each genre. For example, the personal essay can also be a memoir, a conflict narrative, a personal essay based on an interview of another person, or a "dialectical" essay (defined as a paper that moves back and forth between a text and the writer's experience, using each to illuminate the other). The critical essay must incorporate textual analysis and synthesis, but it may also be a critical review or what we call a "text-to-text" essay: an essay that uses the ideas in one text to examine and discuss the ideas in another text. Two of the three essays are further revised for the portfolio. The portfolio also includes a reflective essay, which incorporates features from each of the three other essays.

## Works Cited

Anson, Chris. "Response Styles and Ways of Knowing." *Writing and Response: Theory, Practice, and Research.* Ed. Chris M. Anson. Urbana, IL: NCTE, 1989. 332–66.

Bean, John C. *Engaging Ideas: The Professor's Guide to Integrating Writing, Critical Thinking, and Active Learning in the Classroom.* San Francisco: Jossey-Bass, 1996.

Elbow, Peter. "Ranking, Evaluating and Liking: Sorting Out Three Forms of Judgment." *College English* 55.2 (1993): 187–206.

Palmer, Parker. *To Know as We Are Known: A Spirituality of Education.* San Francisco: Harper and Row, 1983.

Tobin, Lad. *Writing Relationships: What Really Happens in the Composition Class.* Portsmouth, NH: Boynton/Cook, 1993.

# 25. The Teaching Portfolio: Practicing What We Teach

## Margaret Lindgren

Learning to teach and learning to write are much alike. Both require practice and consistent attention to specific rhetorical situations, and both benefit from critical reflection. That's why writing teachers often ask students to assemble portfolios. Writing portfolios present multiple texts for evaluation, encourage revision, and often invite students to reflect on their work and thereby "try on" the identity of a writer speaking to an audience about her or his work. Similarly, faculty who prepare new writing teachers ask them to create teaching portfolios, where new teachers gather materials that illustrate their best work, articulate the philosophies and theories that influence them, and "try on" their teaching identities by describing for an audience how these materials and their theoretical contexts combine to create good teaching. Since 1994, I have asked new TAs at the University of Cincinnati to compose teaching portfolios as the concluding assignment for a set of teacher preparation courses.

In "Graduate Writers and Portfolios: Issues of Professionalism, Authority and Resistance," Nedra Reynolds uses examples from her graduate students to illustrate how portfolios can provide the writing instruction and practice that are often missing in graduate school. She begins by challenging a common assumption, that graduate students "will surely get writing experience—and direct writing instruction—in their courses and seminars" (203) and cites Patricia Sullivan's research as a reminder of how infrequently either the content or the process of professional writing is directly addressed with graduate students. While the traditional seminar paper is perceived to be practice for producing a journal-worthy essay, students get little formal help with such genres as conference proposals, grant applications, or query letters. In addition, Sullivan found that although writing was assigned in most graduate courses, professors seldom commented on drafts or asked students to respond to one another's work-in-progress.

Reynolds argues that portfolios can address this gap and that they are valuable because they emphasize "the kind of writing that the profession expects" even as they allow "students to 'try on' certain discourses, and different identities" perhaps even "to explore resistance of varying degrees to dominant forms of academic discourse" (204). In this essay I address a type of writing Reynolds does not: representation of one's teaching philosophies and practices. I illustrate how teaching portfolios can benefit new teachers and the programs that prepare them. First, I explain the teacher preparation program at UC and how the portfolio assignment functions within it. I then analyze some features of portfolios submitted by nine graduate students from UC, looking especially at self-constructions and assumptions about audience. I conclude by describing how these portfolios pose important questions for me, for our program, and, ultimately, for our profession.

## THE CONTEXT

The English Composition Program at the University of Cincinnati provides a three-quarter sequence of required writing courses for approximately 2000 students each quarter. In September 1999, we scheduled ninety-six sections of composition and employed fifty-one teachers, eighteen of whom were new teaching assistants. As in most large composition programs, entering students are placed in one of several courses; about 80 percent begin with English 101, the first of a three-quarter sequence. At the end of 101, each student submits a portfolio of essays that is judged by her teacher and at least one other 101 instructor as certifying (or not) her writing abilities. After several years of research and consultation with multiple constituencies, Lucille Schultz, Marjorie Roemer, and Russel Durst gained department approval in 1990 to institute this portfolio assessment program to replace an ineffective exit exam. The program relies on teachers' collaboration in determining the criteria for and certification of first-year students' writing abilities.[1]

Graduate students at UC seek MA and PhD degrees, and many find teaching jobs after graduation at four-year institutions where they teach literature and composition courses. MA students must teach for at least one quarter, usually during their second year, and are either awarded graduate assistantships or paid as adjunct instructors. Most PhD students are awarded graduate assistantships and teach every quarter.

Teacher preparation in the English Composition Program at UC happens in stages. TAs attend a three-day orientation workshop the week before classes begin, enroll in two teaching-related seminars during fall quarter—a composition readings course and a practicum—and complete the formal preparation with a second practicum during winter quarter.[2] Orientation provides an introduction to both local and global issues. Because many new TAs were exempt from English composition as undergraduates or studied literature rather than writing in their freshman courses, we spend time at orientation talking about the history of composition studies and situating our program within that history. We identify some theoretical approaches operative in the field and, in that context, explain our course sequence, discuss the placement process, and troubleshoot problems that can arise as the quarter begins.

With this orientation as background, then, TAs begin teaching a section (twenty-six students) of English 101. The four-credit-hour composition readings course in which the TAs are simultaneously enrolled introduces them to current conversations about teaching writing and the research (and kinds of research) that contributes to these conversations. TAs read historical, theoretical, and pedagogical texts to situate their classrooms and develop a critical attitude toward the teaching of writing.

TAs enroll in the practicum for their first two quarters of teaching. As two-credit-hour courses, the practica assure time for both preparatory and reflective activities. Because many TAs have no teaching experience, we anticipate upcoming units and problems. Although the TAs receive a grade for each practicum, I announce early in the course that everyone who completes all assignments thoughtfully and on time will receive an A. While I use this grading strategy primarily to diminish competition, build community, and emphasize intrinsic motivations and rewards, it also eases evaluative challenges posed by the second, and perhaps more important, dimension of practicum: its reflective component. It is in the practicum, however, that TAs reflect further, within the context of their portfolios, on the relationship between their teaching and the readings.

My predecessor, Marjorie Roemer, instituted the practice of having new TAs keep teaching journals and use excerpts from those journals as texts for discussion during the practicum seminar. Following Roemer's structure, TAs submit weekly journal entries that are copied, distributed, and used to focus class discussion. Each week, that is, teachers reflect on their experience—posing problems gleaned either from their scholarly reading or from their interactions with students (or both), speculating about possible ways to address those problems, and engaging their colleagues in dialogue about pressing pedagogical issues.[3] The most significant benefit of this process is its ability to foster a consciousness among the TAs of the complexities of teaching and the divergent ways in which any rhetorical situation might be addressed. Just as writing is still viewed by many as a talent bestowed upon a select few, the perception that pedagogy is an "'art,' the effective performance of which ultimately depends on a teacher's act of divination" (Salvatori 88), continues to influence TAs. The reflection on experience that this journal process fosters serves to resist this romanticization, to cause TAs to look beyond the image of the "great teachers" so often the subject of experience (and film), and to recognize the complexities of teaching and learning.

Building on this foundation, I further revised the practica by attaching reflective requirements to other activities. When TAs observe one another, for example, they write not an account of the experience, but a reflection on how the experience helped them think differently about their own teaching. When they give me student essays on which they have commented, they include a memo reflecting on their comments. When TAs meet with me to debrief after I've visited their classes, they bring written texts articulating their reflections on the experience, and we begin our conversation by addressing their perceptions and concerns. From these assignments, I learn not only what the TAs are "doing" as teachers but also what they think about what they're doing. While the former is certainly important, especially as I write letters of recommendation that represent these young men and women as good teachers, the latter—the abilities of TAs to become conscious of themselves as teachers and curious about the reactions they expect as well as those they receive—is more likely, I would argue, to enable teachers to critique and reform the profession rather than simply reproduce it.[4] The teaching portfolio is the final and perhaps most significant reflective activity of the sequence.

## THE TEACHING PORTFOLIO ASSIGNMENT

As most recently phrased, the teaching portfolio assignment reads as follows:

---

### THE TEACHING PORTFOLIO

Hiring folks in our business look carefully at the teaching philosophies and practices of candidates. Here are two ways in which this request was presented to me a few years back:

"Our Personnel Committee has read your letter and CV, and would like to know more about you and your work. Would you please send us. . . . Finally, we would like to see representative samples of your teaching materials (about ten pages), especially for composition and writing-intensive courses, such as course descriptions, syllabi, student evaluations, handouts, assignments or other writing about teaching (e.g., conference papers or proposals) you have done."

"Could you please send us a dossier that contains the following materials: . . . Evidence of teaching effectiveness, such as a brief (no more than two-page) explanation of your teaching; a syllabus from one of your best courses, along with a brief (again, no more than two-page) explanation of why and how you designed the course as you did; or two or three exemplary assignments, along with a brief explanation of them."

To prepare you to respond to such requests, and as a concluding assignment for our Practicum experience, I'm asking that you assemble a portfolio of teaching materials. While this is likely to be an "active" file in your professional life (changing as do your experiences and interests), what you gather at this point will be an important start.

The two quotes above indicate types of materials you might want to include. We will brainstorm a longer list together, but keep in mind that syllabi and assignment sheets provided for you by the program are less useful than original materials. Most importantly, you should include a statement of your teaching philosophy and provide some guidance to your readers as to how the materials you enclose instantiate that philosophy.

The length guidelines presented above (5–10 pages) are worth noting but not worth losing sleep over. Amount is less important than the quality of the materials you collect. Imagine your audience to be the search committee at a college or university (be specific if you like). We will discuss possible ways to organize the materials as we go; I also have samples contributed by previous students that may give you ideas about structure. If you have other questions or just want to chat about any of this at any time, let me know.

---

Although I introduce the assignment during the first quarter, it is during the second quarter—when the TAs have more confidence and more experience on which to reflect—that most preparatory activities for the teaching portfolio occur. When I began teaching the practicum, I had no model for such an assignment. My recent experience on the job market had persuaded me of the importance of representing oneself as a teacher, and I knew that the TAs would have to do the same. I wanted them to be ready. I also wanted to devise a project that would require new teachers to position themselves, to claim a space within the theoretical and practical complexities they had read about and experienced in much the same way as a final paper in a traditional seminar encourages graduate students to position themselves as scholars. The teaching portfolio seemed to address both goals. I present a less prescriptive assignment than others might (see, for example, Anson) because the choice of materials seems as important as their explanation.

Traditionally, syllabi have been primary documents for demonstrating teaching ability. Unfortunately, syllabi often emphasize what is taught rather than how teaching happens. To the extent that a teacher's perception of the learning process is important, other documentation becomes usable. For example, are not the comments that writing teachers inscribe on students' essays evidence of their teaching ability? Handouts illustrate teachers' perceptions of themselves, of their students, and—perhaps most importantly—of the capacities they are aiming to develop. Teachers' reflections on their own teaching can illustrate both their values and their problem-solving strategies. Additionally, looking for evidence of good teaching beyond the syllabus is especially important in our program because, at these early stages, we provide a standard syllabus for new teachers to follow. Thus, the "skill" of constructing a syllabus is developed later, after TAs have more teaching experience.

Although I originally used this portfolio assignment as a concluding project, over time I have incorporated preparatory activities into class time. TAs read a collection of teaching philosophies, for example, for one class, and we imagine audiences and discuss effective and ineffective aspects of these philosophies. In addition to distributing copies of TAs' philosophies from previous quarters, I have used the philosophies of some noted composition scholars as collected in Richard Straub and Ronald Lunsford's *Twelve Readers Reading*. We list criteria for good teaching and the various ways in which those criteria might be instantiated. Finally, TAs "workshop" collections of materials and drafts of teaching philosophies before submitting the collection to me.

In general, the portfolios are interesting and engaging. Because I have worked intensely with these teachers for twenty weeks, I notice especially their efforts to represent themselves as both unique and effective according to professional standards; they want to fit in and to be different. Most claim to be theoretically eclectic, and the assignment encourages them to articulate, even if only tentatively, with which theoretical positions they identify, how those positions speak to one another, and how they translate into classroom practice. The most popular materials included are syllabi, assignment sheets, student evaluations, worksheets, peer review guides, lesson plans, copies of students' essays bearing teacher comments, printouts of Web pages, letters of recommendation, and observation reports. In most cases, the teaching philosophy articulates theoretical influences and explains and contextualizes the enclosures. Consistent with my overall grading policy, I respond in detail to the portfolios but do not grade them. I hope that this process mediates any influence my own particular allegiances might have on the contents of the portfolio and models shared authority.

## PATTERNS AND INCONSISTENCIES IN TEACHING PORTFOLIOS

I frequently receive permission from TAs to retain copies of their portfolios as part of my ongoing assessment practice. Reviewing these materials has convinced me that the value of teaching portfolios goes beyond the benefits they afford beginning teachers. The portfolios challenge my assumptions as one who prepares TAs to teach and to enter the job market as well as the assumptions that inform our teacher preparation program as a whole. As usual, the issues become evident to me through patterns or inconsistencies I encounter as I read the portfolios. Here I discuss portfolios submitted by ten TAs (three male and seven female) submitted between 1995 and 1999 and focus on the difficulties TAs encounter with articulating assumptions about authority and their reticence to represent themselves as teachers-in-process.[5]

### CONSTRUCTING AUDIENCE

Indications of how these TAs construct their audience, a postsecondary hiring committee, are evident as they anticipate and address potential readers' responses in their teaching philosophies. Perhaps not surprisingly, the issue of authority arises frequently. All teachers make choices about how to relate to students and whether and how to involve students in determining course content and processes. These decisions often position TAs on a continuum, with a lecture-based course at one end and a workshop-oriented course at the other. Even as the TAs describe their ideal teacher-student relationship in their philosophy statements, then, they must also address those whose ideals fall elsewhere along the continuum. For example, after describing his efforts to create rapport with his students, Phil states, "Of course, the challenge of my approach is how to develop such a relationship while simultaneously maintaining a high standard of academic excellence." Phil's comment suggests that he thinks readers might feel that being too friendly with students can cause teachers to ask less and students to produce less. Jack explains that respecting students as individuals is his highest priority because he has "heard far too many stories of professorial disrespect and disdain from [his] students" and thus feels obligated "to play a compensatory role." While Jack is less concerned than Phil about being perceived as compromising his standards, he is aware that readers may view his concern about the quality of his relationships with students to be either obvious or irrelevant.

## ADDRESSING ISSUES OF AUTHORITY

TAs also think about issues of authority as they describe how they teach. Susan writes, "While maintaining the written word as the core focus of the composition classroom, I feel that empowering the students through a democratization of the classroom has been an important aspect of my teaching." Susan is aware of debates regarding the "content" of writing classes. In response, although she emphasizes her philosophical allegiances—by placing them in the main clause of her sentence—she simultaneously reminds her readers that she recognizes that her ultimate responsibility is to produce better writers. After Nancy describes her practice of making classroom interactions and assignments "the object of inquiry," she addresses possible readers' responses by saying, "Rather than undermine my authority, this kind of practice reinforces the importance of the kind of questioning I am asking my students to do about their own reading and writing." Nancy addresses the possible concern more fully than Susan, for not only does she position herself, but she also validates her philosophy by claiming it is consistent with her course goals.

Much has been written about the liminal position of graduate students; they are, as Reynolds says, "caught between the positions of novice and professional" (202). When graduate students are also teachers, however, issues of authority are further complicated because responsibility for a class of first-year students imposes institutional authority. The writing of these TAs suggests that it's virtually impossible to describe one's philosophy without becoming conscious of and writing about authority. In addition, the new models of knowledge implied by postmodern theory tend to lead teachers toward approaches that favor shared authority and student empowerment. TAs tend to represent themselves as facilitators, negotiators, participants in the learning process, questioners, and co-researchers. Thus, TAs, writing about their philosophies by identifying particular scholars by name, must work out what they think while attending to what a hiring committee—perhaps comprised of teachers who support such contemporary theories and those who question them—might be looking for.

## POSITIONING ONESELF WITHIN THE FIELD

I was also surprised to notice how these TAs positioned themselves within the field. The contributions of scholars in rhetoric and composition are discussed in the orientation, the composition readings seminar, and both practica; however, only two TAs contextualized their philosophies with the names of particular scholars. Susan writes, "My teaching is significantly informed by such liberatory theorists as Paulo Freire, Susan Jarratt, and Ira Shor." And after Jack describes his view of the "fractured landscape of composition theory and practice," he positions himself in what some would consider a contradictory spot when he states both that his "initial and dominant sympathies are with the Elbow/Murray school," and later, that he "also take[s] seriously Bartholomae's concern that our job is to prepare students to write academic discourse." Although the TAs frequently used terminology associated with particular approaches—verbs such as "empower" and "democratize" and nouns such as "collaboration" and "reflection"—scholarly references are conspicuously absent.

Given that positioning oneself in the field is a common practice in academic writing, I wondered why more TAs didn't mention influential figures. Perhaps they feared being categorized. As new teachers, these young men and women were just beginning to sort through the multiple and often conflicting scholarly approaches, many of which can seem mutually exclusive. Perhaps they hadn't integrated the conversations into their pedagogical decisions; perhaps it would have felt more like a posture than a sincere claim. In addition, the TAs generally approached this assignment with the goal of establishing their identities as teachers. Perhaps it is only after one articulates a self that one can represent that self in relation to others. Clearly, assigning the portfolio to *beginning* teachers has its limitations. Compared to those of us who have taught for years, these teachers have one year of experience on which to reflect.

## CONSTRUCTING IDENTITY AS A TEACHER

The identity a TA constructs as a teacher is perhaps best understood by the materials he or she chooses to include in the portfolio. Chris Anson describes the contents that might be included in a teaching portfolio as "primary" documents—"actual materials from classroom instruction"—and "secondary" documents—"that demonstrate active, critical thinking about instructional issues and materials" (187). Primary documents generally represent certainty reflected in texts such as directions to students or guidelines for assignments or explanations of grading criteria. Secondary documents, are generally more tentative; for example, a teacher might ponder her choice to use writing groups or to revise an assignment. In these portfolios, I noticed that while the TAs clearly valued reflection in their teaching—they often required meta-writing from students with their essays and requested feedback about the effectiveness of activities and assignments as the course progressed—they were reticent to include secondary documents in their portfolios.

Although as teachers these TAs recognized the importance of developing a consciousness of one's writing process, as job-seekers they were unsure about representing themselves as teachers in-process. For the most part, the teaching philosophies were stated in strong, decisive voices. For example, Ellen writes, "In defining myself as a teacher, I must point to three aspects of my teaching which inform what I do in the classroom. I feel that my greatest strengths lie in. . . ." And Sally states, "I think it is essential to recognize that values, politics, and knowledge are socially constructed and inherently connected." When TAs did articulate their limitations, they generally kept the statements brief and undeveloped. After describing how and why she encourages her students to trust her, Sally writes, "While [these methods] sometimes backfire, I still think that many aspects of this approach. . . ." Although she admits that her approach doesn't always work, Sally doesn't detail what "backfiring" might look like or what she might have learned from such an occasion. Perhaps the most noticeable statement of this nature is at the beginning of Susan's philosophy where she says, "[M]y philosophy is still very much in the process of evolving and at times seems very much in flux as I work through each new quarter in the composition classroom." Although Susan appears to be foregrounding her position as a developing teacher, she doesn't explain the changes she's made or the questions she's faced. Instead, she takes on a decisive voice as she continues, listing her philosophical allegiances and her teaching goals.

Only two TAs included secondary documents in their portfolios. Both Scott and Mark submitted the self evaluation statements they had written to debrief me after a class observation. More than any of the examples above, these documents represent their authors learning from experience. After commenting on the successful class discussion the day I visited, Scott describes "the aspect of the class that was probably the least successful": He hadn't made time for students to write about the discussion. In Mark's self evaluation, he describes himself as "still trying to learn how to ask the right question to get [students] to think beyond the easy answers and observations" and disappointed that he didn't refer to his notes because "some good points didn't get mentioned in class." Though Scott and Mark do not refer to their self-reflective documents in their philosophy statements, I read the decision to include them as evidence that the two TAs think some readers might value teachers who reflect on and learn from their experiences. While I'm quite certain that all TAs whose work I reviewed share this conviction, the subordination of it to other convictions suggests to me that perhaps they expect hiring committees to prefer confident and well-theorized teachers rather than reflective ones. As I discussed this issue with a TA recently, he suggested that perhaps folks withheld these materials because I was the "real" audience, and certainly I already knew of their reflective capabilities.[6]

My experience suggests that teachers prefer to speak with certainty, especially when they are being evaluated. Writing self evaluations for reappointment and tenure review and reading teaching materials to determine teaching awards have taught me that many postsecondary educators appreciate process less than product with regard to teaching. Toward the end of her essay, Reynolds describes a dilemma she faces when advising graduate students. She wants both to "help graduate writers figure out what will get them accepted to a conference or get them a publication" and "encourage their interrogation of or resistance to certain conventions of academic discourse" (208). I certainly feel a similar tension. Do I suggest that TAs like Sally and Susan extend their critical thinking? And what response is appropriate to a TA like Mark who begins his teaching philosophy by saying, "Though I am considered a teacher of writing, I do not consider teaching writing my primary responsibility in the classroom." Given the difficult job market, should one take risks with a teaching portfolio? To what degree should a job applicant reflect on her limitations—even if she goes on to explain how she has addressed them?

## TEACHING PORTFOLIOS AND PROGRAM ASSESSMENT

Looking only at the difficulties TAs encounter with authority and their reticence to represent themselves as teachers-in-process leaves me with important questions. Should I more often mention scholars by name as we discuss practice and as I comment on their journals, student writing, and observations? While such connections are in my head, I often get so focused on the problem under discussion that I forget to situate the problem in scholarly conversations, but doing so could show the TAs how their ideas and practices instantiate, extend, qualify, or resist particular theories or philosophies. Should I invite the TAs to consider connections between the processes and products involved in their teaching? The decision to omit secondary documents may be determined by assumptions that reflection is appropriate for class but not for professional situations. Would more structured reflection about such topics help TAs to examine their assumptions and expand their thinking about good teaching?

My findings also lead to concerns about our program. Currently, I leave any follow-up on the portfolio assignment to chance; those who want help ask for it. But perhaps a structure would help those who may need help but don't know it or those who hesitate to ask. TAs and the department could benefit if more faculty members reviewed and critiqued the teaching portfolios. Most importantly, it won't be long before the TAs whose portfolios I read will be reading the portfolios of job applicants. For what should they look? How will they judge? Such questions push our program to articulate its assumptions more clearly.

To date, my primary evidence that preparing teaching portfolios has been useful to TAs is anecdotal. Several TAs have won departmental and university-wide teaching awards after having used their portfolios when representing themselves to the judges. Others have found jobs and used all or pieces of their portfolios when writing application letters and submitting materials. Anson describes a tendency, particularly in research-oriented universities, for faculty members to "define their professional lives in terms of scholarship," a tendency that he claims "systematically devalues teachers (especially in public schools) whose professions are necessarily rooted in classrooms" (190). I am certain that teaching portfolios, particularly the teaching philosophies, help our TAs to practice another genre and improve their writing. Their philosophies undoubtedly enable them to be more competitive on the job market. I hope that, in addition, the portfolios develop in their authors a sense of respect for teaching that will eventually diminish whatever devaluation they encounter in the institution.

## NOTES

1. For a full picture of the portfolio assessment program at UC, see Roemer, Schultz, and Durst.
2. While Practicum II marks the end of course requirements, TAs are mentored throughout their studies. Second-year TAs invite a professor to visit their classes and participate in ongoing professional development activities provided for all composition instructors. In addition, advanced TAs often have the option to teach 200-level, general education literature courses in the department and to teach composition at regional campuses. In both situations, TAs work with designated professors as mentors.
3. Roemer has outlined and discussed this process in detail in a paper presented at CCCC in 1992, titled "Training Teachers: What Difference Does It Make?"
4. Robert Yagelski describes a tension some perceive between the desire to prepare new teachers for the daily demands and the desire to encourage reflection. He attributes the notion of helping students become "reflective practitioners" to Donald Schön.

5. I chose these ten portfolios because only these students had given me permission to use their work for research purposes. Names I used here are pseudonyms, as I promised the TAs anonymity when I included their work in my research.
6. Getting beyond the confines that academic situations place on audience is, it seems, as much of a challenge with graduate students as with undergraduates.

## WORKS CITED

Anson, Chris M. "Portfolios for Teachers: Writing Our Way to Reflective Practice." *New Directions in Portfolio Assessment.* Ed. Laurel Black, Donald A. Daiker, Jeffrey Sommers, Gail Stygall. Portsmouth, NH: Boynton/Cook, 1994. 185–200.

Reynolds, Nedra. "Graduate Writers and Portfolios: Issues of Professionalism, Authority and Resistance." *New Directions in Portfolio Assessment.* Ed. Laurel Black, Donald A. Daiker, Jeffrey Sommers, Gail Stygall. Portsmouth, NH: Boynton/Cook, 1994. 201–9.

Roemer, Marjorie, Lucille M. Schultz, and Russel K. Durst. "Portfolios and the Process of Change." *College Composition and Communication* 42 (1991): 455–69.

Salvatori, Mariolina. "Pedagogy in the Academy: 'The Divine Skill of the Born Teacher's Instincts.'" *Pedagogy in the Age of Politics: Writing and Reading (in) the Academy.* Ed. Patricia A. Sullivan and Donna J. Qualley. Urbana, IL: NCTE, 1994. 88–99.

Straub, Richard, and Ronald Lunsford. *Twelve Readers Reading: Responding to College Student Writing.* Cresskill, NJ: Hampton, 1995. 395–421.

Sullivan, Patricia A. "Writing in the Graduate Curriculum: Literary Criticism as Composition." *Journal of Advanced Composition* 11 (1991): 283–99.

Yagelski, Robert P. "Portfolios as a Way to Encourage Reflective Practice among Preservice English Teachers." *Situating Portfolios: Four Perspectives.* Ed. Kathleen Blake Yancey and Irwin Weiser. Logan: Utah State UP, 1997. 225–43.

# 26. Evolution of a Teaching Notebook: Contents, Purposes, and Assessment

## SARAH LIGGETT

> *Sometimes I lay awake at night, and I ask, "Where have I gone wrong?"*
> *Then a voice says to me, "This is going to take more than one night."*
>
> Charlie Brown

This epigraph—used by Bill, a teaching assistant in my teaching practicum, to introduce the preface to his Teaching Notebook—will be readily understood by teachers who adopt a reflective approach to teaching. The question—"Where have I gone wrong?" (and, I hasten to add, *"and right?"*)—concerns new teachers as well as those who prepare them for the classroom. While coediting this collection, I have reflected on sixteen years of experience preparing TAs to teach first-year English at Louisiana State University. In particular, I have thought—for "more than one night"—about what I've come to call a Teaching Notebook. It is the main project that TAs at LSU complete for the three-hour required practicum taken for credit while teaching their first semester of an expository writing course.[1] In this chapter, I will describe the evolution of the Teaching Notebook; its contents, purposes, and assessment; and changes I foresee, given what I've learned from other contributors to this book.

## OUT OF THE CLUTTER: EVOLUTION OF A TEACHING NOTEBOOK

I began teaching a practicum for new TAs in 1983, the first semester I arrived at LSU, based on how I had learned to teach at Purdue—a combination of undergraduate methods courses, mentoring, an apprenticeship, and graduate seminars in composition studies.[2] While I knew why I was asking TAs to read selected texts and to do particular assignments, I soon learned that they did not so readily connect the professional literature they read on teaching writing with the lessons they planned or link the methods I modeled in the practicum with the activities they used in their composition classes or see the similarities between the assignments they wrote for the practicum and the ones they gave to students. This confusion was often evident in the clutter of handouts, lesson plans, assignments, course notes, and reading notes—from the practicum and from their first-year course—that jammed their backpacks, covered their office desks, and from some reports, threatened to claim whole rooms in their apartments. Thus, I first conceived of a notebook as a simple means of helping new TAs to organize practicum materials and teaching materials, hoping in the process that they'd realize the connections.

Directions for the notebook were easy: Get a binder with some dividers and a three-hole punch and organize assignments, handouts, and notes from the practicum and keep track of lesson plans, handouts, and other stuff (always a necessary category) from the first-year English course. While this setup worked as a filing system of sorts, it did little to help TAs forge links between the practicum they were taking and the composition course they were teaching.

In the late 1980s, sessions at CCCC and conversations with other WPAs prompted me to redesign the notebook as a Teaching Journal, a space for written reflections on practicum materials and teaching experiences. The Teaching Journal became a more meaningful practicum assignment, not just an organizing tool. While it had some of the same divisions as the notebook, TAs now wrote brief observations at the end of each day's lesson plan about what had worked, what hadn't, what was memorable about the class or a particular student. These notes became grist for the reflection mill after each unit, at midterm, and at the semester's end, reflections written in the journal and discussed in the practicum. Without such records, TAs were apt to forget their and students' specific reactions to particular activities as they sought to solve teaching problems.

The Teaching Journal also helped to clarify how practicum assignments parallel major writing assignments in first-year English as presented in Stephen Reid's *The Prentice Hall Guide for College Writers*, the first-year composition text used by all new TAs. The assignments match as follows:

| *Practicum Assignments* | *First-Year English Assignments* |
| --- | --- |
| Remembering a significant event | Remembering a significant event |
| Planning and presenting a teaching unit collaboratively | Investigating and reporting a topic collaboratively |
| Reviewing a professional book | Evaluating a service or consumer goods |
| Solving a teaching problem | Solving a campus or community problem |

For example, for the first assignment on remembering a significant event, TAs wrote the same assignment that they gave to students—following textbook directions from prewriting exercises through peer review. In the next few practicum classes, we discussed differences among TAs' writing processes, developed over years of schooling and practice, and those outlined in Reid's text; ways to encourage students to recognize and develop their individual writing processes and strategies; and the research and theories that have led to the discipline's understanding of writing as cognitive and social processes. As Darin Payne and Theresa Enos remind us in their chapter in this collection, "The complexity of elements of the writing process, such as recursion . . . or social-epistemic collaboration, can be lost in untheorized TA discussions that attempt to instill the linear logistics of freewriting, drafting, revising, and editing" (54).

TAs also talked about the advantages of various peer review methods and practiced responding in small groups to each other's drafts.

Having completed the same assignment as their students, many TAs then used their writing in the freshman classroom to illustrate how they dealt with the challenges of the first essay. Sharing their personal narratives also helped to build a community of writers during those early weeks of the semester. As they placed their own essay along with other classroom materials in the Teaching Journal section on "Remembering a Significant Event," TAs realized the purpose of the practicum assignment: learning by doing—or in this case by writing.

During midterm conferences on the journal and in prefaces to them at the end of the semester, some TAs, especially creative writers, told me of troubles they had reconciling my requirements for a Teaching Journal with their notion of journals, unstructured writings of personal reminiscences, that many had kept for years. One MFA student explained that the "Teaching Journal posed a personal challenge for me . . . not because I was unfamiliar with the concept of the journal, but on the contrary because I was *so* intimately familiar with journals, having kept one since a 10th grade class assignment started me down that path 18 years ago." While the journal had space for reflection, other prescribed sections and an imposed organization (whether mine or theirs) served functions that were not usually associated with journal writing.

Furthermore, TAs and I began to see how the journal had a life beyond the practicum. On their own, TAs used it and reworked it the next semester as they taught expository writing again; they added new sections when teaching the second composition course with its focus on argumentation; and later when applying for jobs, they mined it for materials and insights to create a Teaching Portfolio. Hence, the Teaching Notebook was born a few years ago.

## CONTENTS AND PURPOSES OF A TEACHING NOTEBOOK

The Teaching Notebook begins as an empty three-inch binder and expands during the semester into an organized collection of materials from the practicum and the first-year course that can be arranged and rearranged as the TA connects activities, readings, and reflections. Because it contains materials such as assignments, handouts, and readings, it is more than a reflective journal. Nor is it a teaching portfolio as described by Margaret Lindgren in this collection, since TAs do not showcase their "best" work. Rather, the Teaching Notebook gathers it all—original and "borrowed" materials, successful lessons and "bombs," ideas on what to do next time, reading notes, and practicum assignments—in a flexible organization that makes sense to each TA. While a few TAs separate practicum materials from first-year course materials, most organize their Teaching Notebooks around units, integrating reading notes, planning guides, and reflections according to the major assignments in the first-year writing course. A Table of Contents and tabbed dividers guide them and other readers to the materials at hand. At the end of the semester, TAs write prefaces to their notebooks that introduce the content, justify the organization, and speculate on what the notebook reveals about the teacher who has amassed it. The rest of this chapter describes five practicum requirements—Reading Notes, Book Reviews, To-Read Lists, Graded Essays, and Practicum Assignments—to illustrate the organization, connections, and value of the Teaching Notebook for TAs and for teacher educators.

## READING NOTES

I confess that I began asking TAs to keep reading notes to monitor their assigned readings for the practicum, texts that include Erika Lindemann's *A Rhetoric for Writing Teachers,* Lelia Christenbury and Patricia Kelly's *Questioning: A Path to Critical Thinking,* the coauthored *Scenarios for Teaching Writing,* and a packet of two dozen journal articles on composition theory and pedagogy, as well as the first-year texts we use and their ancillary materials. As this list shows, there is much reading for a one-semester course that also includes presentations of unit plans for first-year English, paper-grading sessions, and visits from campus support staff. We never have time to talk at length about all the readings. And unfortunately (but predictably), when some TAs realize that I assign more than we can discuss, they concentrate on the hundred pages of Derrida and the whole of *Beloved* due next time in their other two graduate seminars, courses that they may view as more directly related to their graduate work. (Only a few of our TAs concentrate in rhetoric and composition studies; all others pursue an MA or PhD in literature or an MFA in creative writing. Ironically, however, most will find careers in small, liberal arts colleges where teaching loads will include more courses in composition than literature or creative writing combined.) Yet when asked to annotate readings or respond to them in journal entries, TAs, regardless of their graduate concentration, need help to engage the literature of composition studies and realize its value beyond the practicum. More concerned with facilitating than monitoring their readings, I now offer TAs a structured Reading Guide, presented in compact form here, to include in their Teaching Notebooks:

---

### READING GUIDE—TEACHING PRACTICUM

Author: _____

Title: _____

Publication date and place: _____

- What question or problem does the author address in this reading?
- What answers, solutions, or main points does the author offer?
- List key words that appear in this article, defining any new terms.
- What key points do you want to remember from this reading?
- What questions do you have as a result of your reading?
- Note other comments on back. You may wish to attach this sheet to your annotated article.

---

Some TAs fill in Reading Guides verbatim for each assignment; others copy the questions to a computer file and adapt them as they see fit. But the basic format requires TAs to pay attention to the scholars we are reading; to become familiar with standard journals in the field; to note dates and developments in the field (readings on cognitive process theory are usually earlier than those on social constructionist theory, for example). TAs read to identify the dissonance or problem, often phrased as a question, that prompted the author to write; they summarize the solution. Key words and definitions are critical to learning discipline-specific vocabulary. For unfamiliar terms, I recommend that they consult Edith Babin and Kimberly Harrison's *Contemporary Composition Studies: A Guide to Theorists and Terms.* The last two questions—"What key points do you want to remember from this reading?" and "What questions do you have as a result of your reading?"—invite TAs to connect their readings to their teaching. When we discuss readings in class, these are often the questions I ask first.

The Reading Guides offer more evidence of TAs' active reading practices than can highlighted flourescent-yellow texts or cryptic marginalia (! or ? or ☺). Furthermore, the guides summarize the readings for future reference. For instance, TAs can recall suggestions for addressing plagiarism by reviewing their responses to Elaine Whitaker's "A Pedagogy to Address Plagiarism." Some TAs keep Reading Guides together in a section of their Teaching Notebooks, grouping similar topics; others pair them with the Xeroxed articles in their course packet; and others place them in sections with the first-year course materials to which they most closely relate. For example, Whitaker's article is a useful reference when TAs teach freshmen to use and cite outside sources. The Reading Guides also model a method that TAs can use to teach students to read critically. Finally, I am convinced that completing Reading Guides helps TAs understand my purposes for assigning the professional literature I do, as this TA's explanation suggests: "Reading composition theory has highlighted for me the complexities and the broader purposes of composition, which make my particular students' efforts to write and my personal efforts to teach writing all the more important."

## BOOK REVIEWS

In another practicum reading assignment, TAs review for their peers a professional text in composition studies. A text may be reviewed by only one TA, and they choose books based on personal interests. For example, an aspiring scholar of gender studies might select Susan Jarratt and Lynn Worsham's *Feminism and Composition Studies,* a creative writer might opt to learn how stories can create knowledge in Joseph Trimmer's *Narration as Knowledge: Tales of the Teaching Life,* or a technology buff can pick Gail Hawisher and Cynthia Selfe's *Passions, Pedagogies, and 21st Century Technologies.* While I suggest book titles, TAs can select any composition-related scholarly text published within the last five years to study in-depth a topic we can often address only briefly in the practicum.

Applying strategies similar to those they are teaching to first-year students for writing evaluations (setting criteria, gathering evidence, making a judgment), TAs write publishable reviews. (For a model, I offer a *TETYC* review of

*Questioning: A Path to Critical Thinking*—a text read in the practicum. Nearly two decades old, this thirty-page booklet offers excellent strategies for generating class discussion through thoughtful questioning.) I limit reviews to 600–650 words because I want TAs to see how quickly they reach a word count that first-year students often struggle to meet. For most TAs, the imposed limit forces them to be concise, an editing skill that most teach but many have yet to learn.

When I first assigned book reviews in the practicum, I wanted TAs to share their critiques with others, but after we struggled to stay awake through a dozen or so oral readings of reviews, I sought an alternative format. Now, in addition to the written review, TAs also prepare a poster, handout, power-point presentation, or another creative representation of their review to display and discuss at a book fair. Other TAs, faculty mentors, and writing instructors attend the event, study displays, question the reviewers about their texts, and enjoy refreshments and teacher talk. Innovative, informative visual aids help TAs to promote or pan their books. Recently, I added an element of competition and prizes: gift certificates from a local book store and book bags filled with office supplies to the three best presenters as voted on by visitors to the book fair.

## TO-READ LISTS

One way I know that the book fair generates interest is that the titles of reviewed books often end up in a notebook section called "To-Read List" where TAs file handouts on books that piqued their curiosity at the fair. They also list articles and books referenced in their readings to read when they have "world enough, and time." For some, this section starts a reading list for a comprehensive exam in composition studies. For others, it begins a bibliography for their final practicum project, a proposal to solve a classroom problem. For all, I hope, it shows that reading in composition studies should not end with the practicum. Rather, TAs have only started a career-long review of literature on the teaching of writing.

## GRADED ESSAYS

A fourth practicum assignment with short- and long-term applications to the first-year course is group grading of student essays, both to model effective summative evaluations of student writing and to standardize grades within the composition program. At the end of each unit, three TAs provide me with three student papers, representing what they judge to represent high, middle, and low achievement. I then select one from each TA (choosing them for a range of achievement and for challenging problems in evaluation) and give copies to other practicum participants to assess (marginal comments, end response, and a grade).

Each time we do group grading during the practicum, I focus on a different aspect of responding to student writing, in an effort to engage in the "ongoing conservation" about evaluation that Donna Qualley encourages in her chapter in this collection. For example, early on we read Donald Daiker's "Learning to

Praise" and practice giving genuine, instructive, positive comments. Another time, we read Muriel Harris's "Mending the Fragmented Free Modifier," Robert Connors and Andrea Lunsford's "Frequency of Formal Errors in Current College Writing," and Richard Haswell's "Minimal Marking" for ideas on how to analyze and mark sentence-level errors. During the grading session, we compare our critiques of the essays and justify a grade, based on the evaluation criteria we originally established when designing the assignment and on a departmental rubric developed by our composition faculty that lists descriptors for superior/good, satisfactory, and poor/failing performance in four categories: content, development/organization, sentence structure, and diction/mechanics.

At the end of each grading session, TAs and I give our marked essays to the student's teacher who then reviews our comments. In a week or so, the teacher returns the essays to the original graders who add them to their notebooks. At the semester's end, TAs have three graded examples of student writing for each unit in the first-year course; they have a clearer notion of departmental grading standards; and they have developed a responding style based on the kinds of written comments they deem most effective on final drafts. In the short term, group grading sessions help new TAs gain skills and confidence in responding to student writing for a particular assignment; in the long term, these sessions give TAs a file of a dozen samples of student writing for which they have a consensus grade that reflects departmental standards.[3]

## PRACTICUM ASSIGNMENTS

Several other written assignments find a place in the Teaching Notebook, including peer observations, unit plans, and a proposal to solve a teaching problem.

Peer observations serve a somewhat different purpose from those Michael C. Flanigan describes in his chapter in this collection, although I found good advice in his "pre-observation" preparations. My reason for having TAs visit a colleague's class is less to evaluate the teacher being observed and more to foster self-awareness and reflection in the observer. For beginning teachers, it is challenge enough to carry out the day's lesson plan with little opportunity in the give-and-take of a fifty-minute class to be highly conscious of one's questioning strategies, facilitation of group work, or gender biases, for example. Yet, sitting in the back of another teacher's classroom, TAs more easily detect a teacher's tendency to cut short student response and answer the question himself or recognize that directions for group work are muffled in the noise of scooting desks or realize that a teacher tends to call mostly on the attentive female students by the window while ignoring a male student in the back buried in the sports section of the student newspaper. Seeing such patterns in the classes of other teachers prompts TAs to reflect on their own behavior and that of their students. The brief reports that they write for me and share with the teacher whom they observed are more descriptive than evaluative, filled as much with suggestions for themselves as for the teacher whose class they visited. TAs file their peer observation reports in their Teaching Notebooks along with other reflective entries.

Unit plans for the expository writing class that TAs are teaching fill a big section in the Teaching Notebook. Since the TAs teach for the first time while taking the practicum, I start the semester by presenting the first unit, usually a literacy narrative based on Reid's chapter on "Remembering." Plans for a three-week unit include a daily schedule listing objectives, readings, and writing; a detailed assignment; suggestions for large and small group activities and accompanying handouts; and peer-, self-, and teacher-evaluation forms. While we work through the first unit in the practicum and the classroom, TAs are assigned to one of three groups with three or four teachers in each group to plan one of the remaining units. TAs then teach their unit to their peers in the practicum about a week before beginning it in the classroom. When they submit their plan to me, they each also write brief individual reports, explaining their role in the group's project and their reactions to working collaboratively. While most TAs espouse theories of writing as social process and incorporate collaborative activities in their writing classes, some resent having to work together on a graduate project. Their reports to me often vent frustration over colleagues' conflicting work habits—Mr. Procrastinator who needs the pressure of deadlines to do his part at 2:00 a.m. the day of the unit presentation, Ms. Perfection who insists on rewriting everyone else's work "so it's right," Mrs. Overburdened who is too busy with other course work and a novel in progress to meet with the group ("just tell me what to do"). For some TAs, the dysfunctional groups they encounter in the practicum or in their writing classrooms provide the topic of investigation for their final practicum assignment.

A proposal to solve a teaching problem is the TAs' last major writing assignment. They review the content of their Teaching Notebooks looking for dissonance between practices and theories, places where lessons or conferences did not go well, topics about which they want to know more. TAs who have devoted a section of their notebooks to "Questions" have an easy time finding a topic to research and reflect upon. The assignment, cast as a proposal to solve a classroom problem, is shared with other TAs in brief oral presentations the last two days of class.

Although the TAs' proposals to solve teaching problems have a context different from first-year students' proposals to solve campus or community problems, TAs face similar rhetorical challenges and develop similar writing strategies as they come to appreciate the demands their assignments place on first-year composition students. By writing assignments similar to those their students compose (narratives, collaborative plans, reviews, and proposals), TAs are themselves enrolled in a writing course as part of the practicum. Thus, I am not surprised when TAs say that their writing has improved as a result of taking the practicum.

From the unit I plan, to the unit they plan with others, to an original plan to solve a teaching problem next semester, TAs grow as writers and as teachers. One TA wrote in her notebook preface, "A few weeks ago one of my students looked up at me and said, 'Miss Younger, you are a great English teacher.' I was pleased and surprised by that compliment. One of my goals is to be able to acknowledge success . . . while still striving to be a better teacher." Three years later, this TA won LSU's prestigious campuswide award for Outstanding Graduate Teaching Assistant, based partly on the Teaching Portfolio she had assembled from her Teaching Notebook and partly because she has continued to work to improve her teaching and writing.

## ASSESSMENT AND THE TEACHING NOTEBOOK

I assess Teaching Notebooks for two purposes: to evaluate each TA's work on the project as it demonstrates development as a writing teacher and to reflect on my methods for preparing TAs through the practicum in general and the notebook in particular.

While TAs generally write positive comments in their prefaces about keeping a Teaching Notebook, they are aware that it counts for 20 percent of their practicum grade and that I consider its logical organization (forecast in a Table of Contents and signaled by dividers); the quantity of materials (required materials are included); and mostly the quality of materials (reflections, reading notes, and other assignments indicate genuine engagement in and understanding of what it means to teach college-level writing). I enjoy reading their prefaces, but I do so with Glenda Conway's caution that writers of portfolio cover letters may be savvy enough to push "just the right 'buttons,'" knowing what "would be in their best grade-point interests" (84, 85) or, in this case, to claim that keeping a notebook contributed to a successful first-semester of teaching. So when a TA writes, "I am glad that I have created my Teaching Notebook. It will be an invaluable resource for me for many years to come. I will never forget the lessons I learned this first semester of teaching," I smile. Then I look for evidence to support these claims.

In "After the Practicum: Assessing Teacher Preparation Programs," I wrote about multiple methods—surveys, analysis of teaching evaluations, an instrument to measure insight, mentor reports, and exit interviews—by which to gauge the outcomes of our work with new TAs. The adaptation of one method, Mary Murray's Insight Test for writing assignments, has proven especially useful for me in understanding how TAs view their notebooks once the practicum is over.[4] Nearly all TAs (twenty-seven out of thirty-one) over a three-year period felt the assignment had increased their understanding of teaching, often leading to insights. In particular, their responses show that writing about teaching clarified their ideas, that they value their notebooks as resources for future use, and that its meaning grows after the practicum as their knowledge about teaching deepens. The long-term value of the assignment is evident too when former TAs confide that teaching portfolios developed from Teaching Notebooks have helped them get jobs.

## FUTURE OF THE TEACHING NOTEBOOK

Authors of this collection have helped me rethink—again—the Teaching Notebook. I have space to explain two changes I plan, one related to reflective practice, the other to theory.

## REFLECTIVE PRACTICE

TAs in my practicum need guidance to make their reflections on teaching more meaningful. While editing Shirley K Rose and Margaret Finders's chapter on their reciprocal reflective model, I was by chance also reading George Hillocks's *Ways of Thinking, Ways of Teaching*. All three authors, stressing that reflective teaching does not happen naturally, build on Donald Schön's frame experiments. For example, Hillocks identifies five features of a writing lesson's frame experiment: (1) analyzing the students' "progress in relation to general course goals," (2) identifying a desirable change in students' writing, (3) "selecting or inventing a teaching strategy . . . to implement the desired change," (4) planning and implementing the teaching strategy, and (5) "assessing the impact of the teaching strategy" on students' writing and critiquing the strategy itself (136). Reflective teaching requires more discipline than merely musing or fussing about what happened in the classroom; it involves learning to discover "in the situation's back talk a whole new idea, which generates a system of implications for further moves" and plans for the next lesson (Schön 64). The notebook entries that TAs write after each class session record impressions of "what worked and what didn't," but the conversation is often one-sided. Hillocks encourages teacher educators "to find ways and means of helping teachers reconstruct their knowledge and stance" (135). Building on Rose and Finders's ideas for a reciprocal reflective model, I envision working more directly with TAs' reflective responses to their classes and to the practicum to make the conversations in their notebooks more dialogic.

## THEORY

The notebook is a collection of teaching practices, and one might question what theories underlie the methods therein. It's true that my practicum begins with practices (TAs must begin teaching immediately) and moves slowly in discussions and readings toward theory (James Berlin, Richard Fulkerson, and James Corder in particular). But Katrina Powell and her coauthors make a strong argument to foreground theory in order to help TAs understand the *whys*—why I lay out the first unit as I do, why I select certain practicum readings, or why the first-year writing program is structured as it is. My next challenge is to find ways for TAs to acknowledge the theories embedded in the practices within their Teaching Notebooks.

Teacher educators discover many ways to introduce TAs to the theories and practices of teaching writing. As this collection shows, we eagerly share our methods with others. I suspect we keep looking for new and better ways because we enjoy teaching and are eager for others to enjoy it too. Actually, Bill, whose epigraph began this chapter, had another one for the preface to his Teaching Notebook. He balanced Charlie Brown's pessimism with Wordsworth's optimism:

what we have loved,
Others will love, and we will teach them how.
*The Prelude*, XIV: 446–7

## NOTES

1. Undergraduate students at LSU take two required writing courses, one in expository writing and the other in argumentative writing. These courses are taught by approximately fifty TAs and sixty full-time, non-tenure track instructors, most of whom teach on renewable contracts. TAs teach one writing course each semester during their first year; after that, they teach two courses in the fall and one in the spring.
2. The apprenticeship was self-imposed. When first teaching business writing, I attended Jeanne Halpern's class from 10:30–12:00 and taught my own from 12–1:30. As chapters by Paul Anderson and colleagues and by Barry Thatcher have explained, like many of my fellow TAs in English, I lacked workplace writing experiences. The examples that Jeanne used with her students and their questions and sample topics provided me with some background I needed to teach my class. I wish also to acknowledge others at Purdue who taught me to teach: William Evans, Lizette Van Gelder, Muriel Harris, and Janice Lauer.
3. TAs also receive feedback on sets of graded essays from their mentors, experienced instructors assigned to work one-on-one with a TA, visiting classes and sharing their expertise.
4. I collected this data from 1994–1997 when the assignment was still evolving from the Teaching Journal to the Teaching Notebook. However, features in the journal assignment that might contribute to insight are also present in the Teaching Notebook assignment as described in this chapter. Hence, I believe the findings would hold true for the notebook as well.

## WORKS CITED

Anson, Chris M., Joan Graham, David A. Jolliffe, Nancy S. Shapiro, and Carolyn H. Smith. *Scenarios for Teaching Writing: Contexts for Discussion and Reflective Practice.* Urbana, IL: NCTE, 1993.

Babin, Edith, and Kimberly Harrison. *Contemporary Composition Studies: A Guide to Theorists and Terms.* Westport, CT: Greenwood P, 1999.

Berlin, James. "Contemporary Composition: The Major Pedagogical Theories," *College English* 44 (1982): 765–77.

Christenbury, Lelia, and Patricia P. Kelly. *Questioning: A Path to Critical Thinking.* Urbana, IL: NCTE, 1983.

Connors, Robert J., and Andrea A. Lunsford. "Frequency of Formal Errors in Current College Writing, or Ma and Pa Kettle Do Research." *College Composition and Communication* 39 (1988): 396–409.

Conway, Glenda. "Portfolio Cover Letters, Students' Self-Perceptions, and Teachers' Ethics." *New Directions in Portfolio Assessment: Reflective Practice, Critical Theory, and Large-Scale Scoring.* Ed. Laurel Black, Donald A. Daiker, Jeffrey Sommers, and Gail Stygall. Portsmouth, NH: Boynton/Cook, 1994. 83–92.

Corder, James. "On the Way, Perhaps, to a New Rhetoric, but Not There Yet, and if We Do Get There, There Won't Be There Anymore," *College English* 47 (1985): 162–70.

Daiker, Donald A. "Learning to Praise." *Writing and Response: Theory, Practice, and Research.* Ed. Chris M. Anson. Urbana, IL: NCTE. 1989. 103–13.

Fulkerson, Richard. "Composition Theory in the Eighties: Axiological Consensus and Paradigmatic Diversity." *College Composition and Communication* 41 (1990): 409–29.

Harris, Muriel. "Mending the Fragmented Free Modifier." *College Composition and Communication* 32 (1981): 175–82.

Haswell, Richard H. "Minimal Marking." *College English* 45 (1983): 600–4.

Hawisher, Gail, and Cynthia Selfe, eds. *Passions, Pedagogies, and 21st Century Technologies.* Logan: Utah State UP, 1999.

Hillocks, George. *Ways of Thinking, Ways of Teaching.* New York: Teachers College P, 1999.

Jarratt, Susan C., and Lynn Worsham, eds. *Feminism and Composition Studies.* New York: MLA, 1998.

Liggett, Sarah. "After the Practicum: Assessing Teacher Preparation Programs." *The Writing Program Administrator as Researcher: Inquiry in Action & Reflection.* Ed. Shirley K Rose and Irwin Weiser. Portsmouth, NH: Boynton/Cook, 1999. 65–80.

Lindemann, Erika. *A Rhetoric for Writing Teachers.* 3rd ed., New York: Oxford UP, 1995.

Murray, Mary. *Artwork of the Mind: An Interdisciplinary Study of Insight and the Search for It in Student Writing.* Cresskill, NJ: Hampton P, 1995.

Reid, Stephen. *The Prentice Hall Guide for College Writers.* 5th ed., Upper Saddle River, NJ: Prentice Hall, 2000.

Schön, Donald. *Educating the Reflective Practitioner: Toward a New Design for Teaching and Learning in the Professions.* San Francisco: Jossey-Bass, 1987.

Trimmer, Joseph, ed. *Narration as Knowledge: Tales of the Teaching Life.* Portsmouth, NH: Boynton/Cook, 1997.

Whitaker, Elaine. "A Pedagogy to Address Plagiarism." *College Composition and Communication* 44 (1993): 509–14.

# Contributors

**Paul Anderson,** Professor of English at Miami University, was the founding director of its master's degree in technical and scientific communication. He is the author of *Technical Communication: A Reader-Centered Approach* and of numerous publications on technical communication and on composition and rhetoric. He is a Fellow of the Association of Teachers of Technical Communication and of the Society for Technical Communication.

**Betty Bamberg,** Professor of English and Composition Coordinator at California State University, Los Angeles, has been involved in teacher preparation since 1980. As Director of the Freshman Writing Program at the University of Southern California from 1984 to 1996, she redesigned the TA preparation and was responsible for the training and supervision of more than 100 TAs each year. Her publications include articles in *Research in the Teaching of English, WPA, College Composition and Communication,* and the *ADE Bulletin,* as well as a chapter in *The Writing Program Administrator as Researcher: Inquiry in Action and Reflection.*

**Sally Barr Ebest,** Associate Professor of English at the University of Missouri–St. Louis, has been the Writing Program Administrator since 1987, a position in which she prepares and supervises TAs. The author of several articles focusing on the professional development of graduate students, her latest project is *Changing the Way We Teach: Preparing the Next Generation of Professors.* She is also the coauthor of *Writing from A to Z* and coeditor of *Writing With: New Directions in Collaborative Teaching, Learning, and Research.*

**Gita Das Bender,** Second Language Academic Writing Coordinator at Seton Hall University's English Department, mentored writing teachers in New York University's Expository Writing Program from 1995 to 1999. She was one of four mentors chosen to participate in a New York State Consortium project, "Preparing Future Professors," funded by the Fund for the Improvement of Postsecondary Education. In addition to mentoring and staff development activities, she conducted interviews of incoming instructors and mentors in collaboration with directors of the program.

**Chris Burnham,** former Writing Program Administrator and current Head of English at New Mexico State University, has been involved in the preparation and professional development of TAs for more than twenty years. His publications include the coauthored *Investigating Astronomy: Model-Building and Critical Thinking,* "Writing to Learn in Journals: Help for the Homeless in the Universe" in *The Journal Book for Teachers of Emerging Writers,* "Expressive Pedagogy: Practice/Theory Theory/Practice" in *The Writing Teacher's Bibliographic Sourcebook,* as well as articles in *College Composition and Communication, Rhetoric Review,* and *WPA.*

**Todd DeLuca** graduated from Miami University in 1992 with a BS degree in economics and worked as a computer professional in graphic arts, marketing, and technical writing before entering its Master's of Technical and Scientific Communication Program in fall 1997. As a teaching assistant, he taught English 313, "Introduction to Technical Communication," in spring 1998. Since leaving the program, he has worked as a technical writer documenting various computer-related hardware and software products.

**Theresa Enos** is Professor of English and Director of the Rhetoric, Composition, and the Teaching of English Graduate Program at the University of Arizona. Founder and editor of *Rhetoric Review,* she has also edited or coedited seven books, including the *Encyclopedia of Rhetoric and Composition: Communication from Ancient Times to the Information Age.* She has published numerous chapters and articles on rhetorical theory and issues in writing. She is the author of *Gender Roles and Faculty Lives in Rhetoric and Composition* and immediate past president of the National Council of Writing Program Administrators. Two forthcoming coedited books are *The Spaciousness of Rhetoric* and *The Writing Program Administrator's Handbook.*

**Christine Farris,** Associate Professor of English at Indiana University, is Associate Chair and former Director of Composition, a position in which she prepared TAs to teach composition and literature. She also leads writing across the curriculum workshops and prepares high school instructors to teach college writing in a dual-credit program. Her ethnographic research, documented in *Subject to Change: New Composition Instructors' Theory and Practice,* investigates how TAs construct, resist, and change theories of composition in practice. She is the coeditor of *Under Construction: Working at the Intersections of Composition Theory, Research, and Practice.*

**Margaret J. Finders** is Associate Professor of English Education at Purdue University, where she teaches courses in literacy and teacher preparation, with a special interest at the middle school level. Her book, *Just Girls: Hidden Literacies and Life in Junior High,* addresses the sociopolitical dynamics of middle school and middle school girls. Her current project is a coauthored book, *Literacy Lessons: Teaching and Learning with Middle Schoolers.*

**Michael C. Flanigan** is the Earl A. and Betty Galt Brown Professor of Rhetoric and Composition at the University of Oklahoma, where he has served as Director of Composition since 1981. He began preparing writing teachers in 1963 when he worked at the Project English Demonstration Center; from 1975–1981, he directed the writing program at Indiana University. Widely published, his works include "Observing Teaching: Discovering and Developing the Individual's Teaching Style" in *WPA* and a series of videos on problems related to teaching writing, available through Indiana University.

**Richard Fulkerson** has been Director of English Graduate Studies at Texas A&M–Commerce for two decades. He teaches two required doctoral courses: "Theory and Practice of Teaching Reading and Writing in College" and "Theory and Practice of Argumentative Discourse." For the latter course he wrote *Teaching the Argument in Writing*. He has published articles on teacher preparation in *Rhetoric Review* and *College Composition and Communication* and a chapter entitled "The English Doctoral Metacurriculum" in *Foregrounding Ethical Awareness in Composition and English Studies*. His composition life story, "How Way Leads on to Way," appears in *Living Rhetoric and Composition*.

**Judith Goleman,** Associate Professor of English at the University of Massachusetts–Boston, has directed its Freshman English Program and codirected its Graduate Teaching Intern Program in composition since 1992. In a three-stage preparation program, she mentors co-teachers, conducts a seminar in the teaching of composition, and supervises a small staff of graduate students who collaboratively design and then teach their own sections of freshman English while meeting weekly. She has published numerous chapters in collections and is the author of *Working Theory: Critical Composition Studies for Students and Teachers*.

**Katherine K. Gottschalk** is the Walter C. Teagle Director of First-Year Writing Seminars in Cornell University's John S. Knight Institute for Writing in the Disciplines. She has been with the program since it became independently situated in 1982. Her work as director, in addition to administration and teaching, includes faculty development and primary responsibility for the preparation of TAs in Writing 700: "Teaching Writing," a course offered for new instructors of First-Year Writing Seminars. Her publications on writing program administration and on the teaching of writing include *Teaching Prose: A Guide for Writing Instructors*, which she coedited.

**Susanmarie Harrington** is Director of Writing and Associate Professor of English at Indiana University–Purdue University Indianapolis and was formerly visiting Associate Director of Composition at Texas Tech University. Her articles on writing program administration, writing assessment, and faculty development have appeared in such publications as *Computers and Writing*, the *Journal of Basic Writing*, and *WPA*. She is coeditor of *The Online Writing Classroom* and *Questioning Authority: Stories Told in School*. She is currently researching basic writing and basic writers in the contemporary academy.

**Muriel Harris,** Professor of English at Purdue University and Director of its Writing Lab, has, for many years, taught the training courses for undergraduate and graduate tutors. In addition to establishing Purdue's Writing Lab in 1976, she began and continues to edit the *Writing Lab Newsletter*, coordinates the development of Purdue's Online Writing Lab (OWL), and is the winner of the 2000 CCCC Exemplar Award. Her books include *Teaching One-to-One: The Writing Conference* and the *Prentice Hall Reference Guide to Grammar and*

*Usage.* Among her articles and book chapters—which focus on writing center theory, administration, and practice—are "Selecting and Training Undergraduate and Graduate Staffs in a Writing Lab," "Peer Tutoring: How Tutors Learn," and "Training Teachers for the Writing Lab: A Multi-Dimensional Perspective."

**Christine Hult** is Professor of English and Associate Department Head at Utah State University, where she has served as the Director of Writing and Director of the Computer Classroom and Lab. She has been involved with TA training since 1982 when she was Director of Composition and Rhetoric at Texas Tech University. She has published numerous books and articles on teacher preparation and writing program administration, including *Evaluating Teachers of Writing.* For seven years she edited the journal *WPA: Writing Program Administration.* Her most recent coauthored book, *The New Century Handbook,* combines information typically found in English handbooks with guidance on using computers throughout the writing process.

**Brian Huot,** Professor of English at the University of Louisville, has served as Director of Composition since 1996, during which time he has required teaching portfolios from all composition staff and revised the graduate seminar to include contemporary composition theory. He has published in *CCC, WPA,* and other venues dedicated to the teaching, learning, and assessment of writing. He is also coeditor of *Assessing Writing,* the only journal devoted to issues of writing assessment theory and practice.

**Rebecca Jackson,** Assistant Professor of English and Director of the Writing Center at New Mexico State University, has been preparing TAs for the writing center setting since 1996. She is a coauthor of "Survey of Doctoral Programs in Rhetoric, Composition, and Technical/Professional Communication" in *Rhetoric Review.* Her current research explores the influence of context on writing group interaction in the prison college classroom and an exploration of writing center consulting as reflective practice.

**Sarah Liggett,** Professor of English at Louisiana State University, has taught a practicum in teaching writing for beginning TAs for fifteen years, ten of which she also served as Director of Freshman English. The author of several articles and a frequent presenter at CCCC, she has recently published chapters in *Expanding Literacies: English Teaching and the New Workplace* and in *The Writing Program Administrator as Researcher: Inquiry in Action and Reflection.* She now works with staff from the Writing Center and the Communications Resource Lab.

**Margaret Lindgren,** Associate Professor and Director of the English Composition Program at the University of Cincinnati, has taught the two-quarter practicum required of TAs since 1994. Her research in feminist theory has been reported in *Feminism and Composition Studies* and *Feminism and Empirical Research: Emerging Perspectives in Rhetoric and Composition,* and her approaches to evaluating texts appear in *The Practice of Response: Approaches to Commenting on Student Writing.*

**Cassandra Mach Phillips,** is Assistant Professor at the University of Wisconsin at Waukesha, where she teaches courses in composition and business writing. She studied at the University of Louisville, where she served as Assistant Director of Composition for one year and co-taught the graduate practicum for TAs. Her research interests include literacy theory, teacher preparation, and the representation of literacy in literature.

**Wanda Martin,** Associate Professor of English and Associate Dean of Arts & Sciences at the University of New Mexico, directed the Freshman English program from 1995–1999. Formerly Coordinator of the Basic Writing Program at the University of Louisville, she has helped prepare new teachers since 1980. Her related publications include "Outcomes Assessment Research as a Teaching Tool" in *The Writing Program Administrator as Researcher: Inquiry in Action and Reflection;* "Tenure, Status, and the Teaching of Writing" in *Farther Along: Transcending Dichotomies in Rhetoric and Composition;* and "Dancing on the Interface: Leadership and the Politics of Collaboration" in *WPA.*

**Lynn Meeks,** Associate Professor and Director of Writing at Utah State University, has been involved in preparing teachers of writing since 1978, as a fellow of the Greater Phoenix Area Writing Project, as Language Arts Coordinator for the Idaho Department of Education, and as a National Trainer for Frameworks, a literacy-based staff development program for K–8 teachers. She has published in *English Journal, English Leadership Quarterly, WPA, Administrative Problem-Solving for Writing Programs and Writing Centers,* and *Teaching College English and English Education: Reflective Stories.* She is working on *Teaching the Way Kids Learn,* a book on teaching methods for pre-service and in-service teachers.

**Peggy O'Neill,** Assistant Professor of Writing, teaches writing and writing pedagogy courses at Georgia Southern University. While a graduate student at the University of Louisville, she served as Assistant Director of Composition for two years. Her scholarship interests include response to student writing, teacher education, and writing assessment theory and practice. Her work has appeared in several journals, and she recently guest edited an issue of *Assessing Writing* on response.

**Charles Paine** is Assistant Professor of English at the University of New Mexico, where he directs the Freshman English Program. He has mentored TAs at Duke University and has helped prepare TAs at UNM since 1994. He is the author of *The Resistant Writer,* a historical and contemporary study of the cultural motivation of composition teachers that argues for the importance of understanding the broad historical, political, and cultural contexts within which composition is taught.

**Darin Payne** is a Visiting Assistant Professor at the University of South Carolina, where he serves as the computer-mediated pedagogy consultant to the Department of English. In that capacity, he founded and codirects the Program for Incorporating New Technologies in English, and he teaches TAs and faculty members in the practice, theory, and politics of teaching

English in computerized environments. He has published in a variety of regional and national journals, including *JAC: A Journal of Composition Theory* and *Rhetoric Review.*

**Katrina M. Powell,** Assistant Professor in English at Louisiana State University, earned her PhD at the University of Louisville, where she served as Assistant Director of Composition for two years. This experience included co-teaching the graduate seminar for TAs and extensive mentoring. She has presented papers on teacher preparation at CCCC, NCTE, and the Watson Conference. Her research interests include self-representation, autobiography, genre, and activity theories.

**Betty P. Pytlik** has been a WPA, a WAC coordinator, the director of a state-sponsored project for high-school and college writing instructors, and Chair of the English department at Ohio University. Her interest in preparing teachers began in the 1960s, when, as a Peace Corps Volunteer in the Philippines, she conducted in-service workshops for elementary and secondary teachers. She has frequently presented papers at NCTE and CCCC on the history of TA preparation. She has studied graduate student writing in methods courses and investigated changes that take place as new teachers gain experience. Currently, she is helping to develop a master of arts in the teaching of English and serves as Director of Composition.

**Donna Qualley** is Associate Professor at Western Washington University where she was Director of Composition from 1995–2000. She was responsible for development of the first-year writing curriculum and the preparation and education of TAs, which included a summer orientation, first-quarter seminar, weekly staff meetings, and all-day, end-of-quarter portfolio readings. Her publications, most notably *Turns of Thought, Teaching Composition as Reflexive Inquiry,* have also served to educate teachers.

**Thomas Recchio** is Associate Professor at the University of Connecticut, where he has been responsible for TA preparation since 1989. Before that he was Associate Director of the Writing Program at Rutgers, New Brunswick, for three years. His articles have appeared in such journals as *WPA, CCC, Rhetoric Review,* and *College Literature,* and he has chapters in *Essays on the Essay,* in *Taking Stock,* and in *Landmark Essays: Bakhtin, Rhetoric, and Writing.*

**Rebecca J. Rickly** is Assistant Professor and Co-Director of Composition at Texas Tech University. She has published chapters and articles on peer tutor training, technology, and research methods in *Computers and Composition, Wiring the Writing Center, Taking Flight with OWLs,* and *Humanities.team@edu.* She has offered national and regional workshops on teaching with technology and coedited *The On-Line Writing Classroom.*

**Shirley K Rose** is Associate Professor of English at Purdue University, where she has mentored TAs since 1994. She served as Director of Composition at Purdue for three years and as Director of Composition Faculty Development at San Diego State for four years. She has published articles on writing program administration and composition faculty development in publications such as *WPA, Journal of Teaching Writing* and *CCC.* With Irwin Weiser, she coedited *The Writing Program Administrator as Researcher: Inquiry in Action and Reflection.*

**Lisa Rosenberger,** a 1999 graduate of the Master's of Technical and Scientific Communication Program at Miami University, has worked as a consultant to industry in information technology and environmental science. She is currently an environmental education specialist for Miami University, where she is helping to redesign a zoology museum.

**Kirsti A. Sandy** is Director of Writing at Keene State College. Prior to that appointment and while working on this chapter, she was a doctoral student at Illinois State University, completing a dissertation on "Learning by Co-Teaching: Graduate Students in a Collaboratively-Taught Intensive Introductory Writing Course." She also served as Assistant Director of Writing at ISU and assisted with the first year of its Graduate Student Mentor Program, which pairs experienced TAs with new MA students for a semester of collaborative teaching. She has written reviews for *WPA* and has presented papers at several national and regional conferences.

**Barry Thatcher** is Assistant Professor of English and director of technical writing at Ohio University. His research interests include technical writing pedagogy, intercultural rhetorics, ESL technical writing, and the history of rhetoric and composition in Latin America. He has published in *The Journal of Second Language Writing, Technical Communication, and Technical Communication Quarterly.* Currently, he is working on a book about professional communication in Latin American and U.S.–American contexts.

**Irwin Weiser,** Professor of English and Director of Composition, has taught at Purdue University since 1981, where he has worked with a wide range of teachers new to Purdue, from first-semester MA students to doctoral students with teaching experience. The preparation of teachers has been the focus of his essays appearing in *Situating Portfolios: Four Perspectives, New Directions in Portfolio Assessment, Evaluating Teachers of Writing,* and *The TA Experience: Preparing for Multiple Roles.* With his colleague Shirley K Rose, he has coedited *The Writing Program Administrator as Researcher: Inquiry in Action and Reflection.*

**Steve Wilhoit,** an Associate Professor at the University of Dayton, was Director of TA Training for eleven years and in 1999 became the Director of Composition. As a TA at Indiana University, he was a peer mentor. At the University of Dayton, he has conducted both pre- and in-service workshops and taught courses in composition pedagogy and rhetorical theory. A frequent presenter on topics related to TA preparation at CCCC and elsewhere, he has, with a group of TAs, coauthored a comprehensive bibliography on TA training for *WPA* and is the author of *A Brief Guide to Writing from Readings* and the forthcoming *Allyn & Bacon Teaching Assistant's Handbook.*

**Kathleen Blake Yancey** is Roy Pearce Professor of Professional Communication at Clemson University, where she also directs the Roy and Marnie Pearce

Center for Professional Communication. Her earlier WPA posts include the UNC Charlotte site of the National Writing Project and the Purdue University Office of Writing Review. With Brian Huot, Yancey cofounded and coedits the journal *Assessing Writing*. She is the author of numerous articles and book chapters and the editor or author of six books, including *Reflection in the Writing Classroom*. The Chair of the College Section for National Council of Teachers of English, Yancey is President of the Council of Writing Program Administrators.

# Index